"A BRAVE BOOK THAT ASKS QUESTIONS WE CANNOT AFFORD TO LEAVE UNANSWERED . . . Spungen's anger . . . comes through with an urgency, a sadness, and an earnestness that is clearly directed at alerting the world to other Nancys and, perhaps, saving them."

*Philadelphia Inquirer*

"Spungen's relentlessly honest and pitiless account of Nancy's life reveals that Nancy's family was even more victimized by her destructive behavior than she was. . . . Spungen raises the legitimate issue of how far parental love and guilt are expected to go when confronted by an offspring like Nancy . . . a courageous book."

*Newsday*

"A POWERFUL AND DISTURBING BOOK. THE PERSONAL RECOLLECTIONS ARE UNUSUALLY SHOCKING, THE WRITING NEVER LESS THAN COMPELLING."

*Penthouse*

# And I Don't Want To Live This Life

## DEBORAH SPUNGEN

FAWCETT CREST • NEW YORK

Grateful acknowledgment is made to the following for permission to reprint previously published material:

Liveright Publishing Corp.: "A Poet's Advice to Students" by e. c. cummings. Reprinted from A MISCELLANY, REVISED, edited by George James Firmage with permission of Liveright Publishing Corp. Copyright © 1955 by e. c. cummings. Copyright © 1965 by Marion Morehouse Cummings, Copyright © 1965 by George James Firmage.

Some of the names of the people and places have been changed throughout the book.

A Fawcett Crest Book

Published by Ballantine Books

Library of Congress Catalog Card Number: 83-48072

ISBN: 0-449-20543-6

This edition published by arrangement with Villard Books

Manufactured in the United States of America

First Ballantine Books Edition: August 1984

# Dedication

To my husband, Frank, whose love, humor, and patience gave me the courage and strength to write this book.

To my children, Susan and David, whose love and trust sustained me in the past and give me faith for the future.

To my daughter, Nancy.
Sweet Baby
  Welcome
I only came to say hello
I cannot stay
Loving arms hold tight
Don't go! Don't go!
But even loving arms could
  not hold the golden thread
She slipped away and never
  said good-bye.

# Acknowledgments

With special thanks for all their help and encouragement:

Milton and Becky Stoloff, Kevin Fee and Eagleville Hospital, Susan Davis, Janet and Myron Waxman, Marsha and Arthur Kramer, Bonnie and Michael Peretz, Mary Ann Caruso, Paula Bram Amar, Ph.D., Lillian Kravis, M.D., Robin Tower, Julia Cass, Robert Krauss, Ellen Portner, Dean Becker, Sylvia and John Walsh.

In sincere gratitude for those who believed in me and my book:

Marc Jaffe, and Peter Gethers of Random House, and my agents, Morton Janklow and Anne Sibbald and to Sue Pollack, who brought us all together.

And to my mother: (Nov. 20 '09—March 2 '83).
Thank you for the legacy of survival.

# Author's Note

I am especially grateful to writer David Handler for the many difficult months he spent guiding me toward what it all meant and showing me how to say it.

# And I Don't Want To Live This Life

# ❑ The Aftermath

The reporters were back.

They crammed our front porch and spilled out onto the lawn, jabbering with each other, jockeying for position close to the front door. There were photographers and television cameramen. There were microphones and tape recorders and lights. One of the reporters rang the doorbell. He kept his thumb down on it so it rang over and over and over again, demanding my attention and cooperation. My husband, Frank, had already left for work but some of our neighbors hadn't yet. As they wormed their cars past the double-parked vans and cars, they craned their necks to watch.

The freak show was on again.

I hadn't opened my door to the press since the nightmare began three and a half months before, when my oldest child, Nancy, was found under the bathroom sink in room 100 of the Chelsea Hotel in New York City. She had been stabbed in the stomach with a seven-inch hunting knife and had been left to bleed to death. She wore only black lace underwear. The man accused of murdering her was the man she shared the room with, her lover—British punk rock star Sid Vicious of the defunct Sex Pistols. He was out on $50,000 bail.

She was twenty years old when she died.

The reporters kept ringing the bell, shouting my name. The neighbors honked. None of them would go away, ever, it seemed, until I opened the door. So I opened it.

"He's dead!" one of them yelled.

"Sid's dead, Mrs. Spungen!"

"Overdose—!"

"Middle of the night—"

"In Greenwich Village—"

"Celebrating being out on bail—"

"Some celebration, huh?"

"Care to comment, Mrs. Spungen?"

"How does it make you feel, Mrs. Spungen?"

"Get what he deserved?"

"Happy?"

"Sad?"

"End of ordeal?"

The shutters clicked, the TV cameras rolled. Pens were anxiously poised. I said nothing. I felt nothing. Just my own pain.

"Don't you want to comment, Mrs. Spungen?"

"How about the criminal justice system?"

"What do you think of it now?"

I closed the door in their faces.

"Wait—!"

"We need a statement—"

The reporter nearest the door began to ring the bell again. I leaned against the inside of the door, the ache in my chest making it hard to breathe. The pain had started right after I had learned of Nancy's death. It would not go away. I'd seen a doctor but he said I was in perfect health. I thought about running from the press. I had my coat on and my keys in my hand. I always did now, so I'd be ready to run. But I knew I'd never get away from them. They'd follow me. They'd find me, wherever I went.

The repeated ringing brought my seventeen-year-old son, David, downstairs. He hadn't yet left for school. Not that leaving was anything more than a token gesture. He rarely made it to school. Mostly, he sat in the public library. He had stopped seeing his friends. He had stopped living. We had all stopped living. I had quit my job; Frank went off to work like a zombie and came back that way; Suzy, who was two years older than David, had isolated herself in her apartment in the city. She seldom went to her classes at the Philadelphia College of Art and we saw little of her.

But the reporters didn't care about any of us, just as they hadn't cared about Nancy. All they wanted was another installment in their ongoing freak show, to sell papers, to boost ratings.

"What's going on?" asked David.

"Sid OD'ed. He's dead."

David nodded grimly. He wasn't surprised. He had no more capacity to be surprised. He had grown up with too much anger and pain and tragedy. He had grown up with Nancy.

"I'll call the police," he declared, and went off to use the phone. I just stood there in the hallway.

A patrol car came immediately. The Nancy Spungen–Sid Vicious case was the biggest story Huntingdon Valley, our little Philadelphia suburb, had ever known. Any call from the Spungen residence brought a quick response.

The officers moved the reporters off our property and sent them on their way. David and I watched from the living room window.

As soon as the policemen left, two English tabloid-newspaper men returned and began to ring the bell again. When I didn't answer, they backed up onto the front lawn and began to yell.

*"How dare you call the police!"*

*"We're not bothering you, Mrs. Spungen!"*

*"We just want to talk!"*

One of the reporters was particularly abrasive. Three days after Nancy's funeral he'd shown up with a copy from a page of an English newspaper carrying the banner headline NANCY WAS A WITCH. He told me if I didn't deny it people would assume it was true. I said "No comment" and closed the door.

Somehow he managed to shove the page inside the door before it shut, then told the police I'd stolen it.

*"We have a right!"*

*"How dare you call the police!"*

David went out the door after the two reporters, fists clenched, face red. Six feet tall and powerfully built, he ran toward them. They turned and took off. He chased them across the lawn and down the block to their car. They jumped in, surprised and frightened, and sped away.

When David came back, I asked him to please go to school, to at least make the effort.

"You sure you'll be okay here all by yourself?" he asked.

"I'll be fine."

"Why are you wearing your coat?"

"I'm cold."

He walked to his car and drove off. The phone rang. I thought about not answering it, but it might be Frank. Possibly he'd heard the news. I picked up the phone. It wasn't Frank.

"Mrs. Spungen, it's Anne Beverley," said Sid's mother, her voice strained.

We had spoken once before. She had phoned two days after Nancy's murder to offer her condolences and to say she was certain Sid couldn't have done it. It had been a bizarre call, but not as bizarre as when Sid himself had phoned me the following day.

"I'm . . . I'm sorry your son is dead," I now managed to say. "I'm sorry for you."

"Thank you. Our children were very special children. I suppose this is the way it was meant to be. You know, no one else understood them except you and I."

"I know."

"Mrs. Spungen, may I bury him next to Nancy?"

I covered the phone, gasping from the pain in my chest. And from horror. How could she ask me to let her bury her son—my baby's accused murderer—next to her?

"May I, Mrs. Spungen? They meant so much to each other."

"You . . . *can't.*"

"Why?"

"It's . . . it's a family plot."

"Then what will I do? Where will I bury him? Perhaps somewhere else in the same cemetery?"

"I can't help you. I'm sorry."

I hung up. The doorbell rang again. More reporters. I let it ring.

I went through the kitchen to the garage and found a piece of heavy, rubber-encased wire with which to hang myself. I'd been thinking about it each and every day for several weeks. In fact, suicide was all I thought about. I kept putting it off. Every day I told myself to wait until tomorrow. Maybe tomorrow the pain would go away. Maybe tomorrow I'd want to live again, have a reason to live again.

But I couldn't take the pain anymore. It was unbearable and there was no end to it. Death was the only way out. I had no other alternative. Today was the day. This was it.

I went back inside the house with the wire, tied a noose around my neck, and looked at myself in the dining room mirror.

Nothing had worked out the way I'd planned.

Once I had looked forward to life. Twenty years before it had been full of promise. I was twenty then, a nice, reasonably attractive middle-class Jewish girl from Philadelphia. I was a college student, a good student. I had plans and ambitions. I had a kind, young husband who loved me as much as I loved him. I had dreams. Twenty solid years of anguish was not one of them. What had I done to deserve this?

Once I had been happy. I had known how to laugh. I had known how to cry. I hadn't cried in twenty years. There had never been any time to cry since the day Nancy was born. No time for the luxury of tears. I had made a promise to Nancy the first time I saw her there in the maternity ward nursery. I had promised her a life of quality and dignity. It took every bit of my strength and my love to keep that promise over the twenty years of my daughter's frightening, misunderstood, tragic life. It took every minute of every day.

I didn't cry when I finally had to admit to myself that she was not like other little girls.

I didn't cry when I realized she was angry and in pain and that nobody, but nobody, could help her.

I didn't cry when she tried repeatedly to end her pain herself, first with a razor blade, then with a needle.

I didn't cry when I knew she could no longer live with us in our home without destroying her sister and brother. She had already come close to destroying our marriage.

I didn't cry when I got the news that she was dead. I held Frank while he wept through the night, my own eyes dry.

I didn't cry at her funeral. I couldn't. By then, I'd forgotten how.

I had never let myself feel the pain. I blocked it. Now I felt it. Oh, how I felt it.

I kept having the same nightmare. Every night in my dreams, Nancy was a small child of five, running up to me waving her hands in front of her face and exclaiming "Look what I have, Mommy! Look what I have!" When she got up close to me, I saw that what she had all over her little girl's hands were track marks from shooting heroin, the track marks she showed me when she was seventeen to let me know she was a drug addict. "Help me, Mommy," she had said in real life, and in my dream, too. "Help me, Mommy," cried little Nancy.

I hadn't been able to. She was dead. And I was alone, totally alone in the world. My life had no meaning. I had no desire to work, to love, to be productive, to see anyone I knew, to smile. I had no desire to be alive.

I shivered. I was cold, even with my coat on.

I really knew Nancy was going to die young. She had wanted to die since she'd been eleven years old. I had long since accepted it as inevitable. It was just a matter of how and when. I had her death all mapped out in my mind for two years before it actually happened. It was my recurring fantasy. We would get a phone call early one morning from the police saying that Nancy was in the hospital from a drug overdose. Frank, Suzy, David, and I would rush to the hospital. Nancy would be in a bed in a private room, conscious. It would be clean and quiet. She would say good-bye to each of us. We would say good-bye to her. Then she would die in my arms.

Nancy's death was dignified in my fantasy. In death, she had at last found the peace she never found in life. The ordeal was over.

It did not work out that way. A murderer intervened. Nancy died under a hotel sink with a knife in her stomach, the whole world there to gape at her. She died the subject of ridicule and scorn. The press called her Nauseating Nancy. Their stories made it seem like she had "asked for it," just like a rape victim in a provocative dress "asks for it." They made it seem like she got what she deserved. In life, the media had made my daughter into a distasteful celebrity; in death, they made her a freak. There was a derisive skit about her on *Saturday Night Live,* jokes about her in Johnny Carson's monologue. Some people were selling Sid and Nancy T-shirts. Others were buying them.

Nobody wanted to hear of her pain, her sadness, her sensitivity. Nobody wanted to understand Nancy. Nobody cared.

I wanted to run to the highest roof and scream "Nancy was my baby! She was my child!" I wanted to yell "No matter what she became, she didn't deserve to die this way—to be *treated* this way!" I wanted to scream "You don't understand her! She was *loved!*"

I wanted to yell so loud that everyone would have to hear, have to understand, have to care.

But I was mute. I could not fight anymore. I ached too much. I was feeling all of the pain, the twenty years of pain I'd accumulated and held in through our tortured life with Nancy. It wouldn't go away. If only it would go away. . . .

And now, as I stood in front of the mirror, noose around my neck, I realized the pain wouldn't go away because I wouldn't let go of Nancy. I couldn't. My odyssey with her wasn't complete. Her murderer had taken more than her life. He'd taken *my* life, my purpose, my focus. He had taken away my right to keep my promise to her. I had promised Nancy a life of quality. Keeping that promise was the basis of my existence. Death is a part of life. Her death of quality was denied her. I had to find a way to give it to her—to keep my promise.

I could not hang myself. I could not give up. I had to fight, to survive. My promise had to be kept. Only then could I let go of Nancy. Only then could I get on with my own life.

At that moment I didn't know how. All I knew was that my path to the future lay somewhere in the past, in our journey with Nancy. Too much had happened that I had never understood, had never let myself *feel*. I had to make some kind of sense of it. I had to figure out how we'd survived. I had to let the pain out.

I had a responsibility—to Nancy and to the others. There were other Nancys out there. Too many. It was too late for Nancy, but it wasn't too late for them.

I had to warn the parents of these other Nancys. They were groping around in the dark just like we had, feeling all alone, feeling somehow to blame for their child's anguish. They weren't alone; they weren't to blame. I had to let them know that. I had to try to spare them from the nightmare we went through. I had to warn them what might happen to their child, to their other children, to their marriage, to their dreams. I knew what happened to ours.

There was hope for somebody else's child. There had to be. Only then would Nancy's life and death have meaning. Only then would the pain go away, the nightmare end, and my life begin again.

Only then could I say good-bye.

# ☐ Chapter 1

The doctor who delivered Nancy had worked his way through medical school as a prize fighter. He was very tall, muscular, and always in a tremendous hurry. I saw him once every month during my pregnancy, and before each visit I prepared a list of questions. (How will I know when I'm in labor? Will it hurt?) Each month the list got longer and longer, because I never asked him any of the questions. I was too intimidated by him. He seemed so busy.

I was twenty years old and I'd never had a baby before.

By my seventh month the list was quite long. On the day of my appointment I examined it nervously while I sat in my religious philosophy seminar—I was in my senior year at the University of Pennsylvania. My friend Janet passed me a little wadded-up piece of paper and giggled. The professor glared at me. Janet had come up with by far the best name to date: Nebuchadnezzar Spungen.

My obstetrician's office was right in the midst of the Penn campus, which spreads across several blocks in West Philadelphia. As I waddled across the campus, I convinced myself

that this would be the day I would have an office talk with
him. I would not be intimidated.

I was quite a sight now in my maternity dress, knee socks,
and saddle shoes, and I got some funny looks from the other
students. You didn't see many pregnant students on campus
in 1958. At Penn, in fact, you saw only one—me.

When I got there, I had my blood and urine tested and sat
down in the waiting room. A pregnant woman who was about
my age came in with her mother and sat down across from
me. We were due at about the same time and had chatted a bit
during previous visits. Now I smiled at her, but she just stared
vacantly ahead. Her mother took her hand, squeezed it, and
turned to me.

"It died," she said softly.

"Excuse me?" I said.

"She's carrying a dead baby. He said she might have to
carry it another month. Maybe longer."

I swallowed, looked away. I was afraid if I looked at the
girl too long maybe it would happen to me, too. I wondered if
such a thing *could* happen to me, and if it did, how I would
tell. How would I feel? I didn't know. My baby was very active, seemed to move around constantly. That was all I knew.

The nurse finally led me into a tiny examining room. It was
cold in there. I waited, watching the traffic down on Walnut
Street, clutching my list, which was moist now.

The doctor had a deep, booming voice. I heard him out in
the corridor, before he burst in. He seemed to fill the room.

"How are we feeling?" he barked.

"Okay," I replied weakly.

He vigorously scrubbed his enormous, hairy hands, dried
them, and put one of them over my bare abdomen. He began
to prod and poke.

"Any complaints?"

"I . . . well, no. But I was . . . I mean, I do have—"

The phone rang. He reached over and picked it up while he
continued to poke around. "How often?" he said into the
phone. "Okay, get yourself over to the hospital. I'll meet you
there. Ten minutes. 'Bye."

He hung up and was out the door in one stride. He stopped,

turned back to me as an afterthought, and smiled. "The baby's doing fine."

Then he was gone.

I sat on the table so long the nurse came in to ask if something was wrong. I wanted to burst into tears, but I did not. I just sat there on the table with my list, feeling very alone.

Frank, my husband, had been stationed at Fort Knox, Kentucky, in the army reserves since the first month of my pregnancy. Actually, he'd already left when I discovered I was pregnant. I kept hoping I wasn't. One day, at a friend's wedding, I thought my period actually *had* started, and I dashed, delighted, for the ladies' room. I was wrong.

Frank and I knew we wanted kids, but we were thinking five years away, not immediately. He had just graduated from Penn and wouldn't start working until he got out of the army, though he had already landed a good job with an accounting firm in New York City. Our plan had been that he would commute to New York every day from Philadelphia until I finished school. Then we would move there. I was majoring in foreign languages and wanted to go into foreign trade. I wanted a career. New York seemed like the very best place for us. We wanted to work our way up together. We wanted to travel to Europe. We wanted adventure.

Unplanned pregnancies were very common then. Just about everyone I knew had at least one unplanned child. Frank and I ended up having two. There were abortionists around, but you didn't go to them—at least not if you were a nice Jewish girl, which I was. And Frank, well, Frank was a nice Jewish boy. Maybe he had been driving a truck when we'd met three years before, when I was still in high school. Maybe he had been running with a tough crowd and had a bit of a wild reputation himself. No longer. He had settled down, gone to college, and worked hard.

We never discussed an abortion. It simply wasn't an option. In 1958 you just made a shift, changed your original plans, and looked forward to your new ones. In 1958 you had fewer options.

With Frank in the army I reluctantly moved out of our little apartment on campus. It had cockroaches and mice and only one electrical outlet, but it was our first home and I loved it.

I moved back into my old room at my mother's row house about ten blocks from campus. Since Mother worked, I made dinner when I got home from school, then stretched out and watched *The Mickey Mouse Club* on TV. In retrospect, it was a very easy pregnancy. I was a little tired and had some back-aches, but my health was fine.

It's just that I was so confused, so lonely. None of my friends had had babies yet. I had no sisters, or brothers for that matter. I tried to be low-key about it with Mother, but during the fifth month I finally sought her out.

It was bedtime. I stood in the doorway of her bedroom and watched her as she sat at her dressing table, brushing out her hair.

Mother was very upset that I was pregnant. She thought I was too young. Also, my father had died during my early in-fancy and I wondered if the idea of someone, anyone, being pregnant reminded her of her pain. So we never talked much about my being pregnant. We talked around it. We discussed a trip to Europe she was planning. We debated current films. We talked about anything we could think of besides what was really on our minds. We were a lot alike in that sense—neither of us was comfortable discussing personal feelings with someone else. We just weren't that sort of people, Mother and I. We got along perfectly okay. Our relationship just wasn't very close.

"I'm nauseated in the morning," I said quietly.

She said nothing.

"Were *you?*" I asked.

"A couple of times. When I had my coffee." She put her brush down, looked at me. "We should buy you some mater-nity clothes."

That was the only conversation we had about my preg-nancy.

I took my list home with me from the doctor's office and added to it "How will I know if the baby is dead?"

A week later Frank came home.

He had a bristly crew cut and big muscles in his arms. He

was very proud of how hard his stomach was and kept kidding me about mine. We talked about names for the baby. I tried out Nebuchadnezzar on him and realized how long he'd been away when, for a brief instant, he didn't know I was kidding.

We looked at baby furniture. We looked at apartments and decided to keep living with my mother while I had the baby and finished school.

As soon as Frank got settled he put on a shirt and tie and took the train to New York to make arrangements for starting his job. He was twenty-three and was starting a new life. As it turned out, his accounting firm now had an opening in their Philadelphia office, and Frank grabbed it. It meant things would be much smoother. Everything seemed to be going smoother now that Frank was back.

We could always move to New York in a year or two.

Five weeks before the baby was due I was sitting in my political science conference course—we sat around a large, round table—when several sharp pains shot through me in rapid succession. They were so strong I gasped.

The professor looked at me with a raised eyebrow, wondering if perhaps I was about to disrupt his class by giving birth to a bouncing baby boy or girl on his conference table. I smiled bravely, wondering if I was, too. Fortunately the pains went away in a few minutes.

Still, I felt heavy and tired when class was over, so I took the bus straight home instead of going to the library. It was a bitterly cold February afternoon, gray, windy, and bleak. There were patches of ice on the sidewalk. I picked my way carefully around them as I walked home from the bus stop. When I got in the house, I took off my coat and shoes and rolled into bed with my clothes on, chilled and exhausted. Both Frank and Mother were at work. I lay there in the silent house, the covers up to my chin. I thought about calling the doctor to ask him about the pains, but I didn't want to bother him. I decided to take a nap instead. Now that I was getting warm, I was getting sleepy. I guess I dozed for about an hour before I awoke abruptly, in terror.

Warm water was coursing out from between my legs.

I didn't know what it meant. I called for Frank, for Mother.

Nobody was home yet. I was alone. Since it was a real physical symptom, I decided to call the doctor. The nurse put me
right through. I wondered if I'd be taking him away from
some other nervous mother-to-be whose stomach his hand
was on.

He came on the line and I told him what was happening.

"It's probably your water bag," he said calmly.

"Does that mean I'm in labor?" I blurted out.

"You might be."

"But I'm not due for another five weeks."

"Or it might mean nothing."

"How will I know if I'm in labor?"

"Just rest now."

"I've *been* resting."

"And call me back if there's any change."

He hung up and I got back under the covers. The phone
rang. It was Frank. He was on his way home. I told him I
didn't think I'd be able to make dinner tonight, if that was
okay. He offered to pick up some Chinese food. I was relieved. He asked me if everything was okay. I said it was, that
I had been leaking a little for a while but that I was fine now.
The flow of water had subsided, after all.

I got back in bed with my books and studied until the water
started to leak out again. I called the doctor again.

"Are you having any pains?" he asked.

"No. No, I'm not."

"Just stay put. Keep in touch. Relax."

Frank came home with the Chinese food. It smelled good. I
was suddenly starving. Whatever was happening to me had
no effect on my appetite. I folded a couple of towels, put them
on a kitchen chair, and sat on them while I devoured my
dinner. I had just about cleaned the plate when I got my first
contraction. It was like a menstrual cramp magnified a hun-
dredfold. It sucked my breath in, doubled me over.

"Are you okay?" asked Frank, eyes widening in terror.

I shook my head. He took my hand and helped me upstairs.
I got into bed and he sat beside me. Ten minutes later I got
another contraction. We called the doctor.

"What does it mean?" I asked.

"What it means," he explained, "is that you're in labor. You don't need to go to the hospital just yet, but when the pains are five minutes apart, you'll want to leave for the hospital. They'll call me when you get there."

"But I'm not supposed to have the baby yet," I protested.

"Evidently the baby has other plans."

I packed a suitcase and gathered my textbooks and papers. Midterms were coming up, and I thought I'd have plenty of time to study. The pains started coming closer together at midnight, so we left.

Frank drove slowly to the University of Pennsylvania Hospital. It had started to sleet and the streets were slick. He was amazingly calm. He drove to the emergency entrance, helped me out of the car, and told me to be careful. He proudly announced to the nurse at the desk that I was in labor and commanded her to phone my doctor. She did.

An orderly appeared with a wheelchair. He told me to sit in it. I did. He grabbed my suitcase, smacked it down on my non-lap, and started to whisk me down the hallway.

"Wait!" I cried. "What about my husband?"

"What about him?"

"Can't he come with me?"

"He having a baby, too?"

"Huh?"

Down the hallway we went. I never got to embrace Frank or say good-bye. I managed a half-wave over my shoulder before I was shoved through a set of double doors.

I was put in a bed. A group of nurses and doctors stood around me, murmuring. I could hear the sleet bouncing off the window.

"How long does it take?" I asked one of the nurses.

"A while," she replied.

"How long is a while?"

"Are you in pain?"

"Uh-huh."

"We can sedate you now."

"Is my doctor here?"

"We'll sedate you now."

She gave me a shot. I was in a twilight state almost immediately. I dozed for a while and awoke sometime during the night, nauseated and in even more pain. Two nurses were at the foot of my bed discussing the merits of the hamburgers they'd just eaten downstairs in the cafeteria.

"I didn't think they were so bad," said one.

"They were okay," said the other, "if you like your meat gray."

I burped Chinese food.

They turned to me.

"Are you in pain?" one asked me.

"Uh-huh," I replied.

"We're gonna give you something for that."

I heard a woman scream somewhere nearby.

"Will I scream like that?" I asked.

"Maybe," one of the nurses replied.

They gave me another shot and I went under again.

Sometime during the night I thought I saw Frank standing next to me, holding my hand. I dreamed that—he told me later he hadn't been there. I also thought I saw my mother standing over me, wearing a white doctor's coat and stethoscope, her cool hand on my forehead. That actually did happen. She was working as an administrative secretary in the medical school and had "borrowed" her boss's coat to check up on me.

Very early in the morning they gave me a needle in the spine. I don't remember anything after that.

Nancy was born at 6:52 a.m. on Thursday, February 27, 1958. I slept through the entire birth.

After it was all over, somebody woke me by pounding on my chest. "You have a baby girl, Mrs. Spungen!" he yelled in my ear. "A baby girl! Six pounds, five ounces!"

*Nancy,* I thought. *A baby girl, Nancy.* Nancy had been my grandmother's name.

I fell back to sleep, only to be awakened again, this time by my doctor, who towered over me in his surgical greens.

"Are you going to nurse?" he asked.

I looked around. I was lying on a gurney in a corridor.

"Huh?" My mouth was dry.

"Are you going to nurse? We have to put her on a schedule."

I seized on the word *schedule* and began to tell him my class schedule at Penn. "I have psychology, um, Tuesday and Thursday, from ten to—"

He broke in with laughter. A bunch of other people stood around laughing at me, too, having a merry old time.

"Go back to sleep," he said.

I did. Later I woke up back in my bed. Frank was there, really there this time, holding my hand.

"Did you see her?" I asked him.

"Sure did."

"How does she look?"

"Beautiful."

He looked funny. Something was bothering him.

"Are you okay, Frank?"

"Of course," he assured me. "The doctor sent me home about two, two-thirty, and then he called me at six. I never got much sleep."

Something was bothering him, though. I could tell. But I was too sleepy to pursue it. He kissed me. He hadn't shaved. He said he'd be back to visit me later. To visit *us* later.

I slept off the sedation but was still a little groggy when I woke up. I drank some water from a pitcher next to my bed and waited for someone to see I was awake and bring me my baby. I wanted to see her.

My obstetrician finally came in about noon. He still wore his green scrub suit.

"How do you feel?" he asked.

"Okay. Can I please see my baby now?"

He sat down on the edge of my bed. I noticed that for the first time since I had started going to him, he was not in a hurry.

"Can I see my baby?" I repeated.

"She's . . . she's experiencing some problems, Mrs. Spungen."

"What kind of problems?"

"She was born cyanotic."

"What's that mean?"

"Blue—her cord was wrapped around her neck, depriving her of oxygen. But don't worry, we gave her a heart stimulant and her intake is improving. We're monitoring her vital signs. I'm not too concerned about it.''

He didn't budge from the bed, though.

"What *are* you concerned about?" I asked.

"Her color. She's jaundiced."

"How come?"

"Well, ordinarily it's caused by an RH-negative blood condition. But your blood has been typed as O-positive, which would rule that out.''

"It *is* O-positive."

"First thing we're going to do is retype it, just in case an error was made. You never know. You might have been negative all this time. It's happened before. That's probably what it is—an error. Anyway, we're going to take some blood from you, okay?"

"Okay. When do I get to see my baby?"

"Soon." He patted me gently on the arm and left.

A couple of minutes later someone came and took my blood.

I called Frank on the phone. "Something's wrong with Nancy," I said.

"You mean about the cord?"

"You already know?"

"He told me this morning. Before I saw you."

"Why didn't you say something?"

"I didn't want to upset you."

"Now it's something else. She's jaundiced. They don't know why. Something to do with my blood or her blood or something.''

"I'll be right there."

But it took Frank over an hour to get to the hospital, during which time my doctor returned in his street clothes to tell me my original blood typing was correct. I was indeed O-positive. He said Nancy's jaundice wasn't improving and that he was calling in a specialist, a pediatric hematologist. The hematologist had requested some additional blood samples from Nancy, and they were being sent to Children's Hospital by police car for processing.

He patted me on the arm again and left.

I didn't know what to think. I was confused and afraid. I didn't know what any of this meant. I didn't know if she was actually going to die and nobody was telling me so as not to upset me. Maybe she wasn't supposed to exist. Maybe she didn't exist. I didn't know. I still hadn't been allowed to see her.

Frank finally arrived. He looked sad and bewildered. He gave me a hug and I clung to him.

"She'll be all right," he assured me unconvincingly.

"What if she isn't? What if she dies?"

"She won't die."

He began to pace nervously around the room. I shared it with one other woman, whose curtain was drawn.

"We just have to wait is all," he said. "Wait."

"Where were you?"

"I had a stop to make."

"Maybe we'll go to New York now. You wanted to."

"Cut it out."

"We both did. We both wanted to."

"That's not important now. Just . . . just forget about it. This'll work out."

"Where did you have to stop?"

"I went to the store where we bought the crib. I changed everything to pink instead of yellow."

"What's wrong with yellow?"

*"She's* yellow. I just thought . . . I don't know what I thought."

I took his hand. He thought changing the color of the crib would make her okay. He sounded like a kid. I sounded like a kid. We *were* kids, confused kids who were unprepared for responsibility, facing a future that seemed to be slipping out of our control.

We met the new doctor, the hematologist. He was thin, dark, calm. He had diagnosed Nancy's problem as ABO incompatibility.

"It's similar to RH-negative, at least in effect," he explained. "Actually it's the opposite of RH-negative. It occurs in firstborns."

Frank and I looked at each other, baffled.

"What do you do about it?" Frank asked.

"We change the infant's blood."

"How?" I gasped, horrified.

"A series of exchange transfusions. We can't change it all in one transfusion—too much of a shock."

"Okay," Frank nodded.

"Why did this happen?" I asked.

"There are a number of causes," my obstetrician said.

"None of which fit this particular set of circumstances," the hematologist pointed out. He turned back to me. "We'll start the exchange series tomorrow morning. First thing."

Frank cleared his throat. "How . . . uh, is it pretty dangerous or what?"

"The fatality rate is fairly low."

"How low is 'fairly' low?" I asked, my voice quavering. Frank took my hand.

The specialist explained that the main concern was Nancy's bilirubin level, which measures the bile in the blood. It presently measured over nineteen milligrams and was climbing rapidly. He said that twenty-two milligrams and above was considered the level where neurological damage—cerebral palsy, mental retardation—could occur. It was imperative, he said, to lower Nancy's bilirubin level.

As I tried to soak all of this information in, it occurred to me that if time was so important, why weren't they going to exchange at once instead of the next morning? But who was I to question them?

We thanked the doctors. Visiting hours were over, so Frank had to leave. He promised to return early in the morning to be with me.

Once again I felt very alone. I had a roommate behind the curtain but we hadn't had a chance to talk. During the feeding hours no one had brought her baby to her, either.

"My baby was stillborn," she said now, from behind the curtain.

"I'm so sorry," I said.

"The nurse told me they put you in here with me because they don't like to put a mother of a live baby in with a mother of a dead baby. I guess they don't figure your baby has much of a chance. But I guess you already know that."

What a mean, bitter thing to say, I thought. It wounded me. But in a way she was right. I didn't feel like a mother. I hadn't seen or touched or nursed my baby. I had no feeling of her being alive. My body hurt; I felt bruised all over. But I didn't feel as if I'd given birth that morning. I just felt empty.

I tried to sleep that night but couldn't. I was awake in the middle of the night when the nurses were padding around out in the hall, bringing babies to their mothers for feeding. I felt like I didn't belong there. I wasn't a member of their club.

A nurse asked me to sign a paper in the morning, a standard form that gave the doctors permission to perform the blood exchange on Nancy. She left before I remembered to ask her if the release was legally binding, since I was still a minor.

Another nurse came in and said, "Would you like to see your baby before they take her to the O.R.?"

"Can I?" I begged.

"Sure, honey. You ought to see her. Just in case . . . well, just in case."

She helped me out of bed and down the hall. I hadn't been up yet and was pretty wobbly. She propped me against the nursery window and went inside. A minute later she opened the curtain.

Nancy was wrapped in a pink blanket. The first thing that hit me was what a tiny, vulnerable human being she was. Her eyes were closed, her face was bright yellow, and she had an amazing amount of thick, dark hair on her head. The nurses had combed it into a little ponytail and put a pink ribbon around it.

I felt love and protectiveness for that tiny infant. I was a mother—that infant's mother.

I gestured to the nurse to unwrap the blanket. I wanted to make sure Nancy had all of her fingers and toes—my mother once told me she had counted mine. The nurse unwrapped the blanket and I duly performed the count. There were indeed ten fingers and ten toes. But each of her heels was covered by several gauze patches held on with tape.

I nodded to the nurse, and she wrapped Nancy back up in

her blanket and closed the nursery curtain. A moment later she came out of the nursery to help me back to my bed.

"Those patches on her heels," I said. "What are they?"

"That's where we take the blood in a newborn, honey," she said. "We take it from the heel. She needed a lot of tests, the poor thing."

Years later, when Nancy had become a heroin addict and I saw her for the first time with needle marks all over her arms, hands, ankles, and the backs of her knees, I remembered the first time I had seen her in the nursery with the gauze patches on her heels.

I got back into bed to wait. Frank was on his way, and the doctors had promised they'd come tell me what had happened when the procedure was over.

I tried to suppress my feelings for Nancy. I still hadn't touched her or nursed her. It would be more sensible if I didn't feel a lot for her, I decided, because she might very well die.

But I *couldn't* suppress my feelings. I had seen her. She existed. I was her mother, and I was going to do my best to give her a life of love, a life of quality—even if that life ended in an hour. This commitment meant I would now have to cope with a great deal of pain if I lost her; I knew that. But I still felt better than I had during the night.

Frank was by my side when the doctors came in at about eight. They were both grinning.

"That's some kind of fighter you have," laughed the hematologist. "She screamed and kicked so much I had to tie her down. First time I've ever had to tie a baby down for that procedure."

"Is she going to make it?" I asked.

"Are you kidding? If she was a boy I'd say you've got the future heavyweight champion of the world on your hands."

He laughed. We all laughed, we were so relieved.

"Can we see her?" Frank asked.

"You bet."

I looked for her through the nursery window. My eyes scanned one infant after another sleeping peacefully in a row. She wasn't one of them.

She was lying in a glass-enclosed isolette in the very back of the nursery, naked except for a patch over her navel, where the transfusion had been done. Her mouth was open and she was screaming hysterically. Her yellow body was thrashing about angrily. The fighter description was an apt one—she looked as if she were in the midst of a battle.

"Is she all right?" I asked the doctor, concerned.

"She doesn't feel any physical pain. Not to worry."

But I did worry. I felt helpless. I wanted to hold her, which was impossible since they wouldn't let me in the nursery or her out.

A nurse removed her from the isolette to feed her and Nancy's little arms and legs flailed wildly. She kicked at the nurse with her tiny feet and screamed. Her minute fists began to beat on her own face. The nurse tried to calm her down but couldn't.

I thought it was a good sign that she was so active. It meant she was alive. But she was in pain. I was sure of it—with a mother's certainty.

We never knew for certain what effect Nancy's traumatic birth—the oxygen deprivation, the ABO incompatibility, the blood exchange—had on her later behavior. There were simply too many unknowns.

But we do know that children who face great life-threatening traumas at birth share many of the same personality characteristics. They spend much of their lives angry. Their behavior is often violent, much of it self-directed, like Nancy's was. I have seen some of these other children and talked to their parents. A common thread exists.

This syndrome is presently acknowledged by the medical community and is being dealt with. This was not so in 1958.

Her bilirubin stabilized after the first exchange, so no more transfusions were necessary. She was four days old when they finally let me hold her.

I heard a commotion outside my room in the hall. Then I heard the nice nurse, the one who'd let me see Nancy before the exchange, say, "I hope that poor girl is lying down because she just may faint."

Then a gang of six or seven smiling doctors and nurses invaded my room. I saw the bundle in the pink blanket, with a shock of dark hair sticking out, and I gasped with surprise and joy.

I took her in my arms gingerly, afraid I was holding her wrong, but she seemed comfortable enough. I felt the warmth of her body, smelled the sweet baby smell, touched the silky skin of her cheeks, stroked her glossy hair.

Her eyes were open and she looked up at me. Her eyes were dark. The iris and pupil were the same color. There was a burning intensity in those eyes. They were like coals.

She wrapped her little fist around my finger. Her skin was still very yellow, but she was very much alive.

The nurses showed me how to nurse her. Nancy began to feed hungrily. I was so happy. I felt like a queen on a throne. My princess was at my breast, her entourage fanned about, watching with admiration.

At last I had my baby.

On the evening of our eighth day there the hematologist came to tell me we could go home in the morning.

"When do you want to see her again?" I asked.

"Don't need to," he replied. "We checked her for central nervous system damage—she's A-one. Reflexes normal. She's gaining weight. As far as I can see, Nancy's a normal baby. Take her home and treat her like one."

So we did. True, Nancy had had a rough beginning in life, but everything was going to be fine now. The baby we took home next morning was a certified healthy and normal baby girl. Almost pink.

# ☐ Chapter 2

Frank had set up a nursery in one of the upstairs bedrooms—my old bedroom, in fact. There was a crib with pink teddy bears on it, and a pink bathinette. My old chest of drawers was now painted white. The room was bright and spotless and beautiful.

I carried Nancy upstairs and laid her in her crib. Frank and I stood over her, beaming. She looked so sweet in her knitted bonnet and starched white baby dress. It was the same baby dress my mother had brought me home in when I was born. Nancy's eyes took in the new surroundings.

"You're home, Nancy," I said. "You're *home.*"

Frank put his arm around me. We hugged. We were so happy. We were a family now. Nancy was the start of a whole new, wonderful life for us.

"Hello, Nanki-poo," cooed Frank. He grabbed her tiny fingers one by one. "Look at that little Nanki-poo finger . . . and *that* Nanki-poo finger . . . and that one . . ."

I undressed her and put her in a pink nightgown. Then I picked her up carefully and sat down with her in the rocking chair Frank had moved in from our room. I began to nurse her. Frank stayed to watch, so filled with pride and love at seeing our child feed at my breast that tears formed in his eyes.

I had never taken care of a baby before. As a gift, Mother had paid a baby nurse to help me for the first two weeks. I was thrilled. This gave me a chance to get my energy back, catch up on my schoolwork, and learn how to bathe and diaper Nancy from an expert. Mrs. Taylor, a cheery black woman in her fifties, was indeed an expert. She had worked with babies her whole life. She was unbelievably relaxed around Nancy.

I wasn't. Especially when it was time for Mrs. Taylor to take her day off at the end of week one. It meant taking care of Nancy all by myself for the first time. I was terrified.

As soon as Mrs. Taylor walked out the door, Nancy began to cry. I went to her crib, picked her up carefully, and cradled her.

"There, there, Nancy. Don't cry," I said. She didn't stop. "Mommy's here, Nancy. Mommy's here."

That made her start screaming. I got frightened and called out to Frank downstairs.

He came up. "What's wrong?" he asked. "Why's she screaming?"

"She doesn't like me," I replied as Nancy squirmed and screamed in my arms.

"Don't be silly. Maybe she's hungry."

"I just fed her."

"Maybe she's wet."

"Mrs. Taylor diapered her before she left."

"Well, something must be bothering her. Babies don't just cry for no reason. Do they?"

"She doesn't like me," I repeated.

"Maybe you're holding her wrong."

"This is the way Mrs. Taylor showed me."

"Sure?"

"Of course I'm sure!"

"Okay, okay. Don't get upset. Here, let me try holding her."

He cradled her tentatively, lowered his head to her, and

made little kissing noises with his mouth. She kept screaming.

"Hello, Nanki-poo," he cooed. "What's wrong with little Nanki-poo?"

She screamed louder.

"What the hell, I must be holding her wrong, too." He handed her back to me.

By this time Mother had come in. "Why's she screaming?" she asked.

"We don't know," Frank and I said in unison.

"Here, let me try," she offered. She cradled Nancy and rocked her back and forth. The bawling didn't let up.

"Maybe," Mother ventured, "she doesn't *want* to be held."

"That's possible," Frank said. "Why don't we put her back in the crib?"

"She was *in* the crib when she started, " I said.

"You may as well try," Mother said.

I put Nancy back in her crib. She didn't stop screaming and crying. She cried the whole day. She cried when I diapered her, bathed her, fed her. She screamed when I came in the room.

I took it very personally. I prided myself on doing things well. I was a good student. I had taught myself to be a good cook. But I was already a total failure as a mother.

She was still screaming when Frank and I went to bed. He was able to get to sleep anyway. I wasn't. I got up, wrapped her in her blanket, and carried her downstairs. I got my papers and books together, poured myself a glass of milk, and went to work on my senior thesis at the dining table. Nancy in one arm.

The sooner I finished my thesis, the sooner I'd get my diploma and become a full-time mother to my baby—a good mother.

After a while she stopped squirming and bawling and fell asleep. My arm began to ache, but I didn't put her down.

I saw the dawn, still writing, still holding Nancy, who was by now wide-awake and screaming again. She was crying when Mrs. Taylor finally arrived.

Exhausted and frustrated, I poured out my failure to her before she had her coat off. I think I may have even whined. Mrs. Taylor immediately went into action. Off went the coat and hat. Into her arms went Nancy. She began walking her around the room and humming.

Nancy magically stopped screaming.

"I *did* that," I complained. "It didn't work. She hates me."

"No, she doesn't. She's been this way all week," Mrs. Taylor said.

"She has?" I'd been so busy with school I hadn't noticed.

"Sure. A lot of babies fuss at first, until they get settled. And her having all that trouble her first day, it's taking her a little longer. It's just her way. Don't you worry."

"I thought it was me."

"Maybe a little," she admitted.

"What am I doing wrong?"

"You're not comfortable. She senses that. As soon as you relax with her, she'll relax with you."

"Makes sense."

It did make sense. Perfect sense. Unfortunately it never worked out that way.

I did get my diploma that June. And we did move into our own apartment, a small two-bedroom duplex at the end of a block of row duplexes. It was on the other side of Philadelphia in Mt. Airy. Right across the street was a playground with swings and merry-go-rounds, and a bus stop so Frank could get to work easily.

But Nancy didn't stop crying and screaming. She screamed all day and all night. She never slept for more than an hour at a stretch, awakening with a scream. I would go to her, cradle her, walk her around. She would stop bawling and eventually fall back to sleep. But as soon as I put her back in the crib, she would start up again.

Babies do cry. But Nancy did nothing *but* cry. She would not be diverted or pacified. Her crying was shrill and constant—twenty-four hours a day. She cried while we ate, talked, watched TV, made love, tried to sleep. We were always aware of Nancy crying. I did everything I could. I checked to see if she needed burping, if she was wet, if a pin was sticking her. I got so frustrated I begged her to *tell* me what was wrong, *willing* her to speak. There was nothing I could do to make her stop.

She began to wear us down, make us irritable.

I described the situation to her first pediatrician, whose office was around the corner from Mother's house. He said she was probably crying because I didn't have enough milk for her. I stopped nursing her and put her on formula. She didn't stop screaming. He said maybe she was still hungry and suggested I try giving her some solid food. I did. She ate everything and began to put on weight. She didn't stop screaming, though.

As soon as we moved into our new apartment, I drove Nancy to a new pediatrician. She loved being in the car and slept peacefully—as long as it was moving. As soon as I stopped for a red light, she awoke screaming. It was as if she had antennae all over her, alert to any slight change in the environment. I was sorely tempted to run every red light in Mt. Airy. It's a wonder I didn't.

The new doctor was young, soft-spoken, and friendly. He examined Nancy, listened to my complaint about her, and said, "First off, you're overfeeding her."

"But the other doctor said—"

"She's eating too much food. Way too much. As for this continuous crying, let me ask you something, Mrs. Spungen. What do you do when she cries during the night? Do you go to her, comfort her, sit with her?"

"Of course."

"That's your problem right there."

"What is?"

"You're spoiling her."

"Spoiling her? How?"

"You're conditioning her to believe that all she has to do in order to get food and love is to cry. She does it to get your attention, and you reward her by giving it to her."

"You mean I should just leave her there in the crib screaming?"

"Exactly. Ignore her. Let her cry herself out. As soon as

she realizes she's not getting any attention, she'll stop doing it.''

His diagnosis fit what I had privately suspected right off—that Nancy's bawling was my fault. I drove her home and told Frank that night what the doctor had said. We vowed not to go to her when she screamed that night.

She cried for two hours after I put her to bed. I fought my desire to go to her. It was hard.

"Maybe she's in pain," I fretted.

"Leave her," Frank said. "The doctor said to leave her."

So I did, and she finally stopped. But she started again when we went to bed—turning off the light switch in our bedroom awakened her. It took her two more hours to cry herself out. Her screaming cut through me like a knife, but I followed doctor's orders.

This went on for a week. Since the sound of a light switch was enough to awaken her, we learned to sit in the dark after I'd put her to bed. My friend Janet and her husband lived nearby. They came over to visit one night and sat with us in the darkened living room, afraid to utter a single word or use the bathroom. We tiptoed around in stocking feet. We served them iced tea without ice because we were afraid the noise from cracking ice would awaken her. Janet and Myron accepted all of this as normal business with someone who had a new baby. We were the first people they'd ever known who had one. At first I accepted it, too, though I was beginning to wonder if all babies were so sensitive and cried so much, if all parents never went to the movies or out to dinner. I did wonder how anyone survived being a parent.

After a week of this "don't spoil her" strategy Frank and I were beginning to snap at each other. He kept complaining that he couldn't stay alert at work because he was so sleepy from Nancy's middle-of-the-night, two-hour screaming sessions. In desperation I called the doctor and complained that his strategy wasn't proving effective. He prescribed liquid phenobarbital to help her sleep.

I kept a baby book for Nancy, in which I noted all of the important days and events in her life as they occurred. I noted the first time Nancy smiled—it was when she discovered that the toy birds in the mobile over her crib would move if she touched them. I pasted in the book a snapshot of Nancy eating her first ice cream cone—most of which ended up on her nose. I noted her first trip to a restaurant—she and I took Frank to Sunken Gardens for Father's Day (though we had to leave before finishing the main course because she wouldn't stop screaming). For Nancy's first birthday I pasted in a snapshot in which she sat with her proud parents watching, a delighted smile on her face and both her hands in the birthday cake.

I didn't note, however, that day in the third month of her life when she took her first drug dose. I should have. It was the most significant occasion of them all.

This doctor, who gave Nancy a drug to control or mask her problems, was the first in a long line. Actually, I think now he prescribed it to her to shut me up. I don't think he believed me when I described Nancy's condition. He probably thought I was a selfish, annoying mother and that the phenobarbital would stop my complaining. Phenobarbital was an easy solution. Unfortunately it also covered up whatever the real problem was.

From phenobarbital to heroin, the road was not paved with good intentions.

It was a red liquid that came in a little amber bottle. I gave it to her on her tongue with an eyedropper. She would scream for twenty or thirty minutes, then fall asleep for an hour, sometimes two. Then she would wake up and scream. I would give her more every four hours according to the directions.

The phenobarbital seemed to have no effect on her activity level, which was increasingly high. Technically, Nancy didn't fall under the category of a hyperactive child. She had no learning disabilities. Far from it—she was tremendously bright and verbal at a very early age. She had a twelve-word vocabulary before her first birthday, including *please, thank you,* and *airplane.* Complete seven- and eight-word sentences quickly followed. Her first was "Fee-Fie-Foe-Fum, I smell the blood of an English muffin." But she was restless. There was discomfort inside her. She was never content, never relaxed. She had an unbelievable amount of energy, most of which she consumed by crawling.

Once she began to crawl, at six months, she crawled every waking moment. She hated confinement and refused to stay in her crib or playpen. She wanted to crawl. She crawled in and out of rooms. She crawled up onto furniture and down off it. Nothing stopped her, not even the heavy metal Dennis-Brown splint she had to start wearing to correct the angle of her legs, which were growing out abnormally. She just dragged the splint around behind her.

When the weather became nice, I took Nancy to the playground across the street in her carriage. Five or six other mothers took their babies there regularly. They sat in a row on the park bench and talked about shades of lipstick, styles of clothing, and hair while their babies dozed contentedly in their carriages or played with little toys. I read a book while Nancy crawled furiously across the playground in her overalls, exploring, getting covered with wood chips.

One time my friend Janet brought her new baby along and we went to the park together. Like the other babies there, Janet's gurgled peacefully while Nancy crawled around like a demon.

I went over to Nancy and picked her up. "Don't you want to sit nice like the other boys and girls, Nancy?" I murmured in her ear.

I began to carry her to her stroller. In response she screamed at me angrily, her face turning bright red. I cuddled her. She reacted by suddenly stiffening her body like a board, arms and legs thrust out straight, head thrown back. She screamed even louder. I tried to relax her limbs but she fought me.

"Is something wrong with her?" gasped Janet.

"I . . . I don't know," I replied, frightened.

I tried to get her into her stroller—*bend* her in, really. She continued to fight me. I finally got her in, so stiff she was almost standing. The other mothers were looking at us now. Again I tried to cuddle her. Again she wouldn't let me.

"What should I do?" I asked Janet.

She said she had no idea.

I pulled Nancy out of the stroller and put her back down. She sped away instantly, blazing a path across the park. I watched her. So did the other mothers, clearly wondering what was wrong with her.

This was my first awareness that possibly Nancy was different from other babies. I was concerned and bewildered. Her pediatrician, however, was not.

"She is a very curious little girl, I'll grant you that," he admitted as he watched her crawl around on the floor of his examining room. "Very active. But not abnormally so."

"What about the way she stiffened up?" I asked. "She keeps doing it. She won't let me hug her anymore. At all."

He shrugged. "That's just her way. She's not affectionate. Don't take it personally."

Nor was he concerned about two physical symptoms from birth that were becoming more and more pronounced. One of her eyes was beginning to cross, and she seemed unable to keep her tongue in her mouth. He said that, taken together, they *could* suggest neurological impairment. But he said she was much too bright for us to worry about that. He said she would outgrow both, no problem.

"How's her sleeping?" he asked me. "Is she still having trouble? Screaming?"

"Yes."

"Let's increase her dosage then."

He gave me the instructions for how much phenobarbital to give her, and I left his office with the distinct impression that he thought I was exaggerating Nancy's problems. I wondered if he was right. I certainly was the only one who was worried. Frank wasn't. But Frank wasn't with her all day like I was. He left her in the morning and didn't come back until evening. She was always on her best behavior then, waiting anxiously for him on a chair by the window, watching the street. Whenever a bus stopped, she clapped her hands and looked for Frank. When he got off the bus, she crawled excitedly to the front door to wait for him. She sat like a little angel on his lap while he ate dinner. Afterward he played her folk songs on his guitar. She seemed to love music.

No, Frank wasn't worried about her.

I decided that the problem was with me. I was fretting un-
necessarily because I was bored. I had no activities except for
cooking and cleaning and following Nancy around. Everything I did was in response to what she wanted. I needed intellectual stimulation. The only adults I saw all day were those
mothers at the park. Suddenly I desperately wanted to get out
of the house. I was cut out to do more than this. I decided I
would go back to school and get my master's degree. That
was the answer.

The trouble was that we couldn't afford a baby sitter. My
mother was only working part-time then and still lived near
Penn, so I asked her if she'd mind taking care of Nancy if I
went back to school. I could drop her off on my way to class.
She said she wouldn't mind at all—she was anxious for me to
resume my career plans.

Since I had never left Nancy with anyone, I thought a test
visit was in order. So I dropped Nancy off at Mother's apartment one afternoon while I picked up some catalogs and applications on campus. I left her there for an hour. Returning, I
was still half a block away from the house when I heard her
hysterical screaming.

Nancy was squirming in my mother's arms, yelling like I'd
never heard her before; there was an animal-like intensity to
it. Her body shook. To this day I've never seen another baby
cry with such ferocity.

"When did this start?" I gasped at Mother.

"As soon as you left," she replied, shaken.

I took Nancy in my arms and tried to comfort her, but it
was no use—she didn't seem to recognize me.

"Mommy's here, Nancy!" I cried. "It's Mommy!"

But she didn't stop.

I held her close to my face. "It's Mommy, Nancy!" Still
she didn't stop. In desperation I took her to the hallway mirror
and pressed her face to mine, in the mirror right before us.

"It's Mommy, Nancy! Mommy's here! Mommy's holding
you!" I repeated the sentence over and over again. After five
minutes she finally seemed to realize I was there. She started
to calm down, but wouldn't let me put her down.

I took her straight home, holding her in my lap as I drove.

After a few blocks she began to doze. When I got her home, she immediately began to crawl around on the living room floor, the incident forgotten.

I stood there watching her, realizing with a sense of sinking despair that I was not, in the near future, going to be able to leave her alone, to go back to school, to achieve my career goals. All of that was going to have to wait. Nancy was my priority now. My life was built around her. Not that I didn't want this to be the case—I loved her. But it struck me at this moment that if I wanted my career it was going to be much, much harder than I'd imagined—that it was going to be *in spite* of her.

Or maybe it was simply never going to happen.

I began to watch soap operas on television during the day. I began to feel trapped, a prisoner. Something had to change.

It did.

I got pregnant again.

# ❑ Chapter 3

I was an only child. Frank had one sister, but she was six years older than he was. We both wanted a lot of kids, and we wanted them to be close together in age so all of us could enjoy the kind of family life Frank and I felt we'd missed out on.

I had so terribly wanted a brother or sister when I was growing up. It seemed as if I was always with adults. I felt very alone. My friends had large families. When I went to their houses, the rooms spilled over with kids and noise and activity, sharing and loving. They seemed so happy and alive. My house seemed so quiet.

Having a brother or sister meant companionship. It also meant a distribution of the burden. Since I was the only child, I was expected to do it all—be smart and pretty and popular and good. If you had brothers and sisters, I thought, you didn't have to accomplish it all. You needn't be perfect.

Frank, meanwhile, loved kids. When we had first started dating, he mentioned several times how much he wanted to have a big family someday. He loved being an uncle to his older sister's toddlers, Dean and Ellen. In fact, the first time

Frank brought me home to meet his parents, he made sure Dean and Ellen were there, too. He even taught them a poem to recite for me and hovered proudly over them while they performed.

We both thought Dean and Ellen were adorable and agreed that someday we would like to have two or four of our own just like them. Never three or five. You weren't supposed to have an odd number, everyone advised in those days. One of them would feel left out or ganged-up on.

During our courtship we often took long walks and talked about what we wanted out of life. Each of us wanted a career. It was important to me to accomplish something on my own. Frank was all for it. We wanted to move to New York and be successes. We wanted not so much to accumulate things as to *do* things. We wanted to find cozy French restaurants nobody else knew about. We wanted to read the newest books, see the most talked about plays, find the truest, smokiest jazz clubs. We wanted to go to Europe.

We wavered about when to have kids, since we did want them and they did tie you down. At first we talked about having them right away. Then, one evening while we were engaged, we were invited to a dinner at a professor's house. He and his wife had just had a baby. She was cute as a button but she cried during dinner. Frank kept making funny faces and noises to cheer her up, but to no avail. He asked the professor's wife if he could pick the baby up. She said yes. He hoisted the tot out of her high chair, bounced her on his knee, and she spit up all over his good tie.

"Let's wait five years," he said to me on the way home. I agreed.

Then Nancy came along, and the life we wanted had to be put on the back burner. So it made perfect sense to have another child right away. I already had to be at home with Nancy. Why not be home with Nancy and her little brother or sister, too?

Her little sister, it turned out. Susan was born September 21, 1959, when Nancy was a week short of nineteen months old. Susan was a beautiful, pink, eight-pound baby. Mrs.

Taylor came and stayed with Nancy while I was in the hospital. She reported that Nancy was difficult.

Frank carried Susan into the house. I came in separately from the new baby so as not to confuse or threaten Nancy. The baby books all said to do that.

Nancy began screaming the second she saw me. I almost cried at that moment. Seeing and hearing her reminded me of how much time and energy she demanded. I honestly wasn't sure I'd have enough strength and love for another child.

On the first day Nancy totally ignored her baby sister until it was time for me to feed Susan. Nancy was walking now. She came over to stand right next to me, watching intently. Suzy's little fist was curled around my finger. Nancy calmly reached over, uncurled the fingers, and removed them. Then she walked away. I gazed after her, chilled inwardly. Nancy's action didn't seem, well, *right*. It gave me the creeps.

Susan was so different from her older sister. She liked to be held and she cuddled into me instead of squirming and protesting. She was calm. She didn't wake with a start if you dropped something or turned off a light. But she didn't seem as bright as Nancy had been during her first few months. She wasn't as responsive to her environment.

Whereas Susan seemed to occupy a middle ground, Nancy was all extremes. We began to think of her as the little girl in the nursery rhyme:

> There was a little girl who had a little curl
> Right in the middle of her forehead,
> And when she was good she was very, very good,
> But when she was bad she was horrid.

Nancy was two when we decided to move to a bigger place. We bought this time—a semi-detached house with four small bedrooms and a finished basement that would be a nice playroom. It was on Welsh Road in greater northeast Philadelphia, a newer neighborhood with a school nearby and lots of kids on the block. My mother loaned us the money for the down payment.

She also had to help us make our mortgage payments for a

few months because right after we got our loan, Frank's accounting firm decided to close its Philadelphia office. He was offered a job in the New York office, but that was out of the question now. He quickly got another accounting job in Philadelphia, but that firm went bankrupt and we were soon on unemployment.

Frank wasn't happy in accounting, never had been. He liked people, not paperwork. He wanted to get out from behind a desk, get out on his own two feet and prove what he could do. So rather than take another unfulfilling job, he decided to make a change. He took a sales position with a paper distributor. The pay was a bit lower than he'd been getting in accounting, but he felt it was something he could really dig his teeth into and someday be a success at. Finding something challenging was very important to Frank. So was working toward being financially secure enough so we would never have to borrow money from my mother again.

Now that Frank's employment situation was settled, we faced another obstacle: Nancy decided she didn't want to move. I couldn't figure out why, but she was very determined about staying. I would pack a carton, she would unpack it. At first I thought she was playing, but she wasn't. I found out how serious she was when the telephone man came to disconnect our phones.

I was in the kitchen, packing, while he worked on the bedroom phone. Suddenly I heard him yell, "Lady, get her the hell off me!"

I dashed to the bedroom. Nancy was attached to one of the man's legs and was pounding at him with both fists, enraged.

"P-p-put my ph-phone back!" she screamed—she was starting to stutter now. "Put it b-b-back!"

"Nancy!" I cried. "We'll get *another* phone!"

She didn't hear me. She continued to attack his leg, frenzied. He tried to shake her off but she absolutely would not let go.

"I'll get her off," I assured him.

"Thanks," he said, eyes wide with fear. Clearly, he had never been attacked by a ferocious two-year-old or met any human being who cared so much about her telephone.

I had to pry her off his leg, first one hand, then the other, then her legs, which continued to kick wildly in midair when I pulled her away. And she continued to scream, "P-p-ut it b-b-back!"

He hurriedly finished his job and left. But it was at least an hour before Nancy calmed down. I had never seen such intense anger in her before. In anyone. It frightened me. I told Frank about it as soon as he got home, but it didn't make much of an impression on him. He hadn't seen the incident, couldn't fathom Nancy's ferocity, couldn't *believe* it. Besides, Frank reasoned, her reaction—however severe—was doubtless a product of her being upset about moving. All kids, he said, have trouble adjusting to it. He felt certain she'd calm down once we were settled. Frank's view made sense to me. I agreed with him.

Nancy had simply overreacted a bit.


Right from the start she didn't get along with the other kids in our new neighborhood. She fought with them. She'd go outside to play in our joint backyards and within ten minutes would be back, sobbing and stammering that one of the children had hit her or taken one of her toys. There was definitely something about Nancy that alienated them. Most of them were two years older than she was. While she was on a par with them verbally and intellectually, none of them were still in diapers. At first I thought perhaps they were taunting her about that. She did, too. Previously she had resisted all of my efforts to toilet train her. But on one of those days that she came running in, crying, she ripped off her diapers, threw them in the trash can, and claimed, "I w-w-want big girl p-pants now."

She was completely toilet trained from that day on.

But that wasn't why she didn't get along. She continued to get into fights. Unable to deal with the frustration outside, she started to spend more and more time inside. But there was frustration inside, too, and Nancy simply could not handle it.

I found this out one afternoon when I was making dinner.

Nancy was sitting at the kitchen table eating a banana. It broke.

"F-f-fix it, Mommy!" she demanded.

"Nancy, you can't put a banana back together."

"F-fix it!" she repeated.

"Look at it this way—now you have two bananas."

*"Fix it!"*

"I can't!"

She began to cry and pound the table with her fists.

"Now, Nancy" I explained, calmly as possible, "There's no point in getting upset about this."

"B-but it isn't *fair*!"

"What isn't fair, sweetheart?"

"It isn't *fair*!"

And with that she threw herself to the floor and began to scream, "It isn't fair! It isn't fair!" over and over again, legs and arms pounding the floor with tremendous force. Soon she was just screaming—no words—and her face was scarlet.

"Nancy!" I cried, horrified.

No response from her. She didn't see me. She rolled over onto her back and began to beat herself repeatedly in the face.

I tried to pick her up. I couldn't get hold of her; she kept whipping around on the floor so violently that a chair fell over. I tried again. She fought me, screaming and sobbing. Finally I managed to gather all of her limbs in my arms and picked her up.

I carried my wild, thrashing two-year-old up the stairs to her room and put her on the bed. She immediately hurled herself off the bed onto the floor and began flopping around like a fish, screaming and sobbing, eyes ablaze.

I didn't know what to do. I wanted to call the doctor but I was afraid to leave her. So I just stood there, feeling totally helpless, trying futilely to calm her. After about twenty minutes she started to hyperventilate, then stopped. She passed out.

I held her in my arms, wiped her moist brow. She was asleep, still gasping.

I picked her up, put her on the bed, put a blanket over her, and phoned her pediatrician, my hands shaking.

"Yep, she's in the 'terrible twos' all right," he said.

"What's that? What's the 'terrible twos'?"

"Lots of two-year-olds get tantrums."

"That was no tantrum."

"From what you described, it sounds to me like a not un-common two-year-old's temper tantrum. Maybe a bit force-ful, but she's an energetic kid. It's just a stage. They outgrow it as soon as they realize they can't always have everything their way. A lot of two-year-olds have tantrums every once in a while. Don't worry about it. She'll be fine when she wakes up."

He was right—she was calm when she woke up an hour later. In the meantime I checked my baby books, and they agreed about the "terrible twos" having the occasional tan-trum.

But Nancy didn't have them occasionally. She started hav-ing several violent tantrums every day, literally from morning to night. She kicked and screamed when it was time to put her clothes on in the morning. She did the same when it was time to get into her pajamas at night. During the course of a day the slightest thing set her off. If I disagreed with her about some-thing—refused to give her a food she wanted, for example—she quickly turned the disagreement into a confrontation and then an eruption. I was not necessarily the catalyst. One time she was quietly coloring with crayons on the living room floor, then suddenly exploded into a frenzied screaming at-tack. Later I looked at the coloring book and saw that she'd accidentally colored outside one of the lines. This was enough to trigger a fit. I was powerless to prevent the fits, and once they started I was powerless to stop them.

I waited for her to outgrow them. As far as I knew, there was nothing else for me *to* do but wait. One day I thought she finally had done that. I was reading on the living room sofa when she came up the stairs from the basement and walked past me with this strange, glazed look in her eyes.

"Where are you going, Nancy?"

"I'm g-g-going to my r-room. I f-f-feel funny, Mommy."

"How do you feel funny?"

She twisted her face, as if she were in pain. "I'm g-going to my room. I'll come o-o-out wh-when I'm better."

She walked slowly upstairs to her room. I followed her up there a minute later and found her sitting up on her bed, staring into space. She didn't notice me, and I left. An hour later she came bounding down the steps, her dark brown eyes all sparkly and alive again, and went back down to the basement to play.

I took this as the promised breakthrough. I thought she had at last come to grips with handling frustration and would be okay now. I was relieved.

I was also wrong. Less than an hour later she had a full-blown fit when she couldn't reach something in the refrigerator. I didn't know how to respond. What could I do? I couldn't control her environment so tightly as to keep her entirely free of frustration. That wasn't possible. All I could do was feel helpless and inadequate.

The tantrums grew with her. As her vocabulary developed over the next few months, verbal tantrums were added to the inarticulate seizures on the floor. At first I didn't recognize them for what they were—another manifestation of whatever was boiling over inside her two-year-old mind.

The first one started in my bedroom. I was making the bed in the morning. She came in.

"I w-want you to g-go outside with m-me, Mommy."

"Okay, sweetheart. Just as soon as I'm finished."

"I w-want you to go outside w-with me, n-n-*now.*"

"As soon as I've made the bed, Nancy. We'll get your things and we'll go outside and play. Okay?"

*"N-now!"*

"In ten minutes," I replied firmly.

"If y-you d-don't go out w-with me right now, I'll t-t-tell you what I'm g-g-gonna do," she warned. "I'm g-g-gonna go into y-your closet, and I'm gonna t-take your b-blue b-b-blouse, y-your red d-d-dress, your g-g-g-green skirt with the l-l-lace on it, and . . ."

She proceeded to name virtually every single item in my closet. I don't know how she knew what was in there, but she did, the list of garments spilling out in a torrent of stammers. I stopped what I was doing and stared at her.

". . . y-your y-yellow sweater. And then I'm g-g-gonna go through your d-d-dresser drawer, and I'm g-g-gonna get all of your n-n-nightgowns and s-s-slips and your underwear and I'm g-g-gonna get a p-pair of sci-scissors and I'm gonna c-c-cut into l-l-little strips your b-blue blouse, y-your red d-d-dress, your g-g-g-green skirt with the l-lace on it . . ."

She repeated the entire list.

". . . a-a-and slips and your u-underwear. A-a-and after I've c-cut them into l-little strips I-I-I'm g-g-gonna take them outside a-a-and p-put them under the c-c-cars in the s-street, s-so they can r-run over them. If-if you don't go with me right n-now, that's what I'm g-g-gonna do . . ."

I just stood there speechless. Such venom, such specific, detailed hate, coming out of the mouth of a two-year-old! She scared the absolute hell out of me.

When I didn't move, she started right over again with the entire list.

"Nancy! Stop!" I screamed.

"Y-y-your g-g-green skirt w-w-with the l-l-lace on it—!"

"Stop!"

But she wouldn't stop. I grabbed her by the arms and shook her. She kept going, screaming now.

". . . Y-your y-y-yellow sweater—"

I picked her up. She began squirming and punching at me. I ran down the hall with her, put her in her room, left her there, and closed the door behind me. She followed me right out and down the stairs, still screaming the list at the top of her lungs.

"Nancy!"

I clamped my hand over her mouth. She bit me. I smacked her hard on the rump. It had no effect. I covered my ears and fled to another room. She pursued me.

". . . Y-y-your g-g-green skirt with the l-l-lace on it a-and slips and under-r-wear a-a-and I-I-I'm gonna t-take them o-outside and p-p-put them u-under the c-c-cars in the s-street s-so they c-c-can r-run them over!"

Then she abruptly stopped, sat down on the living room

floor, and began to play quietly with her coloring book, as if nothing had happened.

I called the pediatrician immediately.

"I've never heard of anything quite that extreme," he admitted.

"What should I do?"

"Stop her. Don't let her continue."

"How?"

"Well, with children like this the best thing is to try and distract her."

"What do you mean by 'children like this'?"

"Or channel that energy."

*"How?"* I pleaded.

He increased her dosage of phenobarbital again. But the verbal assaults continued, some of them lasting as long as an hour.

I wasn't satisfied with either the pediatrician's analysis or his treatment. I had the gut feeling that there was something seriously wrong with Nancy. I thought about taking her to see someone else, but I didn't know who to turn to. One day I opened the phone book and looked through the list of child psychiatrists, but I stopped short of calling one. I thought perhaps I was being silly or overreacting. After all, her doctor said it was just a stage. I was of the naive belief that when your doctor told you something, it should be taken as undisputed fact. I was wrong to stay with a physician whom I was not content with. But I did not trust my instincts then.

I was not content with what he had to say about another problem Nancy was starting to have—violent, recurring nightmares.

Most nights she screamed for me seven or eight times in the darkness. Sometimes she yelled that a man was trying to dynamite her bedroom. Usually she cried that a rabbit had bitten her. Then it was always the same routine.

I went to her, turned her light on, opened the closet door. "There's no rabbit here, sweetheart. See? No rabbit."

"It b-bit me," she insisted.

"Where?"

She showed me a spot on her leg. "Here."

"Want me to kiss it?"

"Yes."

I kissed it. "Want me to bandage it?"

"Y-yes."

I bandaged the leg and she quieted down but didn't sleep. I sat on her bed and talked about nice things—taking picnics on sunny days, going to the beach—and she finally calmed down. As soon as she fell back to sleep, I returned to bed. An hour later she woke up in terror again.

I reported Nancy's night terrors to the pediatrician. He told me that a lot of kids Nancy's age had recurring nightmares.

"It's nothing to worry about," he said. "They forget about them the next day."

Nancy didn't forget hers. She insisted on keeping her rabbit bite bandage on all day and would only let me remove it to change it. She actually believed the attacks took place.

I reported this to the pediatrician.

"That isn't normal," he advised. "I've never heard of that."

This was the best he could do. I finally decided it wasn't good enough. He was a sincere, professional physician, and he was making a genuine effort to account for Nancy's behavior based on what he had encountered previously. Clearly, he'd just never dealt with a girl like Nancy before.

So I tried taking her to a different pediatrician, an older man. He was brusque and impatient with Nancy on our initial visit. After he was done examining her, he handed her a lollipop."

"Y-you know w-w-what I'm gonna do with this l-l-lolli-p-pop?" Nancy said as she took it from him. "I'm g-g-g-gonna take it outside and throw it under the w-w-wheels of the first t-truck I see. Th-that's what I think of y-you and y-y-your l-lollipop."

His mouth dropped open in amazement.

I decided to stay with the younger doctor. It wasn't a different pediatrician Nancy needed. She needed some other kind of help.

I knew Frank would be against it. He had mentioned his distaste for therapy in general several times.

I made Frank's favorite dinner that night—my homemade stew and bread I baked myself. Then I took a deep breath and brought up the idea of taking Nancy to a child guidance clinic.

"You're paying too much attention to the problem," he said flatly. "You're magnifying it. She's not that bad."

"She *is* that bad," I said. "You're not close enough to see it."

"You're *too* close," he insisted. "Look, she's a kid. She's stubborn. That's the way kids are. Maybe she's a little tougher than the other kids. That makes her a tough kid. That doesn't make her sick."

"I want to take her to a doctor."

"You don't go to the doctor every time you get a scratch on your hand."

"Who's talking about scratches? She's sick."

"It's not that bad."

"What about her nightmares?"

"All kids have 'em."

"Not like those."

"Sure, like those."

"How would you know? You sleep through them. Or pretend to."

Frank sighed. "Maybe it's the way you're handling her. Ever think of that?"

"Of course I thought of that," I snapped. "I've tried everything. I've read the books, I've talked to the doctor. I do what they tell me to do. Nothing works. We've got to do *something.*"

My voice cracked. Deep down inside I blamed myself for whatever was wrong with Nancy. I wasn't nearly the success as a mother that I wanted to be, but I didn't know where I was going wrong. I was totally frustrated.

Frank didn't answer me.

"We've got to do something," I repeated.

"Well, we're not going to do that," he declared.

He refused to discuss the matter further. He didn't want to believe that something was wrong with Nancy. And he felt that people like us—who were college graduates and came from good families—solved our own problems. Besides, we were low on money.

I backed down. I was willing to accept his position, mostly because he seemed so sure about it. I wasn't sure of anything. I was looking for answers. He had given me one: no.

So we dropped the subject, until I raised it again about two months later, again at dinner. Suzy had just started to walk. That afternoon Nancy had knocked her to the ground—violently—every time she stood up. (The very first sentence Suzy ever said was "Nancy, leave me alone.") Nancy's verbal tantrums had already exposed such a bottomless pit of rage that I was genuinely afraid she might really go after her baby sister and cause her serious injury. I moved the playpen up from the basement so I could keep an eye on them. And I approached Frank again.

He refused to discuss it and we quarreled. Out of frustration he had joined a softball league at a nearby park, which kept him out of the house every Sunday afternoon. I resented it deeply, and we quarreled over that. Frank finally agreed to take Nancy and Suzy for a drive Sunday mornings before his game so I could get some sleep. Because of Nancy's nightmares I hadn't slept through an entire night in at least two years. Some days I was so exhausted I'd lean against a wall for a second and start to doze standing up. My chief fantasy was to check into a hotel all by myself and sleep straight through for one night.

I worried about Nancy constantly. Soon, however, I had another worry—my period was late.

My knees were knocking when I went to see the obstetrician. I was terrified that I was pregnant again. I desperately didn't want to be, not for a couple of more years, at least. As I drove over for my examination I thought about a dress I wanted that cost twenty dollars, which was a lot of money to us. I made a deal with myself that, because I hadn't bought anything for myself in so long, I'd go out and buy the damned thing if I wasn't pregnant.

I didn't get to buy the dress.

David was born six weeks early, on October 26, 1961. Nancy was three and a half.

She took to David immediately, much more than she had to Suzy. The second I brought him home, she wanted to be with him and hold him. She called him "the boy." She was very sweet to him, caring and compassionate.

When we encountered a couple of health scares during the first few weeks of David's life, Nancy was concerned, loving, and helpful.

I developed a kidney problem right after I got home. The tube between my right kidney and my bladder was twisted. It required surgery and a week's hospitalization. We applied to the Family Service Agency and got financial help for a homemaker. Nancy was cooperative the entire time I was in the hospital, giving neither the homemaker nor Frank a bit of trouble.

When I came home she appointed herself my nurse. She was in my room all day making sure I was okay. I had a pretty ugly scar from the front of my abdomen around to my back. The doctor told me to put cocoa butter on it three times a day to help it heal. Nancy made absolutely certain I did, and insisted on helping me rub it in.

Then, as soon as I got back on my feet, little David developed terrible diarrhea and vomiting. He turned gray and had to be hospitalized for what turned out to be an intestinal obstruction. Again it was Nancy to the rescue. She was very upset that she wasn't allowed to visit him at the hospital. She chose gifts for us to take to David from among her own very favorite toys. She insisted we go shopping so she could pick out a new outfit for him to wear when he came back. She was enraptured the day he did come back—she sat on the front steps all day waiting for the ice cream man so she could buy David an ice cream cone, his first. She doted on him, followed him around the house to make sure he was happy. A few days after his return we had a special celebratory dinner—Nancy's idea. I made a turkey. Nancy and I baked a cake. She insisted on helping. And what an industrious little helper she was. I had to make up little jobs to keep her busy. Her favorite was licking the bowl of icing clean. She got it all over herself.

She had no nightmares or tantrums during this stretch. I felt relieved. Maybe the doctor was right, after all. Time was all she needed. I noticed her playing peacefully by herself one morning and thought about how pleasant life would be if she only stayed this way. I hoped and prayed she would.

She didn't. Once our family health problems passed, her own surfaced again.

The circus was in town. Nancy had seen the commercials for it on TV and wanted to go. Frank decided to take her that Sunday, just the two of them. She was ecstatic and very anxious to go. She hadn't had much time for fun lately, what with her vigils for me and then David.

Frank got the car out of the garage, got Nancy's coat out of the closet, and told her it was time to go. She wouldn't leave the house.

"It's t-t-too far!" she wailed.

"No, it's not, sweetheart," I assured her. "Daddy is taking you in the car."

"That's right, Nancy," he agreed as he put her coat on her and buttoned it.

"A-are we all g-g-going?"

"It's a special day for you and Daddy, sweetheart. Remember?"

"I'm n-n-not going."

"Why?" asked Frank, confused.

"It's t-t-t-too *far,*" she repeated.

"We're going," he stated.

When he picked her up and opened the front door, she began to scream. He put her down. She took her coat off and hurled it to the floor. Frank looked to me for guidance. He'd never seen Nancy like this. I had.

"Nancy, you wanted to go," I said firmly.

"That's right," Frank exclaimed. "The animals will be there. We'll see the bears. And have cotton candy."

She frowned, thought it over. "Okay. I w-w-wanna go." She put her coat back on.

We said our good-byes; they went out the door. I watched from the doorway. They got in the car, Frank started the motor, and she started to scream again. Frank turned off the motor, got out, grabbed a wailing Nancy, and returned.

"She says she doesn't want to go," he explained, exasperated.

Nancy came inside, threw off her coat again.

"Maybe she shouldn't," I said. "If she doesn't want to."

"But I already bought the tickets."

We stood there on the front steps, stuck for a solution.

"Nancy," I said. "Do you want Daddy to take another little girl? Would that make you happy?"

"Y-yes," she replied.

"Then okay," I said. "We'll call Becky from next door and Daddy will go with Becky."

"O-okay," she said defiantly.

We went inside and I phoned our neighbors. Becky was sick and couldn't go.

I told Nancy.

"Then I'll g-g-go," she said. She put on her coat and went out the door to the car, leaving Frank and me standing there in the entry hall, baffled.

He shook his head, followed her to the car. They got in and he started the engine. She started to scream again. This time he didn't cut the engine—he let out the brake and began to back down the driveway.

She screamed even louder. "I d-don't wanna g-go! It's t-t-too far!"

He got as far as the street, then rammed the car into gear and roared back up the driveway to the garage. They got out, returned to the house. She threw off her coat and stormed into the living room.

"I absolutely do not know what to do," Frank said, shaken. "I don't know if she wants to go or she doesn't want to go. I don't know what to do."

I went into the living room. She had turned the TV on.

"Nancy, Daddy's going by himself," I told her.

"O-okay."

Frank was willing to try anything at this point. So he went out to the car by himself, got in, and started the engine. As soon as Nancy heard the car start she came running out of the living room, sobbing.

"I w-wanna g-go!"

I opened the door and waved to Frank. He waited for her. She got in and he backed down the driveway. She started to scream again. This time he didn't stop. He drove away. I could see her through the car window, sobbing, tears streaming down her cheeks.

When they got back, Frank told me she'd been fine as soon as they got away from the house. They had had a wonderful time.

Then Frank looked down at the floor, cleared his throat. "About the guidance clinic . . ."

"What about it?" I said.

He took a deep breath, let it out. "Do whatever you want."

"You think I should take her?"

"It . . . it seems like a good idea to go for some help." Frank looked down at the floor again and swallowed, clearly pained by his unhappy realization. "Something is happening to her. I don't know what."

So glad to have his compliance, I went ahead immediately, fully confident that the professionals would find an easy answer to Nancy's problems—easy and correctible.


The place I drove Nancy to for her first psychiatric evaluation was a child guidance center attached to one of Philadelphia's major children's hospitals. Nancy didn't mind going. I told her we were just going to talk to a doctor. I promised she wouldn't get any shots. She was a month shy of her fourth birthday.

Frank met us out front. It was a gray, shabby old building. We stared at each other grimly, then looked down at our eldest child. She stood there calmly and quietly. We hesitated, wondering if we were making too much of this.

Only one way to find out: We went inside.

We waited on a bench for a while and were finally admitted to the office of a psychiatric social worker. A young woman took Nancy down the hall to a playroom. She went willingly. Frank and I related to the psychiatric social worker what had brought us there. He made notes as we talked.

"We'll have to evaluate her," he advised us. "You'll

bring her back for a series of visits. We'll give her some tests, and then we'll see where we stand. Okay?''

We agreed. I took her there for an hour visit once every other week for six months. I hired a baby sitter to take care of Suzy and David while I was away, and paid her out of the following week's grocery money. I was optimistic, sure the clinic would diagnose Nancy's problem and give Frank and me the proper direction so she'd be all right.

Her visits to the clinic had an immediate effect. Her stuttering began to ease up. By the time her evaluation period was completed and the verdict was in, it had virtually disappeared.

Frank mentioned how pleased we were about this to the psychiatric social worker when we came in to hear the results.

"Well, she was an early-speaking child," he advised. "Stuttering isn't that unusual. She's outgrown it."

He opened a folder and related his findings.

On the Revised Stanford-Binet she had demonstrated an IQ of 134. The Peabody Picture Vocabulary Test yielded an IQ of 129. Both placed her in the category of very superior intelligence.

"Actually she has the functioning IQ of a seven-year-old," he reported. "That pretty effectively rules out any sort of brain damage from her birth, which you mentioned you were concerned about."

We were relieved to hear that.

"Now, we also found that Nancy's motor-visual development is slightly behind her age level. Put together her unusually high IQ and her motor-visual deficiency and you arrive at, we think, her basic problem. She sets high goals for herself. If they're motor-visual oriented, like learning to tie her own shoes or knit, she's unable to perform at the level she's set for herself."

"You mean her head's ahead of her hands?" asked Frank.

"Precisely. This causes her a severe level of frustration, and that's where the tantrums come from. It's an adjustment reaction."

"What can we do?" I asked.

"My opinion is that she'll outgrow her problem as she grows into her intellect."

"That's all?" Frank asked.

He looked over his report. "Yes. The only other area worth mentioning is that her fantasies aren't as rich as they might be for a child her age. She constricts on the Rorschach and Thematic Apperception Test. An average child may see fifty different things in a splotch. Nancy sees one. Always the same one."

"What is it?" I asked.

"A butterfly."

Frank chuckled. "That doesn't sound too dangerous."

"Not at all. It's another area she'll outgrow as she encounters new friends and situations. My feeling is that time and the structured environment of school will be the answer for Nancy. If *you* feel she needs therapy at any time, feel free to return."

We shook hands, thanked him.

"Take her home and love her," he said with a wink as we left.

We were relieved.

We found a nursery school for her, thinking that might help. It did. The teacher was sensitive and seemed to understand Nancy, who adored her. Nancy learned new skills and eagerly awaited going every day. The teacher reported to me that she was already doing first-grade work.

Kindergarten was next. Again Nancy had no problems— short of her inability to hold on to the friends she made. She'd hold on to friends, we reasoned, once she met some nice kids.

The main thing was that she was starting to get the stimulation and channeling she required. We felt certain that she would soon become like other kids.

She was going to be okay.

# ◻ Chapter 4

On the Friday before Nancy started first grade, I took her to have her hair done and bought her a new dress and a pair of red boots that she wanted. She was almost giddy with excitement about starting school—until the night before, when I found her sobbing in her room.

"What's wrong, Nancy?" I asked her.

"I can't go to school tomorrow," she wailed.

"Of course you can." I sat down next to her on the bed. She moved away.

"I can't," she insisted.

"Why not?"

"I don't know how to read and write yet."

I laughed. "But Nancy, sweetheart, that's why you go to school. To learn those things."

She began to scream. I tried explaining again, but to no avail. She sobbed and wailed and rolled around on her bed for several hours.

But she did go to school the next day and performed very well. In fact, she did so well in her first-grade classes that in the sixth week of the term the principal called Frank and me in to tell us he was moving her to a special first-grade class for intellectually gifted students.

We were very proud.

By the end of the second grade Nancy was doing fourth- and fifth-grade-level work in all areas except math (which frustrated her so much she would burst into tears) and penmanship. Her handwriting was a bit clumsy because of her motor-visual problem. Nancy's second-grade teacher recommended on her report card that she skip third grade and go right into fourth. Her only reservation about Nancy, the teacher noted, was that she "was disruptive due to inappropriate laughter." I went in and asked the teacher about this. I had never noticed this behavior in Nancy.

"She seems to laugh at her own little jokes," the teacher explained. "She's tuned in to her own private TV show and just starts giggling."

She did skip third grade, though, and had no problem keeping up scholastically with the fourth graders, even though some were two years older than she was.

Socially, however, Nancy made no progress. She would be tight best friends with a little girl for a week, then they would become bitter enemies. No relationship lasted. Her first new school friend was a sweet, cute girl who lived down the block. Nancy brought her home three or four times to play, then stopped. I asked about the girl, but Nancy refused to answer me and just cried. A few days later I found a note from the girl in Nancy's jeans when I was doing the laundry. It said: "I hate you and you stink and stay away from me forever or I'm going to kill you." I immediately called the girl's parents. They seemed unconcerned about the note, though they did feel it would be best all around if the two girls stopped seeing each other.

Unable to keep friends, Nancy began to take out her social frustration on Suzy and David. She was older, bigger, and smarter than they were and took advantage of it. She manipulated them, bullied them, tormented them, pitted them against each other and their own friends, often with ferocious meanness.

She particularly loved to make Suzy cry. One of her tricks was to exclude Suzy. If Suzy and David were, say, coloring happily on the living room floor, Nancy would come in, grab up all of the coloring books and crayons, and say "Come with me, David, we'll go color in my room. Suzy, you can't color with us. You smell."

Off Nancy would go, little David in tow—leaving Suzy in tears.

Another of Nancy's tricks was to borrow some of Suzy's precious Barbie Doll clothes (Nancy actually had no use for dolls herself) and fail to return them. When Suzy asked for them, Nancy would deny she had ever borrowed them and accuse Suzy of trying to call her a thief and a liar.

If Suzy brought a friend home Nancy would convince the friend to play a board game with Suzy, then tell the other girl how to win so Suzy would lose and go running upstairs in tears. Suzy fought back by no longer bringing her friends home. But if one of them called on the phone Nancy would stand next to Suzy and scream and holler at her to get off because she was expecting a call—even though she had no friends of her own who might call.

Though Suzy was her main target, Nancy occasionally went after David, too. Violently. Once David was playing with slot cars in the basement with his friends and she went down and took his car and hurled it against the wall, breaking it into tiny pieces. Another time she sneaked into his bedroom when he was asleep—on this occasion a reluctant but thoroughly intimidated Suzy in cahoots with her—and bopped David on the head with a weighted, inflatable plastic whiskey bottle. He got quite a shiner from it.

As for Nancy's tantrums, well, we were still living with them. In fact, our household had begun to form itself around her temper. Every Sunday, for example, the Spungen family took an outing. Sometimes we went to Independence Hall, sometimes to the Franklin Institute, sometimes for a drive in the country.

One Sunday we planned to go to a movie that Suzy wanted to see. Nancy flat out refused to go.

"I don't wanna go to the movies," she declared at breakfast.

"We're going to the movies," Frank stated firmly.

"I wanna go to the Franklin Institute," Nancy countered.

"We went to the Franklin Institute last Sunday," I said. "Now, Nancy, we went where you wanted to go last Sunday. This Sunday is Suzy's turn. Be fair."

"I don't wanna go to the movies," she repeated, dropping her spoon defiantly in her cereal bowl.

"We're going to the movies," Frank repeated with grim determination.

"Then I'm not going!" she screamed.

"Oh, yes, you are," Frank replied.

She stood up abruptly, knocked her chair over. "You can't make me!"

"Yes I can!"

She stuck out her jaw. "Then go ahead! Make me!"

"Nancy," I said. "We're going to the movies today."

"I'm not going!" she repeated.

"You're going," Frank warned, "or it's no TV privileges for one week!"

"I already lost them for *two* weeks," she sneered. "Big deal!"

"Then no allowance!"

"That too! You can't do a thing to me! I'll just stay in my room. Starting right now. And you can't do a thing!"

"Oh, yes, I can!" snapped Frank.

Out of sheer frustration he grabbed her and spanked her on the behind. It was always our own frustration that drove us to spank Nancy, since it had no impact on her except to make her angrier.

She screamed at the top of her lungs, outraged, then ran up the stairs to her room and slammed the door.

She would not come out until we backed down and agreed to go where she wanted to.

We wanted our family outing. We couldn't leave Nancy in the house alone. Frank and I exchanged a resigned look. I turned to Suzy. She was already crying. She knew we weren't going to see her movie.

It was this way with all things—Nancy's way. When she wanted something, no matter how big or small, she hollered and screamed and backed us into a corner until we were the ones to back down. We gave in to her. Why? Because there was absolutely no peace in the house until she got what she wanted. And she was impossible to discipline. She was not afraid of us, had no respect for us. Traditional channels like shutting off her allowance were far too puny. Smacking her was pointless and accomplished nothing except to make us feel terrible for losing control of the situation—and to make that situation more intense. So we gave in to her demands, one by one. It was easier that way. Was it really worth enduring a major tantrum just because she wanted to watch a different show on TV than Suzy did? It wasn't—believe me it wasn't, not day in and day out.

And that's how a seven-year-old ran our household. It was not pleasant. In fact, it was so unpleasant it took its toll on our marriage.

Frank's work was beginning to take him to New York two days a week. He would stay over for the night at a hotel in midtown Manhattan, and he would have fun. An old pal of his named Harvey was a talent agent. Harvey often had free tickets to Broadway shows or passes to *The Tonight Show*. They would have dinner out. After the show they would go to a nightclub and listen to jazz. I cannot tell a lie—I deeply resented that Frank was allowed to do all of the things I wanted to do while I stayed home with the kids.

He always called me at six p.m. to see how the day had gone at home. One of the days had gone particularly badly. Nancy had a bronchial infection, David had an intestinal bug, and Suzy had let the bathtub overflow. The water had soaked through the bathroom floor and entry hall ceiling below, causing chunks of it to give way. By the time Frank called, it was raining in the hall and I was hating him for being gone. He was in a restaurant. I could hear music and clinking glasses in the background.

"What's new on Welsh Road?" he asked cheerfully.

"Fuck you," I replied and hung up.

I immediately felt awful for having done that. I just felt so trapped, so lonesome. After the kids were in bed, I tried Frank at his hotel. He wasn't in yet. It was about ten o'clock. I tried again at eleven. He was still out. At twelve, too.

I couldn't sleep now. I phoned him on the hour. When he wasn't there at one, I was afraid he'd been run over by a taxicab. At two, I was afraid he was out with another woman. At three, I was sure he was out with another woman. I thought about grabbing the next train for New York and waiting in his hotel lobby to see who he came in with. I couldn't. I couldn't leave the children. At four, he answered.

"Where were you?" I demanded.

"What are you doing up so late?" Frank asked, confused.

"Waiting up for you. What are *you* doing up so late?"

"I was out with Harvey. We went to a show, got something to eat."

"Are you sure it was Harvey you were with?"

"Who else would it be?"

"How would I know?"

"Can't I just go out and have a good time?"

"I'm home with the kids. I can't."

"Look, Deb, I'm sorry you're stuck there by yourself. But I have to be here—it's my job."

Frank wasn't sorry, though. I realized this a few weeks later. The morning after one of his nights in New York, I phoned his office in Philadelphia and asked his secretary to have him call me when he checked in from New York. I needed him for something.

"But he's here," she said.

"No, he's not," I corrected. "He's going to be in New York all day."

"He's right here, Mrs. Spungen," she said, embarrassed. "The boss called him yesterday. He had a meeting here first thing this morning. I'll . . . I'll connect you."

I was mortified and humiliated. Frank could have come home the night before and been with me and had chosen instead to stay over in New York and drive back early in the morning. He had gone directly to the office. He preferred not to be home.

What was Frank's explanation?

"I'd already checked into my room when the boss called," he said when he came on the line. "It just seemed easier to stay there."

I didn't buy it.

On top of his one night a week in New York, Frank began to go out without me one night a week in Philadelphia. He called it a "boys' night out." He went to a health club and played basketball, or so he said. I suspected otherwise. Sometimes he came home at midnight. Sometimes as late as two a.m. Sometimes we had sex when he got into bed, sometimes we didn't. Certainly, we had less than we used to. I resented his going out another night a week to have fun without me. I was bored and miserable and jealous.

"I want to go out with you," I complained.

"Who's going to stay with the kids? We can't afford a baby sitter."

"So why can't you stay home with me?"

"I'll tell you what," he countered. "You take a night out a week, too, and I'll stay with the kids. How would that be?"

"What on earth would I do by myself?"

"Whatever you want."

"What I want is to be with you."

"Somebody has to stay with the kids," he repeated. "We can't afford a baby sitter."

Married women didn't go out at night without their husbands in those days. It didn't occur to us. We had no real social lives apart from our husbands. I had two old friends, Susan and Janet. Janet had three small children, Susan two. Our social life consisted of one of them coming over for the afternoon with her kids, or me going over there with mine—it all depended on whose husband didn't need the car that day. The kids would play together in the basement playroom and we'd stand in the kitchen drinking coffee and making tuna salad. Sometimes we went to the playground.

But Frank kept egging me to go out without him, so one night I did. I left him with the kids, took the car, and drove around the suburbs of Philadelphia for an hour. Then I went to see a movie by myself. I had a terrible time. I didn't want to be out alone. I wanted to be with my husband. I wanted him to pay more attention to me, listen to my frustrations and problems. I wanted him to love me. I couldn't understand why he didn't want to be with me anymore, why whatever fun he was having he chose to have without me. The only possible explanation was that he had found another woman. I believed I'd failed him as a wife.

Looking back, I now realize that Frank was staying away from home because it was so unpleasant there. Nancy made it so; her presence caused an unusual and intolerable amount of tension. But neither Frank nor I knew that at the time. If just one doctor had said to us, "Nancy is a disturbed child and you are putting up with a very difficult situation that will put a strain on your marriage," we would have understood what was happening to us. But nobody told us that. The doctors insisted that Nancy was a normal child. As a result, Frank and I had no choice but to believe that our problems came from each other. And we did have problems. Both of us felt stifled, trapped, depressed. Both of us felt the pain of failed expectations. Life was not working out the way we'd hoped. But we suffered in separate spheres.

"I'm going to go out and play some ball," he said one night at dinner.

"Why don't you want to be with me? What am I doing wrong?"

"You're not doing anything wrong—except bugging me."

"Frank, are you seeing another woman?"

"No!"

"Why won't you admit it?"

He pushed his plate away. "How can you keep accusing me like this?"

"Because I think you're with someone else."

"Deb, I love you. I just need to get out."

"Where do you really go?"

"Stop keeping such close tabs on me!"

"I have the right."

"Goddamnit, you're smothering me!"

He stormed out. I sat down and wrote him a letter. I apologized for getting on his nerves. I said I was sorry I wasn't a good enough wife and I'd try to be better. I said if there was anything I could do to improve, I'd do it—all he had to do was tell me. I said I loved him. By the time I finished writing the letter it was thirty pages long.

He wasn't home when I got into bed. I left the letter on his pillow. I pretended I was asleep when he got home at two a.m. He sat on the edge of the bed, read by the light on the nightstand. I buried my nose in my pillow and fought back the tears.

He got undressed, turned out the light, and climbed into bed. I stirred as if I'd been asleep.

"I didn't realize you were so upset," he said softly. "I'm sorry."

He made love to me and promised he'd spend more time at home. He did skip his boys' night out—for one week. Then he started up again.

I desperately wished I had someone to talk to about what was happening between Frank and me. But I didn't discuss personal things with anyone then, not my mother, not Janet or Susan. I particularly longed to tell Janet and Susan what was happening—in the hope that they would have some insight, some advice—in the hope that they would say he probably wasn't having an affair. But I couldn't bring myself to air the matter. It just wouldn't come out of my mouth.

So I kept it shut. When David was old enough for nursery school, I began substitute teaching a couple of days a week. A mother's helper stayed with David in the afternoons. It was, on the one hand, nice to be doing something and bringing home that extra eighteen dollars for a day's work. On the other hand, teaching just seemed like an extension of my at-home confinement. Usually I taught at Nancy and Susan's elementary school. I drove them to school with me, waited for them after school in the parking lot to drive them home. I was spending seven days and seven nights a week with children, either my own or other people's.

When Frank and I did go out socially, it was over to Janet's or Susan's for dinner, kids in tow. We seldom had enough money to get a competent baby sitter and also go out for a nice meal or to a show.

So it was a special occasion when a couple we knew

through Frank's business invited us out to dinner one Saturday night to a very nice French restaurant in the country. I felt very good about being able to get dressed up and go out with Frank. I put on a blue and white knit dress my mother had bought for me. I never really had many chances to wear it.

It was a balmy summer evening and the restaurant was lovely, with strolling musicians and an open-air garden dining area. As we were going to our table our friends spotted another couple they knew at a table with three other couples. They stopped to say hi and introduced us. He was in his early forties, with blond hair and a deep tan. She was very loud. They were both expensively dressed. Our friends had mentioned the man before. After all, none of us knew too many millionaires.

After the man had introduced us to the other people at the table, he turned to me and said, "What's that between your eyes?"

He was referring to a birthmark I had there.

"My third eye," I replied, straightfaced. It was my standard reply.

He laughed. His wife did not.

Then we went on to our table with our friends and had a nice dinner.

On Monday morning the man phoned and said he wanted to take me to lunch.

"You're very pretty," he said, "and I'd like to get to know you better."

I was absolutely staggered. I hadn't been approached by a man in over ten years. I was also flattered that someone so sophisticated and worldly would want to spend time with me. Especially since Frank didn't.

"What do you say?" he asked. "We'll eat. Talk. Maybe go for a drive?"

It sounded fantastic. It also sounded very wrong. If you were married you didn't go out to lunch with a man. It was dishonest and clandestine. He would want more than lunch, eventually, and I'd been raised to believe that infidelity was the very worst thing that could happen in a marriage. Nice women didn't sleep around. They didn't even think about it.

"I'd like to," I said. "But I really can't."

"Not even just for lunch?"

"I . . . I'd have to get a baby sitter for my little boy, and if I'm not working, well, I don't have money to pay her."

"I'd be happy to pay."

"Oh no, I couldn't do that."

"Please, the money isn't important. I don't mind."

"Well . . . I don't know."

"Tell you what," he said. "Why don't you think it over. I'll call you in a week. Would that be okay?"

I swallowed. No harm in a phone call. "Okay," I said.

I spent the next week thinking it over long and hard. It sounded so nice, the idea of going out to lunch and talking to someone. I never got to go anyplace. I deserved to get out and have some fun. Frank did—and with women, I was certain. So why not me, with a man. A polite, cultivated man who saw something in me. It didn't necessarily have to lead to anything else. He hadn't said anything about sex. Just lunch, maybe a drive. That's all he'd said.

Looking back at myself then, I suspect I wasn't the most sexually naive twenty-seven-year-old woman in the world, but I must have been pretty damned close to it. I hadn't dated since I was sixteen, before Frank and I started going together. And when I was sixteen, a lunch date was a lunch date. You didn't finish eating, pay the check and say "Let's fuck." You had lunch. Period. I realized that if I continued to see this man he would probably have sex in mind, but who said I had to continue to see him? Lunch. Once.

I needed to be paid attention to. My husband, I was certain, was seeing other women. I felt inadequate. My self-image was low. I had no escape valve, no one to talk to. I was vulnerable.

When he called a week later, I said yes.

Looking back on this experience fills me with such incredible sadness that I wish I could erase it from my memory. But I cannot. It happened, and it happened as a consequence of Nancy.

I didn't sleep at all the night before my lunch date. I just lay there staring at the ceiling, asking myself why I was doing

this. The answer: because Frank was doing it. I was doing it
out of anger. I was retaliating.

I didn't get dressed up. The neighbors would have noticed.
The baby sitter would have noticed. I told her I was going
shopping. It was the first time I had ever made myself una-
vailable. If something had happened that afternoon to one of
the children, no one would have known where to find me.

I drove to the restaurant we'd agreed to meet at. It was in
the Bucks County suburbs. It was a pretty well known place—
the upstairs had been formed out of an old airplane—but no
one I knew, myself included, had ever been there. Our date
was for twelve thirty. I got there at twelve twenty and his
silver Mercedes was already in the parking lot. I sat in my car
for a few minutes, terrified. My hands were cold. Finally I
went in.

He was sitting at a small table in the cocktail lounge. He
smiled when he saw me, got up, pulled my chair out for me,
and sat back down only when he was sure I was comfortable.

"We'll have a drink," he suggested.

"Fine," I gasped.

"We'll talk."

"Fine."

"We'll have lunch."

"Fine."

I ordered a Cutty Sark and water. I don't remember what he
had. I wasn't used to drinking at twelve thirty and the cocktail
relaxed me almost immediately. I began to notice details, like
that he had monogrammed shirt cuffs and manicured finger-
nails. He was the most elegant, well-mannered man I'd ever
met. I found him attractive, but not in a sexual way. He was
just about old enough to be my father.

We talked. He told me about his trips to Europe, his art collection, his yacht. He asked me what I did with my time. I
told him. I mentioned that I was thinking about going back to
school. He was interested in my views on politics and literature. I was glad to air them. I was well informed—I made a
point of reading the news magazines and the Sunday *New
York Times* every week—but never had much of a chance to
discuss my opinions. Nobody was interested in them.

I ordered a second drink.

Our discussion was stimulating. I held my own. I realized, after a while, that I was enjoying myself. It was nice to be having some fun. *I'm not cheating on my husband,* I thought. *I'm having an intelligent conversation.* What was the harm in that? There were no sexual overtones—at least none that I picked up on.

I ordered the least expensive thing on the menu, out of habit.

After lunch we went out to the parking lot. His car glistened in the sunshine.

"It's such a beautiful day," he said. "Do you have time to take a drive?"

I had time. He opened the door, I got in, and he closed it for me. Frank hadn't done that since our earliest dates. The inside of the Mercedes was incredibly luxurious. I soaked in the smell of the leather upholstery, ran my fingers over the polished hardwood dash. I settled back, feeling every bit like a fairy princess.

We drove through the countryside, not speaking much. After a while I realized I was seeing the same road markers and farmhouses again and again. We weren't going anywhere, except around in circles. I assumed he was lost.

"Are we going to go around and around like this all day?" I teased.

He didn't answer me, just swallowed uncomfortably.

"Are you okay?" I asked.

"What I really want to do is make love to you," he said quietly. He turned off the road. There was a motel there. He'd been circling it. He pulled over to the shoulder, stopped the car, and waited for my decision.

I didn't say yes.

But I didn't say no, either.

I could have said no. He would have politely returned me to my car and my husband. I could have stopped it, but I didn't. I was swept away by the afternoon, by the man's elegance. I was already in the wrong by meeting him for lunch. Taking that first step meant that taking the next one was much easier than you'd expect. And I was sexually curious. Frank had

other partners, I believed. I might as well find out what he got
out of it. I had no sexual experience beyond Frank. He was
the only man I'd ever slept with.

I knew it was wrong. I did it anyway. It was an escape, a
delicious escape from Nancy. For an entire hour I'd not
thought of her once, not played referee, not walked on eggs
awaiting her blow-ups, not felt *she* was my existence. For the
very first time I was doing something that took my mind away
from her. I deserved this. Now I understood why Frank was
doing it. This was for *me*.

He pulled into the parking lot of the motel. I waited in the
car while he got a room, my face red and hot from shame. He
came out, got in the car, pulled up in front of our room.

I went in ahead of him. It was a blandly furnished room
with a Gideon's Bible on the nightstand. I wondered if Susan
and Janet could ever imagine me in this place with this man. I
certainly couldn't. This was somebody else, not me.

I felt embarrassed getting undressed in front of a stranger.
He seemed embarrassed, too. We left the lights off and we got
into the bed.

He was very gentle. I kept my eyes shut tight the entire
time. It was not a moving experience; I heard no bells. Nor
was it wildly passionate and adventuresome. I wasn't particularly sexually adept or informed. But it was not unpleasant.
Mostly, I wished he was Frank, that it was my Frank making
love to me. That was what I really wanted—to be with Frank,
to have him care about me the way this man seemed to.

We were there about forty-five minutes. Then I said I had
to get home. We dressed and got back in the car, and he drove
me back to the restaurant with the airplane on top of it. We
didn't talk. I felt very down, very crummy. I felt as if I'd lost
my virginity.

"I'll call you again," he said.

"I . . . I'll have to think about it," I said.

We did not kiss.

I drove home, worried that Frank would be back from work
already. He wasn't—it was still only three o'clock. I felt very
dirty and guilty when I went in the house. I was sure the baby

sitter would *know* where I had been, what I had done. She didn't. I took a long shower.

When Frank came home I immediately wanted to shout "Do you know what I did? I slept with another man!" I wanted him to say "You bad girl! Don't you ever do that again! I love you!"

I wanted him to notice, to care.

That night he wanted me in bed. I thought somehow he'd be able to tell I'd been with someone else. He couldn't. I felt very uncomfortable, very awkward, He didn't notice that either.

The man called me a few days later and asked to see me again. I didn't want to see him. I put him off. Then I got mad at Frank for going out two nights in a row. We quarreled. Like he had before, Frank challenged me to take my own regular night out.

I took him up on it.

I began to see the man about one evening a month. He took me to nice restaurants and to bed while Frank stayed home with the children. Before I left, I always pored over the movie page in the newspaper so I'd be able to tell Frank where I'd been in case he asked. I checked the reviews so I'd be able to tell Frank how it was, in case he asked. He never asked. All he ever said to me when I came in was "Did you have a nice time?"

I was having a nice time. I enjoyed the food, the conversation, the attention. I enjoyed having a piece of my life that was mine alone. The sex? I considered it a price to be paid for the companionship. Never once did we go to bed without me wishing he was Frank. I liked him as a good friend. But I was not in love with him.

It was a bittersweet experience. Obviously I enjoyed it or I would have stopped it. It was a comfortable relationship, with no pressure coming from either of us to make it more than what it was. He wasn't looking to leave his wife, nor I Frank. But I hated the dishonesty, the secrecy. The image of a woman who cheats on her husband was not the image I had of myself. I felt shabby. At the end of each evening I would drive home, glancing at his headlights in my rearview mirror (he always followed to make sure I got home safely, turning off just before we got to my neighborhood) and telling myself that this was the last time, that this relationship was not the answer to my problems.

Meanwhile, I felt fragmented, emotionally drained. If Nancy blew up on a particular evening, I'd wonder if I'd somehow shortchanged her that day by reserving this little space for myself. Nancy never actually said or did a thing to indicate that she was aware of my absences. She wasn't—she was in school or with Frank when I saw the man. Still, I felt tremendous guilt. I felt that I had no right to take something for myself when she needed me so much.

What I really wanted was Frank. What had been wrong between us when the affair started was still wrong. We were not communicating. We were not resolving our problems. By having a secret life, I was certainly not helping matters.

Finally, after about a year, I did end it. I ended it for two reasons. One was that he started getting emotionally involved. We were having dinner downtown one night when he suddenly took my hands in his and said, "We've been seeing each other for a long while now, and I want you to know something I've realized."

I smiled. "What's that?"

"I love you."

I stopped smiling. I didn't want him to love me, didn't want our relationship to threaten my home life. This wasn't part of our "deal."

As I lay in bed with Frank that night, thinking seriously about ending it, Nancy called for me from the darkness. She was having one of her nightmares. I went to her, sat with her, calmed her.

"My friend Cheryl hates me, Mommy," she said. "Cheryl told me she's gonna kill me. She said she's gonna stick rat poison in my lunch and . . ."

Nancy needed me—all of me. She was the other reason why I had to end the affair. She was so desperately unhappy. By fragmenting myself, by reserving a small emotional oasis for myself, I was denying her what I had promised her. I had promised her a hundred percent. I wasn't being fair to her.

So I ended it. I was reluctant to give up my special little world, but I did. He called me about once a month for two more years. I liked hearing from him, liked knowing my escape valve was still there. But I never saw him again. I missed my little world, missed our evenings out—more than I missed him.

I didn't reveal my affair to Frank, at least not until about a year after it had ended. One evening when we went to bed I found him lying on his back, staring at the ceiling. He'd been very quiet all evening, distant and morose. We were still not getting along very well.

"Are you feeling okay?" I asked him.

He didn't answer me.

"Frank?"

"I don't want to be married anymore," he said quietly. "I want to leave."

"Why?" I asked, stunned.

"I'm not worthy of you. I'm a bad father, a bad husband. I'm a failure at everything I put my hands on."

"That's not true!"

"I can't believe this is it."

"This is *what*?"

"My life. This. This home. This job. These kids—"

"And this wife?" I demanded.

"It's not you. It's me. I shouldn't be married. I can't handle all this responsibility. I should get out. Try something else. Somewhere else."

I had trouble catching my breath. I felt like I'd been hit by a truck. "Look, honey, I know it hasn't been great. I know that. But tell me what I can do to make you happy. I'll do anything."

"It's not you, Deb. It's me. I just don't know why I'm here. We got married too damned young. We were a couple of dumb kids. I've never lived by myself. I've never had a chance to have any *fun.*"

"You think I have?"

"I know you didn't, either."

I saw myself in a flash—a divorcée with three kids, one of them impossible to deal with. Who would want me? Nobody.

I'd have to go home to Mommy. Or hide. I'd spend the rest of my life in front of a TV set watching soap operas and getting fat.

I looked down at my husband, sprawled across the bed, an arm across his eyes. I had but one choice, and I'm not ashamed to say what it was. I begged him to stay.

"You're not just going to get up and walk out of here," I said. "You can't. You just can't. What will I do? What will the kids do?"

He shrugged.

"Frank, this *is* your life. We made it together. If it's not working, we have to make it work. You can't just turn your back on it. You can't turn your back on us."

"You'd be better off with somebody else."

"I don't *want* somebody else."

He said nothing.

"Do *you?*" I asked. "Is that what this whole thing is about? Is that why you want to leave? Is it another woman?"

"No. There's nobody else. Not anymore."

It took a second to sink in.

"Not *anymore?*"

"There . . . there was someone. A while ago. A year, two years. But there's no one now."

"So you *were* seeing other women. I knew it!"

"You never believed me when I said I wasn't—and I *wasn't*—so I figured if you were already convinced I was fooling around, I may as well just go ahead and do it. You kept bugging me about it."

"You're saying it's my fault?"

"No, I'm just trying to tell you I shouldn't be married. I'm a rotten husband. Let me go."

"Well, if you're a rotten husband then I'm a rotten wife," I snapped angrily.

He sat up abruptly. "What do you mean?"

"I mean *I* was seeing someone, too."

He just stared at me, in total shock. After a moment his lips formed the word *who* but no sound came out.

I told him. I told him why I started it, why I had continued it, why I had ended it. I told him everything. He told me everything. We talked all night, poured out all of the unhappiness and pain we'd bottled up for years. It was our come-clean session.

Frank was scheduled to go to New York the next morning. He asked me to come with him. Fortunately Mother was able to come stay with the children.

We drove to New York, talked about where we'd gone wrong. We'd been going through the same sort of life crisis at the same time, not realizing it. Both of us felt cheated by life. But we agreed that if life was going to be better, we would make it better together. Seeing someone else was no answer.

Not once did it occur to us that Nancy was at the core of our unhappiness. It would be many years before we would realize that.

We had a very romantic supper that evening in New York.

"Maybe I didn't pay enough attention to you," Frank said. "Maybe I took you for granted."

"Maybe you did."

"Maybe you did."

"I never will again. I'm sorry."

"I'm sorry, too."

"Is it okay if I stay?"

"Only if you want to."

"I want to."

"Then it's okay."

We went back to the hotel and made love. He was my husband again. What he had done was forgotten. What I had done was forgotten. We were together.

When we got back to Philadelphia, I had the birthmark between my eyes removed.

# ☐ Chapter 5

After Nancy gave David the shiner, Frank and I talked about taking her back to the guidance clinic. We chose not to. We decided to believe that her difficult behavior around the house was caused by her inability to make friends at school. We blamed this on the city school system and the types of kids that went there. She was too bright for them, we decided. That was the problem.

We decided to move to the suburbs. The schools there were geared to the bright kids instead of the average ones. The classes were smaller, the curriculum more progressive. The suburbs were the answer, we knew.

We soon found our dream house in a new suburban development in a community called Huntingdon Valley. It was a two-story, four-bedroom colonial on a wide, quiet, gently curving street called Red Barn Lane. It had a big backyard, big enough to maybe even put in a pool someday. A lot of couples our age with young children were moving into the development.

This time Nancy looked forward to moving. She saw it as a

fresh start; she promised me she would make new friends and be happy in Huntingdon Valley. We all believed she would, but that proved to be a fantasy. Even so, for the first few months this fantasy of ours was a reality. Nancy did do well in her new school. She did make new friends. She even found an interest of her own.

On one of the weekends that Frank went to New York for business, I went with him, and we saw the new hit musical *Hair*. We enjoyed the show very much—especially the music—and bought the cast album. We always collected the cast albums of Broadway shows we'd seen and enjoyed, like *The Music Man* and *My Fair Lady*.

When I put on *Hair*, something magical happened. Nancy sat right next to the phonograph, totally absorbed by it. A dreamy, happy look crossed her face. The record seemed to be saying something to her. When the side was finished, she turned it over and played the other side. When that was finished, she turned it over again and listened to the entire album a second time. Then a third. From that day on she played *Hair* at least six times a day, over and over again. She played it so often she wore it out and we had to buy another. When we got a cat, she insisted we name it Aquarius.

At first Frank and I wondered if it was okay for Nancy to listen to this rock musical, which seemed to advocate free love, drugs, and war protest. She was only nine years old. But we let her listen because she loved it. It kept her occupied and happy. She got hysterical if I asked her to turn it off when the phone rang or it was time to eat.

We owned a few other rock albums and Nancy was immediately addicted to those, too. We liked the Beatles very much. She quickly became a fanatic for them, particularly the White Album, which she had wanted for Hanukkah that year. Frank and I also liked some of the softer, more folk-oriented performers like Joan Baez. Nancy didn't care for folk. She liked the harder, acid rock—the harder the better. On Saturdays I took her to the record store. Every cent of her allowance went into albums. She bought albums by The Doors, Cream, the Rolling Stones, Jimi Hendrix, Janis Joplin, Jefferson Airplane, Led Zeppelin.

She sat on the floor right in front of the living room phonograph, legs crossed, when she listened to her rock albums, the volume cranked up to full blast. It seemed to hypnotize her, pull her inside the stereo system with the music. The rock musicians were coming from where she wanted to be. She began to wear her chestnut-brown hair long and flowing. It grew to her waist. She dressed in blue jeans and peasant blouses. She looked like a pint-size hippie.

We bought her a guitar when she asked us for one, but she stopped trying to learn it after a few weeks, frustrated that she wasn't yet as skilled as her idols.

We thought it was nice that Nancy had found an interest in something. Though she listened to her rock albums awfully loud, we understood this to be a typical complaint of parents with teenagers. We were happy she was doing something typical, typical aside from the fact that she wasn't nearly a teenager yet.

She started reading *Rolling Stone* because it dealt with rock music, and quickly jumped to popular counterculture books I didn't think she could possibly understand, but did. At ten she was devoted to Sylvia Plath's poetry and her memoir, *The Bell Jar*. She devoured Kurt Vonnegut, Carlos Castaneda, Richard Brautigan, Ken Kesey, J. D. Salinger. She read and reread several times Tennessee Williams' play *The Glass Menagerie*. F. Scott Fitzgerald was another of Nancy's favorites—not only his novels but the numerous biographies about the author's troubled life and turbulent marriage to Zelda.

On Sundays she read *The New York Times*. She was mostly interested in the Vietnam War coverage, particularly the coverage of the antiwar movement. She identified with the war protesters. They were on her wavelength. Frank and I supported the Vietnam protest, but not actively. We came from the uninvolved generation.

One day I came home from the market with a box of Saran Wrap, and she got furious.

"Mommy, I want you to take that back," she demanded.

"Why?" I asked, confused.

"It's made by Dow Chemical. They're involved in napalm manufacturing."

"Nancy, I'm not taking it back," I put the Saran Wrap in the cupboard.

"You *have* to take it back, or the war will continue."

She waited for me to respond. I didn't.

"Okay," she shrugged. "You had your chance."

She went to the cookie jar, picked it up, and went in the living room with it.

"Nancy, where are you going with the cookie jar?" I asked, following her.

She rounded up Suzy and David, who were watching TV. "You," she said to Suzy, all business. "I want you to get crayons and marking pens. Meet me out front."

Suzy went off obediently on her mission.

"David, find some shirt cardboards," Nancy ordered.

David nodded, "Mommy," he said, "where are the shirt cardboards?"

"Under the sink in the basement, in a big bag," I informed him. Off he went.

"Nancy, what's going on?" I asked.

"We're protesting you," she replied. She patted the cookie jar.

"We'll live on these for as long as we have to. For the duration, if necessary. We're not coming back in this house until you take back that Saran Wrap. Are you taking it back?"

"No, I'm not."

She went out the front door. Suzy and David met her out front a minute later with crayons and shirt cardboards. They wrote WE PROTEST MOMMY AND DOWN WITH DEB on the cardboards and began to picket the house. I watched through a window. Sometimes they chanted "Down with Dow." Our neighbors drove by occasionally and looked at them curiously. In response, Nancy gave them the peace sign.

After about an hour of this Suzy and David got tired and wanted to come back inside. Nancy wouldn't let them. Instead, the three of them got in my car and ate the cookies.

At suppertime I ordered Suzy and David inside and they came in obediently. Nancy got very angry at them, branded them "Establishment pigs" and "sellouts," but finally came in herself a little later.

Every week she had a new cause—whatever she read about in the newspaper. After one of her cousins drew a poor number in the draft lottery, she became insistent that we sneak him into Canada at once. There was something precocious about ten-year-old Nancy's political activism, though she was so serious about it. Frank and I were concerned that she was getting too involved. But we felt that her heart was in the right place.

We just wished she could hold on to her friends. The Huntingdon Valley girls quickly turned on Nancy, just like the girls everywhere else we'd lived. One day I found a note stuck in the front door from her friend Helene: "Stay away from me, you witch." Later that afternoon I saw Helene and two other girls staring at Nancy through our living room window while Nancy read on the sofa, oblivious. I chased them away.

Her relationship with Suzy also continued to be poor. We wanted Nancy and Suzy to be sisters, not enemies. In the hope of bringing them closer together, we suggested to them that they share one of the big bedrooms in the new house. When I was a girl I'd often wished I had a sister to tell secrets to and giggle with when the lights were out. The girls agreed. They picked out matching bedspreads, headboards, and jewelry boxes. They had fun fixing the room up. But they still didn't get along well.

Then, a few months after we'd moved in, the roommate setup backfired. It was on a day that Nancy came home from school in tears. She refused to tell me why, just went up to the girls' room and began to do her homework. Suzy was outside playing. She came inside for dinner, went upstairs, and came back down a minute later, sobbing.

"Look what she did!" Suzy wailed.

"Suzy, what happened?" I asked.

"Just look what she did!" Suzy cried, "Look what Nancy did!"

I went upstairs to the girls' room. Nancy sat on her bed, arms and legs crossed. She stared straight ahead, a sullen pout on her face. Her math book was on the floor next to her bed, the pages twisted and ripped out of frustration.

Suzy's half of the bedroom was totally destroyed.

Nancy had pulled off Suzy's bedspread and ripped it to shreds. Suzy's clothes had been pulled out of Suzy's side of the closet and strewn across Suzy's side of the room, along with the contents of Suzy's half of the dresser drawers. Suzy's jewelry box was broken, the jewelry scattered among the ruined clothes, along with her box of hair rollers, her school supplies, her books.

The sheer precision of Nancy's rampage was frightening.

"Nancy!" I cried.

She just sat there. She didn't seem to hear me or see me.

I repeated her name several times but got no response. So I shook her by the shoulders. Finally I penetrated that vacant glaze.

"Why did you mess up Suzy's things?" I demanded.

"Because," she replied.

"I want you to put it back together right now. I'm very upset with you."

"No!" she replied, suddenly petulant.

"Yes!" I declared.

"No!" she repeated.

I left the room, furious. There was no reasoning with her when she was like this. I went downstairs to calm Suzy. When I went back upstairs, Nancy hadn't budged. She still sat on her bed, arms and legs crossed, that petulant pout on her face—a look we began to see often and quickly dubbed "That Look."

I cleaned up the room.

Frank and I discussed the situation when he got home. We decided it was unfair to Suzy to ask her to share a bedroom with Nancy any longer. At dinner we announced that we were going to move Nancy into the fourth upstairs bedroom, which had been used as a den. Nancy promptly refused to make the move—unless we also agreed to give her her own choice of new wallpaper, her own double bed, and her own Princess phone for the calls that never came from the friends who didn't exist. We agreed.

Again, we thought she was disturbed and should be getting some kind of treatment. Again, we wavered.

Until later that week, when I found Nancy standing at the top of the stairs, holding a brown paper bag over the bannister. She was about to drop it to the floor of the entry hall. Her eyes were glazed. She had That Look on her face.

"Nancy, what's in the bag?" I asked.

"Aquarius," she replied woodenly.

She loved the cat, loved all animals. I couldn't imagine her wanting to harm him.

"But why is Aquarius in the bag, Nancy?"

"I'm gonna throw him downstairs and see if he still lands on his feet, even if he's inside the bag."

"But Nancy, you'll hurt Aquarius."

"I want to."

"No!" I wrestled the bag from her. In response, she tried to smack me in the face. I overpowered her in time, shook her.

She blinked, looked around, looked at me, looked at the bag.

"Mommy, where are we going?"

"What?" I asked, confused.

"Why are we standing here?"

I looked deeply into my daughter's eyes. She wasn't playing a game. She really had forgotten why we were at the top of the stairs, forgotten what she'd been about to do.

"You wanted to hurt Aquarius," I explained.

She frowned, took the bag from me, and opened it. The cat jumped out and darted away. Then Nancy turned and went into her new room. She stared out the window for an hour, then sobbed uncontrollably for another hour.

The next day I commenced researching the guidance clinics in the area. I found one that appeared to have a good program for pre-adolescents. It was a sprawling, antiseptic institution affiliated with a major private psychiatric hospital.

The director was an older man with a rather prominent bald head. Frank and I met with him and described Nancy's belligerent, disruptive behavior, her violent tantrums, the glazed look she was getting, her inability to hold on to friends, our inability to control her. We told him the findings of the child guidance center evaluations administered to Nancy when she was four. We told him we were concerned that Nancy's crossed eye still hadn't straightened out.

He agreed to test her.

Nancy was angry with us but agreed to submit to a battery of tests. I think she was, deep down inside, becoming as frightened by her behavior as we were. She wanted help. Over several visits a psychology intern administered to Nancy a Bender Gestalt, Wechsler Intelligence Scale for Children, Wide-Range Achievement Test, Rutgers Drawing Test, Draw-a-Person, Rorschach, and Thematic Apperception Test. The evaluation was submitted to the head of the institute on October 22, 1968, when Nancy was ten and a half years old. The examiner described Nancy as a "somewhat big girl for her age who walks awkwardly and speaks in a soft, hoarse voice."

The results of the intelligence tests were consistent with what we already knew. Nancy's verbal IQ of 135 placed her in the category of Very Superior. Her full-scale IQ of 129 ranked her in the Superior range of intellectual activity. The Wide-Range Achievement Test placed Nancy as highly advanced—college level—in reading (grade equivalent of 12.9, ninety-ninth percentile) and spelling (grade equivalent of 14.5, ninety-ninth percentile), while almost a half-grade behind her expected level of performance in math (grade equivalent 5.7, forty-seventh percentile).

Nancy's performance on the Bender Gestalt and Rutgers Drawing tests yielded the same story we'd heard six years before. The examiner cited "difficulty in the fine motor area with some attempt at compensation through compulsivity."

But the examiner's evaluation of Nancy offered new insights.

Nancy perceives interpersonal interactions negatively; either as uncomfortable and discordant or as controlled and emotionally sterile. At a deeper level she views her parents as ignoring and rejecting her. Nurturance from her mother, whom she perceives as controlling, is conditional as there is perceived pressure from the latter for independence and intellectual achievement which Nancy perceives as leading to approval and love.

Nancy feels highly insecure about her inability to do things on her own. She sees herself as small and helpless in relation to a potentially dangerous environment and feels that she needs more support and is not getting as much as she needs and wants. She seems to react to her unmet dependency needs with angry feelings (especially toward her mother) which are anxiety arousing and which she must defend against albeit imperfectly by denial and reaction formation.

It seems, however, that tension can build up within Nancy and that she is hard pressed to deal with it as she senses difficulty in maintaining adequate delay and control. Despite her high level verbal ability she does not have a well developed rich imaginative fantasy life with which to bind impulse and affect. Rather she attempts to use rigid cognitive control as a compensatory mechanism, and she seems to relate to the external world without spontaneity.

Her high level verbal ability is not translated into personality functioning in an in-depth way and one does not see the deeper resources in her dealing with personality concerns. Her difficulty with internal control, though well compensated for at the cognitive level, thus appears to influence personality functioning and may have been initially based on some organic difficulty. . . .

Because there is much investment in dealing with basic concerns centering around support and security, she does not show signs of having reached an appropriate and age expected level of psychosexual development and she finds the area of heterosexual interaction and identity threatening and confusing.

Two weeks later the director of the institute held a diagnostic and planning conference with four other staff members, including Dr. Blake, who was to become Nancy's therapist. According to the report of this conference, Nancy's condition at that time was summarized as follows:

She impressed as an emotionally hungry child who feels herself as receiving less than others. This arouses anger which is displayed with sometimes poor control toward peers and siblings. Thought of accepting responsibility for these angry bouts then is sometimes projected onto others.

In reference to parents she reacts with anger but also with concern that she will lose love, nurturance, and protection. Her relationship with mother appears particularly conflictual. Self-concept is inadequate as she would prefer to be prettier, and nicer. Nancy's conflicts seem to be partially internalized, and there are evidences of anxiety, nightmares, and possible phobic features. Compulsive striving in academic work is seen as compensatory efforts at establishing her adequacy. Additionally, she seems to use denial and projection extensively, which might represent more characterological methods of defending herself.

> Finally, the family environment seems to be one in which hol-
> lering and physical punishment are common, which provide both a
> model and instigation for aggressive behavior.

(I don't know where this reference to physical punishment
came from. Frank and I did not believe in it. Nancy might
have made it up in an interview for shock value.)

Out of the planning conference came two recommenda-
tions: individual therapy for Nancy, as well as both individual
and group therapy for Frank and me.

This was relayed to us by the director the following week.

"You two have a lot of problems," he said. "Until you are
able to work them out, individually and as a couple, Nancy
will never be okay."

We were stunned. He was saying it was our fault that
Nancy was the way she was. She was disturbed because we
had a lousy marriage. Admittedly, ours had not been a perfect
marriage. We had had some problems. But we had not said
anything to the doctors about our infidelities. We felt that our
problems as a couple were working themselves out, that our
marriage was solid now. Clearly, the director did not think
so. He saw something wrong. He pinned the blame on us. He
was saying we were rotten parents. True, Suzy and David
were fine, healthy children. But that was just an accident! We
were lucky we hadn't destroyed them, too!

I felt awful and worthless as Frank and I crossed the parking lot to our car. Here I had devoted myself to being a good
mother and wife, only to turn up a total failure. It meant I was
a failure as a human being.

If only I had realized then that doctors are human beings,
too. They make mistakes. Their diagnoses are speculation,
not gospel. But I didn't know that then. Back then doctors
were God to their patients. And I was intimidated.

My instincts told me he was wrong, that something was seriously wrong with Nancy—regardless of her environment.
But I couldn't bring myself to doubt the director or disagree
with him. He knew what he was talking about. I was a house-
wife. I remember thinking I had hit bottom. I didn't know
then that there was still a long, long way to go.

# ☐ Chapter 6

I went to the clinic twice a week, once for my individual therapy, once for my group. Frank also went twice. Nancy started out just going to individual therapy, but soon she was also in group.

Dr. Blake, Nancy's therapist, wore a red dress to their first session. She was a middle-aged woman with a European accent. Nancy seemed to like her and didn't mind going. But she absolutely detested group and after a few weeks refused to go. I couldn't get her in the car.

"I don't want to go and sit there talking to a bunch of dumb, sick kids," she protested. "I don't have anything in common with them."

Dr. Blake said it was all right for Nancy to stop going to group.

I couldn't blame Nancy, actually. I disliked the group session myself. So did Frank. It didn't help that Frank and I were forbidden to attend the same group session.

Six or eight parents sat around in a circle. A doctor chaired the session. We just sat and stared at each other until someone

spoke up. The doctor didn't speak until someone else spoke.
One week I spoke up. I said I was upset with my mother be-
cause she was smoking excessively against doctor's orders.
He yelled at me.

"Who are you to judge other people!"he barked. "In your
own way, you know, you're not much better off!"

The doctor put everyone in the group down like that. It re-
inforced your tentativeness and feeling of helplessness. You
didn't come out feeling cleansed. You came out feeling like
garbage. Nevertheless, Frank and I went every week for almost a year.

Frank complained bitterly about his group sessions, mostly
because he said they never focused specifically on whatever
was supposed to be wrong with our marriage. Actually, Frank
didn't believe we had serious problems. He disagreed with
the clinic staff that Nancy's difficulties were rooted in her
home life. He felt something else was wrong with her. But he
didn't have the confidence to disagree with the professionals,
either.

In my individual sessions I met with a social worker, who
functioned more as a liaison with Nancy's therapist than as a
therapist for me. Each week I reported what had gone on at
home since we'd last spoken. She passed on what I said to Dr.
Blake, then reported Dr. Blake's comments back to me the
following week. As the year went on, the events I reported
became more painful and bizarre, the comments less and less
helpful. Frank and I, meanwhile, grew to feel more and more
helpless.

The first major episode I reported was prescription-drug-
related. Drugs again. Nancy, who was continually plagued
with allergies and respiratory infections, came down with a
particularly bad throat infection and high fever shortly after
we started at the clinic. Her pediatrician gave her antibiotics
for the infection and recommended aspirin for the fever.
When the aspirin failed to reduce the fever or the restless hy-
peractivity it was causing, he told me to fill a prescription for
Atarax, a mild sedative, so she could rest. I did, and gave her
one.

It was evening. The kids were in their rooms. Frank and I

were watching TV downstairs. About forty-five minutes after
Nancy had taken the Atarax I heard her screaming from her
room. I also heard a loud, rhythmic thumping noise that was
strong enough to shake the house. I ran up the stairs to Nancy's room.

She was sitting up in bed, banging her head repeatedly
against the wall with tremendous force and pulling her hair
out of her head in handfuls. Her eyes were glassy. She was
screaming, a guttural, animal yell I'd never heard before.

*"Nancy!"* I cried.

She was possessed, demonic. She was hallucinating and
she had no idea I was there. I grabbed her by the shoulders,
tried to wrestle her down on the bed so she'd stop hurting herself. In response she snarled, whipped around on the bed until
she was free of my grasp. Then she sprang across the room to
her bureau and began to smash it with her fists. She pulled the
drawers out, hurled them across the room, and kicked a leg
out from under the desk, which toppled to the floor.

I yelled for Frank. He came immediately. Nancy didn't
recognize him either. He wrestled her kicking and screaming
back into bed—barely. She was very strong. She had his
square, broad-shouldered build and was getting heavy.

Nancy lay on her back screaming, then abruptly stopped
and began to sing random half-phrases of familiar songs like
"Happy Birthday," "I'm a Yankee Doodle Dandy," and
"We Wish You a Merry Christmas." Then she stopped and
started to scream again.

"I'll call the doctor," I gasped to Frank. "You hold her."

"I'll try," he replied.

I turned to find Suzy and David standing wide-eyed in the
bedroom doorway in their pajamas.

"What's wrong with Nancy?" Suzy asked.

"She's upset. She's not feeling well," I said, trying to
sound calm. "Please go back to bed. Go to sleep."

"But she's making so much noise."

"Try. Please."

They did. I ran to call the doctor.

"It must be an allergic reaction to the medication," he

said. "I must admit I've never heard of such a reaction to Atarax."

"What should we do? Take her to the hospital?"

"No, keep her there. You'll just have to wait it out. Try to keep her from hurting herself."

I was frightened and confused. It seemed to me that Nancy belonged in a hospital. I was genuinely afraid she was going to hurt herself or have severe convulsions or some other physical breakdown we wouldn't be able to handle. But the doctor was adamant. Again, who was I to argue?

I went back to her room and reported the doctor's recommendation to Frank. He had Nancy pinned to the bed. When he turned his head to listen to me, she squirmed free of his grasp and began to punch herself repeatedly in the face. He struggled with her until her arms were again pinned against the bed.

"Who are you?" she screamed. "Who are you people? Why are you doing this to me? *Why?*"

She began to laugh hysterically. Then she began to sing. Then she started to sob.

"Where is she?" she sniffed. "Where is she?"

"Where's who, Nancy?" I begged.

"Her."

*"Who?"* Frank asked.

"The lady in the red dress. Where's the lady in the red dress. I want her. I want the lady."

Dr. Blake had worn a red dress at Nancy's first therapy session. I phoned her at home. She agreed with the pediatrician that Nancy was probably suffering an allergic reaction.

"He said we should not take her to the hospital," I reported.

"I agree," she said. "Nancy will wake up there and think that she did something very bad. Then you will have to explain to her what happened. If you leave her in her own bedroom she will not remember the episode tomorrow. It will be better."

Nancy screamed and sang and fought us the entire night. Suzy and David huddled in blankets on the den sofa, trying to sleep, while Frank and I took turns holding her down, wiping her off with cold cloths, making coffee to keep us going. By dawn the ferocity of the episode began to subside—the singing took over from the screaming. Then she began to talk.

"I know you," she said to me abruptly.

"You do?"

"Yes, you're the nice lady from last night." She looked over at Frank, who sat at her desk, bleary-eyed and stubbly. "And you're the nice man from last night."

She began to sing gaily, like a drunk. At around nine o'clock she recognized us.

"Mommy, where were you all night?" she asked me.

"Right here, Nancy,"

"Oh," She frowned, terribly confused. "What day is it?"

"Saturday."

"Can I watch cartoons in your bed?"

"Do you want to?"

"Yes. Please, can I?"

She got unsteadily out of bed and we walked hand in hand to our room. The bed was still made—Frank and I had never used it. I pulled back the covers and she got in, propped herself against the pillows, and began to happily watch Bugs Bunny, singing merrily. I brought her some breakfast and she ate hungrily.

Frank had promised Suzy he would go with her to buy a bicycle that Saturday, her very first two-wheeler. He shaved, showered, and took Suzy and David out to buy the bike. He wanted to get them out of the house and calm their fears.

I stayed with Nancy. By the afternoon she was totally recovered and had no memory of the episode.

I ran into Dr. Blake in the corridor at the clinic when I went for my individual session that week.

"It was the Atarax," she repeated. "It was a drug-related psychotic episode."

"What should we do?" I asked.

"Don't give it to her again," she snapped, then turned and walked away.

I didn't view this as particularly constructive. But the people at the clinic failed to offer much explanation of what happened in New York City a few weeks later, either.

Frank had a weekend convention there, and his company didn't mind if he took his family along. We got a family room with two double beds and a rollaway at the City Squire Hotel. On Saturday I took the kids shopping and sightseeing while Frank worked. Nancy was excited and happy the whole day. She bought some rock albums. She seemed to like New York. Saturday night I got a baby sitter for the kids while Frank and I went to dinner with some of his business acquaintances. The children thoroughly enjoyed themselves, the sitter reported. They ordered up from room service and watched TV. Nancy was no trouble. Sunday proved to be a gorgeous April spring day. The blossoms were on the trees; the sun was warm. After breakfast we took the children for a walk in Central Park so they could get some exercise before the drive home.

When we got into the park, we found ourselves amidst a swarm of young people with long hair, thousands and thousands of them. They were all heading for a large, open grassy area called the Sheep Meadow. Policemen were everywhere, setting up barricades, barking instructions to each other through walkie-talkies. Frank finally asked one of them what was going on.

It was a special event. The first anniversary of the musical *Hair* was being commemorated by a free performance of the show that day in Wollman Rink.

Needless to say, Nancy was thrilled at the chance to see her favorite rock album performed live.

"I wanna stay for it," she said.

"We have to leave, Nancy," I said. "It'll be too late to head back when it's over."

"I wanna stay," she repeated.

"Nancy, we're leaving," Frank said firmly.

The clinic people had told us to be firm and not get into an argument with her.

We didn't get into an argument. Nancy simply evaporated. One minute she was there; the next minute she was gone into the crowd.

There were about 100,000 people sitting there in the grass in the sunshine. It seemed like all of them had flowing brown hair and wore faded blue jeans like Nancy. It was hopeless to try to find her.

We located a policeman and asked him to help us. He told us that the department had set up a temporary precinct headquarters behind the stage. He offered to take us there to talk to the district commander. Frank and I decided to split up. He took Suzy and David to the fountain in front of the Plaza Hotel to wait. I went with the officer.

By the time we got backstage, *Hair* was underway. I reported to the district commander that Nancy was missing. He put out a general notification by walkie-talkie that there was a lost ten-year-old girl named Nancy in the park, with long brown hair, blue jeans, and a green and white T-shirt. Then he told me to wait there.

I did. I was terrified. What if she went off with someone? What if she were attacked? There were so many people out there. So much marijuana smoke. Who knew what could happen? I sat and waited.

At intermission the district commander asked Michael Butler, the show's producer, to make an announcement about Nancy. He went out on stage, went up to a microphone, and said, "We're looking for a lost little girl named Nancy Spungen."

The immense crowd cheered derisively.

"That's Nancy Spungen," he repeated. "Age ten. If you're out there, Nancy, come backstage. That's where your mom is. She's waiting for you."

I waited there for her through the entire second act. She didn't show up. Then the show was over, and the performers and musicians were leaving and the crowd was beginning to disperse. Still there was no Nancy. The district commander kept shaking his head and apologizing to me. There was nothing more that he could do.

About an hour after the show was over, just when the temporary police headquarters was being dismantled, a call came in. A patrolman had found a girl who answered Nancy's description sitting on a park bench. He had asked her if her name was Nancy. She had failed to respond.

Somehow I knew it was her. A patrolman escorted me

through the rapidly emptying park until we met up with another patrolman, who had Nancy by the hand. I was so relieved, so happy to see her, that I ran up to her and hugged her.

She didn't return the hug. Her eyes were glazed. She didn't talk, didn't acknowledge my presence. The patrolman was concerned. He asked if I wanted him to call a doctor. I politely refused, thanked him for his trouble, and led Nancy away. We found Frank and the other kids at the Plaza fountain, where they'd been waiting for hours.

Frank was livid, until he saw That Look on Nancy's face. He said nothing. We were all afraid to say anything to her, for fear she'd start screaming and lose control. So we didn't punish her. We just plain didn't speak the entire way home. Nancy stared out the window. When we got home, she got out of the car, went up to her room, closed the door. She didn't come out or talk or eat for the entire night.

I was both angry and confused. Part of me felt that Nancy was in total command of herself, had run away because we wouldn't let her stay for the concert, didn't give a damn about the grief she'd put the rest of the family through. The glaze was a deliberate, calculated, defensive move to stop us from punishing her. She was simply a rotten kid.

Part of me wasn't so sure. Deep inside I felt that something Nancy had no control over had pulled her, that she wasn't responsible for her actions, that the glaze was a genuine one.

I asked myself if I was ever going to understand what was wrong with my child. I asked myself when this was going to end, *how* this was going to end.

The next day Nancy acted as if nothing had happened. She didn't mention the episode. I honestly couldn't tell if she was pretending not to remember so as to avoid my wrath, or if she really didn't remember. None of us could tell.

She never once acknowledged that she'd seen *Hair* performed live, even though she played the cast album that day and every day thereafter.

I reported the episode to my social worker, who reported it to Dr. Blake, who said that Nancy had run away because she wanted to see the concert and had been forbidden to do so.

She added that I should have punished her immediately and was negligent in not doing so.

My fault, again.

Dr. Blake said I also handled the beads incident wrong when I reported that a couple of weeks later.

A popular hobby with girls at that time was stringing tiny Indian glass beads into necklaces and bracelets. As soon as the hobby shop in the neighborhood shopping center would get a new color of bead, it would sell out immediately.

The girls used to gather in a circle on someone's front lawn and string the beads. They let Nancy join them. She loved to string beads, in spite of her hand-eye difficulty.

One day I noticed Nancy with them on the lawn across the street. A few minutes later I heard Nancy scream.

*"It isn't fair!"* she cried. *"It isn't fair!"*

Then I heard the other girls scream.

I ran out of the house. They were standing around her, horrified and frightened. They parted to let me to her. Nancy was face down in the grass. She was screaming and crying and pulling her hair out at the roots, just like she had during her Atarax attack. I turned her over on her back and pinned her arms down with mine.

"What happened?" I asked as I struggled with her.

"Her . . . her beads slipped off the wire, Mrs. Spungen," one of the girls said, eyes wide with fear as Nancy bucked and screamed underneath me. "Her beads went in the grass and she couldn't find all of them."

"She's okay," I assured them. "She's just upset."

Nancy's sobs gave way to deep gasps for air. She began to hyperventilate.

"Could one of you please get me a paper bag?" I asked.

One of the girls ran into her house and came back with a brown paper bag. I put it over Nancy's mouth and nose, but it didn't stop her from hyperventilating. I gathered her up, got her into the car, and drove to the hospital.

She was still hyperventilating when I got her to the emergency room. The doctor had her stretch out on a table. He couldn't find whatever it was he wanted to give her, so he left the room for a second to get it.

I was right outside in the corridor.

"She'll be fine," he assured me as he came out.

No sooner had he said that when Nancy leaped from the table like a panther and slammed the glass emergency room door shut in our faces and locked it. She stood there, pointing at us, laughing. She was having no trouble breathing now. Nobody could get the door open. A nurse had to send for a security man who had a key. When he got the door open, Nancy was sitting on the table, still laughing.

"I'm smarter than you," she said to the doctor. "I'm smarter than all of you stupid motherfuckers."

I'd never heard Nancy curse before and I was shocked. I scolded her but she totally ignored me. When I got her home, she went upstairs and slammed her door and put on the stereo very loud.

The other girls were still sitting on the lawn across the street. I'd seen them watching our return and now I went over to them. I thought it was important to talk to them. I didn't want them to ostracize Nancy or gossip about her.

"Sometimes things get to be too much for you," I said. "And you have to blow off steam. Nancy's pretty sensitive sometimes and she just got real upset."

They nodded. They were shaken, but they seemed to understand. They were a couple of years older than Nancy, thirteen and fourteen. They made an extra effort to remain friends with her. I felt better for talking to them.

I didn't feel better for talking to my clinic social worker. She took down my report of the episode, relayed it to Dr. Blake, and came back to me with the following counsel.

Of the beads seizure, Nancy's therapist advised, "She'll just have to learn how to control herself." As for the emergency room lockout, Dr. Blake suggested, "She's looking for attention. She's acting out something she probably saw on TV." Dr. Blake also suspected the cursing was acting out, possibly acting out something she read in one of her books. Dr. Blake's response to my query about how I should handle a similar situation in the future: "You should have ignored her. Go about your business."

"Would you please explain something to me?" I asked

Frank that evening while we lay in bed, both of us too upset by the day's events to sleep. "Would you please tell me how I'm supposed to 'go about my business' while my oldest daughter is pulling her hair out at the roots on our neighbor's front lawn?"

"I'll be goddamned if I know," Frank said, heaving a sigh. "I don't know what to do. To tell you the truth, I'm beginning to wonder whether they do, either. We do everything they tell us to do and none of it has any impact on her. I wish I knew what the hell was going on with her. I wish I knew what the story is. This is just so goddamned frustrating and confusing."

It was. Here she was, getting reputedly topnotch professional care, yet her behavior was getting worse. We feared Nancy was periodically not in control of herself. Her therapists still saw her as a smart, headstrong girl who knew exactly what she was doing. There was no acknowledgment from the clinic that any other diagnosis or treatment might be required, even though Nancy wasn't responding to anything they were prescribing. The clinic was either unwilling or unable to deal with Nancy as anything besides a bright, sensitive child who came from a troubled home. We couldn't exactly blame them. Ours *was* a troubled home. But was Nancy the source of the trouble or the result? Was her behavior our fault? Or was it, once again, simply outside the realm of experience of those treating her? We didn't know. We were young and naive. We trusted the medical community. We didn't challenge the doctors, didn't press for answers, didn't take Nancy elsewhere. We left ourselves in their hands and accepted our feelings of doubt and helplessness as a fact of life, something we'd have to live with.

Our daily life was a total misery. Typically, I had put out two or three brushfires by the time Frank got home— brushfires started by Nancy. On one particular afternoon the flames started over a pen.

Nancy and Suzy were doing their homework in their rooms after school. I was downstairs.

First I heard Nancy yell, "You fucking brat!"

Then I heard Suzy yell, "Mommy!"

I went upstairs. Nancy was in Suzy's room. She wanted to borrow a pen, the very pen Suzy was doing her homework with.

"You stupid fucking brat. Give me the pen."

"It's *my* pen," whined Suzy. "And I'm *using* it. Make her leave me alone, Mommy, Please make her."

"Why don't you borrow a different pen?" I asked Nancy.

"I want *that* pen," Nancy said.

I sighed. "All right. Suzy, why don't you give her that pen and I'll give you another one, okay? How would that be?"

Suzy looked down at the floor, reluctantly nodded, and handed over her pen to Nancy, who smirked triumphantly.

"Got ya, ya fucking brat." She laughed.

"Nancy, I've warned you about your language. I won't tolerate it. I don't like it."

"Who gives a fuck what you like, you stupid bitch."

*"Nancy!"*

She went in her room, closed the door, and put on Hendrix full blast.

I went downstairs, got Suzy another pen, and brought it to her.

"I don't know what to do, Mommy," she said. "I try to be nice but it doesn't make any difference at all."

"I know. Just try to, well, try to avoid being a troublemaker."

"But I *do* try."

I gave her a hug. "I know you do."

I felt so badly for Suzy. She always seemed to get the short end. So did David. Frank and I did our best to give them special, undivided attention. Once or twice a month Frank would take David to a ballgame, just the two of them. Or I'd take Suzy shopping. Sometimes Frank took the two of them for a drive in the country and lunch while I stayed with Nancy. We made every effort we could to give them what was our idea of a more normal childhood. But it meant fragmenting the family unit. It meant getting them away from Nancy.

I went downstairs to make dinner. Ten minutes later Nancy started hollering at her sister again.

"Fucking crybaby brat!"

"Mommy!" Suzy yelled.

Back up the stairs I went. Nancy was in Suzy's room again.

"Mommy, make her leave me alone," Suzy begged. "I'm trying to do my homework."

"Nancy, why don't you let Suzy do her homework?" I asked, in my reasonable voice.

"I want her to listen to a record with me," Nancy replied.

"But she's busy."

"I don't care."

"You *have* to care."

"Says who?" she demanded.

"Says me," I declared.

"What do *you* know? You don't know a fucking thing about anything. You married Frank, didn't you? He's a bastard. He's a fucking shithead bastard."

I almost slapped Nancy in the face, but I stopped myself.

"Go ahead, hit me. Hit me, bitch."

I walked away. Dr. Blake had told me to ignore her when she was like this. I went back downstairs. She followed me, the expletives and abuse spewing out of her, just like when she was two and had threatened to cut up everything in my closet. She followed me right down the stairs.

"Why don't you get rid of him? Throw him out! You don't need to be married to that son of a bitch! We don't want him here! Get rid of him!"

I chewed my lip and busied myself in the kitchen.

"He doesn't love us! He's not a nice man! He's mean. He's a mean fucking bastard."

Mercifully, she stopped short and went outside. She came back a minute later with David, who had been playing outside. She pulled him up the stairs by the scruff of the neck. He was too little to fight her.

"Where are you going with David?" I demanded.

She didn't reply. She went to Suzy's room and pounded on Suzy's closed door.

*"I don't need you, brat! I have David! David and I are gonna listen to records!"*

Then she dragged David into her room and put a record on, leaving the door open so it would annoy Suzy more.

After a few minutes she let David leave.

Then Frank came home from work, exhausted. He slumped onto the sofa with a drink and turned on the news on TV. He couldn't hear it because of Nancy's stereo, even though her door was now closed.

"Does she have to listen to her records that loud?" he complained.

"Believe me, this is the quietest it's been all day. Let it be."

He nodded with weary resignation and made the TV louder. We stared at it for a few minutes, too tired to move.

Then it was time for dinner. I called the kids to the table. Suzy and David and Frank were already seated at the dining room table by the time Nancy came down. She had left her music on upstairs.

"Nancy, why don't you turn that off when you come down?" Frank asked.

"I want to listen to it."

"Well, I don't," Frank said.

"So?"

"So, you're not being fair. It's our house, too."

"If it's your house then why don't you throw her out?"

"Throw who out?" asked Frank confused.

"Mom. She hit me today. In the face, hard."

"Nancy, I did not," I protested.

"She's a liar. She hit me. She hits all of us. I think you should throw her out. Get rid of her. Divorce the ugly bitch."

Frank threw his fork down. "Young lady, I told you I'm not going to have you talk that way in this house!"

She whirled, glowered at Suzy. "What are you staring at?"

Suzy quickly looked down at her plate. "Nothing."

"You were staring at me! I saw you!"

"I *wasn't!*"

"*Were!*"

"Nancy, leave her alone," I ordered.

"*Not until she stops staring at me!*" Nancy hurled her full dinner plate against the dining room wall. It shattered.

"*Tell her to stop staring at me!*"

I sighed. "Suzy, stop staring at your sister."

"But I *wasn't.*" She began to sniffle.

"Don't be a troublemaker," I warned.

"Crybaby," gloated Nancy.

Suzy ran, sobbing, to her room. I ran after her, apologized, and calmed her down. I tried to explain, but I was putting her in an impossible situation, asking her for more comprehension than she was capable of at age nine.

We dried her tears and came back downstairs to the table.

Frank was pointing to the mess Nancy had made with her dinner plate.

"Nancy, pick that up!"

"There's the crybaby!" laughed Nancy at Suzy, ignoring her father. "Look at the crybaby!"

Suzy sat down and resumed eating, eyes glued to her plate.

"Pick it up, Nancy!" Frank repeated.

"Make me, you son of a bitch." She sneered.

"Do it!"

"No!"

"Do it!"

"Fuck you!"

"Do it or I'm going to take away your goddamned record player! For good!"

*"Lay one hand, one fucking hand, on my record player and I'll go out the door and never come back. Just try and touch it, you bastard!"*

Frank threw down his napkin and got up. "You've got a deal!" He started up the steps.

Nancy shrugged, got up, and ran out the front door of the house, leaving it wide open.

*"Nancy, come back here!"* Frank screamed.

Too late. She was gone.

"You happy?" I demanded. "You happy you got her to run away?"

"Thrilled to death," he replied bitterly as he closed the door behind her.

"Aren't you going to go get her?"

"She'll come back."

"Go get her, Frank. It's your fault she ran away."

"Why is it *my* fault?"

Suzy and David watched us like it was a Ping-Pong match. They were used to us fighting over Nancy.

"Because you gave her no choice. You backed her against a wall."

"What else was I supposed to do? I try to do what's right. I don't know what else to do."

"You can start by going out there and getting her. It's cold tonight. She hasn't got a coat."

He sadly put on his coat, got Nancy's coat, and went out after her.

There was a big field behind the house that hadn't been developed yet. She was crossing it. He caught up to her, demanded she come back. She called him every name in the book, refused to come with him. He grabbed her arm to pull her back. She struggled to get free, and in so doing pulled her arm out of its socket.

She came back to the house, screaming in pain and anger.

"Look what your fucking cocksucker husband did to me!" she yelled. "He broke my fucking arm!"

We drove her to the hospital emergency room. She was quiet during the drive. As soon as we got to the ward she began to yell.

"Look what my father did to me! He beats me, see? I want him arrested right now! I want you to call the police this instant!"

The doctors and nurses on duty exchanged a look. They remembered Nancy from when she had locked everyone out of the emergency room. They ignored her ranting, took her inside, and popped her arm back into its socket. She calmed down immediately. They did not leave her alone in there this time.

"How's that feel?" the doctor asked.

She rotated the arm easily. "It still hurts."

"It does?" he asked, surprised.

"A lot. Can't you give me a sling or something."

"Okay, a sling might be a good precaution for tonight."

He put the arm in a sling. Nancy insisted on wearing it for ten days, even though the arm was fine. She went up and down the block with it, shouting, "Look what my father did to me!" to the other girls in the neighborhood.

She seemed to enjoy dramatizing her own suffering, particularly at Frank's expense.

Frank was heartbroken by the incident. I was too, for yelling at him when Nancy ran away. We both felt sad and guilty. She was constantly prying us apart, pitting us against each other. We fought out of frustration. I told him I knew he hadn't meant to hurt Nancy's arm, that he was only trying to be firm. We talked all night.

Once again, Dr. Blake blamed us for the incident.

"There's conflict in the house," she said to me, through my social worker.

"Of course there's conflict!" I complained. "As long as we try to handle her there's going to be conflict. You told us to be firm!"

The social worker had nothing to say.

I informed Dr. Blake a few weeks later that Frank had a sales meeting to attend in New York. The other wives were going, and I was expected to go, too. I asked her if she thought it would be all right to leave Nancy, Suzy, and David with a sitter for the weekend. Dr. Blake said she thought it would be okay. In fact, she said, it would be a good idea because it would show Nancy that we trusted her.

I hired an experienced neighborhood baby sitter for the weekend, a college girl who came highly recommended. Just before we were to leave, I got cold feet and asked my mother to stay at the house, too. She agreed.

We left on Friday afternoon. I called home several times while we were gone, and each time my mom and the sitter reported that everything was fine. Still, I didn't enjoy being away. I couldn't relax, couldn't wait to get home. I wasn't comfortable leaving Nancy. I was afraid she might get belligerent and curse.

I was in no way prepared for what did happen.

Frank and I drove back on Sunday morning. It was afternoon when we turned onto Red Barn Lane. Our neighbors were out washing their cars and mowing their lawns. It was a hot, sunny summer day. Frank and I waved to them as we passed. Instead of waving back they looked away.

We pulled in front of our house. Nancy was sitting on her bike in the driveway, wearing her bathrobe. Her eyes were glazed. She had That Look on her face.

Mother was inside, badly shaken. She burst into tears when she saw me.

"We had just an awful experience this morning. Just awful."

"What? What happened?"

"She . . . she . . ."

Frank came in with the bags. "What happened?"

"She . . ." Mother trailed off, sobbing.

From what she told us when she calmed down, and from what the sitter told us later, we pieced together the story.

Nancy called David a "fucking little brat" at the breakfast table.

"You know, Nancy," the sitter scolded, "it isn't nice to talk to your brother that way."

In response, Nancy ran upstairs to her room, pulled the window screen off, and jumped out on the roof of the garage in her bathrobe and slippers.

She began to scream at the top of her lungs, *"I wanna die! I wanna die! I'm gonna kill myself! I wanna die!"*

Everyone in the neighborhood could hear her.

Mother and the sitter tried to coax her back into her room from the window. Nancy finally agreed to come back in when the sitter apologized for what she'd said to her at the table. That seemed to satisfy her.

No sooner had Nancy climbed back in the window, though, than she grabbed a pair of scissors from her desk drawer, brandished them over her head, and hissed to the sitter, "I'm gonna stab you to death, you fucking bitch."

The sitter screamed and ran from the room.

Nancy ran after her. She chased her down the hall, down the stairs, around the living room, hissing at her, "Fucking bitch, fucking bitch." She chased her back up the stairs, then back down again.

Finally Mother got Nancy to the floor by tripping her. She

pried the scissors from Nancy before she could recover. The sitter ran home, terrified.

Then Nancy's eyes glazed over. When Mother released her, she wandered out the front door and sat on her bike until we got home.

"I didn't know she was this bad," Mother said to me, "I didn't know she was this bad."

Frank calmed her down while I went out to see Nancy. I said her name several times. She didn't see me. I held my hand out to her. She took it, came willingly with me into the house. Then she went up to her room and sat on her bed and stared at the wall. I looked in on her a few minutes later and she was asleep. I pulled a blanket over her.

I went to see the baby sitter. I apologized to her and to her parents. I told them that Nancy was indeed undergoing therapy, but that she'd never exhibited this sort of violent behavior before. I swore to them that we wouldn't have left Nancy with a sitter if she had. They were surprisingly understanding and compassionate.

I phoned Dr. Blake when I got home.

"She's acting out," Nancy's therapist said. "She wouldn't have really stabbed the girl."

"It certainly looked that way to my mother," I said.

"No, no, no. She wouldn't have."

"How do you know that?"

"She isn't violent."

"Aren't you listening to me? I just told you, she tried to stab her baby sitter with a pair of scissors!"

"She's acting out," Dr. Blake repeated calmly.

"Acting out what?" I demanded.

"I'll talk to her this week and we'll find out."

I hung up the phone, furious. The clinic refused to acknowledge that Nancy was in serious trouble. But Frank and I knew she was deeply disturbed. It wasn't only her behavior that had deteriorated over the past few months. It was her appearance, too. She was ballooning in weight, so much so that I had to buy her new clothes every two weeks. And her facial expression had changed. When Nancy had started her treatment at the clinic, she still smiled, still had an alert, warm gleam in her eyes. Now the light was gone.

I have snapshots of her at age ten and age eleven. The contrast is alarming. The ten-year-old Nancy is our Nancy. The eleven-year-old Nancy, the Nancy who stood on the garage roof and screamed that she wanted to die, is not. She is glaring vacantly through you, her thick dark brows knitted into a frown.

Whatever was pulling her had taken her away from us. But the experts didn't believe us. They still thought we were the trouble.

They needed to see it for themselves, and finally they did.

Ever since Nancy had started with Dr. Blake, she'd been very curious about the source of the therapist's accent. Dr. Blake was from one of the Eastern European countries, I believe. But for some reason she preferred not to tell Nancy where she was from. It became a major point of contention.

When Nancy arrived for her first session after the near-stabbing, she was armed with a list of at least ten European countries that Dr. Blake might have come from. She intended to confront her therapist.

I waited outside Dr. Blake's office on a couch, as usual. A few minutes after their session started I heard Nancy scream, "I know you're from somewhere, you fucking bitch! Where are you from? Where?"

Then I heard a loud smash, followed by another, then another. Another therapist hearing the commotion came running down the hall and into Dr. Blake's office. I followed him.

Nancy was destroying the woman's office. Everything on the desk was smashed. The books had been swept off the shelves. A clock had been hurled through the closed window and out into the parking lot. A bottle of blue ink was all over Dr. Blake, dripping down from her hair onto her face. She was definitely frightened.

The man pinned Nancy's arms behind her and sat her down hard on the couch. Dr. Blake motioned for me to come out in the hall with her.

"Nancy got *very* angry," she said, with total surprise. Clearly, she had not believed any of my reports over the past year. "Angry over absolutely *nothing*. I think you had better take her home." Dr. Blake looked warily over her shoulder into the office. "When she's calm."

"Do you still think she's acting out, or is something else wrong with her?" I asked.

Dr. Blake hesitated. "She really did try to stab the baby sitter, didn't she?"

Finally Nancy calmed down a little, and as we left she turned, pointed a finger at Dr. Blake, and said, "I warned you, you bitch." Then she marched down the hallway, me struggling to keep up with her.


Nancy's fall term at school started soon after that. She was excited about going back to school, though she did get upset when we had to buy her new jeans because the old ones didn't fit anymore. I couldn't understand why she was blowing up so fast. She wasn't eating much.

She was very quiet when she came home from her first day of classes. She went to her room and read and listened to records. She came down for dinner but ate little and said nothing. She went to bed early.

Her screaming woke me in the night. I ran to her room, turned the light on. She was cowering on the floor in the corner, her arms over her head, gasping in fear. Her face was white.

"They're after me!" she screamed. "Help me."

"Who?"

"They're after me!"

*"Who,* Nancy?"

"Sharks. Sharks are after me. They're gonna attack me. Eat me up!"

She began to crawl furiously around on the floor on her hands and knees, trying to escape the terror only she could see.

She was awake. This was no nightmare. This was a hallucination.

"Where, Nancy? Where are they?"

"They're gonna get me!"

I sat with her, just like I used to when she was little and thought a rabbit had bit her. I tried to soothe her. We talked about going to the seashore. I quieted her. After a while she fell asleep in my arms, her legs still kicking.

In the morning she refused to come out of her room to go to school. She locked us out and no amount of threatening would get her out of there.

"I'm not going and there's no way you can make me!" she yelled through the locked door.

I got Suzy and David off to school, then called Dr. Blake.

"Nancy must go to school," she said. "She absolutely must. Get her out of there. Take the door off at the hinges if you have to, but get her out of there. She *must* go to school."

Frank took Nancy's bedroom door off. She was huddled in the corner on the floor like the night before, her eyes wide with terror. "Don't make me go," she begged. "Please don't make me. They hate me. My friends, the teachers, they all hate me. They're all against me. Don't make me go. You can't."

Frank and I looked at each other. She didn't seem to be in any condition to go to school, but Dr. Blake was quite emphatic about this.

"Come on, Nancy," Frank said, "I'll drive you."

"Drive me where?"

"To school."

She screamed. He pulled her to her feet and dragged her to the top of the stairs.

"No, no! Don't make me go! Don't make me go."

She wrapped her fingers around the wrought-iron bannister and held on for dear life. Frank tried to pull her down the stairs but she held firm. The bannister began to creak.

"They're against me! Don't make me go!"

I peeled her fingers off the railing, one at a time. When one hand was loose, Frank was able to drag her down a step. She grabbed hold again. Again I peeled her fingers off, one by one, and Frank pulled her, screaming, down one step. After twenty minutes of this we had her downstairs. Frank dragged her, kicking, punching, screaming, into the car. He started the motor, backed out the driveway, and hadn't gone halfway down Red Barn Lane before her door flew open. She tried to jump out of the car. He pulled her back in, slammed the door shut. He yelled. She screamed. They drove away.

Frank got her to school, then came home to have breakfast before going to work. His hands were shaking.

"I know the therapist said she had to go," he said, "but to tell the truth, by the time I got her there she was in no condition to go to class. I took her to the counselor, and she said she'd take care of her until she was calm enough to go to class."

I poured Frank a cup of coffee. Before he had time to take a sip of it, the phone rang. We both looked at the phone and then at each other. There was no doubt who it was. I answered it.

"Mrs. Spungen, I'm so sorry," the counselor said, her voice quavering. "Nancy was right here, she was sitting right here in my office. Next thing I knew she got up and just walked right past me out of the office into the hallway. I ran after her, Mrs. Spungen. I called her name. But she didn't see or hear me, I swear. It was like she was in a trance. Her eyes were . . . were . . ."

"Her eyes were blank."

"Yes, that's it. She just kept going out the front door of the building. She's gone, Mrs. Spungen. She's gone. I'm so sorry. Do you want me to phone the police?"

"We'll find her. Thank you." I hung up.

"She's gone," I told Frank.

"I'm not surprised," he said.

We started out the door to look for her. The phone rang. It was Nancy.

"I'm at the Buck Road Mobil station," she said in a wooden monotone. "Come and get me."

"Nancy, why did you leave?" I asked. "Why aren't you at school?"

"Come and get me."

"Stay there. Don't leave. We'll be right there."

"Come and get me," she said again.

Frank followed me in his car. Nancy was waiting by the phone booth at the gas station she mentioned. She got in my car. She had That Look. When Frank saw that she was calm, he kept on going to the office. I drove Nancy home.

"I'm never going back to school ever again," she said quietly.

"But Nancy, you *have* to go back."

"I don't need to. I already know everything I need to know."

"But you won't be able to go to college if you don't go back to school."

"I'm not going."

I was surprised and very disappointed to hear her say this. Until now, Nancy's intellect had been the one thing she could hold on to. She was proud of it. She read constantly, knew a great deal about what was going on in the world. College had always been her goal. Frank and I had encouraged her. Here was one area in which she excelled and could have a positive self-image. Moreover, pointing her toward college kept her headed in the direction of a normal life—a life we still hoped she could have. College was her anchor to a useful adult life. By repudiating school, she was, in effect, saying she didn't believe she'd ever have that normal life. She was setting herself adrift. This upset me deeply.

When we got home she went straight up to her room, sat on her bed, and stared at her feet. I went in, sat down next to her on the bed, and put my arms around her. She didn't push me away, but she didn't return the hug, either. It was like holding a dead person.

"I wish I could make you happy, Nancy," I said. "I love you so much. You're my firstborn, and you're special to me. You'll always be special to me. I want you to be happy. So does Daddy. We both love you."

She just stared at the floor.

I left her. I phoned the counselor at school to let her know Nancy was safe. She was relieved.

"Mrs. Spungen, I . . . I . . . well, what I have to say isn't easy."

"Yes?"

She cleared her throat uncomfortably. "I don't think

Nancy belongs in school. At least not this school. I don't think she ought to come back. I'm sorry.''

I hung up, staggered. The public school system was no longer able to handle Nancy. It was as if a door had been slammed in our faces.

I called Dr. Blake and told her. Then I poured out my frustration.

"We don't know what to do," I said, trying to choke back the emotion in my voice. "We do what you tell us to do and it doesn't work. We don't know what to do."

"I have spoken to the director," she said coolly. "He agrees with me that a reevaluation is called for. He would like to see Nancy tomorrow, then meet with you the following day. Can you bring Nancy tomorrow at ten a.m.?"

I said I could, and I delivered Nancy to the director of the clinic the following morning at the appointed time. He held a lengthy individual session with her. The details of his reevaluation, dated September 29, 1969:

> My session with Nancy today was at the request of Dr. Blake who had expressed serious concern regarding Nancy's recent exaggerated behavior.
>
> From my interview with her, it was quite clear that she is a seriously disturbed child who has regressed considerably in recent weeks. Her affect [level of emotion] is bland and her thinking inappropriate and marked by poor judgment.
>
> With respect to her avoidance of school, she says that she plans never to return again and can see nothing irregular about her attitude. She will not attend school because "all the kids are against me, even my best friend."
>
> She showed little concern about her extreme behavior at home and was casual about the recent episode of attempting to stab her baby sitter. The extent of projection that she uses appears to have reached the point of almost adult-like paranoid schizophrenic ideation with evidence of underlying mild depression often seen associated with such projection.
>
> My diagnostic impression of Nancy is that she is a schizophrenic girl who is currently in a state of decompensation and regression with suggestions of probable continuation of her regression. The latter I base on her inability to see the degree of her poor judgment, the blandness of her affect, and the frequent bizarreness of her ideation.
>
> The extreme rapidity of her regressions suggests that careful neu-

rological studies be carried out to rule out the possibility of any organic determinants.

The director's evaluation was thorough and concrete and
signified a major change from a year before, when he had
seen Nancy as a bright girl with a personality problem that
stemmed from her troubled environment. He now believed
what we had long believed. He now put a label on it. He now
thought Nancy was schizophrenic. In recommending neurological studies for "organic determinants," the director was
referring to brain tumor as a possible explanation for what he
perceived to be Nancy's marked deterioration.

He did not, however, share any of this information with us
when he ushered us into his office the following day. I only
obtained it years later, when Nancy was already dead, at
which point I felt bitter vindication—I had been certain for a
long time that Nancy was seriously ill—but no satisfaction.

What he told us that day was that Nancy was being terminated from the clinic because she needed more care than they
were capable of giving her.

He did not share with us his diagnosis of schizophrenia.
Rather, the diagnosis he chose to offer was basically a continuation of his original one. He acknowledged that she was
worse, but he still put the blame on us.

The clinic's own report of this meeting, which I also obtained after Nancy's death, jibes with what Frank and I recall
of that day.

He [the director] strongly recommended and concurred with the therapy team, that Nancy should get all the help that she needs at this
time. He also impressed on the Spungens that if they were to follow
through with this it would be highly important that they make a point
of getting involved themselves, because what is going on at the present time is not only due to factors in the present, but also due to multiple factors and interactions which have been on-going over many,
many years.

What is seen now is purely a product of what has been fed into the
situation in the interactions between the parents and the child over the
past few years. The Spungens were essentially satisfied, and our con-
tacts with them were terminated at the time.

The clinic report makes no mention of the director saying anything to us about schizophrenia or about recommending a neurological study for Nancy. That's because he didn't.

I asked him that day, point-blank, for a diagnosis. He told me, point-blank, that he had none. I asked him what our next step should be. He made a steeple of his fingers, looked me in the eye, and replied, "Damned if I know." Not a word about a neurological work-up.

If the director had been more candid with us that day, we would have had a better understanding of what was wrong with Nancy and of where to search for treatment. We wouldn't have had to stumble along blindly like we did. Maybe it wouldn't have altered the course Nancy's life took. Maybe it would have. If nothing else, we wouldn't have felt so helpless and confused, so lost.

Why wasn't he more candid? Doctors now tell us that up until about five years ago it was not uncommon to "spare" the parents of a seriously impaired child—just as they did the parents of a terminally ill one. The director probably felt that Nancy needed a hospital-like psychiatric setting, and was fully aware that not one such place existed for an eleven-year-old then in the Philadelphia area. So for him to have spelled it out to us straight would have been for him to say, "You're going to have to live with this for as long as you live—there's no hope." That would have been just like telling us our daughter had incurable cancer.

Doctors also tell me that psychologists find it much more difficult to diagnose schizophrenia in a child than in an adult—so many of the dream-world symptoms are natural behavior in a child. But even if a psychologist does suspect schizophrenia, he or she will still be reluctant to use that label for behavior the child may outgrow. This is especially applicable to Nancy's case, since she was such a bright child and since the director may have wanted to see the results of a neurological work-up before disclosing his suspicions to us.

Why didn't the director himself undertake the neurological testing before electing to terminate Nancy? Why didn't he advise us to have the tests done? I don't know. I have no explanation.

All the director did was stand up, wish us good luck, and shake our hands.

Frank and I reeled out to the parking lot, just like we had a year before—only now we knew even less. All we knew was that we had a disturbed eleven-year-old daughter who neither the school system nor the clinic could deal with.

We drove back slowly through the quiet afternoon streets of our suburban development, not saying a word. We had no idea what to do with Nancy. If the professionals didn't know, how were *we* supposed to know?

I wanted to cry, but I stopped myself. There was no time to cry. No time for the luxury of tears. Tears meant giving up, and I wouldn't. I had made a commitment to Nancy that day eleven years before in the nursery, when I saw her fighting for her life. I had promised her a life of quality. Now that promise had real meaning, real direction. I had to find a way out of this maze. I had to do everything in my power to keep my promise to my child. I took several deep breaths. I did not cry. I would not cry.

# ☐ Chapter 7

I sought out Nancy's pediatrician for help. He saw her a few days later and was concerned about her physical condition. He said her pulse rate was unusually high and her pupils dilated. He gave her a blood test on the spot. When I asked why, he said he wanted to see if she was taking drugs. This surprised me—drugs were not yet a problem with the kids in our neighborhood. Besides, Nancy was only eleven.

She was clean. There were no drugs in her system. She was speeding on her own.

Through the pediatrician, I found a psychiatrist who was willing to see Nancy. I scheduled an appointment, and though Nancy didn't want to go, she did. I sat outside in his small waiting room.

Within five minutes I heard a crash, then a thump, then a scream. Then another crash.

He opened the door. His forehead was bleeding. His glasses were smashed and hanging from one ear. His wristwatch was shattered.

"Please come in" he said.

Nancy had swept everything off his desk. The floor was covered with papers and the broken remains of his family photo album. She sat on the couch smirking.

"We've had some problems here," he said quietly. "Please take Nancy home and call me." He turned to Nancy. "I'll be seeing you later."

"I'll do it again," she warned.

"Call me," he said to me.

I did when I got home.

"I'm very concerned," he confided. "I think she's a very disturbed girl. All I did to provoke her was ask why she walked out of school."

He agreed to take her on—provided I sat in on her sessions. He pointed out, though, that he regarded his involvement as an interim step. He said my top priority should be to place Nancy in some sort of full-time residential treatment center/school facility. He gave me some names and addresses.

He made no mention of having Nancy neurologically tested. I guess he didn't feel there was any need for it.

I spent every day and night with Nancy over the next five months. Much of the time I was on the telephone trying to locate her school records, trying to find a school to place her in.

I wasn't having an easy time. I called private schools all over the country. They were prohibitively expensive—some as high as $20,000 per year, which was Frank's entire income. The state of Pennsylvania did operate schools for disturbed children, with sliding-scale fees based on income, but it seemed that Nancy's circumstances were unique. She didn't fit the model of the emotionally disturbed child: usually, children who exhibited behavior like hers were also learning-disabled. The state schools weren't equipped to offer any education beyond the level she'd already reached. There just didn't seem to be any school that fit Nancy's problem. So I kept looking.

She found some of the brochures one day and got so upset that Frank and I were "sending her away" that I had to begin hiding the brochures and applications under the underwear in my dresser, and making whatever phone calls I needed to make before nine thirty in the morning, when she got up.

She rarely went outside. Mostly, she read and listened to raw, hard rock albums in her room. Once, when I was cleaning up her room, I found a piece of paper on the floor that she'd scrawled a note on. Evidently, it held significance for her:

> To be nobody but yourself in a world which is doing
> its best, night and day, to make you everybody else
>     means to
> fight the hardest battle any human being can fight; and
>     never stop fighting.
>
> —e.e. cummings.

She was still fighting, just like the day I saw her in her isolette in the hospital nursery, screaming and kicking at some unseen enemy. I wished I could help her, but I didn't know how.

The shark nightmares were becoming a regular occurrence now. I sat with her practically every night when she woke up screaming. Then they began to spill over into the daylight. She began to see sharks all over the house, even when she was wide-awake.

Once I found her in the den, trying to crawl under the couch.

"They wanna eat me!" she screamed. "They wanna eat me!"

I sat her down on the couch and tried to calm her. She began to bang her head against the wall and pull her hair out. She was wild-eyed. I pinned her arms down and spoke to her. After a few minutes she came out of her hallucination. She looked at me gravely.

"Mommy," she said, "I want to die. Let me die. Please."

"I love you, Nancy," I said. "I don't want you to die."

"If you loved me you'd let me."

I hugged her helplessly. She pushed me away.

"I wish I'd never been born," she said.

A few minutes later I found her going through my medicine

chest, collecting what was left of some old prescriptions for muscle relaxants, cold pills, painkillers.

"Nancy, what are you doing?" I cried. "Give me those."

She gave them up without a struggle. She'd collected about eight or nine pills.

"You don't love me," she said woodenly. She walked away. I threw out all of the pills in the house.

She spoke to her psychiatrist that week about the sharks. "They want to kill me," she explained to him, simply.

He asked her why. She had no explanation.

But verbalizing the hallucination to her psychiatrist did seem to have an effect. The shark attacks seemed to diminish over the next few days—only to be replaced by something far worse.

It was a Sunday afternoon, Suzy and David were playing in the living room. Nancy and I were watching TV in the den. Frank had gone out on an errand.

"This is a dumb movie," Nancy said abruptly. "Let's go to the Franklin Institute."

"It's too late," I pointed out. "The science museum closes in half an hour."

"I *want* to go," she repeated.

"No," I repeated.

At that moment I looked down at the coffee table. David had been trying to fix something and had left a hammer there. Nancy saw me looking at it, grabbed it before I could stop her. She hefted it in her hand and smirked. "Take me or I'll kill you."

"Give me the hammer, Nancy," I said sternly, trying hard not to let her know that I was afraid, for the first time, that she might actually hurt me.

"Take me or I'll kill you," she said.

"You won't."

"I *will!*"

"You *won't.*"

She struck me hard on the shoulder with the hammer. It gave me a jolt down to my fingertips. Then she did it again.

"Stop that! Give me that hammer!"

She struck me on the arm. I fought the pain and went for

her. I tried to wrench the hammer away from her, but I couldn't get it out of her grasp. She may have been five inches shorter than I was, but she outweighed me by ten pounds and was filled with animal fury. We began to wrestle. She struck me repeatedly on the shoulders and arms. I couldn't overpower her. It took both my hands to grab hold of the arm that was striking me with the hammer, and when I did grab it she began to punch me in the chest with the other fist. I wouldn't let go. I didn't know if she was capable of killing me or not, but I didn't want to find out. She was in a blind rage. She didn't see me.

Far away, I could hear the sound of Suzy and David playing and giggling innocently. I thought about calling them for help, but they were smaller than I was—they could be seriously hurt. I didn't call.

I held her off for an hour or longer. She just wouldn't quit. I was reaching the point of exhaustion. My battered arms were losing their strength. But I had to hold out just a little longer, until Frank got home. I just had to hold on, hold on.

At last I heard Frank's car pull up. His car door closed. The front door opened.

"I'm home!" he yelled cheerfully.

*"Frank!"* I screamed.

He rushed in, wrestled the hammer away from her, and threw it into the hall. She began to punch and claw and kick at him, totally out of control. He overpowered her, put her down on the floor in a wrestling hold, face down. He put his knee in her back to contain her. She continued to whip around and curse and snarl.

Suzy and David watched from the doorway, cowering in fear. I just lay there on the floor, panting.

"Are you okay?" Frank asked me, straining to hold her down.

"Uh-huh," I gasped. "Just in . . . just in time."

"Can you phone?"

I nodded, crawled over to the telephone, and dialed the psychiatrist at home. I hoarsely related what happened. He could barely hear me over Nancy's screams.

"Lock her in a room," he advised. "Lock her somewhere

where she can't hurt herself and let her get all of that anger out.''

"None of the bedrooms lock from the outside," I said.

"Oh . . . how about a punching bag? You got a punching bag?"

"A what?"

"Something she can punch."

"Just me."

"How about the basement? Can she hurt herself down there?"

"No, I don't think so."

"Put her down there. Call me when she quiets down."

Frank pulled Nancy kicking and screaming to her feet and into the kitchen. He took her halfway down the basement steps, released her, ran up the steps, and locked the door. We stood in the kitchen, watching the door and waiting. She ran up the steps and began to pound on it with her fists.

"Let me out, you motherfuckers!" she screamed through the locked door. "Don't do this to me! Don't do this to me, you bastards! You motherfucking bastards!"

She kept pounding and kicking at the door. She began to slam at it with her shoulder. The frame strained against her weight and I was afraid it might give way.

She gave up on the door. She ran screaming down the steps and began to throw open the storage cupboards down there. She pulled out cartons and suitcases and the lawn furniture and hurled all of it to the floor. She destroyed the furniture, broke lamps, broke the luggage, ripped our winter coats into shreds, ripped the boxes up. She destroyed the entire basement. The rampage went on for two hours, interrupted only by an occasional run up the steps to throw herself against the door.

Then it was quiet.

We unlocked the door and tiptoed warily down the steps. Nancy was sprawled across the rubble of our belongings, spent. She was gasping for breath, her body quivering. Frank carried her to her room and put her to bed.

I called the psychiatrist. "We have to do something," I cried. "We can't live like this."

"Calm down," he said. "I know that. I've been on the phone trying to find a hospital for her. But she's too young— none of the psychiatric hospitals take children, not even the one I'm on staff at."

"So what do we do?"

"I'll keep working on them. In the meantime our only alternative is to put her on heavy medication to keep her calm."

I drove to the drugstore, the bruises on my arms beginning to throb. I picked up a prescription for Thorazine, a very powerful tranquilizer. Then I came home and collapsed.

The Thorazine did the job, if you call turning Nancy into a vegetable doing the job. The drug put her in a perpetual zombie state, neither awake nor asleep.

During the day she just sat on the den couch and stared at the TV, absorbing none of it. Occasionally her head would droop over to the side and she would be asleep.

At night she wandered around the house in a stupor. I slept with one eye open. I could see her doorway from my side of the bed. When she was up, I was up. One night she went in the kitchen. I heard the kitchen drawers being opened and shut. I followed her in there. She was calmly gathering up all of the knives.

"Where are you going with those, Nancy?"

"To stab them," she replied dreamily.

"Stab who?"

"Them. The brother and the sister."

I took the knives away from her—she was so stoned that she was really quite docile. I suggested she go back to bed. She obeyed.

From that night on I ordered Suzy and David to sleep with their bedroom doors locked from the inside.

Another night I found her in the den, slowly collecting things and piling them onto one another in the middle of the den floor—a few encyclopedia volumes, a lampshade, some paintings off the wall. She hummed while she worked, eerily humming in a singsong manner those exact same melodies she'd sung the night of her Atarax attack, songs like "Happy Birthday" and "We Wish You a Merry Christmas."

"What are you doing, Nancy?"

"They don't like me," she explained softly.

"Let's put them back. Then maybe they'll like you."

"Gee, you think so, Mommy?"

"Uh-huh."

"Okay." She began to put everything back.

"And then we'll go back to bed."

"Okay," she said meekly.

This was a stranger. This wasn't Nancy.

Whenever she came out of her stupor and became herself again, she immediately began to pull her hair out, bang her head, and scream, "Help me! Help me! Put me somewhere! Help me!" After fifteen minutes of this she would fall asleep.

It broke my heart to see her either way, but these were the only two choices.

Finally her psychiatrist came through. He persuaded the Psychiatric Center (which was, ironically, affiliated with the clinic we had taken her to) to admit Nancy to their adolescent unit, even though she was too young. He told us to meet him there at seven thirty that night. We agreed.

Frank and I sat Nancy down. We told her she'd asked us for help and that we were going to take her to a hospital so she could get it.

She didn't fight it. She seemed relieved, actually.

I packed some things for her. When it was time to leave, she followed us meekly to the car and got in. It was a damp, cold night, the night before Thanksgiving, when we drove to the hospital. Christmas decorations were up on the houses in the neighborhood. The lights were on inside the houses. It looked warm in each one.

We were committing our child to a mental hospital. It was incomprehensible that it had come to this, but it had. There was no alternative. Thorazine was certainly no answer. She had to be put somewhere. For her safety, and for the safety of the rest of the family. She could not live in the house anymore in this condition.

The psychiatrist who admitted Nancy to the adolescent ward was wearing cufflinks that didn't match. I don't remember much else. I didn't hear a word he said. He led my daughter away.

Then Frank and I drove home. We didn't speak. To talk meant to admit aloud what we knew to be true: our dream had died that night. By giving our first baby to the mental hospital, we'd given that up, too. The life we'd wanted for Nancy and for ourselves when she was born, the future we'd planned, was never going to happen. We knew it. There was no need to talk about it, no desire to talk about it.

The next day I made a turkey, stuffing, cranberry sauce, mashed potatoes, and apple pie. The four of us sat down to Thanksgiving dinner and tried not to look at Nancy's empty place at the dinner table. None of us ate much.

Our family had died that night, too.

The next day there were visiting hours at the mental hospital. Frank and I went to see Nancy. We were issued passes at the front desk and took them to the adolescent ward. The nurse there checked our passes, led us down the hall to a different door—the one that led to the locked women's ward. She began to unlock the outer door with a key attached to her belt.

"Wait," I said. "There must be a mistake. Our daughter is in the adolescent ward."

"Your daughter is in here," she replied calmly.

"No she's *not,*" I insisted.

*"Please* follow me," she said.

She took us through one locked door, then another and another until we arrived in a large, central room with several doorways that led off to the lockup rooms. The room was dark and dingy and there were benches running along the walls. One woman was sitting on a bench, staring straight ahead. Several sat there shouting to themselves. One woman was standing and urinating on the floor. Another lay face down on the tile floor, mumbling. It was like something out of the Middle Ages.

In the midst of all this stood our eleven-year-old child.

She ran to me and hugged me hard. She was shaking. "Mommy, get me out of here," she begged. "I'm not like them . . . I swear I'm not. Take me away. I'll go to the psychiatrist. I'll go to school. I'll be good. I'll do whatever you want. Just get me out of here, Mommy. Oh, *please.*"

I held her tightly to me, as if to protect her from the madness around her. I believed her. I *wanted* to believe her.

"We're getting her out of here," I said to Frank.

He agreed, his face registering the horror of the ward.

We left, promising Nancy we'd get her out of that awful place at once. We didn't tell her we had no idea what she was doing in there in the first place.

I found a pay phone in the hospital lobby and called her psychiatrist. I demanded to know what she was doing in the locked women's ward.

"The hospital people called me," he said. "They said they didn't think the adolescent ward would be safe for her. They've got sixteen-, seventeen-year-olds in there with criminal behavior—drugs, rape. They weren't sure she'd be safe. They were worried about homosexuality. I told them to go ahead."

"Don't you know what it's like in there?" I protested.

"I do. But you have to keep in mind, Mrs. Spungen, Nancy's in a mental hospital, not the Holiday Inn."

"But don't you think you should have discussed this with us before going ahead?"

"It was for her own safety," he repeated.

"We want her discharged immediately."

"That's impossible."

"Why?"

"It takes at least two days to process the papers. Besides, what are you going to do with her when she's discharged?"

"I don't know. That's not important. The important thing is to get her out of this place."

He sighed. "You'll have to keep her on the Thorazine."

"Fine."

"Very well, Mrs. Spungen. I'll arrange to have her discharged."

He was right—it did take time to process the discharge papers. Nancy was stuck there for the entire weekend. We picked her up on Monday morning. She hugged me again and held my arm tightly until we were out of there. She breathed the fresh air deeply and gratefully. We got in the car and Frank started the engine. Nancy started to giggle.

"What's so funny, Nancy?" I smiled, happy to see her laughing.

"I'm not gonna do any of those things I promised." She giggled. "I only said them so you'd get me out of there. Tricked ya. Ha ha ha."

She laughed all the way home.

I was back on twenty-four-hour duty. I pressed forward with my search to find Nancy a residential school.

Through my state senator I put pressure on the Pennsylvania state school to at least grant Nancy an interview. Frank and I no longer cared if the school was unable to provide education at her level—which was presently college level in all areas except math. The schooling was unimportant now. What good would a gifted intellect do her if she was unable to function in the outside world?

Nancy's interview at the state school was memorable for its absurdness. The social worker who conducted it chewed on her hair the entire time. When Nancy asked her for a tour of the facilities, she snapped, "Be quiet."

In the car on the way home Nancy said she would not go to that school. It didn't matter—they didn't accept her anyway.

I began working the phone again. One of the private schools I contacted was the Darlington Institute. Darlington was headquartered in one of Philadelphia's Main Line suburbs but had over twenty units throughout the country, as well as a summer camp system. Darlington took retarded and disturbed children of various ages and degrees and placed them in what they considered to be the appropriate setting. It was exclusive and expensive. The application blank was over twenty pages long.

It took the Darlington people a long time to decide whether or not they wanted to interview Nancy and, if so, for which unit. An admissions officer I spoke to on the phone told me that if Nancy was as disturbed as we thought, she might belong in their locked unit, which was in Texas.

Frank and I discussed this. We were upset at the idea of sending Nancy so far away, but we agreed that she had to be placed somewhere.

So I pressed Darlington for an interview at the Texas unit. They agreed. I made plane reservations, then had to cancel them because Darlington cancelled the interview. They gave no reason.

I pressed them to see us at the Main Line headquarters. I was desperate. Now that the state school had fallen through, Darlington seemed like our only hope—no matter how much it cost. They finally granted us the interview.

The three of us drove out there. After a series of morning interviews Frank and I were asked to leave Nancy for the afternoon. We did.

We returned to hear the first good news we'd heard in a long, long time. After evaluating her, the Darlington people had decided Nancy wasn't suited for the Texas unit, but would be right for a small facility they had just opened in Connecticut. It was called Barton. Nancy could go there if we wanted.

I couldn't believe my ears. "When?" I asked, incredulous. "When can she start?"

"Immediately," the admissions officer replied.

At last we'd found a place for her. A place where *maybe* she could get better.

The fee was $850 per month. It was more than we could afford, but we'd manage somehow. The important thing was that we'd found her a school, a good school. And relatively nearby—about a three-hour drive from Philadelphia.

We said we'd be there tomorrow afternoon and took Nancy home to pack.

"I don't wanna go, Mommy," she said that night while I was folding her clothes and putting them in a suitcase.

"I don't want you to go, either, Nancy," I replied softly.

I really didn't want my Nancy to go away. But this Nancy who sat there on the bed wasn't my Nancy. It was a different one, a stranger. I would only get my Nancy back if I sent this one away.

"Then why do I have to go?"

"Because you don't go to school. You have to. It's a law."

"But I don't *want* to leave."

"We don't want you to, sweetheart. Believe me, we don't want you to. We'll miss you. A lot. But you have to. And when you feel better, you can come home and go to regular school again. Okay?"

"Promise?"

"Promise."

"Okay, but I'm gonna be back real soon."

"Sure you will," I agreed.

She insisted I pack all of her books and board games. She refused to say good-bye to Suzy and David because she was certain she'd be back in a few days.

The drive to Barton was a silent one, each of us lost in our thoughts. I knew we were doing the right thing, but I wondered. I wondered who would get up in the middle of the night to sit with her when she had her nightmares. I wondered who would hold her. I wondered who would love her. She was only eleven years old. My heart ached at having to separate from her. It is so impossibly hard to finally admit to yourself that your child must leave you. You're admitting that no matter how much love you've given her, it hasn't been enough. It *won't* be enough. It means you're not enough to make your child happy and well.

But this was the only alternative. And part of me was still optimistic. Maybe Nancy would get well and come home. Maybe she could still become like other girls.

When we got to western Connecticut, we stopped at a diner for lunch. Nancy was very calm.

"I'm coming right back," she assured us. "This isn't for long."

"Of course it isn't," Frank agreed, doing his best to be cheerful.

I said nothing. I knew if I opened my mouth I would cry.

Then we got back in the car and drove our daughter to her new home.

# ☐ Chapter 8

The town in Connecticut where Barton was located was a postcard New England village. There was a church with a tall white spire. The lawns of the neat houses were covered with snow. Kids were sledding. Barton was a few miles outside of town, in the woods.

We pulled into the Barton driveway and were totally overwhelmed. The school was headquartered in the most beautiful mansion I'd ever seen. It was a huge old stone place with formal gardens, stables, a pond, a swimming pool. We came to a halt before the front door and just gazed in awe.

The massive oak front door opened. Mr. and Mrs. Bebee, a handsome older couple who were Barton's headmaster and headmistress, came out and greeted us. A big, friendly dog bounded out the door behind them and began to lick Nancy's hand, his tail wagging like crazy.

"Mommy, I forgot," she said, frowning. "Who's gonna take care of Cupcake?"

'We'd gotten a new cat, a friend for Aquarius.

"I will, sweetheart. Don't worry."

"Promise?"

"Promise."

Mr. Bebee helped Frank unload Nancy's bags. We went inside. There was an immense pipe organ in the living room. A fire crackled in the fireplace.

Nancy's room upstairs had a fireplace, too. She had the room to herself.

"Boy, I wouldn't mind moving in here myself!" exclaimed Frank.

A few of the girls watched us shyly from the hallway as we parked Nancy's things. Altogether there were twenty boys and girls—ages eleven to fourteen—living in this wonderful mansion.

Nancy checked out the view from her window. "Look, Mommy. There's a skating pond!"

Mrs. Bebee smiled kindly. "Do you like to ice skate, Nancy?"

"Uh-huh."

"So does Annabelle, your next-door neighbor. Oh, Annabelle!" she called.

A tall girl in a slouchy felt hat, torn jeans with peace sign patches, and a baggy sweater appeared in the doorway. Mrs. Bebee introduced them. They acknowledged each other with a nod, their eyes firmly fastened on the floor.

"Annabelle, how would you like to introduce Nancy to the pond?"

"Okay," she replied softly. "Do you need skates?" she asked Nancy.

"Got 'em right here," Nancy said, grabbing her skates. Off they went.

Mr. Bebee smiled at us warmly. "Coffee?"

We went back down to the living room and sat before the fire while Mrs. Bebee served us coffee.

"Before I forget," I said, digging into my purse, "here's Nancy's Thorazine and the prescription."

Mr. Bebee took the pills and the slip of paper. "We'll keep this stuff for you, but we don't think much of pills. They're no solution. We expect to have her off them very soon."

"Well, you have our complete support there," I said.

"If you can manage her without the medication, that would be great," agreed Frank.

"We will," Mr. Bebee said firmly.

"We hope you'll write Nancy often," Mrs. Bebee said. "We generally ask parents not to phone at all for the first three weeks. We'll contact you."

Frank and I nodded, finished our coffee.

"I hope you won't think we're bad hosts," said Mr. Bebee, "but we'd also appreciate it if you left now, before Nancy comes back. It'll be easier on her."

From the car window I could see Nancy and her new friend skating merrily back and forth on the pond. The Bebees stood in the doorway and waved to us as we drove away.

It was a dream come true. At last Nancy was in a place where she could get better, a place staffed by caring people who would make her a happy, healthy, functioning child. No price was too high to achieve that. Not the financial burden, not being separated from her.

"It's so lovely here," I said to Frank.

"Very nice. Very nice people. I was glad he said that about the pills. I'd like to see her off those."

"I think we did the right thing."

"It'll be good for her. No question."

Frank took my hand and held it most of the way home.

When we got there, Suzy asked me if she could sleep in Nancy's bed.

"Why?" I asked, surprised.

"I just want to, Mommy. I miss her. Can I? Please? I won't touch anything. Promise. *Please?*"

"Well, okay. But don't let her know about it."

"I won't."

Suzy was frightened of Nancy. Sometimes she even hated her. After all, Nancy was seldom nice to her. But Nancy was still her big sister. Though it may seem hard to believe, Suzy looked up to her and loved her. Most of all, she wanted Nancy to love her.

From that night on, Suzy did her homework in her own room, then went to bed in Nancy's room, with its psychedelic posters and antiwar stickers.

Life was very strange around the house with Nancy gone. There was stability, order. Frank and I were no longer adversaries. Our romantic life blossomed. Often, he would bring home flowers and wine. Suzy and David would make us a special dinner. Suzy would carefully scroll fake French words on a menu. Frank and I would eat late, after the two of them had eaten and gone to bed. Afterward there was time to talk, to be gentle.

Suzy and David quarreled from time to time—siblings do quarrel—but if I told them to stop they did. No escalation to full-scale war. All four of us savored the quiet and tranquility. We ate out as a family together, went for rides, to movies. We were all glad Nancy wasn't there, yet at the same time we missed her very much. But she needed help and was someplace where she could get it. She would be back.

Mr. Bebee phoned at the end of Nancy's first week.

"Just wanted to let you know everything is fine," he said. "We had ourselves a small problem yesterday. Nancy didn't want to go to class and when I told her she had to, she started cursing like a sailor and went up to her room and broke her bed up practically into kindling. She's a strong girl, isn't she?" He chuckled.

"Yes," I agreed.

"Well, we had ourselves a little talk about it. I'd like to see her talking out her problems more."

"Instead of acting them out?"

"That's right. So we discussed what was bothering her. It seems she thinks a particular girl she shares a class with doesn't like her. She felt a lot better after we talked about it. Then I asked her if she'd like to help me put her bed back together again so she wouldn't have to sleep on the floor. Kind of cold on the floor. So the two of us put her bed back together. We had a real nice time."

Mr. Bebee's firm, patient, one-on-one way of handling Nancy pleased me. She needed the attention and the understanding. Clearly, if she agreed to help him put the bed back together, it was what she needed.

During her second week she began to see a therapist, Dr. Pritchard, once a week. There was no group therapy.

Since there were only twenty students at Barton, classes were more like tutorials, with a teacher and two or three students. Nancy was so advanced in some areas that she often had a teacher to herself.

Afternoons, evenings, and weekends, the Bebees kept the students busy participating in the running of the house. It was a highly structured environment. Each student had responsibilities—helping to prepare and clean up after meals, taking care of the horses and chickens, toting firewood. When they weren't working they hiked, played sports, and took field trips. There was a music room where they could listen to records. Barton was very much like a big family.

And Nancy responded almost immediately. Mr. Bebee's first progress report was extremely positive:

> After a rather difficult initial adjustment period, there has been great improvement in Nancy's adjustment to the overall program. She is more accepting of guidance, and is less sensitive to the reaction of her peers. She has become much less demanding.
>
> In the academic setting she has been able to apply her real ability to a much greater degree. Her attitude has become much more positive and she voluntarily contributes to class discussion.
>
> All in all, we are quite pleased with Nancy's overall adjustment.

The Bebees preferred that Nancy write to us rather than phone us. We soon began to receive her letters. Her scrawl was crooked and clumsy and the lines wandered up and down the page—her handwriting was almost as bad as mine. But it was big enough to be legible.

She seemed content. She was certainly well fed.

*Dear Family,*
*We went to a boat show in New Haven yesterday. It was great. We ate dinner at Kentucky Fried Chicken. Right across from there was a kosher foods place and we bought lox and bagels and knishes. Then we went to Dairy Queen and I had a banana split. All this is in New Haven.*

*Please see if I can come home on March 19 for*
*Easter break. It's three weeks long. If not maybe I will*
*be satisfied here. If you can't arrange for me to come*
*home then I guess I will have a pretty good time here for*
*a few days. The Reeders [one of Nancy's teachers and*
*his wife] said us girls can come over to their house for*
*some of the vacation and you are allowed to watch TV*
*during the day, and as late as you want to. And we go to*
*a lot of places. So don't worry about it if I can't come.*
*Leslie, Jane and Valerie are staying here for vacation.*
*Well all for now.*

                                        *Love, Nancy*

At the end of February the four of us drove to Barton for
Nancy's twelfth birthday. I could already see the difference in
her. She was happy. Her eyes were agleam again; she was
alert and smiling. She even hugged us. We took her to New
Haven for lunch and gave Nancy her presents. We gave her
the three albums she had asked for—*Déjà Vu* by Crosby,
Stills, Nash and Young, the new Paul McCartney album, and
John and Yoko's Plastic Ono Band album. We also gave her a
cloth-covered address book, a diary, and stationery. She was
delighted with the gifts. We were delighted with her. She
seemed so much improved.

When we brought her back to school, we asked Mr. Bebee
if it would be all right for Nancy to come home for at least part
of the Easter break.

"I don't see why she can't come home for a week," he
said. "She's stabilized. I think it will be helpful to see how
she responds to being home."

Nancy was ecstatic when we told her the news. She ran off
immediately to tell her friend Annabelle. "I get to go home!"

Before she came home for Easter, she participated in a
small Passover seder at Barton.

*Dear Everybody,*
*Yesterday we had a seder here. It was Alice, Lois and I.*
*I made horosis. That is apples, nuts, honey and grape*
*juice. Alice made matzoh ball soup. It wasn't very*

*good. We also had gefilte fish, horseradish, shank
bone, matzoh. Tomorrow we are walking through
Goose Creek and we are going to clean it up. We are
doing this because of Earth Day which is an Ecologist
movement.*

*Bye bye. See you soon! Don't let the pigs get you
down! Power to the people!*

*Peace.*

Her visit home for Easter week was peaceful. She was
pleasant and relaxed. No hostility or violence. She slept well,
without nightmares, and there were no tantrums. Of course,
we did whatever we could to avoid them. I stocked up on her
favorite brands of pretzels, pickles, and soda. I served her favorite meals. All of us took her to her favorite museums and
shops. We bought her jeans, records, books. She was aware
of the effort we were all making and seemed to appreciate it.
The visit was a success.

Until the night before she went back to school.

It was pouring rain so we decided to stay home for the evening. We were watching TV in the den.

"I want a Big Mac," Nancy announced.

"We want to stay in, Nancy," Frank said. "It's wet out."

"I want a Big Mac," she repeated, jaw stuck out firmly.
"You promised me I could have one."

"We'll get you one tomorrow on the way back to Barton,"
I offered.

"I want one *now*. Let's go!"

"Nobody else wants one," Frank said. "It's not fair to
make us go out."

"You promised me a Big Mac," she insisted.

"I'll make hamburgers," I said. "How would that be?"

"I want a Big Mac!" she yelled.

*"No!"* Frank yelled back.

*"Fucking asshole!"* she screamed. *"Fucking bastard!"*

She stormed upstairs to her room, slammed her door shut,
and began to pound on the floor with a blunt object over and
over again. Her room was right over the den. The noise was

extremely irritating and she knew it. She kept at it for thirty minutes.

Frank and I exchanged a look. It was a look that said many words. It said, "Let us not delude ourselves. Let us be realistic. She is not completely better. She is not going to change overnight. She is still Nancy."

She complained bitterly about having to go back to Barton the next morning.

"You promised I wouldn't have to go back," she protested.

"Nobody promised you that, Nancy," I said. "Besides, I thought you were happy there."

"This is my house. I wanna stay here."

"You will. It's not time yet, but soon."

"When?" she demanded.

"When you're better. When you can go to school here."

She pouted, but she did get in the car when it was time to leave. She didn't fight us or try to jump out or anything like that, but she was very sullen and wouldn't speak.

She slid quickly and happily back into her Barton environment. We got another very positive evaluation from Mrs. Bebee.

> Nancy has done remarkably well recently. She is learning to handle problems with her peers in a much more appropriate manner, asked for and has been given a "paying job" running the dishwasher after the evening meal—with one of the younger boys, and has taken it upon herself to help him with his reading and writing.
>
> Today, after her session with Dr. Pritchard, she asked to speak with me. She said that for the first time she was able to talk freely about her problems and was setting herself a goal of June of next year to be well enough to go home for good. Nancy also asked if I thought this was realistic, and had numerous questions as to what plans would be made for her after she left here; how such decisions would be made; and who would be involved in making them.
>
> She seemed satisfied and pleased when I explained that plans for all students leaving were made after much discussion with the family, the therapist, the student, and us.

Mrs. Bebee advised us that our discussion over Nancy's progress would be held on Parents' Day, the last day of the semester, when there would be a picnic and activities. She recommended that Nancy then go directly from Barton to Darlington's summer camp in Maine. We were instructed to bring her summer things with us, if we agreed with her rec- ommendation. We did.

> *Dear Everybody,*
> *Mrs. Bebee told me today that you are coming up soon. I will be happy to see all of you. Mrs. Bebee said that if I keep acting like I am I will get out next year.*
>     *My hamster died and I gave the cage to Leslie. What's a four letter word for intercourse? T-A-L-K! Thanks for the stockings. We stayed up to watch "The Pit and the Pendulum" the other night. It was good and scary, and you better tell the Bebees that if they make me tie my hair back you will have every lawyer in the state on their backs! Please!*
>     *How are Suzy + David? Hope you are fine. How is Aquarius and Cupcake? Give them my love. Has Aqua- rius been catching any mice? I am enclosing some cat food coupons.*
>     *So far in the last two weeks these are the people that have ran away. Annabelle ran away three times, Sue Gilmore ran away two times, Alice ran away and Anne ran away. But they all got caught! Well all for now. We are supposed to have watermelon this Sunday. See you soon!*
> *Love,*
> *Shoily from 34th above the delicatessen in the Bronx*

Our meeting on Parents' Day was held in the Bebees' of- fice. They were there along with Dr. Pritchard, her therapist, who was young and friendly. And Nancy was there, her face scrubbed, eyes bright, hair neatly brushed. Her bad eye still wandered a bit, but it was not nearly as marked as before. Her weight had dropped. Though she was still a bit chunky, she was not nearly as bloated and puffy as she'd seemed before. It was the prettiest and happiest she'd ever looked.

"I'm very pleased with Nancy's progress," Dr. Pritchard said.

The Bebees smiled in accord. So did Nancy.

"She's really beginning to open up and verbalize a lot more," Dr. Pritchard continued. "Mr. and Mrs. Bebee and I have discussed Nancy, and we feel that after one more year here at Barton, the possibility is very strong that she'll be ready for a small, private boarding school environment, someplace structured. We have a list of several schools we can recommend when the time comes. We would see this as a kind of interim step. After a year at boarding school, assuming she proves herself there, which she says she will . . ."

Nancy nodded her head vigorously.

". . . then she should be able to finish up high school at home."

"At public school?" I asked.

"At public school," he replied.

"See?" Nancy beamed. "I'm coming home!"

"Why, that's just wonderful," I gasped, delirious with joy.

"Great," Frank exclaimed. "Just great."

"She's doing very well, Mr. and Mrs. Spungen," Dr. Pritchard said. "We have high hopes for Nancy. High hopes."


I went into business while Nancy, Suzy, and David were away at camp. I opened a health food store in Jenkintown, a suburban village right next to Huntingdon Valley. I had become more and more interested in natural foods over the previous year, and no such store existed in the area. I had the time to devote to a business now. Frank and I hoped that if The Earth Shop made a go of it, the profits would take care of Nancy's tuition and board at Barton. We needed the money.

I found it very satisfying to organize a store, establish contact with suppliers, and cultivate a regular clientele. I was accomplishing something on my own, and I enjoyed working, especially because business started off brisk and stayed that way.

Frank still had to go to New York one night a week, but with all three children away, I was now able to join him. Every Wednesday when I closed the store I drove to the Trenton train station, parked, and took the train to New York. I got there in time for us to have a nice dinner and a bottle of wine. Afterward we'd go to a movie or listen to jazz. I'd spend the night at the hotel with him, then get up real early, catch the train back to Trenton, and make it back to the store in time to open up. It was an idyllic summer for Frank and me, the best ever.

Nancy came home after camp for three weeks, tan, trim, and bubblier than we'd ever seen her. She took immediately to the health food store.

"I wanna help," she declared, and help she did.

She rode to work with me every morning. She sorted merchandise, stocked the shelves, waited on customers. She was such an eager, tireless worker that I quickly ran out of work for her—it was a small store. That didn't stop her. She found more work elsewhere. Within a few days she was busy unpacking and tagging dresses at the women's clothing shop a few doors down. The owner was a friend of mine.

At the end of the workday she rode proudly home with me.

"Does this make us commuters, Mom?" she asked one evening grinning.

"Sure it does," I replied. "After all, we do have our own business."

"That's right, we do! Spungen and Spungen!"

She began to giggle. I did, too. It made me so happy to see Nancy happy.

Then it all unraveled.

The Bebees didn't come back to Barton that fall. Darlington reassigned them to another unit. Nancy detested their replacement, Mr. Grant, on sight.

He was a perfectly pleasant man in his thirties, tall with dark hair. But he was cool and formal and he kept a professional distance, unlike the Bebees, who were so warm and caring that they functioned as surrogate parents. Nancy had gotten very attached to them.

"I'm sure Nancy will have a very nice year with us," he said quietly and shook our hands. His handshake was limp.

"Sure. You bet." Frank assured him.

Mr. Grant then went inside while we pulled Nancy's things out of the car.

"Mr. Grant seems like a nice man," I ventured hopefully.

"Mr. Grant," she replied, "is a dumb fucking bastard."

"Give him a chance, Nancy," said Frank. "You have to give people a chance."

"I miss the Bebees."

"You'll get to like Mr. Grant," I said. "You just don't know him yet. As soon as you do, you'll feel the same way about him as you did about the Bebees."

"Do," she corrected, glaring at me. "Do. Not did. *Do.*"

"Okay. *Do.*"

She turned away angrily. She had That Look. "We may as well go in."

The house itself had changed that fall, too. It had been remodeled to accommodate twice as many students. New walls broke the spacious downstairs living area into classrooms and offices. Upstairs, bunk beds had been installed in the bedrooms, along with second desks and dressers. No more private rooms.

Barton's warm family atmosphere was gone. It was now an institution. Nancy's new roommate's things were already unpacked. Nancy looked uncomfortable at this stranger's books and family pictures neatly arranged on one of the desks, clearly feeling threatened.

"I'll bet she's a real nice girl," said Frank, trying to cheer her up.

Nancy slumped sullenly onto the bottom bunk. "It's not the same anymore. It's just not the same."

She said it matter-of-factly. This wasn't an observation. Her mind was made up—she was simply not going to enjoy Barton ever again.

Frank motioned that we ought to leave. It was best to let her get settled. She wouldn't allow us to hug her or kiss her. She just sat on the bed staring at her feet.

We went downstairs and drove away with a strong sense of

foreboding, a feeling that was thoroughly justified by a phone call from Nancy a few nights later.

"Did Mr. Grant say it was all right for you to call us, Nancy?"

"Fuck Grant. He's mean and he doesn't like me and I wanna come home."

"You can't, sweetheart."

"Why not?" she demanded.

"You have to go to school. It's a law."

"Why can't I go to school at home?"

"Because you're not ready."

"Am, too," she insisted.

"Nancy, you were at the evaluation meeting at the end of last semester. You heard what Dr. Pritchard said."

She said nothing.

"Have you seen Dr. Pritchard?"

No reply.

"Nancy?"

"No."

"Are you going to?"

"I don't know. He's in Hartford or somewhere. I wanna come home."

"You can't," I said firmly. "Not until Christmas."

She slammed the phone down.

But she called again the next night.

"Nancy, I don't want you calling unless it's an emergency. You're supposed to write us."

"I can't write you," she snapped, very agitated. "They stole my stamps."

"Who stole your stamps?"

"The sickies."

"What sickies?"

"They're all sickies here. They take twitch pills."

"Twitch pills?"

"Tranks. *Tranquilizers.* They twitch out all over the fucking place. Have fits, shit like that. And they stole my fucking stamps and my stationery and . . . and my new Hendrix album. They're all against me. They hate me.

They're all sickies. You have to get me out of here. You have to. You *have* to!''

"You're staying, Nancy."

She slammed the phone down.

I was very concerned. She sounded as though she'd deteriorated, slipped back into her paranoia. I phoned Mr. Grant and reported what she'd said.

"There may be a few more peer problems in general this year," he admitted. "We have more students and we're a bit understaffed. But let me assure you—there's no specific campaign against Nancy by anyone. She's making that up."

"She said the other girls are stealing from her."

"She's imagining it."

"Is she going to be seeing Dr. Pritchard?"

"Yes, she will. Not quite as often as last year. He's doing his residency in Hartford now. But she'll be seeing him at least once a month."

"Once a *month*?"

"Possibly every two weeks."

"Wouldn't once a week be better?"

"Possibly, though not necessarily."

"Tell me, Mr. Grant. Is she . . . is she all right?"

"Her schoolwork's fine.

"But she sounds so upset."

"She's been a little difficult, I must admit. She's not getting on well with the other girls, and she's disrespectful of authority. Hostile. Curses a lot. It's most likely a readjustment problem. New faces, new environment. I wouldn't worry."

But I did. So did Frank. We weren't sure whether Nancy was deteriorating or Barton was. How could they be understaffed if we were paying them $850 a month? Nancy didn't write us at all that fall. She phoned a couple of more times, agitated, and demanded to come home. When I said she couldn't, she hung up on me.

At Christmas she came home. She was nervous and unpleasant. She refused to do anything other than what she wanted. One of the things she wanted to do was work in my store again. I hesitated. Her manner was rude, her language foul. I told her I'd think it over.

On her first day back, she and Suzy went into Philadelphia —supposedly to shop—while I was at the store. Suzy told me that night that she and Nancy never did go shopping; as soon as they got off the train Nancy took her directly to a storefront youth help center, where she requested legal help. Nancy claimed that her parents physically abused her, kept her locked in her room, and now had her locked up in a school. When the worker asked Nancy for her name, address, and phone number, she called him a "fucking pig" and stormed out, Suzy in tow.

I decided to let her work in the store. She'd been so happy there during the summer. Maybe it would make her happy again. At least I'd get a chance to be with her. At least I'd know where she was.

I wasn't sorry. She was very friendly and helpful her first day on the job. She happily organized and shelved the stock. She made each customer, many of whom were young and long-haired, feel that their health and well-being were vital to her own.

That night Frank, Suzy, and David met us at the store at closing time and the five of us went to the Chinese restaurant across the street for dinner—per Nancy's request.

The restaurant wasn't too crowded yet. We took a round table in the middle of the room. Nancy happily began to list all the things we were going to order.

". . . and spare ribs and shrimp and chicken chow—"

"Oh nuts," I broke in.

"What's wrong?" Frank asked.

"I forgot to call my vitamin supplier. Maybe he'll still be there." I got up to use the pay phone next to the kitchen.

"Mom, where are you going?" asked Nancy, frightened.

"Just to make a call, sweetheart."

"Why?" she cried, her fear suddenly becoming terror. Her eyes were wide and glassy. "Who are you calling?"

The rest of us exchanged worried looks.

"I . . . I have to place an order," I said calmly.

"With *who*!"

"Vitamins, sweetheart. I'm ordering vitamins."

The waiter came by to take our order.

"Go ahead and order what you want," I said. I went to make my call.

Nancy ignored the waiter. "Who is she really calling, Daddy?" she cried. "Tell me! *Who*?"

"Just who she told you, Nancy. Relax."

"No, she's not!"

"Of course she is. Who else would she be calling?"

I got to the phone and began to fish around in my purse for a dime. I waved reassuringly to Nancy.

"She's calling someone about me!" Nancy suddenly screamed. "She's calling someone about me! They're gonna take me away. Make her stop! Stop her! Daddy, stop her!"

The other customers turned to look at Nancy, alarmed. The waiter flushed nervously.

"Don't let her call!"

I went right back to the table without making the phone call. As I approached, Nancy jumped to her feet.

"No! You told them to take me away! They're gonna come get me!" She whirled, bowled over the waiter, and made a dash for the entrance, barreling into a couple who were coming in the door. Frank threw down his napkin and went after her.

He found her down the block, trying frantically to get into my car, which was locked. He was able to calm her by promising to take her away in the car. The two of them went for a long drive into Bucks County while I took Suzy and David home in his car and made them dinner. Frank and Nancy stopped for a hamburger along the way. When they got home she went right upstairs to bed.

"Nothing she said made sense," Frank reported. "Just a lot of stuff about people being after her, like the 'twitchies' at school. She's in trouble again, Deb. We're right back where we started."

I sagged into Frank's arms. He held me. We didn't discuss it further. There was nothing to say that hadn't been said already.

Nancy forgot the incident the next day. She also forgot that she'd wanted to work in the store. She just stayed in her room, listening to records at full blast.

That Sunday we had a cousins get-together in town, a holiday ritual. Nancy always enjoyed these family assemblages. She was big on holidays and especially liked to see her cousins Dean and Ellen, Frank's sister's children, who were in college now. The get-together was held at the new apartment of one of my cousins. It was a big place, and my cousin invited some of her friends to the party along with the relatives.

Nancy strongly resented the presence of these nonfamily members. Even though they were extremely nice people, she refused to be introduced to them or speak to them. She was very uneasy. When we sat down to eat, she erupted.

"What are you looking at?" she demanded of one of my cousin's friends, who was sitting across the table from her.

"Excuse me?" the man asked.

"You heard me! I said what the fuck are you looking at?"

"Nancy!" I said sharply.

She turned to me. She had That Look. "He was staring at me! I saw him!"

"No, he wasn't," I assured her.

"No, I wasn't," he assured her.

"Were too!" she screamed. "Goddamnit, you were!"

All conversation and chewing stopped. Nancy became aware of the silence. She looked around, frightened, at the surprised faces of the strangers and the not-so-surprised faces of her relatives. She bolted.

She grabbed my coat from the pile on the bed and took off out the front door.

"Nancy's a little uncomfortable with people she doesn't know well," I explained to the man.

"Don't worry about it," he said cheerfully. "Know just how she feels."

The party resumed.

"Don't you think you should go after her?" I asked Frank. "She doesn't know this neighborhood."

"She'll be back."

Frank was right. She slipped back in about an hour later. We didn't make an issue of her return for fear it would start her up again. She went off in a quiet corner and talked to her cousin Dean until it was time for us to leave.

Dean phoned later that night.

"I have something to tell you," he said, "but you have to promise me you won't say a word to Nancy about it. Okay?"

"Okay," I said.

"Nancy told me tonight that she takes drugs. She said she's been addicted to heroin for several months. She also said she'd been pregnant and had an abortion so you wouldn't find out."

"C'mon, Dean. She was pulling your leg. She's twelve years old."

"I know she has a way of, well, exaggerating things sometimes. But she was so deadly serious about this that I thought I should tell you."

I thanked him for calling, told him I'd handle it and not to worry. She was telling tall tales. I was sure of it.

But just in case there was even the tiniest grain of truth to it, I phoned Mr. Grant at the school the next day.

"No, absolutely not," he said. "Nothing of that sort is happening here. We're very isolated. If drugs were coming in, we'd know about it. Believe me. And we keep close tabs on the boys and girls. These are youngsters. There've been no pregnancies here."

"So she made it all up?"

"Yes. A form of boasting, I suppose. To get attention, seem more mature. It's all a figment of her imagination."

I phoned Dean to set his mind at ease. I said nothing about it to Nancy. I'd promised Dean I wouldn't.

We took Nancy back to Barton after New Year's. The phone calls home started immediately.

"If you don't get me out of here," she vowed, "I'll run away. You can't make me stay here. I'll leave."

"Nancy," I reasoned, "You *have* to go to school."

"I'll run away," she repeated.

I didn't respond. She hung up on me.

The following day Nancy ran away from Barton.

"I'd not be too concerned," Mr. Grant said over the phone. "One of our people is out in the car looking for her.

She hasn't been gone long and she only has two dollars. She's probably walking into town. But I wanted you to know in case she calls you. If she does, try to find out where she is, so we can pick her up."

I agreed to. "Is there any specific reason why Nancy ran away?"

"I'm not certain about that. I took away one of her privileges this morning for some disruptive classroom behavior. She spoke back to a teacher."

"What privilege did you take away?"

"Her use of the music room for two weeks. Where the girls listen to records."

They found Nancy in town. She was by the side of the road, trying to hitchhike home.

"She was very angry," Mr. Grant reported to me over the phone. "Yelled and cursed. But they got her in the car and now she's back safe and sound. Pretty calm, too."

"Will you discipline her?"

"Yes. I'm afraid this means a grounding—no trips to town. And I'll be taking away her phone privileges for two weeks. She won't be calling you."

A few days later I got a letter from Nancy. It consisted of a terse one-line message:

"They can't keep me here."

She didn't run away from Barton again, at least not that I was informed. But as spring arrived she got more and more disruptive. Mr. Grant's evaluations grew increasingly negative. She was fighting with the other girls and with authority figures. For the first time her schoolwork was beginning to suffer. She refused to do it—as a form of rebellion.

By the end of the semester, when we arrived at Barton for our Parents' Day evaluation session with Mr. Grant and Nancy, the idea of her moving on to a small boarding school had been abandoned.

"We feel that Nancy belongs in our Avon unit this fall," Mr. Grant said. "The students are older, and she needs the scholastic level they can offer her there."

Nancy sat up stiffly in her chair. She was very angry. "You *promised* me I could leave after this year!"

"Nancy," he said. "You still need a structured environment."

"Don't listen to him," she commanded Frank and me. "He's a liar."

Mr. Grant shook his head. "We told you you'd be able to leave *if* you continued improving like you had been. I'm afraid you didn't keep up your end of the bargain, Nancy."

"I'm okay!" she insisted. "Mom, don't listen to him! I'm okay!"

"We don't think she's capable of handling a boarding school. If you wish to keep Nancy in the Darlington system, then she's to go to Avon after she gets back from camp."

Darlington was still the only school system we'd found that was equipped to deal with Nancy. The Avon school was more expensive than Barton—$1,000 a month. But it was also closer, about forty miles from Huntingdon Valley in the Main Line suburbs. We agreed to enroll her there.

It was at Avon that Nancy became involved with drugs. This time it was no figment of her imagination.

# ☐ Chapter 9

The Avon unit was called Lakeside Campus. Its ten-acre grounds were situated in countryside that was giving way to suburban development. The students lived in two old mansions, one for the boys, one for girls. Joint classrooms and a gym had been added on. There were forty boys and forty girls at Lakeside Campus, ages fourteen to eighteen. Nancy was the youngest. She was thirteen.

Most of the girls were already there, slouched on sofas in the mansion's downstairs living area or on the floor, smoking cigarettes and catching up on summer news. A stereo blasted the Jefferson Airplane from somewhere upstairs. They were unkempt girls, barefoot and braless, wearing patched jeans, torn T-shirts or workshirts, and hostile expressions on their faces.

Some of them paused to check out Nancy, the newcomer. She stood next to us in the front doorway, clad in a clean, puffy peasant blouse, jeans, and sandals. She looked uncomfortable. So did Suzy and David, who had come along to say good-bye.

I looked around for the supervisor. There were no adults anywhere, so I tried to find one of the college students who were supposed to be around part-time as child-care workers. I approached the only clean-cut girl in the room, who sat alone on a sofa.

"Do you work here?" I asked.

She stared straight ahead, eyes glassy. She was in some kind of fog.

"Hello? Excuse me?" I said.

She blinked. "Huh?"

"Do you work here?" I repeated.

No answer.

"Hello?"

"I live here," she replied.

I tried one of the other girls, who wore a paisley headband and was deep in conversation.

"Excuse me?" I said. "Could you direct me to the supervisor, Mallory Brooke?"

The girl pointed over her shoulder with her thumb. "In her office. Brooke's in her *office.*"

I signaled to Frank and the kids and we went to the back of the house, where we found Mallory Brooke, girls' unit supervisor, in her office. She was in her mid-thirties, tall and thin, with close-cropped hair and no makeup. She looked like a gym teacher. She gave Nancy a firm handshake.

"Hello, Nancy," she declared. "Mallory Brooke. Call me Brooke. Everyone does. I'll take you up to your room." She pushed past us and marched through the living area. We followed.

The girls sitting on the great curving staircase parted grudgingly to let us pass. Three or four stereos blared upstairs. Several girls were taping psychedelic posters to the corridor walls.

There were three beds in Nancy's room, two of them already made up. The furniture was chipped, the curtains were shabby.

Nancy looked around at all of this, then glared at me. "I got no fucking room here," she said.

"We'll make room," Brooke said. "Plenty of it."

Frank went back downstairs to get the rest of Nancy's things from the car. We left quickly. Having us hanging around was making her feel like even more of an outsider.

"Mommy?" Suzy said as we got in the car. "Mommy?"

"Yes?"

"Mommy, I don't like it here."

"It'll be fine," I said, trying to convince myself as much as Suzy. I had an uneasy feeling about the place, too. But I knew of nowhere else for her to go.

She phoned that night.

"The food is crap here," she said. "Nothing but fat. Total crap. And the kids are sickies and weirdos. I don't like it here. I wanna come home."

"Do you have permission to phone, Nancy?"

"What's wrong, don't you wanna talk to me? Your own daughter?"

"That's not the point, sweetheart. You're supposed to be getting settled and—"

"I wanna come home," she demanded.

"You can't."

"How about this weekend?"

"You just got there. I don't think you'll be allowed home yet."

"Brooke gave me permission."

"She did?"

"Yes. She said it was okay."

"Well . . ."

"Don't you wanna see me?"

"I'll talk to Brooke, see what she says about it."

"She said it was *okay*. Don't you believe me?"

"Of course I do. I just—"

Nancy slammed the phone down angrily. I dialed Brooke.

"No," she said emphatically. "I absolutely did not give Nancy permission to come home. Certainly not this weekend. She's not even set up in her classes yet. Absolutely not."

I spoke to Nancy, told her Brooke denied having given her permission. She called Brooke a liar and hung up on me again.

Later, after Suzy and David had gone to sleep, Frank and I

were watching the news on TV in the den. I felt a cool breeze behind me, and turned. Nancy stood in the foyer, That Look in her eyes.

"Nancy!" I cried. "What are you doing here?"

"I live here," she replied quietly.

Frank got up, closed the front door behind her. "But honey," he said, "you're not supposed to be here."

"I wanted to come home."

"How did you get here?" he asked.

"Hitched."

"This time of night?"

"Nothing's gonna happen to me," she said.

"It's dangerous," I protested.

"What would you care? You don't love me. Either one of you."

"Of course we love you," Frank insisted.

She glowered at us, went into the den, and sat down on the couch with her coat still on. She stared defiantly at the TV set.

We were not pleased. Nancy didn't live with us for a very good reason—we couldn't handle her. That was why we had relinquished our supervisory role. That was why we had gone to the great expense of placing her in the Darlington system, reputed to be one of the finest in the country. They were supposed to be able to handle her. Clearly, they weren't living up to their end of the bargain.

Frankly, Nancy's arrival was also an intrusion. I was not proud to admit this, but the truth was that our life was better when our first child was not there.

I went to the kitchen and phoned Brooke to tell her Nancy was safe and that we'd return her the next morning. She had no idea what I was talking about.

"Nancy's gone," I said, confused. "She must have been gone for hours. She ran away. Didn't you know that?"

"No, I thought she was in her room. I can't watch her all the time. I'm sorry."

"But don't you have help?"

"Not right now."

"You mean you're keeping track of forty girls all by yourself?"

"I do the best I can, Mrs. Spungen. But you have to re-member this isn't a locked campus. If a girl wants to leave, there isn't much I can do—even if I had a dozen assistants."

Barton hadn't been a locked campus, either. But Barton *had* been isolated. Lakeside Campus wasn't. It was within easy walking distance from Winfield, a commuter town with a train station and access to the major turnpikes.

Nancy still sat in her coat, staring at the TV. I made her a sandwich and a glass of milk. She ate, but said nothing else. She seemed very depressed. Frank and I sat quietly with her until she abruptly got up, went up to her room, and went to sleep in her clothes. I dropped her off at Lakeside Campus the next day.

She phoned constantly. She accused the other girls of hating her, conspiring against her, threatening to hit her, stealing her clothes, her records, her spending money. I checked with Brooke. Most but not *all* of Nancy's accusations were products of her imagination.

"We have had rip-offs," she admitted. "We can't watch them all the time."

Nancy was not in therapy. This bothered us and I called Brooke after a few weeks to find out why Nancy wasn't seeing anyone.

"It's taking time," she said. "You see, most of the girls already have a therapist from last year. But don't worry. She'll get one soon."

She didn't. Weeks passed and Nancy still hadn't been assigned a therapist. So I phoned Mr. Sylvester, Brooke's boss at the Lakeside Campus unit, and demanded one.

"We're working on it, Mrs. Spungen," he said.

"That's simply not good enough," I said. "Your brochure promises therapy. We're paying you a thousand dollars a month. Nancy's supposed to be in therapy and I want her in it—*now!*"

She got her therapist assignment, though the sessions didn't actually begin for another two months.

She came home for Thanksgiving. She arrived after school on the Wednesday before, looking like many of the girls we'd seen that first day. Her jeans were frayed and filthy, her hair and complexion untended.

She went straight for the kitchen, which I had, of course, stocked with her favorite brands of pretzels, cheese, and pickles. She gathered the goodies in her arms, sat down at the kitchen table with them, and dove in. I joined her in the kitchen and began to make dinner.

Almost immediately I smelled smoke.

I turned to find Nancy smoking a cigarette at the kitchen table. A pack of Marlboros and a book of matches sat there. She glared at me, daring me to say something about it. I went back to my cooking.

After a moment I quietly said, "I see you're smoking cigarettes now."

"So what?" Nancy demanded.

"So, they're bad for you. So, when Daddy smoked you made him stop because you said they would kill him."

She laughed derisively. "Like, I mean, who wants to live. Ya know?"

"No, I don't know."

Frank pulled his car into the garage and came inside through the side door. He exploded the instant he saw Nancy smoking.

"Put out that goddamned cigarette!"

"Fuck you!"

"I said put it out!"

"And I said fuck you!"

I heard two doors slam upstairs. Suzy and David were now hiding in their bedrooms. This had become their standard response when the yelling started.

Frank stopped, made an effort to control himself. He lowered his voice. "Nancy, you're not going to smoke in this house."

"I'll do what I want!"

*"No you won't!"*

*"Yes I will!"*

Frank crossed the room, yanked the cigarette from her mouth, and threw it in the sink. She immediately lit another.

He turned to me. "I can't deal with this." He stormed out, stomped up the stairs.

Nancy laughed.

"Nancy, I wanted to tell you before Daddy got home . . . he's, uh, he's pretty down right now."

Frank was, in fact, very down. Both of his parents had just suffered crippling strokes. Neither of them was able to talk or function, and he had had to place them in a nursing home. On top of the emotional burden, he now had to face closing down their jewelry store and selling their house. The strain had given him stomach ulcers. And a short fuse.

"He's got a lot on his mind," I pointed out, "and he's not feeling that well."

"What do you want me to do about it?"

"Go easy on him."

"I mean, I liked Grandma and Grandpa, too."

"I know, sweetheart. But try to go easy on him, okay?"

She shrugged, popped a pickle into her mouth. "He's still an asshole."

She simply didn't care about Frank's problems, didn't care about anyone but herself. I wished she hadn't come home. As soon as she walked in, the house revolved around her. She ruled us. She also created an immediate rift between Frank and me. I deeply resented it.

He resented it, too. His reponse had been to blow up at her. On the one hand, I was glad he had. I wanted to myself, but I couldn't. Why? Because I was afraid that once I started, once I let the lid off, I'd not be able to stop. I'd shake that meanness out of her; I'd slam her against the wall; I'd beat at her with my fists. I couldn't let that lid off, not only because I was afraid of myself but *for* myself. She had attacked me once with a hammer. Who knew what she was capable of doing if provoked?

It was vital to me to try to keep the emotional level turned down and to urge Frank to do the same. I went upstairs to talk to him. I tapped lightly on the kids' doors to let them know the storm had blown over, then went into our bedroom.

Frank was washing his face, his shirt off. He looked up.

"How the hell can you let her just sit there, smoking in your face like that?" he demanded angrily.

"I was *dealing* with it, Frank!" I protested. "I was trying to reason with her about the health hazards and . . . and . . ."

"*Reason* with her? What good is that going to do?"

"What good did *your* way do?"

"No damned good at all," he admitted.

"Do me a favor?" I asked Frank quietly.

"What?"

"Try to be more patient with her. She's going to be here for four days. At least things will be quieter."

He nodded with weary resignation. "Whatever you say."

There was very little dinner conversation. When Nancy finished eating, she lit a cigarette. Frank and I kept quiet.

"Ugh," said Suzy, who was still eating. "Why are you smoking?"

"Mind your own fucking business."

Suzy fastened her eyes on her plate and kept them there. David's were already on his plate.

After dinner Nancy wanted to watch a particular show on TV in the den and sit in the easy chair. Suzy was already sitting in the chair, watching something else. Nancy changed the station.

"Hey!" Suzy protested.

"I don't wanna watch that," Nancy snapped. "Get up!"

"What for?"

"I wanna sit there!"

"No!"

"Why don't you sit somewhere else, Nancy?" I offered. She ignored me. "Get the fuck up, you little shithead!"

"No!"

"*Get out of that fucking chair you fucking goddamned shithead!*"

Frank spoke up. "Don't talk to your sister that way, Nancy."

"Or what, asshole?"

"Or . . . or . . ."

Nancy crossed her arms, glared at him. "Go ahead, hit me, why don't ya?"

The color rose in Frank's face.

"Frank, don't start with her," I cautioned.

"She *can't* talk to her sister that way!"

"You're rising to her bait! I *asked* you not to! Let it be!"

"You're rising to her bait by letting her get away with her crap!"

"Stop yelling," begged David. "I'm trying to watch TV."

"Don't *you* start opening your big fat mouth!" ordered Frank.

"Don't take it out on David!" I cried.

David stormed out, ran upstairs, and slammed his door.

Nancy still stood over Suzy. "I wanna sit in that chair!"

"Suzy, let her sit there," Frank commanded.

"No," Suzy said. "I'm sick of doing things just because *she* wants to."

"Please, Suzy," I begged. "It'll be easier if you do."

"But it isn't *fair,* Mommy!" She sniffled.

"Suzy, I order you to get out of that chair at once!" yelled Frank.

She got up, fighting back tears, and angrily left the room. Her door slammed.

Nancy triumphantly sat down.

"You happy now?" Frank demanded of her.

"Shut the fuck up," she said. "I'm trying to watch the show."

Nancy still ran the household, just as she had when she was seven. Only now her impact was more pervasive, more insidious. She set us against each other, made us say and do things to each other we later regretted. She was the catalyst. Because of this relatively tiny incident—who gets to sit in a chair—I was angry at Frank, Frank was angry at me, David was angry at Frank, Frank at David, Suzy at both of us. This anger wouldn't just disappear when Nancy left. It would take us weeks to forgive and forget, weeks to erase Nancy's presence in the household. By then she'd be back home for another holiday.

Meanwhile, just as when she was younger, Nancy still delighted in manipulating, bullying, and dividing Suzy and David. She was still older and smarter. They, in turn, looked up to her, feared her, loved her. They played right into her hands.

Suzy was still her favorite victim. Whereas before she'd exclude Suzy from coloring or a game, now she'd deny her admittance to her inner sanctum, her room. Suzy had long ago stopped sleeping there.

When she first came back for Thanksgiving, for example, she flatly refused to let Suzy in her room. "You're fat and ugly," she said. "I don't want you in here. Only my adorable, sweet baby brother." Then she invited David in and closed the door on Suzy. David came gladly. It was a treat to hear Nancy's newest records and Lakeside Campus stories.

Just before Nancy went back to school after Thanksgiving weekend, she finally admitted Suzy to her room. Suzy joined her, thrilled. Nancy closed the door, put on a record.

"If I tell you something, you promise you won't tell Mommy?" Nancy asked.

"Uh-huh."

"You better not, because if she finds out, I'll know where she heard it."

"I won't," Suzy insisted. "Tell me."

"I get stoned all the time and I've taken acid seven times," she announced triumphantly.

Suzy told me about it that night, wide-eyed with fear. "Don't tell her you know, Mommy, please. Please don't tell her. But I *had* to tell you. I don't want her to get in trouble."

I assured Suzy I'd keep quiet. Then I sank into a chair, devastated.

I believed it this time.

I had seen and heard the other girls at Lakeside Campus. These were girls who either already used drugs or were prime candidates to be drug users. They were angry and rebellious. They were hurting. They were lonely—most of their parents lived out of state. And, as Brooke had told me, she couldn't watch them all of the time.

For Nancy, drugs were a natural outgrowth of her life. Drugs were a badge of rebellion and, for a thirteen-year-old, of maturity. They offered her a passport to a different, "better" reality. Drugs could take her somewhere else, take her where her beloved hard rock music was. She had continually been on prescription drugs since her infancy—to mask discomfort, restlessness, anger. It was only natural for her to move on to the illegal means to the same end.

I phoned Brooke. She denied that there was a drug problem at Lakeside Campus. Still, I believed it. Frank was ambivalent.

"She *might* experiment with grass," he said when we were getting into bed that night. "But no way she's a user. She's exaggerating, Deb. To impress her kid sister."

"How do you know?"

"Because she doesn't act any different. Don't you think we'd notice a change in her behavior if she'd taken LSD seven times? Even *one* time?"

"How would we be able to detect it? She'd start acting weird? She was weird before."

"Good point." He mulled it over. "Well, how about money? All she gets is twenty bucks a month, doled out by Brooke. And judging by the way she's going through cigarettes, that'll just about cover her in smokes. She hasn't got any money for drugs. Somebody might turn her on once, but nobody gives grass and pills away for free."

Now Frank had a point. Maybe she had only experimented once or twice and had stretched the truth to impress Suzy. We both wanted to believe that. Desperately.

Frank and I had a dinner party to go to a few nights after Nancy had gone back to Lakeside Campus. While I dressed I noticed that Frank was sitting on the edge of the bed in his underwear, staring at his knees. He was totally down. It hit both of us periodically: we worked hard, tried to be good people, tried to do the right thing, yet life just seemed to be an unending stream of misery. Nothing went right. When you looked around for causes, it was impossible to *always* blame Nancy. It was impossible not to say to yourself, "Maybe it's *me*. Maybe *I'm* the problem. Maybe *I* should go away, let the others flourish."

I sat down on the bed next to him. "I think about it, too. Leaving."

He seemed relieved that I knew what was going through his mind. "For somebody else?"

"No."

"Me neither."

"You know what stops me?" I said. "I ask myself how I could leave you to handle Nancy by yourself."

He nodded. "I know. I couldn't leave you with her."

"And if I did meet someone else and remarry, could I expect that someone else to understand her? Nobody else could. Just you and me. So even if we did split up, we'd still be together because of her. We'd have to deal with the phone calls, the traumas, the decisions. Nobody else would take that on. *Could* take it on."

Frank said, "I was thinking the other day, when she was here, that she's like a wedge driving us apart. But you know, sitting here, talking like this, makes me realize that she also holds us together."

"She sure does," I agreed. "Like glue."

"Do you think she knows it?" he asked.

"I don't know. I'm not so sure I've thought of it myself quite that way before."

He smiled sadly, put his arm around me. "So what do we do?"

"Survive."

He kissed me, got up, and went into the bathroom to shave. I finished dressing, then opened my jewelry box to discover that the one piece of jewelry I was most attached to was missing. I searched carefully through the box. It wasn't there.

"My diamond wedding band is gone," I cried out, distraught.

"How do you know?" Frank asked, emerging from our bathroom with lather on his face.

"Because it's not here."

"So maybe you misplaced it somewhere."

"I didn't," I insisted. "I keep very careful track of my jewelry. And I *always* put my wedding band back in the same spot. It's not there."

"You saying somebody took it?"

"Somebody must have."

"That's crazy. We haven't had a break-in. Is anything else missing?"

"No."

"So who would have come in here and taken that one piece? And why? I didn't do it. Suzy wouldn't do it. Nancy wouldn't . . ." He trailed off.

We looked at each other sadly. Nancy *would*. And *had*. She had stolen my wedding band to buy drugs. She'd found a source of money. There was no doubt.

"I'll get you another one, Deb," Frank said quietly.

Then he held me. He got lather all over my face and hair. I didn't care. I needed to be held. I felt so helpless.

Nancy came home a few weeks later for Christmas break. This time, Suzy reported to me, Nancy showed her a piece of paper with a man's name and address on it and said, "This guy deals right near campus. Everybody buys from him. I'm gonna buy an ounce of weed and some Ludes from him as soon as I get back."

Then Nancy shoved the piece of paper into one of her textbooks.

As soon as Nancy went out for a walk, Suzy showed me which book. There was indeed a piece of paper with a man's name and address on it. I copied down the information and returned the paper to where I'd found it. I couldn't let Nancy know I knew. I couldn't confront her—if I did I'd get Suzy in trouble.

I phoned Brooke and gave her the information. She was far less skeptical when confronted with hard evidence. She thanked me and said she would contact the authorities. Later that night she called to say the police had arrested the man for possessing large amounts of marijuana, hashish, Quaaludes, and LSD.

"Will you be searching the girls' luggage when they come back from vacation?" I asked.

"No. Why?"

"I think some of them will be bringing drugs back with them from home. At least that's what Nancy told her sister."

"In that case," she said, "I'll be searching the girls' luggage."

And she did. When we brought Nancy back after the holiday, there was a long line of grumbling girls waiting to get up the stairs with their things. Brooke wouldn't let them up until she had inspected their luggage and purses.

Her search turned up numerous one-ounce bags of marijuana, grams of hash, and bottles of pills. She confiscated the lot.

Nancy's bags were clean. Brooke found no drugs in them. Nor did she find my opal pin or my Danish sterling silver ring. Those two pieces were missing from my jewelry box when we got back home.

I did confront Nancy about my jewelry. When she called a few nights later, I mentioned that several pieces were missing.

Her response was silence.

"My wedding band is gone," I went on. "So is an opal pin and a silver ring."

"Yeah, but they were insured, weren't they?" she asked.

"Yes, they were."

"So you got nothing to worry about. You'll get your bread back."

"That's not the point."

"What is?"

"They were dear to me."

"Oh. Gee, I'm real sorry, Mom. But I don't know anything about it."

After we hung up I wrote Mr. Sylvester a letter. Lakeside Campus had no drug counseling program at that time. Seemingly, none of the supervisors knew they had a drug problem. I suggested he start a program. He agreed that it would be a good idea. A drug counseling program was started soon after that. I don't know if it helped any of the girls. I hope so. It did not, unfortunately, help Nancy.


The four of us pulled together as a family in Nancy's absence that winter, due to a bit of adversity. Frank took David skiing in the Poconos for a weekend and David broke his leg the first day—a bad compound fracture. He was in a cast for four months.

He was unable to go to school for the first few weeks. All he could do was mope around the house, bored and in pain. Afternoons, he sat with his nose against the living room window, watching the kids in the neighborhood—Suzy included—sled down their driveways on the new-fallen snow. He was very unhappy.

One afternoon I was surprised to hear him crying from his living room perch. He was twelve and didn't cry much anymore. I went into the living room and found him face down on the floor, sobbing hysterically, kicking with his one good foot.

"I wanna die!" he screamed. "I wanna die! I wanna die!"

This was a Nancy thing to do and I was suddenly seized by terror. Could her behavior be spreading to another child?

I went to him, knelt. "Why are you crying, sweetheart?" I begged, heart pounding.

He put his head in my lap. "My leg hurts and I wanna go out and play."

"You don't *really* want to die, do you?"

He thought it over. "No, I guess not. I'm just unhappy, Mommy."

I hugged him tightly and planted kisses all over his face, laughing with relief. "That's right. You're just unhappy. That's right."

But his Nancy-like behavior surfaced again the next afternoon. I panicked again. This time I phoned our pediatrician and told him about it. He told me not to be concerned.

"The first child tends to set the emotional tone of the household," he explained, "whether positively or negatively. David is reacting to his unhappiness by doing what his older sister would do in response to pain. It's something he picked up. I wouldn't worry. Just try to make him happy."

So we did. Frank made a special effort to get home early so the four of us could have dinner together. Then we would gather in the living room and Frank would make a big fire in the fireplace. We'd pop popcorn and play games. One evening Suzy brought her paints down—she was discovering both a love and a talent for art—and painted the foot of David's cast so it looked just like a Philadelphia Flyers skate, with laces and eyelets. Above that she painted a Flyers orange-and-black striped sock. He was delighted.

Once David was able to go back to school, on crutches, the school bus driver was nice enough to stop in front of our house for him. But it seemed as though it never stopped snowing that winter, and David couldn't negotiate our walkway unless it had been shoveled. Suzy happily went out first thing every morning and shoveled it for him. Then she carefully tied a plastic bag around his foot. She grumbled good-naturedly, but she really enjoyed helping him, and he was grateful. Frank and I were delighted to see their relationship develop this way.

The night David had his cast taken off, the four of us went out to dinner to celebrate. As it happened, the subject of drugs came up. Frank and I explained that it was important for them to understand that Nancy was troubled, that it was likely she was involved with drugs, and that drugs would do nothing but compound her problems. Suzy and David volunteered to keep us informed, in confidence. Then we advised them that they themselves might soon be exposed to drugs at school, and we wanted them to feel free to discuss the pros and cons with us, not sneak around behind our backs. They agreed. It was a good talk.

The phone was ringing when we got home. It was Brooke. Nancy had cut up her forearm with a pair of scissors.

Frank and I drove over the following morning.

Nancy was sitting on a sofa in the living area, reading a book. Her forearm was bandaged. I sat next to her on the couch and tried to hug her. She wouldn't let me.

"Why did you do that to your arm, Nancy?" I asked.

She looked down, depressed. "It's your fault," she said softly.

"Our fault? Why, sweetheart?"

"I . . . I wanted to talk to you. You weren't home."

"We just went out for a little while," Frank said. "To eat."

"If you'd been there, I wouldn't have done it," she insisted.

"We're here now," I said. "What did you want to tell us, Nancy?"

"I wanted to die," she replied.

"Why?" I asked.

"I don't wanna be here."

"Look, Nancy," Frank said. "I don't want to go to work every day. I'd much rather sack in, go skiing, go see a movie. But you can't always do what you want. And just because you can't is no reason to end your life."

"You have to adjust, sweetheart," I added.

Nancy said nothing, just sat there in misery.

She was so unhappy with this place, with life. We didn't know how to cure her misery. I thought briefly about looking for a different school system to place her in—maybe Darlington *wasn't* the only game in town. But that seemed pointless. She'd be miserable anywhere.

In truth, we were having trouble affording the fee at Lakeside Campus. Frank was making a good living. My store was in the black. But a thousand dollars every month was a lot of money. We applied to the state of Pennsylvania for funding aid and were told that the state would indeed help parents of children the public school system was unable to serve—provided those children were brain damaged. In those days the state would not aid the parents of socially or emotionally disturbed children who needed a boarding situation. Now they have to.

It was solely because of this ruling that Nancy was finally administered the neurological testing that the clinic director in Philadelphia, as I later learned, had recommended three years before. If a neurologist were to determine that Nancy was brain damaged, then the state would cover about half of her tab at Darlington.

Nancy's allergist recommended a neurologist, whose associate agreed to examine Nancy and give her the necessary EEG at a major teaching hospital in Philadelphia. Brooke agreed to let Nancy leave school for the day. Nancy took the

train in by herself from Winfield on a drizzly spring morning.
I met her at the station and drove her to the hospital.

The test results were inconclusive. The neurologist found
no evidence of a brain tumor. Nor did he find *conclusive* evidence of brain damage caused by Nancy's troubled birth.
However, after he had completed his testing and diagnosis, he
admitted to me that the testing procedures were not very sophisticated or broad-based. He described Nancy as "living in
a gray area."

I later obtained a copy of his findings. His report to the
commonwealth of Pennsylvania, dated May 8, 1972, concludes:

> Although the neurological examination does not reveal any abnormality, her history and behavior characteristics are those seen in the presence of dysfunction of the Central Nervous System and her deviant performance seems directly or indirectly related to her neurological condition.
>
> It is commonly held that a distinctively behavioral syndrome occurs in certain children with organic brain dysfunction with a perinatal history such as this girl. The syndrome may vary from hyperkinesis to anti-social behavior (with events such as lying, stealing, truanting, sex offenses and cruelty). Extreme anxiety often with panic catastrophic reactions may be accompanied by increase in the CNS deficit, including ritualistic compulsive behavior to avoid anxiety.
>
> It is almost impossible to observe the contribution made by the abnormality of the brain to the total situation of the emotional disturbance shown by this girl, but it will be helpful in the understanding of the psychodynamics if there has been a brain injury.

Based on this report, the state granted us four thousand dollars in aid toward Nancy's annual fees with the Darlington
school system. We were thankful for this.

And so, surprisingly, was Nancy. She wanted to stay now.
Her attitude toward Lakeside Campus changed dramatically
at this point. She didn't necessarily improve. She just found
something else to occupy herself with. She met Jeff.

# ☐ Chapter 10

"I have a boyfriend in the band," she told me proudly on the phone one day.

"That's nice, Nancy. What band?"

"The dudes in school. They got together with a band. Jeff plays guitar. Rhythm, mostly. Some lead."

"Jeff is your boyfriend?"

"Uh-huh. Angela and Spring go with two of the other guys. We have a, like, well, it's like *family*. I mean, we hang out together and like kinda watch out for each other, you know?"

"Yes, I know."

"Yeah, it's just really nice."

I didn't know if the rock band was any good. I didn't even know if it had a name. All I knew is that Nancy had found a place for herself, an identity. She was a lady of the band.

We met Jeff when we visited Nancy one Sunday. He was taller than Frank and had a wiry, muscular build, wildly uncombed shoulder-length hair, and a scraggly mustache. He wore torn jeans and a long-sleeved T-shirt with a big star on the chest. He was fifteen, a year older than Nancy.

They held hands.

"Mom and Dad," she said, "this is my boyfriend, Jeff."

He gave us a nod and sort of half-wave. Then he began to examine the lawn at our feet. Like the other Lakeside students we'd seen, he seemed sullen and uncommunicative. I don't know why he was there. His mother and father were divorced. He visited his father in Connecticut on vacation breaks.

"Very pleased to meet you, Jeff," Frank said enthusiastically.

"Yes," I agreed, "we've heard so much about you."

He looked away. "Yeah," he said vaguely.

"I understand you have a rock band," Frank said.

He nodded, fished a bent pack of cigarettes out of his back pocket, and lit one. He cleared his throat.

"Well . . ." I said, groping for conversation.

"Hey, I gotta split," Jeff said. He raised an eyebrow mischievously at Nancy. "Gotta jam."

They kissed—with considerable passion and familiarity. Frank and I looked at each other a bit uncomfortably. They parted. Then he gave us that same half-wave, said "See ya" to us, and was off.

"Nice meeting you, Jeff," Frank called after him.

"Yes, see you soon!" I added.

Nancy gazed after him lovingly as he slunk off to the boys' house, shoulders slightly hunched, bare feet shuffling on the grass.

"Isn't he just unbelievable?" she said.

"He seems like a very nice boy," Frank said.

She was so excited. Jeff was her first boyfriend.

I assumed they were having sex. It was unrealistic not to. I didn't condone it, but at the same time I knew there was nothing I could do about it. So I looked on the bright side. She was holding on to a relationship—this was a positive thing. She seemed to have found someone to care about her, other than us. She seemed happier.

Still, I decided I would have a talk with her about sex and love as soon as the opportunity arose.

The relationship with Jeff did improve Nancy's overall outlook. She started getting more involved with the other kids. She became manager of the boys' soccer team—doubtless because Jeff was on it. She also found an interest in photography. She joined the school photography club and learned how to work a 35 millimeter camera and develop pictures in the school darkroom. I still have some of Nancy's black and white photographs. They are all very dark and brooding, interesting in a grotesque way. Perhaps they show what was going on inside her mind better than her words did at the time. One picture, for instance, is of a log smoldering in the middle of a barren field. Another is of an old bathroom sink that someone had abandoned in a cornfield. I think Nancy had a gift for photography. She might have gotten pretty good at it, if someone hadn't stolen the school's cameras and darkroom equipment.

Her relationship with Jeff continued through the summer. They both went to the Darlington camp in New Hampshire. While she was there, Nancy got a hold of some ink and a needle and tattooed Jeff's name on her chest. She also tattooed a flower on her thigh.

Nancy also tried to abort herself with a wire coat hanger that summer. Her counselor found out when Nancy started to hemorrhage. She rushed her to the hospital.

"I've treated her for a perforated uterus," the doctor told me over the phone. "Your daughter just went ahead and stuck a hanger right in there. She bled a lot, but she's okay."

"She was pregnant?" I asked.

"She seemed to think she was, but I examined her. There's no evidence she was or is pregnant."

I asked to speak to her. Nancy got on the phone.

"Nancy, why did you do such a foolish, dangerous thing?"

"I had to," she said, her voice flat, almost wooden.

"But why?" I begged.

"I was pregnant."

"The doctor says you weren't."

"I was."

"But why didn't you *call* me? I'm *here* for you. I love you. You're my baby. Why didn't you call me?"

"I couldn't."

"Why?"

She didn't respond.

"Nancy?"

"I took care of it," she said.

I was upset and frightened. So was Frank. She was acting out her emotional problems by means of self-mutilation. This was a continuation—a worsening—of when she had carved up her arm. It was irrational and dangerous behavior. Was it drug related? I didn't and don't know.

She was apparently taking LSD at this time. She came home from camp for a few days before going off to visit Jeff at his dad's house in Connecticut. She wrote Jeff a postcard and left it out on her desk before she sent it. I couldn't help but find it when I was tidying up her room.

> Dear Jeff—
> By the time you get this we'll be on windowpane acid and fucking our brains out.
>
> Love, Nancy

She was trashing her life and she was flaunting it. There was no doubt in my mind that she had purposely left the card out to rub my nose in what she was doing. I despised her for it.

I confronted her.

"What'd you do?" she demanded. "Go through my shit?"

"You know I wouldn't do that. You left it out and I noticed it."

"So?"

"So . . . I thought maybe we could have a talk."

"About what?"

"About love."

She laughed contemptuously. "I've fucked four hundred guys. What are *you* gonna tell *me?*"

I wondered how many men—boys—she *had* slept with.

"What are you looking so shocked for?" she asked. "Didn't you fuck anyone before you got married to Daddy?"

"No."

"Not even Daddy?"

"No."

"God, I don't *believe* you people. Look, mind your own fucking business. I do what I want. And don't try to tell me I can't go to Jeff's, because I'll just run away and not come back. Ever."

Part of me wanted to hold her in my arms, love her. She seemed to have no comprehension of love—for a man, for her family. She was unable to give it or receive it. I couldn't understand why. I felt incredibly sad for her.

And part of me wanted to smack her in the face. She so totally frustrated me. I could not have a reasonable, rational discussion with her. I wanted to *beat* reason into her. But I couldn't. I had to keep that lid on. The alternative was too dangerous. So I walked away. I went into my room, shut the door, and sat down on the bed. I took one fast, deep breath after another, eyes clamped shut. When I had counted to a hundred, I opened my eyes to find my fists still clenched. I relaxed them and calmed down a bit. The anger didn't go away, though. I had merely succeeded in pushing it down, burying it deep inside me. It was always there.


Her relationship with Jeff continued into the fall of Nancy's second year at Lakeside. It ended abruptly when Jeff left the school a few weeks into the semester. I don't know why he left or where he went. I don't know if Nancy ever saw him again, though I think not.

At Thanksgiving she brought home a new boy from Darlington. She described him as "just a friend." His name was Roger. Roger was very clean-cut, with short hair, a tie, and a sportcoat. He had very nice manners. He was from Virginia. Nancy had picked up his southern accent.

"Mama and Daddy," she drawled, "I'd like y'all to meet Roger. Roger, that there's Suzy, my kid sister. And that's David, my sweet li'l baby brother."

She acted like the model daughter. It was quite a performance. She proudly took Roger on a tour of the house, helped him get settled in the guest room, made sure he had everything he needed. She offered to help me make dinner (I nearly fainted). During dinner her table manners were flawless. She took a keen, sisterly interest in Suzy and David's school activities. She asked how Frank's new paper business was going (he nearly fell out of his chair). She complimented me on the turkey, pointed out to Roger what a wonder her mama was, running a store and a household, too. When we were done eating, she helped me clear the table.

Then she decided to take Roger for a walk around the neighborhood. She invited Suzy to join them.

"*Can* I?" exclaimed Suzy, delighted to be included.

"Why shore," Nancy drawled.

Off they went on their walk. Frank and David and I chuckled over the "new" Nancy. They went into the den and turned on the TV. I started in on the dishes, humming to myself. Maybe Nancy's behavior was fake. At least she was being pleasant. And this Roger seemed a nice boy, a good influence.

After a few minutes I heard giggling in the street and looked out the kitchen window. Nancy, Roger, and Suzy were standing together under a streetlight. Roger was holding a match to a small pipe and Nancy was smoking from it. She took a deep drag, held it in, and offered the pipe to Suzy. Suzy took it eagerly, puffed on it, coughed. The other two laughed at her.

I couldn't believe it. Suzy was smoking marijuana. She was barely twelve. Nancy was turning her on!

My heart began to pound; my face flushed. I felt like I'd been kicked in the belly. Here was my worse fear realized— that Nancy would use her influence over Suzy to make a drug user of her. She had the power to pit Suzy against us, to undermine our authority. And she was using it.

Why? Looking back, I believe it was Nancy's own way of trying to make Frank and me love her more. By turning Suzy on, she was hoping she'd tarnish Suzy so we'd love Suzy less and give that love to her. There was never enough love to satisfy her.

I didn't see it that way then, though. All I saw was a child who was making it so impossibly painful for me to love her.

I said nothing to Frank about what I'd seen until Nancy and Roger returned to school. When I did, he wasn't surprised. There was no outburst. He accepted the news with weary resignation.

We now had a new, urgent reason for keeping the girls apart, we agreed. Suzy had to grow up free of Nancy's poisonous influence. Meanwhile, we had to keep our relationship with Suzy as open as possible. We had to reassert our authority. Our influence over Suzy had to be greater than Nancy's was. *Had* to be.

We decided a come-clean session about drugs would be a good starting point. Suzy, however, denied she had ever gotten stoned.

"Suzy, sweetheart," I said. "I know you did it. There's no point in lying. The important thing is for us to be honest."

"I'm *not* lying! I've *never* done it!"

"Suzy, I saw you."

"God, who do you think you are, my jailer? I don't *believe* you!"

It was a Nancy response. Frank and I glanced at each other nervously. How *much* was rubbing off?

"Suzy," Frank said. "Mom and I are very disappointed in you for this. We expect more of you."

"Meaning what?" she demanded, jaw stuck firmly out.

"We expect you to be *you*," I said. "You're not Nancy."

She broke down and began to sob. She ran off to her room. I followed her up there. She wept in my arms. Still, she would not admit she'd gotten stoned.

We kept an eye on Suzy when Nancy came home for Christmas. We now regarded Nancy as a threat. We didn't like feeling that way, but we did. We discussed searching her things, but I wouldn't do it. I believed in my privacy. If you want privacy for yourself, you have to respect the privacy of others. Frank and I agreed—we wouldn't go through Nancy's things. Instead, we kept the two of them apart as much as possible, or together in our presence. It was not a pleasant stay. Fortunately Nancy went back to Lakeside early because there was a New Year's Eve party she wanted to go to.

Frank and I had a New Year's Eve party to go to also.

David planned to sleep over at a friend's house. Only Suzy had nothing to do. Her crowd was having a party, but she had no date. She was going through her awkward phase—she felt a bit heavy—and was dismayed that none of the boys had asked her. She sulked around the house all day.

"Everybody has a date except me," she pouted. "I'm so fat and ugly."

I tried to cheer her up. I told her not to worry, that she'd get a date next year. But she was inconsolable.

Before Frank and I left, I went up to her room to try cheering her up one more time. Frank went out to warm up the car.

Her door was closed. I knocked. She didn't answer.

"Suzy?" I called. No answer. I checked the crack under the door to see if her light was on. It was.

"Suzy?" I called louder.

Still no answer. I tried turning the knob. The door was locked from the inside.

"Suzy!" I screamed. I panicked. I believed she was trying to kill herself in there because she'd not gotten a date. Nancy would have. Why not Suzy?

"Suzy!" I screamed again. I rammed my shoulder against the door, threw my weight behind it. It wouldn't give.

Then I heard a rustling in the room. Suzy unlocked the door and opened it a crack. I shoved it open, stormed into the room. It was freezing. The window was wide open. The room reeked of marijuana. She had been smoking a joint.

I glared at her. Her eyes rolled around for a second, then she fainted in a dead heap on the carpet. I gasped. I didn't know what she had taken, or if she'd overdosed or what. I got down on the floor next to her and shook her. She came to, as confused and frightened as I was.

"What are you on?" I cried.

"I was . . . I was just smoking a joint."

"Where did you get it?"

"From Nancy."

"I knew this was going to happen. I knew it. You're going to see a shrink, young lady!"

I overreacted. I immediately lunged for professional help, terrified that Suzy was drug-involved and in serious trouble.

"W-why do I have to see a shrink?"

"Because I said so!"

"O-okay," she agreed. She was so scared she'd have agreed to anything.

She went to see a therapist twice. Then she came to me and said she wanted to stop. I asked why.

"Because I don't wanna go. Because I'm not Nancy."

A few days later Nancy ran away.

"Don't be concerned," said Brooke over the phone. "We think she's in New York City."

"New York City!" I cried.

"Yes, we've called the NYPD and they're looking for her. One of the girls gave us an address there. If you hear from her, let us know."

We waited by the phone. Nancy didn't call. This was something new and disturbing. She had run away before, but always with the purpose of coming home to us. If indeed she was in New York, well, she was fourteen. You heard stories about what happened to runaway girls in New York City, about how they become prostitutes and drug addicts.

We waited by the phone. "Don't worry, she can take care of herself," Frank said at one point, unconvincingly.

Neither of us slept that night. Brooke called the next day, just to say there was no word.

I slept fitfully the second night Nancy was missing. I dreamed I was driving to the store in the morning and passed a group of teenage girls waiting at a school bus stop, giggling and talking. As I drove by them, I realized that one of them was Nancy. She was smiling and happy. I'd found her! I stopped the car and called out to her. As soon as she saw me she glowered, then ran off. I couldn't catch her.

After three days the police found Nancy at the Port Authority Bus Terminal. She was okay. Brooke said she was being put on a bus for Avon.

Nancy was back at school that evening.

"Why did you run away?" I asked.

"It's your fault," she replied. "You wouldn't take me out of here. So I got away on my own. I had to."

Clearly, Nancy was not responding positively to the Darlington environment. Far from it. She was using drugs. She was becoming a runaway, in danger of ending up a teen prostitute, one of those pitiful girls they find dead in some Times Square fleabag with a needle in her arm—an entry on the New York City police blotter. This was too nightmarish to even conceive of. We had to get her out of there. I had to find her another school. There had to be another one out there somewhere. Maybe I'd missed one on my prior search.

I picked up the trail where I'd left off four years before and found a school in Florida that seemed capable of treating Nancy, but part of the entire staff had just been arrested for smoking pot. Then I found a fine school in Topeka, Kansas—Menninger's Clinic. They worked with emotionally disturbed children of Nancy's age. They also charged $18,000 per year. There was simply no way we could afford it.

I even went so far as to see the senior rabbi at our synagogue. He was a learned, prestigious man. Maybe *he* could help us.

Frank and I weren't devout members, but we did like to go to Friday night services sometimes. We both found comfort in the ritual and prayer. The temple was a retreat from Nancy.

The rabbi saw us in his office. He listened with great patience and empathy as we told him of Nancy's pain and of our confusion. We asked him if he knew somewhere she could go. We asked if he could help us, if the Jewish Federation could help us, if *anyone* could help us.

He was kind, but he was no help.

"You have a dilemma," he said, "to be sure. I am sorry to say, however, that I have no answer. As far as I know, the Jewish Federation will be unable to help you. I wish I myself could ease your burden, but I cannot. I know of no place for your Nancy."

We were lost again. We had no idea where to turn.

Then one day I read an article in a health magazine about Dr. Allan Cott, a psychiatrist in New York City who believed that certain types of mental illness, particularly schizophrenia, were caused by chemical imbalances in the body. Thus, he felt, talking therapy was meaningless. His unorthodox and controversial method of treatment, called orthomolecular medicine, involved treating patients with chemicals, large doses of vitamins, and a sugar-free diet. There were a few other psychiatrists practicing this orthomolecular medicine— none of them very popular with the American Medical Association.

What attracted me to Cott's ideas was that the article referred to the case histories of several children who had shown remarkable improvement under him, children who had, from infancy, been restless, poor sleepers, angry, and incapable of holding on to friends. Children like Nancy.

I mentioned the article to Frank. Coincidentally, he'd just been speaking to a customer whose problem child had been helped by Cott, helped so much that he was now able to function at home.

"Do you think we ought to talk to him?" I asked.

"She's not getting any better where she is. It's certainly worth a try. What have we got to lose?"

We had nothing to lose.

I made an appointment with Dr. Cott. It was two months before we could see him—evidently a lot of other people had similar problems and were anxious to talk to him. A week before the scheduled appointment he sent us a very detailed twenty-page questionnaire covering Nancy's physical and behavioral development. We filled it out. Then Frank and I rode up to New York City to see him.

As we drove I began to understand the plight of the families of terminal cancer victims. Often they will seek out controversial treatment for their loved ones. And why not? It's impossibly difficult to stand by and watch someone you love deteriorate right before your eyes. So you begin to grasp at straws. This is not to say that Dr. Cott was a straw, but he was unpopular with the medical establishment. So what if he was? Here was a chance to administer another form of treatment. The present one wasn't working.

His office was on East Thirty-eighth Street. He was a small, slightly built man with gray hair and a concerned manner. He had thoroughly digested our questionnaire.

"Mr. and Mrs. Spungen, I have a few more questions about Nancy. Some of them may sound a bit odd to you, but please bear with me. They could be important. Okay?"

We nodded.

"Was Nancy an affectionate infant? What I mean to say is, did she like to be cuddled or did she react negatively by, for example, stiffening her limbs?"

I gasped. "How did you know that?"

He made a note in her file. "Would you call her affectionate now?"

"She doesn't like to be hugged," I said. "At least, not by us."

He made another note. "You mentioned this psychotic episode she had at age ten, an apparent allergic reaction to Atarax. You mention she inflicted punishment on herself. By that, do you mean she began to bang her head and pull her hair out? That sort of thing?"

"That's exactly what she did," exclaimed Frank.

"And she continued to do it during other episodes?"

"Yes!" we both cried, excited. Cott was the first professional we'd ever seen who actually seemed to know Nancy!

"Does she take drugs?" he asked.

"Yes," I replied. "We think she does."

"What kind?"

"Marijuana. Pills."

"Hard drugs? Heroin?"

"No way," Frank assured him. "Nancy's hysterically afraid of needles."

"Even so, I'm afraid she's a real candidate for serious drug problems. She's vulnerable. She was overmedicated as a child, and society has failed to provide the means to ease her pain."

"What exactly is *causing* the pain, Doctor?" Frank asked. "What's wrong with her?"

"Well, I'd have to examine her before I made a definite diagnosis. But based on reading your report, and talking to you, I'd say Nancy's a schizophrenic."

At last, after fifteen years of searching, someone had told us what was wrong with our child.

# ☐ Chapter 11

"Can you help her, Doctor?" I asked.

"I believe I can, yes. I'd need thirty days to stabilize her. I'll put her in a hospital so I can control her intake, get the sugar out of her diet. I'll feed her megavitamins. Then we'll see."

"What are the odds?" Frank asked. "What are the odds you can help her?"

Dr. Cott took a deep breath, let it out slowly. "I can't make you any promises. It wouldn't be fair to you. All I can tell you is that I have seen other young people like Nancy and I have helped them."

"We didn't know there were others like her," I said. "We've always gotten the impression that . . . that . . ."

"That she's some kind of unique specimen? A freak? She's not. She's just misunderstood. Nobody's gotten to the root of her problem, which, in my opinion, is chemical. Give me thirty days. There will be a dramatic improvement in your daughter or none at all. There doesn't seem to be a middle ground with this kind of treatment. If it doesn't work, I'll be the first to tell you."

Frank and I looked at each other, nodded. Then Frank stood up, beaming, and stuck his hand out across Dr. Cott's desk.

"You've got yourself a deal!"

We practically sailed home on our enthusiasm. He'd given us hope, the first real hope in ages. We were so thrilled.

I phoned Walter Froelich, a staff social worker Mr. Sylvester had assigned to us, and told him about Dr. Cott. I explained that Dr. Cott thought she could be schizophrenic, that he wanted to examine her and, if his diagnosis held, withdraw her from school for a month so he could hospitalize her. Froelich said he would have to discuss it with Mr. Sylvester.

Mr. Sylvester's response was swift and negative. He phoned personally.

"We had a boy here last year who had been on this Dr. Cott's program," he declared. "He wasn't any better at all. The whole thing is a lot of meaningless garbage, a scheme to peddle a lot of vitamins."

"We don't see it that way," I said. "We see it as an opportunity to help her."

"It's not," he snapped.

"We'd like to withdraw her for a month," I said firmly.

"Fine, but I can't guarantee her place will still be here."

"What are you saying?"

"I'm saying we have no such thing as a leave of absence here. If you withdraw your daughter she won't automatically get back in. She'll have to take a place on the waiting list."

"How can you do this to us?" I cried. "We're trying to *help* her!"

"And I'm trying to save you unnecessary grief and expense, Mrs. Spungen."

I hung up, enraged, and phoned Dr. Cott. He was sympathetic.

"You've got a difficult decision on your hands," he said.

"What do you advise?"

"I'm not going to lie to you, Mrs. Spungen. There's a good chance I can help Nancy. There's also a chance I can't. If I can't, and Darlington won't take her back, then there won't be any place for Nancy to go after her month is up, except home. She has to remain in a school environment. She can't just move back in with you and not go to school.''

"So we should forget it?" I asked, not wanting to hear his answer.

"For now, I'm afraid so. I can't take the responsibility for pulling her out of the Darlington system. It's the only system I know of that can handle her. There's certainly nowhere else in this area. It would put you in a terrible position if she couldn't go back there. I'm sorry."

"So am I," I said, crushed.

"If they change their minds, let me know."

Frank and I discussed it that night. Reluctantly, we agreed that there was no way we could risk freezing her out of Darlington. We had no choice. We were forced to abandon the Cott alternative.

We were furious with the Darlington Institute for extinguishing this spark of hope. We simply could not understand Mr. Sylvester's motive in denying us a chance to help Nancy. We still can't.

I phoned Froelich and asked him to tell Sylvester we would not be withdrawing Nancy. He said he would. This done, we thought the matter was closed. It wasn't.

We hadn't told Nancy about Dr. Cott. We saw no purpose in it, at least not until we knew the treatment was going to come off, at which point we planned to explain it to her as openly as possible. Since it did not come off, we said nothing to her.

Somehow she found out what had happened—I don't know who told her—and took our intentions the wrong way.

She phoned, screaming.

"You bitch! You're trying to prove I'm a schizo so you can put me in a fucking hospital! You want me locked away! You never wanted me, and now you're trying to get rid of me!"

"Now, Nancy, that's just not so! We weren't—"

"You tried to hide it from me! You *know* you did! But I found out! I found out that you wanna put me in a hospital for fucking schizos!"

"We're *trying* to help you! We had some conversations

with a doctor. He seemed familiar with your problems. That's *all* that happened!''

"You're the one with the problem! Not me! *You!* You're the one who's fucked up!"

My head began to throb just over my left eye. I took several deep breaths. The lid. I had to keep the lid on. "Nancy, how can I make you understand that Daddy and I love you?"

*"I hate your fucking guts!"*

"Nancy, if you're going to talk to me—"

*"Hear me? I hate your fucking guts!"*

"—talk to me like that, I'm going to hang up."

*"Go fuck yourself, you fucking bitch!"*

I hung up on her, shaking.


By now, Nancy was in the spring of her second year at Lakeside. Frank and I were called in for a meeting with Mark Meadows, the Lakeside schoolmaster, Mallory Brooke, and Walter Froelich, at which time we found out that they'd pretty much had it with Nancy. They came up with a novel way of ousting her. Meadows informed us that Nancy would be ready to graduate in June.

"We wanted you to know," he said, "because she should be getting her college applications out."

Frank and I just sat there staring at him, mouths agape.

"You've got to be kidding," I finally said, incredulous.

"Not at all," Meadows said. "Scholastically, she's ahead of her age in most areas. She's a very bright girl."

"Look," Frank said, "she may be ready academically to handle college work, but she's also fifteen years old. Don't you think you're rushing her a bit?"

"She's ready," Meadows insisted.

"But even a well-adjusted child isn't emotionally ready for college at fifteen," I countered. "And Nancy is *not* well adjusted. She has to stay here for another year. *At least* another year. She *has* to."

They said they would let us know. A few days later Mr. Froelich called to say that Lakeside would keep Nancy for one more year, but that she would definitely be graduated after that, at age sixteen.

"We feel that by then she'll have caught up emotionally to her scholastic level," he reported.

I had to laugh.

"What's so funny?"

"Nothing. It's just that people have been telling us that since she was four years old."

Within a few days Nancy had found out that Lakeside had been ready to graduate her until we insisted she be kept there for another year. Her response was to slash the veins in her left forearm with a razor blade.

Brooke took her to the hospital, where the wound was pronounced not serious. Nancy was stitched up and sent back to school.

Two weeks later Nancy tried to kill herself again. This time she almost succeeded.

She had gone up to her room to listen to records. One of the girls found her in there, sitting on the edge of the bed bleeding all over the floor. A razor blade was in her left hand. She'd slashed her right forearm this time. She was just sitting there, staring at the blood.

They rushed her to the hospital in serious condition. The surgeon who treated her reported that she was about five minutes away from bleeding to death. The wound required twenty-one stitches—fifteen on the outside of her arm, six on the inside.

Brooke relayed the story to me over the phone, obviously shaken.

Nancy was not playing games anymore.

For the first time it hit me—the sickening realization that Nancy was going to die before I was. I'd battled so hard for her life. Now she was against me in that fight. She wanted death. She was reaching out to it and I could do nothing to stop her. She was not a little girl anymore, a baby I could hold in my arms, protect. She was fifteen years old. She was making a choice. She was choosing death.

I felt empty inside. There was nothing in me.

I was not going to live to sit around the fire with my Nancy and her husband and their babies. The natural order of the generations was not going to apply to this child. She had a terminal disease. She was going to die. I was going to see her die. I was going to bury her.

She wanted to die. She *would* die.

I was overwhelmed by dread and horror. Little did I know that within three years I would be praying for her to succeed.

# ☐ Chapter 12

I sold my store that winter. I was considering going to law school with the profits. The law seemed like an attractive, fulfilling career to me. Then one day I ran into a man I knew who worked at Western Union and who respected my sales skills. The chance encounter led to a job with Western Union as manager of Mailgram sales. It was basically a headquarters job that called for me to work on sales literature and sales training programs, but it did involve some travel, particularly to New York to coordinate projects with ad agencies. I enjoyed the fresh challenge. I thrived.

That winter also marked the death of Frank's mother. She passed away about a year after his father did. She had lived for almost two years after her stroke had left her unable to talk or function. They were both gone now, and Frank's ordeal was over. He had already sold their house and business and put the money in the bank. He and his sister divided it. Frank's share was six thousand dollars. We talked it over and decided to put the money to use in a way the entire family could enjoy. We built a swimming pool as soon as spring came.

Nancy calmed down quite a bit that winter. She saw that her stay at Lakeside was nearing its end, and she turned her sights to getting into college.

We still didn't think she was ready. Frankly, I was terrified at the idea of Nancy out on her own somewhere, unsupervised. We thought she might need a year at boarding school prior to taking the plunge.

But the folks at Lakeside did not. They set the machinery in motion without our knowledge. Mark Meadows arranged for her to take the SAT tests, to choose several possible schools, and to send out applications. Nancy's education was spotty in the areas that frustrated her, particularly math and science. Despite this, and despite not yet having reached her sixteenth birthday, she scored 1030 on the SAT tests—good enough to qualify her for many of the mid-range universities. She applied to the University of Colorado because she liked to ski. She got in. We didn't even know she'd applied until she called us with the happy news.

"They accepted me, Mommy!" she cried with joy on the phone. "I'm going to a real college! I don't have to be with sickies anymore!"

Now we had to decide whether or not to let her go.

All we knew about the place was that it was a big skiing school. When we mentioned the University of Colorado to friends, we found out it also had a reputation as a big party school.

"There are drugs everywhere," Frank said. "She'll either find them or she won't. Here or in Colorado. Going to one school or another won't make any difference."

"The question is whether she's ready to go anywhere," I mused aloud.

"What will she do instead? Live here? She can't. She's too disruptive. She's a bad influence on Suzy and David."

"Do you really think it's okay for her to go off by herself?" I asked.

"No, not necessarily. I have doubts, too, Deb. But she did do well on the tests. And she got in. And, well, she *has* been on her own since she was eleven."

"*With* supervision. She can barely handle herself under

those circumstances. What will she be like without any supervision at all?''

"We don't know. All we know is that being accepted at Colorado is giving Nancy a healthy image of herself. I think it would be counterproductive to tear that down.''

"I know," I agreed. "Possibly . . . maybe the Darlington kids were rubbing off on her. Maybe when she gets into a more normal environment she'll be—'' I stopped. I suppose even then I knew it was wishful thinking.

With reluctance and trepidation, we agreed to let Nancy go. The university accepted her with the stipulation that she begin by attending the six-week summer session. Nancy didn't mind at all. In fact, she was delighted.

The week before Nancy graduated from Lakeside there was a senior prom. Nancy put down the whole idea of a prom— until one of the boys asked her. Then she got very excited. She asked me if she could buy a new dress for the big dance, which was to be held in a private room at a restaurant near the school. I said that she could and gave her a budget. She went into Philadelphia by herself to buy it.

"It's the most beautiful dress in the whole world!" she jabbered excitedly when she came home, clutching the box.

"So let me see it, sweetheart!" I exclaimed, sharing her excitement.

"Not until I put it on!"

She dashed into the bathroom, closed the door. A minute later she came out in an unbelievably slinky lime-green matte jersey dress with a bare midriff.

"Isn't it just incredible, Mom?" she cried, anxious for my approval.

I wasn't about to ruin it for her. "Yes, sweetheart. Very nice. It makes you look very . . .''

"Mature?" she ventured hopefully.

"Mature. The very word I was groping for.''

"All riiiight!"

It was not your typical prom dress. But Nancy loved it. That's why we chose to bury her in it. It wasn't your typical burial dress either, but we thought it was important that she be wearing something she'd picked out herself and had enjoyed. Even if it was slinky and lime-green.

Her graduation ceremony was held on the Lakeside Campus lawn. It was a bright, sunny day. Suzy and David came with us to see Nancy, in her cap and gown, receive her diploma. She looked so pretty and proud. It was a lovely ceremony, a happy, smiling occasion.

When it was over, the kids cried and kissed and vowed to stay in touch. Then we took Nancy out to lunch and gave her one of her graduation presents—a wristwatch.

Her other present was driving lessons, which she took during the three weeks she spent at home before leaving for summer school in Colorado.

Surprisingly, she was a calm, pleasant dream during this stay. She shopped and packed up her belongings with great enthusiasm. Excited about being away from Darlington, she saw this as a fresh start.

"I'm in the real world now, Mom," she told me. "I'm normal. You'll see. I won't let you down this time. You'll be proud of me."

"I know I will, sweetheart."

"Because I'm not a sickie anymore."

I let a ray of sunlight creep in. I wondered if maybe, just maybe, she *was* going to be okay.

Nancy took her six driving lessons but she flunked the test for her license. It made her angry. She took it again a few days later and flunked again. This made her furious. Then she took it a third time and flunked a third time. So she stole my car.

I wasn't home. I had gone to work—with the company car Western Union had given me. My own was in the driveway when Nancy's driving teacher dropped her off after her third attempt at getting a license. She stormed into the house. Suzy told me Nancy screamed, "Goddamned stupid motherfuckers! I'll show them!" Then she grabbed my car keys and split.

She was still gone with my car when I got home. I waited out on the driveway, livid, for her to return.

She waved to me as she drove up. Then she parked the car,

calmly got out, and said, "Hi, Mom! Did you have a nice day?"

"Goddamn it, Nancy! You cannot drive a car without a license! You cannot just . . . just *go off* in somebody's car—*my* car—because you feel like it! You are *not* a certified driver! Do you understand? You have *no* insurance! None! If something had happened to you we'd be in a *lot* of trouble!"

"No use in getting upset about it. Nothing happened. Besides, it's their fault."

"Whose fault?" I demanded.

"Them. They wouldn't give me the license."

God, how frustrating it was to try to deal rationally with someone who wasn't rational! It was also asinine and meaningless. It accomplished nothing. Still, I had to try. I calmed myself down a bit.

"Nancy, you *can't* blame someone else because *you* failed the test. You just have to try to do better next time."

She shrugged. "I didn't hit anything."

"That's not the point! Don't you understand me?"

"Don't talk to me like I'm a sickie! I'm in the real world now!"

"Well then, *act* like it. Living in the real world means you *must* consider the consequences of your actions! You *must* learn the meaning of responsibility!"

"Fuck you."

She went in the house. Two days later she left for college.


Frank and I flew to Denver with her. She was very quiet in the car on the way to the airport. She was clearly tense about going off to college.

I made one attempt to talk to her. I said, "Well, we certainly got a nice day to fly, didn't we?"

"Go fuck yourself," she replied.

She wanted to sit by herself on the plane, in the smoking section. We let her. I passed by her on my way to the lavatory once. She was leafing through a magazine, puffing on a cigarette.

"What are *you* looking at?" she demanded loudly.

The people who were sitting around her looked at her, then at me.

"I'm *not* looking at you. I'm just going to the bathroom."

She glared at me. I kept going. On the way back I looked the other way.

"Steer clear of her. If that's the way she wants it, screw her," Frank said.

We rented a car in Denver and drove to the university in Boulder. It is a gorgeous modern campus in the foothills of the Rockies. Her dormitory was a two-story building. We helped her unload her suitcases and cartons. Her roommate, a Chicano girl, arrived. Nancy was polite and friendly to her but would *not* speak to us. Since the dormitory wouldn't be serving food until the next morning, we offered to take Nancy into town for lunch. She agreed to come. We had Mexican food. She was hostile through the whole meal. Afterward we walked around in Boulder, looked in the shops. She saw a pair of Earth shoes she wanted and asked us to buy them for her. We did. Then she saw a blouse she wanted and asked us to buy it for her. We did. Then she saw a sweater she wanted and asked us to buy it for her. We said no, that was enough. She began to curse at us on the sidewalk.

"Why don't you just leave me the fuck alone? Get the fuck out!" she screamed.

We took her back to the dormitory, said good-bye. We had planned to stay another day and went to Rocky Mountain National Park without her, then drove to Denver and caught our flight back to Philadelphia. I wasn't happy about leaving her like that but it was for the best.

It was a quiet, relaxing six weeks. Suzy and David were in camp; Frank and I spent a lot of time by the pool. We seldom heard from Nancy. When we did, it was positive. She adjusted to her new environment, made friends. She wasn't there long enough for her usual social problems to arise. She took two courses—journalism and marketing. I don't know if she did well in them; I never saw a transcript of that summer's work.

There was a three-week break between the end of the summer session and the beginning of the fall semester. Nancy came home for it. Frank and I picked her up at the airport, and I couldn't believe what I saw when she got off the plane. Nancy had blossomed. Her face was relaxed and tanned. She looked fabulous. She smiled sweetly when she caught sight of us, waved and hugged and kissed both of us.

Frank went to get the car. Nancy and I walked together to a bench in front of the airline terminal and sat down to wait for him. She was wearing jeans and an orange T-shirt with little silver clouds on it. Her beautiful chestnut-brown hair curled around her face, framing it.

She smiled. "You know what, Mom? I'm happy for the first time in my life. Really happy. I'm not a sickie anymore. For sure."

My heart soared. We hugged each other.

I had never been so happy. Nancy was healed! The veil had been lifted! I immediately forgot all about her chronic troubled behavior. Past history was erased. The evidence was there—the look on Nancy's face was enough to convince me she was going to be okay now. I so desperately wanted to believe it that I did. The human mind is pretty amazing that way. In those few moments while we waited for Frank to bring the car, my whole life seemed to turn around. I had waited for sixteen years to see my Nancy find joy in life. That had been my goal. And now, at last, it had been realized. I thought to myself, *No matter the cost, the pain, the sacrifice—it has been worth it.*

Fortunately I could not see into the near future. I was able to enjoy that special moment. It remains one of my most precious memories.

I didn't know at that moment that Nancy was about to get much worse, that her behavior was about to grow more horrifying and insidious with each passing day, that she was about to eat away at the four of us like a malignant growth. Soon we would openly despise Nancy. Can you hate your own child? Sure you can. Yet you still love that child, still hope that someone will step in to set her right. But over the coming year we would finally realize our inability to even come close. Over the coming year, as each door was slammed in our face, our anger and outrage would give way to numbness and despair. Nancy was about to back us deeper and deeper into a nightmarish corner until; beaten down, all feeling and hope gone, we would have but one choice left. We would have to cut that malignancy out.


Things fell apart the instant Nancy got home. Suzy and David had just returned from camp the day before, and David was still very proud of his new wall-unit desk. We'd had a carpenter build it in while he was away. We'd offered Suzy one, too, but she didn't want one. She was happy with her bedroom-set desk. David dragged Nancy upstairs to show it to her. We went with them. She immediately seized on the fact that David had something Suzy didn't have.

"How come *David* got one?" Nancy demanded.

"He has his homework to do," Frank replied. "He needs a proper place to do it."

"But what about Suzy? Doesn't she have homework?"

"Yes," I said. "But she turned us down. She didn't want one."

"I don't believe that shit for a minute. Suzy, get in here!" she called out.

Suzy came in from her room.

"How come you didn't get a desk like David's? Because you're dumb?"

"I didn't want one," Suzy answered. "And I'm not dumb."

"Are," insisted Nancy.

"Am not," countered Suzy.

"Nancy, leave her alone," Frank said. "You're off base."

She ignored him, plowed on. "David got one because he's smart. He got all A's on his report card. You didn't get a single A. That's why you didn't get a desk."

"That's not true!" Suzy cried, upset.

"David's so good and sweet and perfect. You're not!"

"Nancy, stop it!" I ordered.

Suzy began to cry. "He is *not* sweet and perfect." She sniffled.

"*They* think he is," Nancy said.

Suzy turned to me. "You think he's sweet and perfect? He's not. He's *not*. He gets stoned. She turned him on. *She* did it!"

"Shut up!" David cried out, too late.

Suzy clamped a hand over her mouth, eyes wide with horror. Nancy smirked. Frank and I froze. There was an ominous silence.

"Uh-oh," David said.

Suzy turned to David, tears streaming down her face. "I'm sorry." Then she ran out. Her bedroom door slammed.

I finally swallowed, turned to David, and said, "Is that true?"

He put his head down, nodded.

It was a total shocker. Twelve-year-old David, who got good grades and was popular and outgoing, smoked pot. It was so unexpected.

"Nancy," Frank said. "Please leave us alone."

She shrugged, still smirking, and went downstairs. Frank closed the door. He and I sat down on David's bed. Nobody said anything for a minute. Frank and I were too devastated to speak. Here, surely, was the last blow to our family's innocence. I looked at David.

"Don't look at me like that," he said.

"Like what?" I asked.

"Like . . . like I was the last best hope for the Spungen family and now I'm doomed to a life of crime. It doesn't mean anything. Everybody does it. Everybody at school gets stoned. Somebody else would have turned me on if it hadn't been Nancy. Don't blame her."

"You mean most of your friends get stoned?" Frank asked.

"Some of them."

"Suzy and her friends, too?" I asked.

"Suzy and her friends, too," he replied.

"How often do you do it?" Frank asked.

"Just about every day after school. It's fun."

"It's dangerous," Frank said.

"Not if you don't get into anything else. And you don't have to. I won't. I won't be like Nancy."

"What else has Nancy done?" I asked.

"I don't know for sure. Acid, Ludes, THC."

"Suzy?"

"Just pot. Same as me. Nancy won't let us try anything else. She's really kind of protective of us. I asked her if the pills she had were Ludes and she wouldn't let me touch them. Said she'd break my arm if she caught me trying anything other than pot."

"It's against the law," Frank pointed out.

"The law's wrong," David said.

Both Frank and I were too dizzy and confused to say anything more to him. We talked in bed that night. The world, we realized, had certainly changed since we'd been kids. Maybe a total of two kids in my high school had taken drugs, and they were definitely the type that would land in prison someday. This was different. David and his crowd were good students, good kids. Achievers. We didn't get it. We didn't condone it. But we didn't think there was anything we could do about it, so we faced up to it: Suzy and David were recreational marijuana users. All we could do was impress upon them to be responsible—not to ride in a car with someone who was stoned, for instance; not to go on to stronger drugs. Not to be Nancy.

Suzy and David smoked marijuana regularly for several more months. In a way, it was Nancy who stopped them. She got worse, and they reached a point where they no longer wanted to be like her in any way, shape, or form.

Nancy finally passed her driver's license test during her three-week stay at home. She also got friendly with a girl named Linda, who had been Suzy's friend. She sort of stole Linda from Suzy. She and Linda began going in Nancy's room together and closing the door on Suzy. Suzy resented it deeply. "I'm sorry I introduced them," she said, sulking. "Linda was *my* friend."

Now Linda introduced Nancy to a new crowd of friends, and Nancy fit like a glove. They were just like the Lakeside bunch. She would have them up to her room, the whole pale-faced, sour, disreputable bunch of them. They'd close the door and stay in there for an hour, the stereo blaring. Then the door would open—releasing a blast of cigarette smoke—and down the stairs they'd slink. I disliked them intensely, hated having them in the house.

We were delighted when Nancy went back to Colorado for the fall semester.

She was placed in a different dormitory when she returned, and didn't like her new roommate. Her old roommate and the other students she'd been friendly with over the summer were scattered around the campus. There were many more students on campus now, and she seemed less comfortable.

Toward the beginning of October, Frank had to be in Oregon on business. On his way back he stopped in Boulder for the weekend to see Nancy. He got in at about six p.m. on Friday. She seemed to be happy and was doing okay in her classes. Her new dormitory was a high-rise. She warned Frank that her new roommate was an "asshole." Actually, her roommate turned out to be a very nice Jewish girl who was studying pre-med. Frank asked her to join them for dinner, and she did. He called me from his motel that night to say they'd had a very pleasant time.

On Saturday he took Nancy shopping and then joined her at a party she'd been invited to at a student's apartment in Boulder. It was a small party; about eight people were there. Some of them were students. Some of them were "street people"— nonstudents who hang around college towns, using and usually selling drugs. A hash pipe went around at the party. Nancy smoked it. Frank felt very uncomfortable but said nothing. This was what college kids did, he decided, and he shouldn't try to judge them.

Frank was bothered that Nancy seemed to be associating with the street people element, but otherwise he thought she was doing fine. He left on Sunday morning. It had been a pleasant weekend.

The phone calls started soon after he returned.

We were in the midst of planning David's bar mitzvah, which was scheduled for the end of October. Nancy had elected not to come home for it. Since we couldn't afford the plane fare for her to come home both after the summer session break and for David's bar mitzvah, we had given her a choice. She chose to come home after summer school.

Now she phoned and said, "I need to come home."

"You mean for the bar mitzvah?" I asked.

There was a very long pause.

"Huh?"

"Nancy, are you all right?"

There was another long pause.

"Something's . . . wrong."

"What is it?"

"Huh?"

"What's wrong?"

"Uh . . . something."

"Are you on something, sweetheart?"

No answer.

"Nancy?"

Clearly, she *was* on something—something heavy like angel dust or LSD or THC—and wasn't doing well with it.

"Something's *wrong*," she repeated. She sounded scared, like she'd gone off the deep end again. "I need to come home," she said.

"But we made a deal about the bar mitzvah, Nancy."

"Oh."

"Let me talk to Daddy. I'll call you tomorrow. Okay?"

"Huh?"

"I said I'll call you tomorrow, okay? To let you know about coming home."

"I have to go now, Mom."

She hung up. I was very concerned. That night Frank and I discussed her coming home for the bar mitzvah. We thought maybe we would send her a ticket. When I called her the next morning to tell her, she sounded very confused.

"Why would I wanna come home?" she asked.

"You said yesterday you wanted to."

"What for?"

"David's bar mitzvah, I think."

"Nah, I'll send him a present. I saw a really nice turquoise ring. He'll like it."

So Nancy did not come home for the bar mitzvah. These rather strange phone calls continued, each one seemingly isolated from the previous one. She called me several times at work. Once she mentioned a guy she liked—a street person—who didn't like her. Most of the time, though, I was never quite sure why she was calling.

She did not come home for Thanksgiving. Instead she went skiing with friends. It was just as well, since I had to spend the holiday in the hospital for some tests. I hadn't been feeling well. My doctor had initially diagnosed my problem as hypoglycemia and had put me on a special diet, but I hadn't improved.

My condition was then diagnosed as a possible nonmalignant tumor of the pancreas. Exploratory surgery was scheduled for when the surgeon returned from vacation in two weeks. I was discharged from the hospital until that time. I went back to work but felt weak and down. I took the train home from the office instead of driving each day. Frank picked me up at the station on his way home.

On the Friday before the Monday I was scheduled to go in to the hospital, I got off the train to find Frank staring straight ahead in the car, very upset. He gripped the steering wheel so tightly his knuckles were white.

"What's wrong?" I asked. "What happened?"

"I just got a phone call from the Boulder police," he said. "Nancy's been arrested."

"For what?" I gasped.

"Receiving stolen property. Skis. Apparently she got mixed up with a bunch of these street people who were stealing students' skis. They were stashing the skis in her room."

Frank started up the car and we drove home.

"Is she in jail?" I asked.

"The guys are in jail," he went on. "They put her in a county juvenile detention center, since she's only sixteen. We have to get a lawyer for her. I guess I'll have to go out tomorrow and try to clear it up."

"I'm going with you."

"No. You're not up to it. And you have the hospital Monday. Who knows how long I'll be out there."

Suzy and David took the news pretty calmly. They made dinner while Frank and I called our lawyer. He contacted a law firm in Boulder, and a lawyer there went to work on Nancy's case that night. Our lawyer said the man in Boulder would be ready to meet with Frank and fill him in as soon as Frank got in on Saturday morning. Then we called the airlines and got Frank a seat on the earliest flight out.

We didn't sleep that night. We were too tense, too angry at Nancy. *She had been busted.* We were respectable, responsible citizens. We were *not* the kind of people who had their child thrown into a juvenile detention center. Or so we'd thought. But we had been wrong. We *were* that kind of people. Nancy had made it so. She had brought crime into our family.

It was hard—*very* hard—to remember she was ill. She couldn't help herself. She wasn't responsible for her actions. No, that kind of perspective didn't come easy. Self-pity did.

How could she do such a thing to us? Where would it end? How much worse would it get?

Frank got to Boulder on Saturday afternoon. Pending a Monday morning juvenile hearing, Nancy was released from the detention home to Frank's custody. She was the only juvenile involved in the case.

"You *believe* those bastards?" she demanded. "Blaming *me*? I didn't do a thing. They had no right."

"Didn't you suspect anything when those guys wanted to put all those skis in your room?" Frank asked.

"No, why should I?"

Frank checked them into a Sheraton for the weekend. At this point there was nothing they could do but wait. Same with me. I called Janet, Susan, and my mother and told them Nancy had been arrested. They were very supportive, said if we needed anything—including money—to just ask. I took Suzy and David for a drive. And I paced a lot. Now that it looked like Frank wouldn't be back on Monday morning, I made arrangements to get a ride to the hospital.

Nancy's lawyer told them to report to his office on Monday

morning. When they got there, a juvenile officer and the lawyer were conferring. Frank was asked to join them and Nancy was told to wait outside for a few minutes.

Then the juvenile officer informed Frank that Nancy had managed to get herself involved in something very serious—much more serious than the other charge. She had bought drugs from somebody and that somebody was in actuality an undercover federal agent. It was only a small part of a large Boulder drug operation. The investigators had infiltrated it and were almost ready to shut it down—almost, but not quite. They needed about two more months before they'd know who the main dealers were. They were not that interested in Nancy. They felt she was a harmless kid who'd been influenced by her peers. Their undercover operation was the important thing. They didn't want it blown. Frank was informed that if Nancy left school and Boulder immediately the ski theft charge would be held in abeyance for a year and then expunged from her record. In addition there would be no federal warrant issued.

Frank really had no choice. If he didn't accept the deal and take her home, she'd be left subject to prosecution. But Frank couldn't tell her that the real reason for leaving Boulder was the federal drug bust.

They brought Nancy in. The attorney and the juvenile officer informed her that she was being expelled and that she had to leave Boulder immediately to avoid prosecution on the ski theft charges. She blew. She went into a blinding, red-faced rage.

*"You can't do this to me, you fucking goddamned cocksuckers!"* she screamed. *"I didn't do anything wrong! I didn't do anything wrong!"*

As usual, she refused to accept any blame for her actions.

*"You piece of shit! How could you fuck over your own daughter! You bastard! I hate you! God, I hate your fucking guts!"*

A horrible burden had been placed on Frank. He had to be the bad guy. Nancy couldn't know why she was being taken out of school. She hated him for it and never forgave him. He finally told her the truth after the drug operation had been shut

down, but it was too late. Her dream world had been destroyed. As far as she was concerned, Frank had done it.

He got seats on a Tuesday morning flight to Philadelphia
and helped her pack her belongings. She was totally uncoop-
erative. She punished Frank by flatly refusing to speak to
him. I felt Frank's pain deeply when he phoned to tell me
what happened and I wished I could be with him to absorb
some of it. We were stronger when we were together. But he
had to suffer it alone.

I was driven to the hospital that afternoon. For selfish reasons, I wished Nancy hadn't done such a foolish thing so that
Frank could be with me. Suzy and David were left on their
own, too. They made their own dinner that night, did their
homework, and waited for Frank and Nancy's return.

Frank called me at the hospital when they got in on Tuesday afternoon.

"Well, I packed her up and got her here," he said, sound-
ing upset and harassed. "She hasn't said a single goddamned
word to me since the hearing. She's up in her room. I'll be by
as soon as I can."

I decided not to have the surgery. Frank needed me too
much. So did Nancy. With her home under these circumstances, there was no way I could be laid up in the hospital for
several weeks after surgery. I called Frank right back and told
him to come and get me at once. I could hear the relief in his
voice. Then I had my surgeon paged. While I waited for him,
I got out of bed, threw off my hospital gown, and put on my
clothes. When the surgeon came, I told him I was clearing
out. He was furious but I didn't care. Frank and I had to see
this thing through with Nancy together. When Frank got
there, we clung to each other for a long time. Then he picked
up my suitcase and we took off.

I never went back for the surgery. It turned out later that the
diagnosis had been wrong and it wasn't necessary.

She was up in her room sitting on her bed when I got home,
very depressed, surrounded by unpacked cartons and suitcases. I gave her a hug. She didn't return it.

"Tell him to get the fuck out of my room," she said
quietly.

Frank was standing in the doorway. I motioned for him to leave us. He did, clearly hurting inside.

"Why won't you talk to Daddy?" I asked her.

"He's an evil scumbag."

"No, he's not. He loves you."

She said nothing.

"Can't you at least talk to him?"

"Never."

"You can go to school somewhere else, you know. There are other schools besides Colorado."

"There's no point," she said quietly.

"Why not?"

"Because I'm gonna die before I'm twenty-one. I'm gonna go out in a blaze of glory. Like . . . like, *headlines.*"

"What makes you say that?"

"I just am. It's something I know. For sure."

It was no surprise to me that she wanted to die, but her reference to headlines baffled me. I couldn't imagine what she could possibly do to make someone want to put her death in the newspaper.

Nancy's return from Colorado was the turning point of her life. Never again did I see the slightest ray of light. She had genuinely believed she was well enough to function in the real world with regular people—without us, without Darlington. Now she knew she couldn't. Her failure in Colorado meant she had to admit to herself that she wasn't like other people, that she really *was* a sickie. For her, this was the last straw. No more dreams. No more will to live. The episode left her purposeless. It left her with nothing to do or be or believe in. Her only commitment now was to death. She took the fast lane so she could get it over with as soon as possible. It took her four years to fulfill her prophecy.

For us, Nancy's failure in Colorado meant she was back home again, ours. The burden was back on us. I was petrified. How were we going to be able to handle her? She was as bad or worse than before. But what could we do? We couldn't close our home to her, could we? We didn't know what we were going to do, how we were going to cope. All we knew for certain was that she would take control of the house again—at a time when Suzy and David were coming of age, in need of room to grow, to be free of her influence, to have friends, to have a life. Was there any hope? Any alternative? The only thought that occurred to us was to try hospitalizing her with Dr. Cott, now that she was free of Darlington. But she would never stand for it. The mere mention of his name sent her into a rage. We would have to physically drag her there, incarcerate her.

We didn't know what we were going to do.

She sat on her bed all afternoon that first day she came home. She wouldn't unpack. It was as if unpacking were an admission that she was really home. She didn't come down for dinner. That evening she unpacked her stereo and put a record on. Then she dressed up in one of her ski outfits and came down the stairs to model it. She wore red, iridescent skin-tight ski pants with a matching sweater, yellow ski boots, and yellow mirrored sunglasses. She seemed very proud of the outfit. She posed and smiled so David could take her picture. Then she went back in her room, piled all of her ski clothes and boots together and dropped them over the bannister to the floor of the entry hall. They landed with a thud.

"Nancy!" I called up the stairs. "What do you want me to do with all of this?"

"Get rid of it!" She slammed her bedroom door.

She never mentioned skiing again. It was as if she had never skied. She never mentioned Colorado, either. As far as she was concerned, it didn't exist.

She didn't do any more unpacking the next morning, just sat there on her bed, head down. I stayed home from work to be with her.

"Do you want me to help you unpack, sweetheart?" I asked her.

"I wanna die."

I noticed that her right hand was closed, as if she were clutching something.

"I'm gonna do it now," she said.

She opened her hand. She had some Valium my doctor had given me, about eight of them.

"You're wasting your time," I said. "Those won't kill you. You can't OD on Valium."

"I can't?"

"No." I held my hand out. "Give them to me."

She did. I flushed them down the toilet. She stretched out and stared at the ceiling, morose. I sat on the edge of the bed.

"Nancy, have you thought about what you want to do now that you're home?"

"Yeah, I wanna—"

"Besides die."

"No."

"You don't want to go back to school?"

"No."

"How about working? What would you think about getting a job?"

"Okay." She shrugged.

*"Okay?"* I asked, surprised.

"May as well make some money." She sighed. "I don't care."

That afternoon I loaned her my car, a four-year-old Volvo, and she made the rounds of the nearby malls. She found a part-time job at a clothing store, starting the next day, which we thought was a step in the right direction. That night Linda and a couple of the boys from the neighborhood came over and sat in her room with her with the door closed. We thought that *wasn't* a step in the right direction, but we had to allow her some freedom.

She had to use my car to get to her job. I wasn't too crazy about that idea, but I wasn't using it during the day—I took the train to work. So we let her have it. She worked on Friday and Saturday afternoons. On Saturday night she asked us if she could use the car to go out for a pizza with Linda and two boys. One of the boys was named Stephen. He was a musician. I don't remember the other's name.

We had some qualms, but we said okay. After all, we couldn't lock her in her room. We reminded her that she had to be home by midnight as a condition of her Pennsylvania junior driver's license. In the commonwealth of Pennsylvania, sixteen-to-eighteen-year-olds are not allowed to drive past midnight. She promised to be home by twelve.

The phone woke me at two a.m. It was a Philadelphia policeman. Nancy had wrecked the car on her way home from a downtown rock club. She had never gone to the local pizza parlor. She'd driven off the side of an expressway ramp, rolled three times down a twenty-foot embankment, and landed upright on the road below. Miraculously, no one had been seriously hurt.

Nancy was being held at a police station in Philadelphia. She was apparently under arrest, though the policeman was vague as to what the charges were—beyond driving after midnight. She had been tested for drunk driving; she was not drunk. The test revealed a .03 alcohol level in her blood, equal to about half a glass of beer and well below the level that constitutes drunk driving, which is .10. No drugs were found in her system.

She got on the phone.

"Are you okay?" I asked.

"Of course I'm okay," she replied angrily. "The cop's a liar. I just bent the fender is all. A fucking bent fender. Get me out of this hellhole, will ya?"

The policeman got back on. He said that because Nancy was a minor, she would have to be processed by the Philadelphia Juvenile Aid Division. Since we were not residents of Philadelphia County, she could not be released into our custody without the presence of a juvenile aid officer. It was a Saturday night. The officers were swamped with arrests. None were available.

As a result, Nancy was held in a cell until six a.m., when she was transferred by paddy wagon to the Youth Study Center, Philadelphia's juvenile detention center.

We waited there in the parking lot with our lawyer for the paddy wagon, not having slept a wink since getting the phone call. It had been some week: Nancy had been arrested twice and had destroyed our car. I wondered if I had a breaking point, or if I would just keep bending. At that moment I didn't think I could take too much more. There was no more emotion left in either of us. We were burned out, defeated.

"What's going to be next?" I asked Frank.

"I really don't know," he replied. "You imagine the worst . . . the *worst* . . . and it happens. Sure enough, it *happens.*"

The paddy wagon pulled into the driveway. A policeman hopped out and opened the back doors to reveal Nancy handcuffed to a bench. She wore a rabbit fur jacket, satin skirt, and platform heels. As the policeman unlocked her cuffs, she blinked at the sunlight. She looked pale and frightened; she was shivering and she had a bruise on her forehead. Getting out, Nancy teetered a bit on her high heels until she got her balance.

The policeman laughed. "Look how looped she is, Sal," he said to his partner, who joined in the laughter.

"Has she been checked by a doctor?" I asked the policeman.

"What for? She's fine," he replied.

"I'm cold," my daughter told me. "They made me lay on the floor in a cell."

He took her inside and we followed. At that time the Youth Study Center was a genuine inner-city house of horror—dingy, overcrowded, understaffed. Kids were reportedly sleeping on bare mattresses in the corridor.

There was an informal hearing with a juvenile aid officer, who informed us that Nancy was being held for reckless driving and driving after midnight on a junior license. Since we lived in a different county, he would not release her to us. She would have to stay at the center until a preliminary hearing, which wouldn't be held for several days.

"Isn't there any other course we can take?" our lawyer inquired.

"Just one," the officer replied. "You can have her committed. Put her in a mental hospital or leave her here. It's up to you."

It was quite a choice.

We chose to commit her.

# ◻ Chapter 13

In my heart, I guess I was still looking for an answer. There had to be a way of helping Nancy, a magic pill. There had to be an end to all of this pain. Nancy seemed totally out of control, dangerous to herself and others. We were afraid of what she would do next if she wasn't stopped.

Nancy didn't take the news of her commitment to a hospital well, but she was so shaken and exhausted at that point that she didn't fight it.

There was still the problem of finding a bed for her in a mental hospital. I phoned Mallory Brooke at Darlington. She concurred with our decision and gave me a list of a few possibilities. Then she wished me luck.

The first hospital I called took teenagers but didn't have a bed available, not even for an emergency. They referred me to a nearby state hospital, which had a ten-day evaluation program. I spoke to them and they agreed to admit her for evaluation. At the end of ten days they would make a determination as to how to proceed.

The juvenile aid officer was satisfied with this and released

Nancy into our custody. He said we would receive a summons for a hearing in about a month.

Nancy dozed in the car on the way to the hospital. Our route happened to take us past the wreck of the Volvo, which sat—totaled—by the side of the road. She woke up when Frank and I gasped at the extent of the damage.

"It can be fixed" was all she said.

We spent several hours at the hospital. Nancy was examined individually by a psychiatrist, then slept on a couch while Frank and I were interviewed by a team of doctors and psychiatrists. Then they asked us to wait while they discussed Nancy's case. We sat on a sofa across from Nancy and I watched her sleep. Her hair was spread wildly over her face; her makeup was smeared. Her satin skirt was torn and had dried blood on it. But still, asleep, she looked like my little Nancy, my baby.

The psychiatrist joined us. He spoke softly so he wouldn't wake Nancy up. "We're against admitting her for the ten-day examination. I'm sorry to drag you over here and put you through all of this, but it's our feeling that Nancy has simply had herself a real bad week. She's upset, exhausted. Take her home. Love her."

"What the hell are you talking about?" I demanded.

He smiled. "She's fine."

"No, she *isn't* fine," I argued. "She is a lot of things. She is disturbed, troubled, unhappy, in pain, miserable. She is *not* fine!"

"Uh, Mrs. Spungen—!"

"Don't tell me she's fine!"

He looked at Frank uncomfortably. "We can't keep her here."

We had to place Nancy somewhere. That was the condition of her release.

Suburban Psychiatric Center was the last name on the list Brooke had given me, so I phoned. They had a bed and were willing to evaluate her, possibly admit her. We woke Nancy up and drove over there. She was still very groggy and didn't fight us.

Suburban Psychiatric was a large, new private hospital.

Again, a team of doctors and psychiatrists spoke to us and to Nancy. Then we waited for their verdict. This time Nancy was awake and eating a candy bar.

The doctor who sat with us was young and casually dressed. "We think Nancy should be here," he said. "We'd like to admit her."

Nancy's response was the most shockingly violent I'd ever seen. She hurled her candy bar at the wall and began to scream. She went berserk with rage—all of it directed at me. It spilled out in a nonstop torrent like the verbal tantrums she had had when she was two.

*"You motherfucking bitch cunt shithead evil motherfucking bitch cunt! You'll die for this! You'll die!"*

"Now, there's no reason to get upset, Nancy," the doctor said calmly. She ignored him.

*"I'll have you killed! I'm not staying here! I'll leave! I'll have you killed. You wanna know how I'll have you killed, bitch cuntface? I'll have them tear your fucking head off and gouge out your fucking eyeballs with a fucking icepick and tear off your fucking arms and break off every finger . . . and you fucking cunt you can't lock me up here—"*

"Now, there's *no* reason to get upset," the doctor repeated, a little less calmly. People had stopped what they were doing all over the hospital, and watched.

*"I'm not gonna stay! I'll kill you myself! With my bare fucking hands! You know how I'll do it? I'll stick a knife up your motherfucking cunt and rip you wide open!"*

I covered my ears with my hands, horrified. I couldn't listen anymore.

*"That's how I'll do it! I'll cut your cunt and you'll die! Die! Die like an evil shithead motherfucking cunt!"*

She was sobbing now, her voice hoarse from yelling.

"Perhaps," the doctor said to me, "you and your husband should wait in my office."

We did. It was down the hall. Though we closed the door, we could still hear her screams and curses.

*". . . gouge out your fucking eyeballs you fucking cunt!"*

I sagged against Frank, my insides melting. My child hated me with such a vengeance. Such venom and ugliness came out of her mouth. I had seen and heard her rages before, but never like this. Never. It broke my heart. All I was trying to do was save her. I loved her. I was doing whatever I could.

I guess they led her away. Her screaming faded and mercifully died out.

"I don't care what happens," I said weakly to Frank. "I'm never going through this kind of scene again. Ever."

He nodded, dazed.

If the law interceded and had her forcibly committed, fine. But we were agreed: we wouldn't try it again on our own. We couldn't. This door was too horrible to go through. We closed it.

The doctor came in a moment later.

"Don't be concerned," he said. "We'll take care of her. We can help her. I'll call you."

We went home. It was a Sunday. Suzy and David had been home alone all day. They had made dinner and were waiting for us. We explained everything that had happened. They were upset and saddened.

"Do you think she'll ever come home again?" Suzy asked.

"She can't stay at the hospital for more than a month," Frank said. "Our insurance will run out. So I guess she will. Yes."

And then what? I couldn't look ahead. Ahead I saw nothing but pain. I saw a life of trying to get through each day, one at a time. I saw no other priority besides surviving. No hope. No optimism. Ahead, I saw no kind of life. How could we live with this child in our home?

I crawled into bed and slept fitfully. I was still weak and tired in the morning, when the psychiatrist called.

"She's calmed down quite a bit," he assured me. "I'm about to have another talk with her. I suggest you not see her for a few days."

We set up an appointment with him for Friday afternoon, by which time he hoped to be ready to discuss Nancy's condition in depth. After the appointment we'd be able to see her.

I phoned the clothing store and told the owner that Nancy would not be coming back to work.

Nancy still hadn't unpacked. One night later that week I

decided I'd do it for her. Somehow I thought it would make
the transition easier for her. I opened the cartons and suitcases
and began to remove the contents.

There were books—her textbooks in English, psychology,
and marketing, and a frayed paperback copy of Hunter
Thompson's *Fear and Loathing in Las Vegas*. Tucked into
the paperback was a small bundle of notes the other students
on her dorm floor had left her when they heard she'd been
expelled. I glanced at them. They were nice notes. One of
them said, "You're too smart to fuck up. Get it together and
come on back." There were cosmetics and some bottles of
shampoo, several pairs of jeans, some longjohns, turtleneck
sweaters, hiking boots. There was a workshirt. When I unfolded it, several syringes, a rubber catheter, and some
spoons spilled out onto the bed.

I stared at them for a second. Then I screamed.

Frank came running. He stood there next to me, staring at
the drug paraphernalia. It looked so ugly and evil, its presence
seemed to refute everything we stood for. I was numb with
horror. I could barely breathe.

"So now we know," he said softly.

My Nancy. An addict. Sticking needles in herself. I shuddered as we continued to stare—neither of us could take our
eyes off it.

"What . . . what should we do?" I asked hoarsely.

"I don't know. We've got the meeting at Suburban Psychiatric on Friday. We'll bring it with us and talk to them about
it."

"Okay. But what should we do with . . . it until then?"

"Wrap it in a towel. Stick it somewhere. Somewhere we
don't have to look at it."

I wrapped it up, searched for a place to put it. No such
place existed. I tried every nook and cranny in every room. I
ended up putting it in the garage.

We went to our meeting at Suburban Psychiatric that Friday. I had the syringes in my purse. We met with the young
psychiatrist in his office, along with another doctor. The psychiatrist immediately told us that he was discharging Nancy
the next day.

"Why?" Frank asked, shocked.

"There's no point in keeping her here." The psychiatrist stopped, made an effort to be as tactful as possible. "You see, you only have thirty days on your insurance. There's no way we can make any impact on Nancy's condition in one month. She's too sick. This is a longstanding problem. I'm afraid you waited too long to get her help."

Waited too long! I was aghast, outraged. My face got very hot. I couldn't speak.

Frank finally spoke up. "If . . . she's, as I understand it, too sick to be treated, then how can she come home?"

"Good question, Mr. Spungen. But I think we've got a solution for that. Nancy's agreed to sign what we call a behavioral contract. We'll go over all of the things you want her to do as part of your household. We'll draw it up together. Nancy will sign it and abide by it."

"Are you kidding?" I demanded, incredulous.

"Far from it. We've had great success with this technique. It helps the patient understand her responsibilities and obligations."

"A piece of paper won't matter to this girl!" Frank snapped angrily.

"But she's agreed to sign it," the psychiatrist countered. "That's an important step. We'll just have to try to work with her as an outpatient. It would be futile to attempt treatment here in thirty days—unless, of course, her present condition were drug-predicated."

"Wait!" I cried out. "It is!"

I opened my purse, pulled out the syringes, and dumped them on his desk. He looked at them, turned to the other doctor. "This makes a difference."

The other doctor nodded.

The psychiatrist turned to us. "Let's call Nancy in and confront her."

Nancy was brought in. She looked at us blankly when she saw us. Her facial expression didn't change when the psychiatrist pointed to the drug paraphernalia and asked her about it.

"Where'd you find that?" she asked, her voice flat.

"Your mother found it," the psychiatrist replied.

She sneered to me. "So you went through my stuff, huh?"

"No," I said. "I was unpacking for you."

"Well, it's not mine," she told the doctor. "I was just keeping it for a friend."

The doctor questioned her further but Nancy had all the right answers. Frank and I knew she was lying, but the psychiatrist bought her story, didn't pursue it further. He wanted to believe it. Whether she was using drugs or not, he knew there was no way he could help her. He wanted to free her bed for someone he *could* help. There was no point in fighting him any further. His mind was made up.

"In that case," he said when he was satisfied, "let's gather around this table and draw up our contract."

We all sat around the table. He pulled out a pen and legal-size pad.

"Now, Mr. and Mrs. Spungen. The idea is for you to bring up what you would like Nancy to do. Nancy, if you agree to do it, we'll put it in the contract. Then both parties will sign it, just like a regular contract. If you violate it, Nancy, you'll get demerits, which means you'll be punished. Understand?"

Nancy nodded. She thought this whole thing was a joke. It was. I knew Nancy would agree to do anything at this point, and then do whatever she wanted once she got home. But we went ahead and drew up the ridiculous contract anyway. It was an option we couldn't afford not to try, since we had so few. Besides, I thought it wouldn't hurt to at least verbalize how we wanted her to behave.

BEHAVIORAL CONTRACT BETWEEN NANCY SPUNGEN AND MR. AND MRS. FRANKLIN A. SPUNGEN

1) I will keep my room neat.
2) I will not curse at my parents.
3) I will not curse at my sister and brother.
4) I am not permitted to drive until authorized by my parents.
5) When I have been authorized, I will not take the car without permission.
6) I will look for a job.
7) I will go regularly to therapy.

8) I will do my share around the house.

9) I will obey my 12:00 a.m. curfew.

We signed the contract. The psychiatrist dated and witnessed it, then folded it, put it into an envelope, and gave it to us, with the name of a recommended therapist for Nancy. He smiled and wished us the best of luck. He felt he'd discharged his responsibilities.

It was too late in the day for Nancy to be checked out. She had to spend one more night at the hospital. We agreed to pick her up in the morning.

On the way home we passed a darkened, deserted commuter railroad station.

"Pull in there for a second," I ordered Frank.

"What for?"

I pulled the towel with the syringes in it out of my purse. "I don't want this stuff in my house anymore."

Frank nodded, pulled into the station. We looked around carefully. There were no people in sight. I felt like we were about to commit a crime.

"Turn off the lights," I said.

Frank switched off the headlights. I jumped out of the car, dashed to a trash bin on the outdoor platform, threw the towel into it, and ran back to the car.

"Go," I commanded as I hopped in.

We sped off, lights still out. We didn't turn them on until we were half a mile away.

Nancy came home the next morning. By noon she had twenty-seven demerits.

"Fuck your demerits," she snarled.

"That's twenty-eight, Nancy," I pointed out. "This calls for disciplinary action. You agreed to abide by the rules of the contract."

"Fuck your contract. I just signed it to get out of that fucking hospital."

Frank and I decided then and there that the contract wasn't going to fly. We stopped keeping track of demerits.

It was a Saturday. Nancy called Linda but her parents wouldn't allow Linda to see her—they were suing us.

Our insurance company eventually settled out of court for ten thousand dollars, then dropped us. It wasn't easy for us to get insured again, and it was very expensive.

So Nancy stayed in her room alone that first day playing records. When she came downstairs to join us for dinner, she was surly and unpleasant. She still would not speak to Frank—did not, in fact, say one word to him for over a year. She spoke around him. At dinner, for example, she said to David, "Tell him to pass me the potatoes." This became a standard means of address. The word *Daddy* was no longer part of her vocabulary.

I was afraid of her. The pure hate for me that had spewed out of her when we'd committed her could surface at any time, I felt. I was nervous, particularly at night. I couldn't sleep that first night. I just lay there in bed, from where I could see the crack of light under her door. Once she opened the door and went downstairs. My heart began to pound out of fear—I remembered the time I'd found her collecting knives in the middle of the night. I lay there tensely, heart pounding, afraid to breathe, afraid to move. It was as if I'd awakened to hear a prowler in the house. I heard the refrigerator door open and close, then cupboards. I heard her coming back up the steps. Then she appeared in her doorway, clutching a bag of pretzels and a glass of cola. She went into her room and closed the door. I relaxed, but not enough to be able to sleep very well.

I had made an appointment for Nancy to see the new therapist on Monday morning. Frank and I took off half-days so we could go with her. An hour before we were to go, she went out the front door and didn't come back. We went without her.

The therapist was a young, idealistic behaviorist. This constituted a new wrinkle. We had been through Freudian therapy and family therapy, but not behavioral. He mapped out a new strategy for handling Nancy, one emphasizing behavior modification through positive reinforcement.

"Now, give me an idea of something you want her to do,"
he said.

"Get a job," I replied.

"Okay. What you do is suggest she go through the classifieds and circle three jobs she's interested in. Tell her that
when she does it, you'll give her a dollar. That's the positive
reinforcement. When she gets a job, buy her something she'd
like. A record or a blouse. What you're doing is reinforcing
compliance."

"Isn't that sort of like housebreaking a dog?" Frank asked.

The therapist laughed. "It works. But you're going to have
to modify some of your behavior, too. For one thing, you
must never argue with her."

"How do we do that?" I asked.

"It takes two to argue. If you want Nancy to do something,
say to her 'Nancy, this is what you're going to do . . .' State
it to her as fact. If she argues, walk away."

"What if she follows?" I asked.

"If the situation gets undesirable, say 'Time out' and explain to her why it is undesirable. If you're angry, tell her
you're not mad at her but at what she's doing. Don't lecture.
Don't yell. Simply say 'You must not do this . . .' Don't
quarrel between yourselves. Be calm, be consistent. If you
two disagree, don't let her know that. Present a united front,
then discuss your differences later."

It sounded positive. It sounded like something to do. He
gave us a book called *Families* by Gerald R. Patterson and
scheduled us for a once-weekly session. He suggested we
come without her. He said he would help us learn new and
better responses.

Nancy still wasn't back when we got home from work
that evening. She finally got in at about seven. Frank and I
were in the den and Suzy and David were doing their homework.

"Nancy, you missed an appointment with your therapist
this morning," I said calmly. "That was wrong. I'm angry.
I'm not angry at you, but I am angry at your behavior."

"Who cares?" she said and went upstairs.

"I've got to admit," said Frank, "there *is* less arguing this way."

We tried the behavioral approach to controlling Nancy. She circled three jobs in the classifieds the next morning. I gave her a dollar. She was happy to take the dollar. When she cursed at me for suggesting she call about the three jobs, I ignored it. I told her I was angry. I told her I didn't like it. When she responded by hurling a napkin holder against the kitchen wall, breaking it into numerous pieces, I didn't get angry. I simply said "You must clean that up." When she refused, I told her I didn't like her behavior, and, because of that, she could not go over to Linda's house that night. (Linda's parents had relented and she was now allowed to see Nancy.) When she responded by climbing out her bedroom window after dinner and not coming home from Linda's until four a.m., I took several deep breaths, told her in a calm voice that I was angry at what she had done, and said she was grounded for two weeks.

"Keep it up," the therapist encouraged us at our second session. "Just remember—you don't have to explain yourself. When she starts in on 'Why,' don't mix it up with her. Just repeat yourself and start walking. It's your house. You are the law. She has to understand that."

She responded to her two-week grounding by lifting my car keys from my purse and stealing my car while Frank and I were at a hockey game. It was impossible to be calm. We took Frank's car and drove around the neighborhood. The car wasn't at Linda's or Stephen's or the houses of any of the other members of the crowd. Frank wanted to call the police. We called our lawyer first. He told us not to.

"You'll have to press charges against her, and you don't want to do that," he said. "Wait it out. She'll be back tomorrow."

She wasn't back in the morning. We went to work. I phoned the house in the afternoon. David was there but Nancy was not, he said. She finally got home at dinnertime. I went in my room for a minute so I wouldn't blow up at her—actually, what I really wanted to do was punch her in the

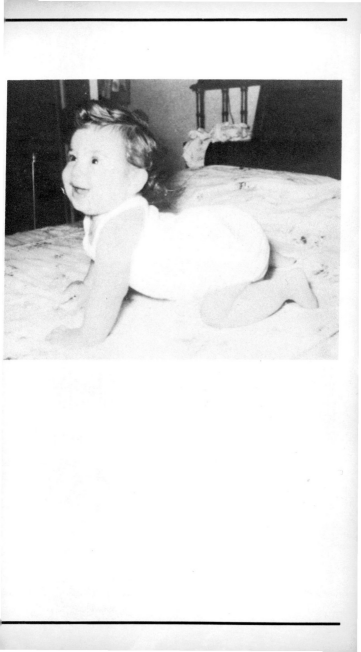

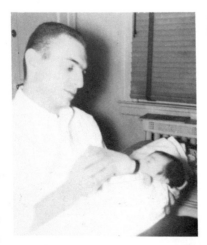

*Frank and Nancy,
two weeks old.*

*Nancy, fourteen months.*

*ABOVE: Nancy dressing up for Halloween, her favorite holiday.*

*BELOW: Nancy, age six, had a fit over this picture. She thought she looked ugly and insisted the photo be reshot.*

*RIGHT: Frank and David.*

*Age 10½.*
*School photo.*

*Age 11½. "The Look."*
*Nancy left school—*
*7th grade—several days*
*after this was taken. She*
*never went back to public*
*school.*

*Nancy, age 14. Sent to the family after her funeral by a classmate of Nancy's at Lakeside Campus. The note said this is the way he remembered Nancy, not the way the newspapers described her.*

*Susie, Deborah, Nancy and David outside the health food store. Nancy is 15.*

*Nancy, age 16, and Deborah on graduation day.*

*Nancy, age 16, after she returned from Colorado. She wore the outfit once and then threw it away.*

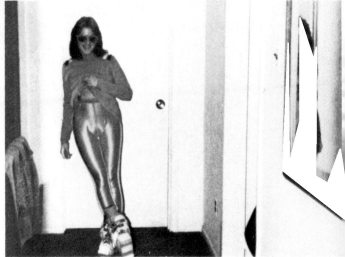

*Age 17 in St. Thomas. Nancy's favorite photo of herself, she carried it with her until her death.*

*The Spungens— David, Susie, Deborah and Frank (left to right).*

face—and then I took the behavioral approach. Frank stood by, chewing on his lower lip.

"Nancy, you had no right to take my keys from me and take the car," I said, calmly but firmly.

"I went for a drive," she snapped. "So what?"

The doctor had said not to explain myself.

"You're not to do it," I said.

"And what if I do?"

"Ever again," Frank commanded.

"I'll do what I please. It's my fucking house, too." She went up to her room, slammed the door, and turned her stereo on full blast. She began to throw stuff around the room and bang on the floor, just to let us know it was her house, too.

"I'm going to take the distributor cap off your car," Frank said. "She might have copied your keys."

So we kept the distributor cap off the car whenever we went out.

When we met with the therapist that week, we told him what had happened. He was pleased with the way we'd handled the situation.

"But it didn't do any good," Frank protested.

"You can't ask for overnight results, Mr. Spungen. It takes time. Be firm. Be consistent. Don't give in to her demands. Ignore her threats. You'll see, she'll come around."

Frank was skeptical. So was I. But we kept at it. That Saturday, when Nancy wanted the car, we said no.

"If you don't let me have the car," she threatened, "I'm going to take my fists and put them through a window."

"I'm sorry you feel that way, Nancy," I said. "And I understand that you're upset."

"Then I can have the car?"

"No, you cannot."

"You'll be sorry!" she cried.

She ran upstairs. A door slammed. Then there was a tremendous smash of broken glass and a scream. Frank and I ran up the stairs.

Nancy was in the bathroom. She'd followed through on her threat. She'd rammed both hands through the bathroom window and, since it was winter, the second storm window too. There was blood and broken glass everywhere.

"See what you made me do?" she screamed, holding out her bloodied hands, one finger nearly severed. "See what I had to do?"

Fine. We had done what we were told. We had called her bluff. Look where it got us. Clearly, she was *not* responding to this kind of treatment. Clearly, she was *not* controllable.

What were we going to do with her?

We took her to the hospital. A doctor in the emergency room stitched her up. He said she'd severed the tendon of the dangling finger, which meant she'd have to see a hand surgeon. I took her on Monday. He fitted her with a splint and said she'd need to wear it for two weeks. Surgery might be required if the splint didn't do the trick.

"I want surgery now!" she demanded.

"It might not be necessary. It might heal itself," he explained.

She began to scream and call him vile names. He began to scream and call her vile names. She stormed out. He refused to see her again. As it happened, she didn't wear the splint and it did heal.

Frank and I related the entire incident to the therapist that week. His eyes widened in shock and horror.

"I didn't realize she was this disturbed," he said. "She's much more disturbed than I thought. I don't know what she'll do to herself—or to someone else—if we continue on this path."

"You mean you don't think it's going to work?" Frank asked.

"I can't see you anymore," he said. "I'm sorry. I can't help you."

Another door slammed in our face—the last door. This was the last time we sought therapy or professional help for Nancy. We had tried every known form and failed. We had tried committing her and failed. No one would keep her. We had run the gamut, exhausted every possibility. She was our problem, our responsibility. No one else existed who could help us.

We were alone.


Nancy still had her juvenile hearing to face in Philadelphia. The subpoena arrived about a month after the accident. Nancy and I went with our lawyer. The hearing took place in a crowded, open courtroom. I had hoped, perhaps foolishly, for help from the court—possibly some kind of intervention or supervision. Some magic.

This was not to be. The judge, an older man with white hair, lit into *me* with a fifteen-minute tirade about rich suburban parents who gave their children cars of their own and allowed them to do what they pleased, without discipline or supervision.

"What kind of mother are you!" he demanded. "How dare you give your daughter a car and let her drink and stay out until all hours! It's *your* fault! *You* caused this accident!"

Who was he to sit in judgment of me? He was insensitive and uncaring. I got angry. Nancy, however, got *furious*. She tried to protect me.

"Stop yelling at my mom!" she shouted.

"Nancy, keep quiet," our lawyer hissed.

"You have no fucking right to yell at my mom!" she screamed. "Leave my mom alone!"

"Nancy, ssh," he repeated, literally clamping his hand over her mouth.

The judge abruptly stopped his tirade.

"Not guilty," he said. "Next case."

We were momentarily stunned. Then we got out of there as quickly as possible.

"The facts just weren't there," our lawyer explained in the corridor. "They had nothing on her."

"I'll kill that motherfucker with my bare hands," steamed Nancy. "He had no right to treat you that way, Mom. I'm real sorry."

I think it was the first time—the only time—Nancy was

made to realize that we had to take the brunt of the consequences for her actions.

"I'm just real sorry," she repeated. "I don't *believe* that
motherfucker. Don't worry, he'll die for this! I'll get somebody to kill him."

At that moment we bumped into a man I knew through
Western Union. He was an officer of the traffic court, and I
had helped him set up a Mailgram billing system for parking
tickets. When he saw how upset Nancy was, he invited us into
his office, gave us coffee, and stayed with us until Nancy
calmed down. He was very kind.

Nancy never forgot his kindness. Three years later he was
being tried for accepting bribes. He asked me to be a character
witness, and I agreed to. I mentioned it to Nancy over the
phone. She was in New York with Sid. She immediately
wanted to rush to the defense of this man who had been so
nice to her.

"Hey, if he wants me to be a character witness, I'll be
happy to go."

I pictured her getting on the witness stand with her wild
white hair, punk clothes, heroin track marks, and sickly,
translucent skin. This was not exactly the sort of character
witness he needed.

"I'll tell him, Nancy, but I don't think it'll be necessary."

"Whatever it takes. I wanna help."

"I'm sure he'll appreciate it."

I've never forgotten Nancy's readiness to help someone
who had once helped her. I've never forgotten that phone conversation. It was our last. She was dead four days later.

# ◻ Chapter 14

We didn't need a therapist to tell us that Nancy was going to have to find something to do with herself.

She got very upset when I suggested she go back to school somewhere.

"I won't!" she screamed. "You can't make me!"

"It's only a suggestion, Nancy."

"I won't go! I just won't!" She ran into her room and slammed the door.

That was the last time college was mentioned as a possibility.

A job, then. We were determined she find work—so she would have not only money but some element of structure in her life. She was amenable to the idea. She wanted to have some money. She was qualified to be a salesclerk or a typist. Every morning she scanned the classifieds for jobs. Her geographical options were pretty limited—she was isolated in the suburbs and she wasn't allowed to drive. Her best option was to find something in Philadelphia, which was accessible by commuter train. She made phone calls, but nothing panned out. It was January. The Christmas rush was over. Stores weren't hiring.

One morning when I was going to work I saw a HELP WANTED sign in the window of the dress shop that was downstairs in my building. Nancy rode into town with me the next morning, applied for the job, and got it. She began the next day as a salesgirl. The store was small and sold fashionable, youthful women's clothes. Nancy was excited about the job. She liked the girl she worked with, whose name was Randi. Randi introduced her to another girl, Karen, who worked at the store's other branch a few blocks away. The three of them had lunch together on Nancy's second day.

"Everything's working out," Nancy enthused when she got home that night.

The manager of the store called early the next morning when Nancy was still in bed. I woke her up so she could take the call. Nancy spoke to the woman for a moment, hung up, and went back to sleep. I roused her a while later.

"You'd better get moving, sweetheart. Time to go to work."

She said something into her pillow.

"What'd you say?" I asked.

She turned over, glared at the ceiling. "I don't have a job. She fired me."

"Why?" I cried.

"No reason at all."

"I'm sorry, sweetheart. We'll find you another job."

"What's the point? I'll just get fired again."

I wondered why she had lost the job, but it wasn't my place to intervene and find out. I never did learn the reason.

Nancy rolled over and went back to sleep. She was very discouraged about losing the job. It confirmed her negative self-image. In response, she closed this option off, just as she had school. She refused to look for another job.

She was only interested in two things from this point on—music and drugs. The harder the better.

She'd sleep all day, get up at about the time Suzy and David were coming home from school. After a cigarette and a cup of coffee she'd go up to her room and put a record on—

she was big on Lou Reed now—and make plans on the telephone.

If it was a weeknight she'd usually stay home in her room listening to music, reading, and smoking. Sometimes she went over to see Don and Carol, an unmarried couple in their twenties whom she'd gotten friendly with. She often stayed out all night. She was no longer friendly with Linda and the neighborhood kids.

If it was a weekend, she'd take the train into Philadelphia and meet up with the two girls she had gotten to know at the dress shop, Randi and Karen. The store closed at six. The three of them would go to Randi's apartment (Randi and Karen were older than Nancy, in their early twenties) and fix up their appearances.

Nancy's overall look was beginning to change from flower child to street tough. The workshirts gave way to tight black T-shirts. The patched and faded denim flares yielded to very tight new straight-legged jeans. She wore platform heels, the higher the better. At 5 feet 1 inch, she thought she was too short. She also began to wear a lot of eye makeup and plucked her eyebrows. Her lovely, full chestnut-brown hair was cut to shoulder-length shag and streaked blonde.

The three of them would go to *the* rock club, which in those days was a place called the Hive. It was their hangout. They would drink Black Russians—Nancy easily looked as old as the other girls and had no trouble getting served—and meet guys. When the Hive closed at two a.m., they'd move on to an after-hours club called High Society. It had a dance floor. They'd stay there until about five or six, and Nancy would come home on a morning train. She'd see the guys she met at these places one or two times—never longer. Always, there were drugs. The neighborhood kids, I later learned, were mostly smokers—marijuana and hashish—and LSD users. With her new friends, Quaaludes were the big drug. Karen didn't like to smoke, she recently told me. But what was enough for the other kids wasn't enough for Nancy. She had to get higher. According to Karen, Nancy began to shoot speed when it was available. Karen tried to talk her out of it—

she was afraid Nancy would kill herself. That argument, of course, held no water with Nancy. She *wanted* to kill herself.

"She was always reaching for something that wasn't there," Karen told me recently. "She needed for some guy to come along and set her straight, some nice guy. She'd do whatever a guy told her to."

Years later Suzy told me that one afternoon when she came home from school Nancy called her into the bathroom. She was shooting up. She ordered Suzy to tie her off with the hose. Suzy, always the dutiful sister, did. Then she watched in horror as Nancy repeatedly punched at herself with the needle until she found a vein.

Years later David told me he answered the phone one Saturday morning. It was Randi. She advised him to check Nancy's room to make sure she was still alive.

"She took ten Ludes last night," Randi said. "She took enough to kill a horse."

David checked. Nancy was fast asleep. He tried rousing her, and, after a moment, was able to get her awake—mumbling and cussing, one eye open. She was alive.

We didn't know this sort of thing was going on at the time. Suzy and David didn't tell us. They were afraid of incurring Nancy's wrath. They were also trying to protect us, I think. We did figure Nancy was getting stoned. We did know her neighborhood friends were troublemakers. But we had no idea how seriously drug-involved she was, or that Suzy and David were being forced to witness her exploits. Had we known at the time what was going on, I suspect we would have sent Suzy and David away from Nancy to boarding school. It would have meant depriving them of a family life, but it would have been our only choice. We couldn't do a thing with Nancy.

Where was she getting money for drugs? She stole some more of my jewelry. I was forced to begin to keep it locked up. Then she intercepted a $300 refund check from the University of Colorado, forged our signatures on it, and cashed it. When we discovered this and angrily confronted her, she made up three or four different stories. She said she'd get the money back from someone she'd given it to. We never saw the money.

We were not totally naive. We suspected even then that she was financing her drug usage by doing some low-level dealing. Three of the guys in the neighborhood were definitely dealers. She was often dropping by their places for a few minutes. Worse, they were often dropping by ours. They'd go up to her room with her, stay thirty seconds, then come downstairs, smirking. Never would they make eye contact with us on their way out. Who knew what they'd brought into our house. The thought terrified me.

We would not have our home serving as an illegal drug marketplace. Frank and I considered calling the police anonymously and having the boys busted. Nancy, too. We went so far as to ask our attorney what would happen to her. He said that since she came from a comfortable suburban family and still—despite her numerous brushes with the law—had a spotless record, she would probably be put on probation and sent home to her parents. We just plain couldn't win.

The only way the legal process could help us, our attorney advised, would be to declare Nancy a ward of the court. But to make Nancy a ward of the court, we would have to relinquish our rights as parents. Frank and I wouldn't do it. It would be like leaving your baby on somebody's doorstep in a blanket, a five-dollar bill pinned to her diaper.

She was our child, so she stayed in our home—where she remained a disruptive, divisive influence. Worse than ever before, actually. How could we raise Suzy and David responsibly when there were two sets of rules, one for them and one for Nancy? They had to be up at a certain time and off for school. Not Nancy. They had to be home by a certain time. Not Nancy. Sometimes she never came home at all. If we got angry at her for staying out, she'd tell us to "get fucked." Or worse, she'd bring some boy home with her at two a.m. on a weeknight, lock her door, and "entertain" him right there in her room while the rest of us tried to sleep. The talking and loud music would wake the four of us up. Frank and I were outraged by this. It was *our* house. She was violating our family unit. Frank would have to get up and throw the boy out.

After one such nocturnal visit, I went downstairs in the morning to find a young man with long hair sprawled on the living room sofa, asleep. I didn't know who he was. I tried to wake him up, was unable to. I called Frank down. Frank was unable to rouse him. He really appeared to be quite comatose. Before we called an ambulance we woke up Nancy. She told us not to worry.

"He's just tired." She yawned. "He was too tired to drive home, I guess. He's cool—just let him sleep."

So we went about our morning routine with this strange person passed out on our couch. David said he was still there when he got home from school. When Nancy came down at about four o'clock, she woke him up and he left. Later I found out from David that he had been on Quaaludes.

Even now, I wonder how we could possibly have put up with this. But thinking back, what could we have done? We had tried *everything*. There was no solution, no hope. All we could do was cope. Most of the time, we felt so defeated that we had no capacity for anger. Anger accomplished nothing but to make us feel worse, anyway. Certainly it had no effect on Nancy. Nothing did. More than once I asked myself *Why me? What did I do to deserve this?* More than once I fantasized that someone would kill her, put her and us out of our misery. I really did. I'm not ashamed to admit it.

We went through the motions of living. We were prisoners in our own home. We literally could not leave. Then one night both Frank and I had to be out of town on business, Nancy responded by inviting half a dozen couples to sleep over. They took over the house—used our bed, David's bed, Suzy's bed. David told me there was humping and moaning and naked people running up and down the stairs all night long, not to mention two very large dogs. He and Suzy were forced to spend the night on the sofa while this went on around them.

This was going on while Suzy, at fifteen, was starting to date boys and formulate her opinions about sex. I knew that Nancy and Suzy's generation was more promiscuous than mine, that having sex on the first date—not kissing—was now considered by some to be the way a girl showed she liked a boy. So I tried to emphasize to Suzy the difference between sex and love—a distinction Nancy was never able to comprehend. Nancy was right there to contradict whatever I tried to impress on Suzy. She egged Suzy into losing her virginity.

"You should go out with more guys," she told Suzy one afternoon. "Don't any of 'em dig you or what?"

"Joe likes me," Suzy said defensively.

"So you oughta fuck him. You're too old to be a virgin."

"Nancy," I said sharply. "That's *Suzy's* business, not yours."

"I don't like him," Suzy said, ignoring me, as Nancy was.

"What difference does it make?" Nancy demanded. "Everybody balls everybody."

"That's not true!" I cried. "Everybody does *not* do that. There is such a thing as romance, Suzy. I don't want you—"

"Mom," Nancy interrupted.

"Yes?"

"Fuck off. I'm trying to set my baby sister straight."

I was furious—especially when Suzy didn't come home Friday night.

She told me she was sleeping over at her friend Laura's house. When Frank, David, and I were in the middle of dinner, I remembered that Laura's parents had forbidden her to have sleepovers. I called Laura. She was home. Suzy was not there. She said she didn't know where Suzy was, but Laura must have contacted her, because Suzy was afraid to come home the next morning. She hid at another friend's house. David interceded and found her. She came home that afternoon, sobbing.

"I don't like what you did," I told her. "More than anything, I don't like to see you lie."

She apologized. I grounded her for two weeks.

Frank and I fretted over Nancy's influence on Suzy and David. It ate away at us that they still looked up to her, respected her, wanted to be like her. After all, she was getting more erratic and irrational with each passing day.

One time she didn't come home for two days. She finally called from a train station in Philadelphia. She said she'd been beaten and robbed. When I picked her up, she was bruised and pale. Her wallet and watch were missing. She was totally vague about what had happened.

"He beat me," she said softly, as if she were under a spell.

"Who did, Nancy?"

"*He* did."

"Where?"

"I don't know . . . I don't know."

"I'll call the police," I said.

"No! No! You can't!" she suddenly screamed. "You can't call! No, *please!*"

I didn't call. I took her home and put her to bed. She stayed there for a day and a half.

Another time I dropped her off at a mall to buy some records. It was early on a weeknight. The mall closed at nine. We didn't hear from her until midnight. She told us she'd been abducted by a man at gunpoint and driven around. Again, she sounded very vague, as if under a spell.

"Did he rape you?" Frank demanded, barely able to contain his agitation.

It was maddening. We didn't know if the crime was real or a product of Nancy's imagination.

She didn't answer.

*"Did . . . he . . . rape . . . you?"* Frank repeated.

"No. He just wanted to kill me . . . to kill me. He drove and he drove and he . . . then he just drove back to where I am now."

"Where are you now?"

"Uh . . . the mall."

I said we'd be there as soon as we called the police. Again, she got hysterical. I brought her home and put her to bed. We never did figure out what happened either time.

Then, one weeknight, Nancy brought home a boy named Stephen at around three in the morning. He was about twenty, a guitar player with long hair. Her stereo woke us up. Frank banged on the door and told him to get out.

There was no response.

"You hear me in there?" Frank screamed, pounding on the door with his fist.

Still no response. He tried the knob. The door was locked. He stormed back into our room, picked up the phone.

"I'm calling the goddamned police!" he fumed. "And get that lousy sonofabitch out of my house."

"Wait!" I cautioned. "Maybe they'll get up, now that they've heard you. Wait a minute."

He slammed the phone down. "I know what I'll do! I'll take the door off! That's what I'll do!"

By now, Suzy and David were standing in their doorways in their pajamas, yawning, annoyed.

"What's going on?" asked David.

He got no answer from Frank, who took Nancy's door off to reveal Nancy and Stephen lying on the bed, fully clothed, so zonked on drugs and Southern Comfort that they were barely stirring.

"Out!" Frank screamed. "Get out!"

"Okay, man. Okay," Stephen mumbled. "Don't get crazy. No need to get crazy."

*"I'll get crazy if I want to! This is my house and you're in it! O-u-t!"*

Frank came back in our room, cursing. We could hear the two of them talking. Suzy and David closed their doors and went back to bed. Then Nancy showed Stephen to the front door. We heard it open. We didn't hear it close. A moment later she came back upstairs. Stephen started up his car, drove away. He had a loud sports car. We could hear it circle around the block, pull back up in front of our house, and stop. He turned off the engine, got out, and came back in the house through the open front door.

Frank leaped out of bed, intercepted him before he'd gotten halfway up the stairs. Stephen was surprised to see him.

"Oh," he said. "How ya doin', man?"

*"What do you think I am, some kind of stupid schmuck? Some asshole?"*

"Look, don't get, like *hostile,* man. No hassle. It was just like your daughter said I should come back. No hassle."

*"Get out! Now! Or so help me I'll beat the living crap out of you!"*

"Hey, like I said, you don't have to get *hostile*. I'm splitting."

He did. Frank slammed and bolted the door behind him. Nancy's light was out when he came back upstairs, her unhinged door resting against the hallway wall.

"Your friend had to leave!" he shouted into the darkness. "I hope you don't mind!"

She didn't answer.

We went to bed.

This was not the end of the incident, though. In the morning we discovered that our cat, Sake, had disappeared. She'd gone out the door that Nancy had left wide open for Stephen.

And because of this incident, Suzy and David saw how irresponsible her behavior was, how intolerably inconsiderate she was. They understood why Frank had been so upset. They were upset, too.

They cooled toward Nancy.

For instance, when we, were having dinner that night—breakfast for Nancy—she told Suzy to get her a cola. She often ordered Suzy around. Ordinarily Suzy obeyed. Not this time.

"Get it yourself," she snapped.

Nancy was so surprised she had no retort. She got it herself.

Suzy did more than stop waiting on Nancy. She stopped emulating her. She stopped wearing jeans to school, began to wear a dress with stockings and heels. She got her hair done.

"Going to somebody's sweet sixteen party, Jappy?" Nancy sneered at her when Suzy came home from school one day. "Jappy" was something of a family insult, deriving from "Jewish American Princess."

Suzy just walked away.

Nancy laughed, turned to David. "Doesn't she look ridiculous?"

"I think she looks very nice," David replied.

Undaunted, Nancy turned to me. "Why is she dressing like such a JAP?"

"She dresses the way she wants," I said.

Nancy shook her head, went up to her room, and closed the door.

When Nancy invited Suzy to a concert later that week, Suzy said she was busy.

David, meanwhile, avoided Nancy. He stopped hanging around the house. He never brought friends over anymore. If they did drop by, he didn't introduce them to Nancy.

After a couple of days, miraculously, Sake came home. The cat's return didn't alter the way Suzy and David now felt about Nancy. They loved her as a sister, but they didn't look up to her anymore, didn't respect her opinions, didn't want to be like her. If anything, Nancy now pushed them in the opposite direction. They became more considerate, more responsible. They stopped smoking marijuana.

Frank and I were very proud of them.


Like her involvement with drugs, Nancy's becoming a rock groupie was a natural outgrowth of her troubled life. She was into the anger, the rebelliousness, the oversimplified, hard-edged morality, the sound of the music. Always had been. The only boyfriend she'd ever had had been Jeff, the musician. Otherwise, at age seventeen, she had proven herself unwilling and unable to handle the complex demands of a mature relationship—the intimacy, the sharing, the caring, the love.

In Nancy's mind the best thing in the world that could happen to her would be to meet and get involved with a guy in a famous band. Someone who was a big deal. By becoming his lady, she herself would then be a big deal. I suppose most teenage girls have this fantasy for a little while, just as most teenage boys probably have the fantasy of being that famous musician. Most boys and girls outgrow it.

Not Nancy. Music was *everything* to her. There was nothing else in her universe that mattered. All she wanted was to belong to the music. All she wanted was a musician.

And her friend Randi provided her with a means to make her dream come true.

There was a big rock concert in Philadelphia once every

four or six weeks, usually on a Saturday night. I think Nancy
and Randi went to about half a dozen of them over the course
of that spring and summer. For Nancy, each was a major
event.

She spent hours getting ready, trying on and discarding
practically every garment in her closet. Her outfits began to
get totally outrageous—she looked like she bought her clothes
at the same place Rod Stewart did. She wore skin-tight orange
spandex pants, black satin scarves or a purple kimono in place
of a top, immense multicolored platform heels. She wore lots
and lots of makeup and silver or black nail polish.

She'd check herself out in the mirror. When she was sure
she looked just right, she'd lift up one leg and do this little
dance maneuver of hers, a form of the twist that for her was
almost like revving up her engine. Her eyes would light up.
She'd cry out *"All riiiight!"* and then head off to the train station.

Somehow she and Randi got backstage.

There'd usually be a party going on backstage before the
concert, then another afterward. Later on the party would
continue at the band's hotel suite. Randi and Nancy would go
along, often by black limousine.

One time a limousine dropped Nancy off at our house the
next morning while Frank and I were having breakfast. The
kids were upstairs getting dressed. In she stumbled, exhausted, disheveled. Her outfit seemed particularly preposter-
ous next to our bathrobes.

"Where were you all night?" Frank demanded, stirring his
coffee.

"Tell *him*," Nancy said to me, "that it's my business."

Then she stood over him, glaring until he threw down his
napkin in disgust and left the room. As soon as he was gone
her mood changed completely. She erupted in girlish delight.

"Guess who I met last night, Mom!"

"Who?"

"Guess!"

"I don't know, Nancy."

"*Queen!* Do you *believe* it? We went backstage and talked
to 'em. Just, like, rapped about music. Do you *believe* it?

*Queen!* And then there was like, there was like this all-night *party!*"

"That's very nice, sweetheart," I said halfheartedly. I had never heard of the group.

"Boy!" she cried. "Wait till I tell Suzy!" She kicked off her platform heels and ran upstairs to find her sister.

I stared at the misshapen shoes there on the kitchen floor and sighed. No, I'd never heard of the rock group. But I had heard of what reputedly went on at the sort of party Nancy said she'd just come from: drugs and sex in multiple variations. It was no secret.

Frank and I discussed Nancy's newest social development at length. It seemed as if every week she got wilder, further and further from our control and our sense of right and wrong. Our morality meant zero to her. She would simply step over the line, draw a new one, and then step over that. We were also revolted. It was ugly and distasteful and we hated to see such a bright child throw her life away—trash it, really. But we were powerless to stop her. Nothing we could say or do would have any impact.

Actually, we were never really sure how much of the backstage scene Nancy was intimately involved in then. We still aren't. She bragged about her sexual exploits to Suzy and Karen, providing them with all of the steamy details of her conquests. We never knew, however, how much of it was true.

She told Suzy, for instance, that her first band was Bad Company. The whole band. She ranked each member's performance. She kept a Bad Company poster on the wall in her room to commemorate the occasion. It said, "Does your mother know you've been keeping Bad Company?"

Then there was Aerosmith. She told Karen that after she had taken on the whole group, two of the guys wanted to set her on fire and throw her out the hotel window. She was willing, she said. It sounded like a pretty great way to die, she said. Aerosmith chickened out, she said.

She told Karen and Suzy about her sexual involvement with other bands—The Who, the Allman Brothers, J. Geils. How much of what she said went on actually did go on is a matter of conjecture.

Karen recently told me that she didn't believe a lot of what Nancy was telling her at the time, and still doesn't. She thinks Nancy was making it up to shock and impress her. Suzy says the same thing. I tend to agree. Obviously, as Nancy's mother, it is preferable for me to have that point of view. I admit that. There's no question in my mind that she'd have been involved in whatever drugs were going around. And I guess I think she was involved in some sex—she would, after all, try anything once—but not as much as she led Suzy and Karen to believe. Possibly she herself believed it.

The one firsthand indication I had that she was socializing with rock groups was when I came home from work one day to find two station wagons parked outside and an entire British band parked inside. There must have been seven or eight of them—all with long, stringy hair, bad teeth, sallow complexions, and high-heeled blue suede shoes. A couple of them were in the den drinking beer, eating last night's leftovers, and watching television. A couple of them were frolicking in the swimming pool. I didn't check to see if they had trunks on. I figured they didn't take swimming trunks on tour with them. The rest of them were up in Nancy's room with her, sprawled on the floor, smoking cigarettes and listening to her records, the stereo blaring. Suzy and David were in their rooms trying to do their homework, their doors closed.

"Hey, Mom," yawned Nancy when I appeared in the doorway. "This is Pretty Things. They just rolled into town. Told 'em to look me up when they did. Guys, this is my mom."

"Hello, Nancy's mum," they said almost in unison.

They left almost immediately. I told Nancy it was unfair to her brother and sister to have so many people over like that, to raise such a ruckus. She told me to "eat shit."

What worried me most during this period was that Nancy would get pregnant, convince herself it was by some famous rock star, and then want to keep the baby. At one point she actually thought she was pregnant, though she refused to tell me by whom. She simply told me she hadn't had her period in three months. I took her to my gynecologist. He gave her a lab test, which showed that she was not pregnant, but she refused to believe this. She insisted she was pregnant. To satisfy her, the doctor performed a D and C on Nancy at the hospital. The D and C also showed that she was not pregnant. Furthermore, the doctor advised me, Nancy's uterus was so underdeveloped that if she ever did get pregnant, she would doubtless have a miscarriage in the second or third month. I never told her that, for fear of upsetting her.

Nancy would not accept the results of the D and C. Instead, she chose to believe she hadn't had one at all, but rather an abortion. She mentioned her "abortion" several times over the remainder of her life.


We couldn't live this way. We were desperately unhappy—stretched so taut we were ready to snap. We began to reach for crazy solutions, solutions that weren't really there. One night in bed, Frank and I actually discussed changing all of the locks on the house after she went out one night. Our good sense got the best of us, though. We realized she'd simply break a ground-floor window to get back in. We also talked about renting her an apartment in Philadelphia. What was money if it meant we wouldn't have to live with her anymore? But we decided that wouldn't be a solution, either. She'd be too nearby, with ready access to us, to the kids, to the house.

But we couldn't live this way.

We sent Suzy and David away to camp that summer. We felt they deserved the normal life Nancy's presence in the house deprived them of. They were grateful to get away.


I got a promotion that summer to director of Mailgram sales for Western Union. I was delighted. It was nice to be considered good at something. It meant spending one, sometimes two nights a week at the headquarters in Upper Saddle River, New Jersey, and doing some traveling as well. I didn't mind. In fact, I liked it. It became for me what New York had been for Frank earlier in our marriage: an escape. Frustrated and unhappy at home, I was glad to get away and leave Frank in charge of Nancy. The irony of this role reversal was not lost on me.

As for Nancy, she had abandoned all notions of employment—unless it had something to do with music.

"I wanna do like sound mixing," she said. "You know, studio stuff. Or maybe arranging gigs."

"Have you tried looking for that kind of work?" I asked.

"There isn't any here." She shrugged. "There isn't anything in this town. They don't have any concerts even."

"Where is it?"

"New York. London. L.A., but it's really plastic in L.A."

"How do you know it's plastic? You've never been there."

"*Believe* me. It's plastic."

As it happened, Frank needed some extra clerical help at his office that summer. We asked Nancy if she'd be interested.

"Would I, like, get paid?" she asked.

When Frank said yes, there would be money involved, she agreed to come to work for him. Transportation was no problem—she drove to and from work with Frank every day. The problem was getting her up in the morning at seven thirty. We bought her a clock with the loudest alarm in creation, but still she'd go right back to sleep. We had to keep rousing her, and she got nasty and abusive. It was not a pleasure to go through every morning.

Of course, there was also the communication problem between Nancy and Frank. She still would not engage in conversation with him. Their rides in the car were totally silent. At the office, however, she would willingly take orders from Frank and the other employees. But after a couple of months she flatly refused to get up in the morning, and quit.

With just the three of us around the house, her presence began to take its toll on our marriage again. Both Frank and I were upset about Nancy most of the time. In bed we were either tense about her being home—with company—or not being home. There was no time for gentleness. Romance seemed long ago and far away. Most of the time we existed in sadness.

It didn't help that she was up to her old tricks of pitting us against each other.

One time she went through my purse in search of money (I never kept any in it for fear she'd take it to buy drugs with) and found a business letter I'd received from a male business acquaintance. As soon as Frank got home, she started in.

"Why don't you tell him?" she sneered.

"Tell him what, Nancy?"

"That you have a letter in your purse. From a man. Why don't you tell the asshole?"

Frank looked at me, concerned.

"Cut it out, Nancy," I ordered. To Frank I explained, "It's just a business letter. She's just being impossible."

But the seed of doubt was planted in his mind. After all, we had had our painful bout of infidelity years before—infidelity, I should point out, that none of the children knew anything about. By the time we got into bed that night, he was still stewing over it.

"You know," he said seriously, "if you're seeing someone again, Deb, well, I won't get upset about it as long as you tell me the truth. I just want to be told the truth."

"Frank, I did tell you the truth. I'm not seeing anyone. I wouldn't see anyone. It was a business letter."

"Honest?"

"Honest."

I could see that he wanted to believe me, *did* believe me, but there was still the tiniest element of doubt. I got out of bed, went downstairs, brought up my purse, and gave him the letter to read. He did. Then he apologized and kissed me.

Nancy did this kind of thing constantly. She wanted to start trouble between us. She had it in for Frank. If he was away on a business trip and I was home with her, she'd keep hammering at me.

"What do you think he's doing right now?"

"At this very moment?"

"At this very moment."

"I'd say he's probably sitting in the Portland airport, waiting for his flight."

"Do you *really* believe that's what he's doing? Don't you know what he's doing? He's fucking some woman. He doesn't love you. He told me. He never loved you. Why don't you divorce him? Why don't you dump the sonofabitch?"

We tried to ignore her attempts to drive a wedge between us. It was impossible. We grew farther apart.

The day Suzy and David were due back from summer camp, Frank and I sat Nancy down and made what I suppose you could call our last possible appeal. We told her she had not, thus far, been a very considerate sister to them; they deserved a peaceful night's sleep free of nocturnal visitors to her room; they deserved a chance to discuss their schoolwork and activities at dinner without fear of their sister screaming and hurling dishes if someone looked at her "the wrong way"; they deserved a chance to be the people that they wanted to be, that we wanted them to be.

We had previously tried to appeal to Nancy on every conceivable level of decency and courtesy, to no avail. We appealed now for Suzy and David, hoping it would have some effect on her. It did. She went crazy.

"You don't think I'm gonna take that kind of bullshit from you, do you? I'll have you fucking killed. I have Mafia friends! Everybody I know is connected! I'll have you fucking killed! Don't think I won't!"

She continued to scream death threats and obscenities at us for several minutes, then went upstairs and slammed her door.

When Suzy and David got home, she refused to come out and say hello to them. When I told her through the door that the four of us were about to go to a Chinese restaurant for dinner with my mother and that she was welcome to join us, she opened the door.

"Don't expect the house to look the same when you get back!" she warned.

"Meaning what?" I demanded.

"My friends are gonna wreck it. My Mafia friends. They'll smash every single piece of furniture. They'll break every window. They'll pour paint all over everything. They'll destroy the whole fucking house! Hear me?''

I turned to Frank. "Let's go," I said quietly.

The four of us turned and left, Nancy threatening us as we went down the steps and out the door.

*"Go ahead! You'll see! They'll dump everything out of the closets and set the fucking place on fire! There won't be a house left when you get back! Go ahead!"*

We kept going. She stood on the front porch, shouting at us as we got into the car. *"You'll see! Go ahead, you'll see!"*

We drove away.

We were silent in the car for several blocks. Finally I broke the silence.

"Do you think she'll actually carry out any of those threats?"

Frank shrugged. "Deb, I honestly don't know."

We picked up my mother and went to the restaurant. It wasn't much of a coming-home celebration for the kids. We were all very quiet and had little appetite. We didn't tell my mother about the incident or why we were so quiet, but by now she, of course, knew it had something to do with Nancy.

I spent the entire meal visualizing our furniture being smashed, our walls being smeared with paint. I wondered if Nancy really would do those things. Certainly, she was capable. I wondered how we could sit there in a restaurant after our eldest child had threatened to murder us and have our house destroyed. I wondered how this could be happening and how we could be so powerless to do anything about it. I wondered, as I did so often, what we had done to deserve this.

The ride home was interminable. When we rounded the bend in Red Barn Lane, we saw that the house was intact, the lights off. We got out and went inside. Nothing had been touched. The house was fine. Nancy was gone.

Frank and I sat up the entire night talking. This incident was, for us, the last straw. I don't know why this one particular episode among a sea of episodes put us over the top, but it did. Possibly because it was our *home* she wanted to destroy now. All we possessed was our home. She'd already destroyed the people inside it—our lives, our dreams. All she had left us with was the physical structure, the shell. She could not be permitted to destroy that, too. And we did believe she *could* do it. The house, we felt, would have to be guarded from now on, day and night.

We had to do something. This could not continue. She was holding us captive. We could not subject Suzy and David to her any longer. Or ourselves. She would have to leave. Have to.

My promise to her? I'd kept it. I'd done everything in my power to give her a good life. To keep it any longer would be to jeopardize the futures of Suzy and David.

We had lost her. We could not control her any longer. All we could do was try to save the other two children. We had to get Nancy out for their sakes. And yes, for ours. On this we were in achingly painful agreement.

The only question was how. We had exhausted the resources of the medical profession. Committing her to a hospital was not an alternative. We had tried that and it hadn't worked. Besides, her response to it had been such a bottomless pit of rage directed at me that I would not go through it again. Turning her in to the police, as our lawyer said, was not going to accomplish anything. She was almost eighteen and would no longer be made a ward of the court.

We were out of options. We really had only one choice, and we made it. It was a necessity. Guilt? Guilt is a luxury.

We cut Nancy loose, to sink or swim on her own. We set her free.

# ◻ Chapter 15

We told her when she finally turned up two days later.

"Dad and I have a plan," I said.

"For what?" she demanded impatiently.

"For you," I said. "For what you're going to do."

"Oh, yeah? What am I gonna do?"

"You're going to move to New York."

She stopped short. "I am?"

"You've been talking about how much is there for you,"
Frank explained, "in terms of getting work in the music business. Seems like that's where the action is. So we think you
should give it a shot."

Nancy sat down and lit a cigarette, now very interested in
what we had to say.

"You'll need a place to live, of course," I said. "You and
I could find you an apartment, someplace nice. Nothing
fancy—"

"I wouldn't need anything fancy."

"Right," I said. "Maybe in the two-hundred-dollar-a-
month area. Until you find yourself a job, typing or in the mu-

sic business or whatever you want, we'll cover your rent for you.''

''Six months,'' Frank said. ''That's how long it should take you to get on your feet. We'll give you half that for another six months. After that, we'll still be here for you financially if you run into trouble. But we don't think you will. We think you can handle the responsibility of supporting yourself.''

We never said to Nancy ''You can't live here anymore.'' Nor did we explain why we'd come up with this plan. We simply laid it out for her. We wanted her to think of it as a positive step, an opportunity. In truth, we weren't sure she could handle the responsibility. But there was only one way to find out.

She didn't have to think it over for long. ''I could do that,'' she said. ''Yeah, I could do it. It sounds real good. I'll get a job in the music business. Yeah. Great. Let's do it!''

It was the beginning of November. We picked December first as the target date for Nancy's move.

I can't say Suzy and David clapped their hands when they were told that Nancy was moving to New York, but they did seem relieved.

She and I took the train to New York the following week. She circled apartments in the *Times* classifieds and we discussed the relative merits of the different neighborhoods. When we got to Penn Station, I left her to start looking while I took care of some business. By the time I met her in the afternoon, she'd found a one-bedroom apartment on West Twenty-third street, in Chelsea, that she liked. It was two hundred dollars a month. She took me there. It was about half a block west of the Chelsea Hotel, a nice bright ground-floor apartment in an elevator building. It was clean and freshly painted. The bathroom and kitchen were new. She was very excited about it. I said okay and gave the landlord a deposit. Then we took the train home.

Nancy spent the next two weeks earnestly packing and accumulating old furniture and dishes. From our basement she took an old sofa and a round, wrought-iron and glass patio table. She took her bedroom set, bed, bookshelves, and plas tic milk crates for her records. We made plans for a few of her friends to rent a U-Haul and help her take it to New York the day after Thanksgiving.

I felt very sad watching her pack her things, not because she was leaving but because it had come to this. She was going off to live in New York by herself. She was only seventeen. In many ways she seemed so much older. In other ways, so much younger. I held out hope that she would at last find her niche there.

A few days before she left, Frank and I were driving in the car when he said, "Deb, I . . . I've been thinking. Now that Nancy's going away . . ." He trailed off, swallowed. "It seems like we don't have any life together. I'm unhappy, you're unhappy. Maybe we should just split up. Start over. I'll take David. You take Suzy."

"I know, I've been thinking about it, too."

"You have?"

"Yes, I have."

We drove along in silence for a moment.

"So do you want to?" he asked.

"To tell you the truth, I sort of did until I heard you say it out loud. Now I don't know, Frank. We've been through so much in this past year. So have Suzy and David. Maybe we owe it to them—to us—to try it for a while without Nancy in the house. Maybe it'll work. Maybe we'll have the life we wanted. I still want it with you, nobody else."

"Me, too," he said.

"Why don't we give it a try? Give it six more months?"

He thought it over, agreed to wait it out. Agreed a bit reluctantly, I think, but it turned out for the best. The question of our splitting up never came up again.

On the day before Thanksgiving I came home to find a mysterious message for me: "Call Murray's Delicatessen and tell them when you want your turkey." I had no idea what this was about. I phoned Frank, but he didn't either. So I phoned Murray's Delicatessen. They asked me what time on Thanksgiving Day I wanted to pick up my turkey. I was still very confused until I was able to determine I'd won a fifteen-pound turkey with all the trimmings in a raffle contest. I was de-

lighted, of course. However, I explained, I'd never entered
any raffle. They said I had.

As it turned out, several weeks earlier Nancy had filled out
a raffle ticket in a shoe repair shop in the same shopping center as Murray's. It was she who had won the turkey. She had
left me the mysterious message as a surprise.

It was delicious, and the meal was a special experience.
Nancy was so delighted about winning the dinner that she was
in high spirits throughout it.

"I won this dinner for you, Mom," she beamed.

We had a lovely, happy time, the five of us together. If
someone had looked at us through the window, we'd have
seemed like a happy, prosperous, healthy, loving family enjoying being together on the holiday. For those few hours I
think even we believed that this was so.


The next morning her friends came by with the U-Haul. We
loaded up her belongings and furniture. Then we said good-
bye. Nancy kissed each of us quickly.

"I can't wait to get a job," she said. "You'll come and
visit, okay?"

We said okay. She drove off.

Then the four of us went inside the house, closed the door
and looked at each other. After a moment there was a collec-
tive sigh of relief.


My work took me to New York two weeks later. Nancy and I
made plans for me to drop by. When I did, I was very pleased
Nancy had made a nice, tidy home for herself in the Chelsea
apartment. It was clean, organized, and well equipped. The
dishes were done; the bed was made. She looked happy and
healthy. She proudly showed me around her place.

She'd arranged some stools around the glass-topped patio
table and thrown an artificial fur rug over our old sofa. Her
huge record collection was stored in a wall unit constructed of
plastic milk crates. In the bedroom was her dresser from home
and a couple of Parsons tables as nightstands. She'd put the

double bed on the floor and covered it with a plaid spread. In the bathroom was a litter box. She'd gotten herself a black kitten. I don't remember what she named it except that it was "fuck you" in a foreign language.

She opened up the linen cupboard, ran a hand over its contents.

"See?" she pointed out. "I keep my sheets and towels in here."

Then she opened the kitchen cupboards to display the stacks of plates and cups and frying pans.

"I keep my dishes and cooking shit in here."

Then she opened the refrigerator, which was well stocked with fresh produce, milk, eggs, and yogurt.

"See? I have food. I buy groceries."

I thought to myself, *What other seventeen-year-old could have moved to New York on her own and gotten completely set up in two weeks?* There wasn't a carton to be found anywhere.

"You've done a lovely job, sweetheart. It's really nice."

"Really?"

"Really."

She glowed from my praise. "Thanks, Mom. I was kinda hoping you'd like it. Can I get you anything? A diet soda? I have diet soda."

"Please."

She opened the cupboard and took out a glass, then pulled an ice tray out of the freezer.

"I'll put some ice in it. I have ice."

She put several cubes in the glass, then filled it with diet soda and gave it to me. I took a sip from it.

"Cold enough?" she asked.

"Perfect."

"I mean, 'cause, I have more ice if you—"

"No, it's fine."

"Great."

We sat down on the sofa and watched her kitten smack a rolled-up sweatsock around the room.

"I'm looking for a job," she said. "I typed up a résumé and I'm gonna hit the music magazines next week to see if I

can get something. I'll do anything they want, you know, file
or type or answer the phone or whatever. It'll happen.''

"I'm sure it will, sweetheart."

"I met a couple of my neighbors. One of them's a hooker.
Oh, and you know who lives upstairs? You won't believe it.
Lance Loud! Remember, from the Loud family, the one that
was on the TV series?"

"Uh-huh."

"And I went to Max's. Max's Kansas City. And CBGB's.
I mean, there's really a lot going on here. You wouldn't *believe* it. I met some people in bands. Good bands. Not plastic.''

"Anyone I would know?"

"Not yet, but you will. Yeah, there's really a lot happening.''

I left about an hour later, feeling positive about Nancy's
move. Maybe it would turn out to be good for her. She'd certainly gotten off to a good start.

At home it seemed like life had gotten back to normal.
Suzy, who was sixteen, was concentrating on art as a major
subject. She didn't have a boyfriend, but she had a lot of
friends and baby-sat on Saturday nights. David, who was
fourteen, played basketball nearly every day and did very
well in his classes. He brought his friends home now. Since I
seldom got home before six o'clock—especially on the days I
was called upon to be in Upper Saddle River—Suzy and
David were responsible for preparing dinner. I could count on
them. Both of them were blossoming into reliable young
adults, not to mention excellent cooks.

With Nancy out of the house and the atmosphere much
calmer, Frank and I became close and strong. We could relax
at night, talk, make love, sleep in each other's arms, knowing
that no strangers were under our roof. We could leave the distributor cap on the car, money and keys on the table. It went
unsaid, but life was better at home without Nancy.

It was so pleasant that I wanted to be there more. When
Western Union asked me to spend a greater part of the week
in New Jersey (it was a promotion), I asked instead for a
transfer that would allow me to spend more time with my

family. It meant giving up a professional opportunity, but it was worth it to me.

The first inkling we had that Nancy was having trouble in New York came on Christmas Day, one month after her arrival, two weeks after my visit. The four of us were at my cousin's house for dinner, and Nancy called me there.

"Mom . . . I . . . I . . ."

"What is it, Nancy?"

"Like . . . uh . . ."

She sounded just like she had when she'd started phoning from Colorado—zonked, morose, her voice slurred.

". . . uh . . . I ain't feelin' so good."

"Are you sick?"

Long pause.

"Huh?"

"Are you sick?" I repeated.

"Oh . . . I don't know, I don't have . . . have no *money*. I can't like, I don't have no *money*. Can't pay my rent. Nothin' to . . . nothin' to eat, Mom. Nothin' . . . no food. I can't get me no job. I ain't got no . . . job. Nobody interested. Nobody wants me. Ya gotta send me money, Mom. *Money*."

I knew from her voice that she had found drugs—which kind I don't know. Certainly, it was something hard. Frank and I had agreed not to send her money if she was on drugs. We would not finance her self-destruction.

"Mom?"

"I'll send the rent money to your landlord."

"No, send it to *me*, Mom. Send it to *me*."

"No, Nancy."

"Why?"

"That's the way it is."

"I want it. Send it . . . send it to *me*. Don't you trust me? Don't you, like, *trust* me, Mom?"

"I'll send it to your landlord."

"How'm I gonna eat?"

"I'll be up to see you tomorrow."

"You don't have to do that."

"Yes, I do."

I went alone. Frank stayed with Suzy and David, who were on school vacation. I stopped at a market near her apartment and bought two big bags of groceries.

She looked awful. She was pale and had dark circles under her eyes. She had a bad cough and was unkempt and dirty. This was unusual for Nancy. No matter how outrageous her appearance, she was usually clean. The apartment was a mess—dirty dishes and clothes everywhere. It smelled of overripe kitty litter. I was worried. She seemed really out of it.

"Are you taking care of yourself?" I asked as I tidied up the kitchen and put the groceries away.

"Been sick," she replied weakly. "I been sick. Don't . . . still don't feel so good."

"Are you on something?"

"Uh-uh."

"Really?"

"Uh-uh."

"If you need to go to a doctor—"

"I don't."

"If you do, let me know."

"Did you bring money?"

"I bought you groceries," I said.

"Oh, right. Yeah . . . thanks. How 'bout money? Any money?"

"No. Look, why don't we get out of here for a bit? Get some fresh air, something to eat?"

She nodded. "Sure. Okay."

She put on a ratty old fur jacket I'd never seen before.

"Where'd you get that, sweetheart?"

"Place on Saint Marks . . . where I work. Old clothes."

"You got a job?"

"Just sort through the stuff. Coupla hours a week. Coupla . . . coupla bucks."

I took her to lunch at Feathers, a restaurant in the Fifth Avenue Hotel, just above Washington Square Park. She chain smoked through the meal but ate her food ravenously. She showed me the clothing store where she was working—it was a seedy, damp place in a basement. Then we went back to her apartment. She kissed me good-bye woodenly and asked me again for money. I said I had none to give her. I didn't really—I'd only brought an extra five dollars.

"*Please, Mom.* You gotta give me some *money. Please.*"

I gave her the five dollars. Then I took the train home.

The phone calls started. She called collect three, four, five times every single day for several weeks—stoned, troubled, barely coherent. Often, she called me at the office. I alerted my secretary that Nancy had some emotional problems and should be put through to me even if I was in a meeting. If I was traveling, I left a number where Nancy could reach me. I was forever anticipating her call, wondering when it would come. I began to equate the phone cord with an umbilical cord.

Many times, she called in the middle of the night. I begged her repeatedly not to call after eleven p.m.—the kids needed to sleep; *Frank* and *I* needed to sleep—but she kept at it. So I had to turn the phone off at night. I figured whatever was troubling her would still be there in the morning.

For some reason known only to Nancy, she would speak to no one in the family but me. If she called home and I wasn't there, she would not engage in conversation with Frank or Suzy or David. She had rejected them. "Tell Mommy to call" was all she'd say.

When I did, it would generally be to hear a plea for money. I refused to send it to her. She'd just buy drugs with it. One of the most impossible things in the world, I'm now convinced, is to refuse your own child money. I did my best. I paid her rent and utilities directly and brought her groceries every two weeks. I suggested she get a job. Instead, she began phoning relatives and demanding money from them. She called my mother, Frank's sister, my cousin in Brooklyn. When they refused to give her the money (per my instructions), she got abusive and threatened to have their houses destroyed. I ordered her to stop bothering the family. In response, she hocked the television set we'd given her, which infuriated me. The very next day she called to say someone had grabbed her in the vestibule of her building, held a gun to her, and taken her wallet with the money from the TV in it. When I asked her if she'd called the police, she began to scream and curse. Then she hung up on me.

If it wasn't money Nancy needed, it was Mommy. Just as I had sat with her on her bed in the middle of the night when she was little—making the shark demons of her nightmares go away—now I was soothing her grown-up demon, which was mounting paranoia.

"I went to CB's last night, Mom. Nobody would talk to me. They hate me. What am I gonna do? Nobody likes me. What am I gonna do, Mom? What am I gonna do?"

"I'm sure they'll like you again, sweetheart. Try to be nice. Try hard."

We had this conversation so many times that they all blur together in my mind. She'd sob; I'd do what I could to comfort her. Nothing had changed, really, from when she was a little girl. And she knew that no matter what she said or did, I would always be there for her. She was still my baby. Sometimes I hated her for not being able to cope with the world. God, how she made me hate her. But ultimately I still loved her. She had so much intelligence and compassion inside of her. When I got really angry at her, I'd try to remember the baby, the soft, sweet-smelling baby with the glossy black hair. I had to do what I could to keep that baby alive. I hadn't given up on her yet. In a sense I was playing for time, waiting for someone, somehow, to step forward and save Nancy—ease her pain, allow her to lead a productive life.

The analogy between watching Nancy destroy herself and watching a terminal patient being destroyed by disease popped up again and again in my mind. I never gave up hope. Instead I waited for the discovery of some magic cure. The longer she stayed alive, I told myself, the better the chance that someone *would* come along to rescue her.

The calls tapered off when Nancy settled into a routine of sorts that winter. She made some friends. By January 1975 she'd found a place for herself. That place was the punk rock scene.

As I understand it, punk was an underground backlash against the slick, juiceless, studio-produced sound that had begun to dominate the charts in the mid-seventies. Punk professed to being a return to rock's roots. It was raw, hungry, and angry. It lived for the moment. It was hard and fast. It was Nancy. At age ten she'd been listening to *Hair* and the Beatles. At age twelve she'd graduated to Hendrix and The Who. Now, at seventeen, she was ready for punk.

Like she had when she was living at home, Nancy generally slept all day, partied and got high all night. The clubs where she took to hanging out most of the time, Max's Kansas City and CBGB's, were where the punk bands were playing, drinking, getting high, and, ultimately, getting discovered. Blondie came out of that scene. So did the Ramones, the New York Dolls. Nancy knew who these people were early on, before anyone else did. She mentioned them frequently. She had always seemed to have her finger on the bands that would be popular in a year or two. Now was no different, except that she was there with them.

She wrote several articles of criticism about the punk groups for a local rock paper in Greenwich Village. She sent us the clippings. We were very impressed. She set forth what punk stood for with remarkable clarity. The articles were interesting, perceptive, and surprisingly well written. We complimented her profusely.

"Did you *really* like them?" she begged repeatedly.

"Yes," we replied repeatedly.

She didn't get paid for the articles. The magazines that did pay, she said, weren't hiring at the moment. Unfortunately Nancy didn't stick with it until something opened up. And then the local rock paper folded.

She was most enthusiastic about Blondie and its lovely lead singer, Deborah Harry. She told me they were very talented and that Debbie Harry would be a superstar someday. She was right. She mentioned Debbie quite often.

"She's real good, Mom," Nancy said once. "And pretty. She's my friend. Debbie's my friend."

At the time of her death, Nancy was carrying a photo album portfolio filled with family snapshots, postcards of places she'd been in Europe, the stubs of airplane tickets. Most prominent was a black and white glossy photo of her sitting at a table at one of the punk clubs with Debbie Harry. The two of them are smoking, drinking, and, seemingly, engaging in intimate conversation. She felt they had a special friendship.

Nancy referred to a number of the soon-to-be-famous figures of punk rock as friends. I must point out that my knowledge of Nancy's relationship with them is confined to what she told me then. I have only her version. I never met Debbie Harry or the others she mentioned, like Joey Ramone. Once, when I made my bi-monthly grocery stop, Richard Hell was at Nancy's apartment with her. They were listening to a Bruce Springsteen album and drinking coffee. He seemed quiet and polite. She asked me to give them a lift to an address on Houston Street. I did. Richard Hell, I learned years later, was considered a punk rock visionary. He led pioneering punk bands like Television and the Voidoids, and is credited with coining the punk catch phrase "the Blank Generation."

None of these people came forward after Nancy's death to make themselves known and offer condolences. I thought it over at the time and came up with several possible reasons for their silence. Possibly, they hadn't known or liked Nancy much and didn't care what happened to her. Possibly, they had liked her and were sensitive enough to not want to embarrass or hurt us further. Possibly, they themselves were embarrassed at having known the infamous Nancy Spungen, now that they were successes with somewhat more mainstream images.

There were other friends. Lance Loud looked out for her. There was a tall, striking model named Sable whom she often went to the clubs with, as well as Phyllis, whom she described as "can you *believe* it—a nice Jewish girl with a straight job and a nice Jewish family?" Each joined Nancy and me for lunch on separate occasions. There were Felipe and Babette, a French couple who lived in Chelsea.

Recently I met a girl named June who had a brief encounter with Nancy that winter. June had come up to New York on the train from Philadelphia to meet her boyfriend, a musician, at a party. She told me she got there before her boyfriend and, intimidated by the scene, stood against a wall feeling bewildered and ignored. Then a young woman, Nancy, appeared at her side.

"Hey, I'm Nancy and you need a drink and an ashtray."

And with that, Nancy stuck by June's side until her boyfriend arrived an hour later. She got her the drink and the ashtray, and when she found out June had come from Philadelphia, Nancy introduced her to everyone else at the party as "my friend from Philly." June told me everyone there seemed to know Nancy and made a point of speaking to her on their way in and out. She told me she thought Nancy was so sophisticated and self-assured, and couldn't believe she was not yet eighteen. June added that she thought Nancy was a very considerate, very special person.

Frank and I decided to take a vacation alone that winter—our first. It so happened that the only time both of us could get away from work was during Nancy's eighteenth birthday. We thought it over. After all, Nancy had a way of regarding her birthday as a national holiday. We decided to go. Our relationship needed this.

We arranged for one of the secretaries in my office to stay with Suzy and David. I think they were a bit offended—they felt they were old enough and responsible enough to stay alone for a week. They *were*. We just thought an adult should be there in case Nancy got upset about us being away for her birthday and decided to come home.

I told Nancy we would be going to Aspen on a one-week charter and would be gone for her birthday. She said that would be fine. She wished us a pleasant trip. We sent her a birthday card and a toaster oven as a gift, and I arranged for a Mailgram to be delivered to her on her birthday, which was a Saturday.

We had an idyllic two days and nights in Aspen, skiing and cuddling in front of the fire. On the third day I came down with the flu and spent the rest of the trip in bed with a high fever. I felt like God was punishing me for trying to get away and have a good time.

Our charter flight came back very early the morning after Nancy's birthday. Suzy and David were still asleep. They left a note: Nancy had called continually all day Saturday and was furious to find us absent on her birthday. I crawled into bed, still weak from the flu, and was just about asleep when the phone rang. It was Nancy.

"How dare you go away on my birthday!" she screamed.

"Now, Nancy, I *told* you we were going to be—"

"You forgot my fucking birthday! I don't *believe* you!"

"Nancy, we sent you a card and a Mailgram and a toaster oven. We didn't forget. And we told you we would be away."

Silence from her end.

"You don't love me," she said quietly.

"Of course we do."

"Do you *really?*" she demanded.

"Yes."

"Good. Then I'll get on a train and be there right away. We'll celebrate today. Okay?"

I honestly didn't want her to come home that day. I was still sick and not sure I could handle her first return visit since moving to New York. But how can you tell your own child not to come home to celebrate her birthday with her family?

"Okay, Mom?"

"Okay, sweetheart."

Suzy baked her a birthday cake. I found a roast in the freezer and stuck it in the oven. I went to get her at the train station. She got off the train with her old nasty scowl—That Look—and another look that was entirely new. Nancy was now a blonde.

"Whaddya think?" she demanded.

"It looks very nice, sweetheart," I replied. What else could I say? I thought it looked cheap and awful. I thought it made her look like someone other than my Nancy.

"Yeah. Debbie and I did it at her apartment. She's a blonde, too."

She wore a purple sweater and new, skin-tight black jeans, which she stripped off the second she got in the house and dumped in the washing machine.

"Need to be shrunk," she said. "Let's eat."

So she sat through her birthday dinner in her sweater, her

underwear, and her ridiculous blonde hair, and any time any of us glanced at her, she erupted.

"What the fuck are you staring at, you!" she demanded of David at one point.

"Nothing," he said quickly, shooting a look at Suzy. They exchanged a smirk—both of them thought Nancy looked really silly as a blonde.

"Now you're passing fucking signals," Nancy charged. "Back and forth. I saw you, you two little shits!"

"Aren't!" Suzy protested.

"*Are!*" Nancy returned.

We ate the rest of the meal in silence, our faces in our plates. When we were finished, Nancy blew out the candles on her cake and ate a large piece. We had no more gifts for her. This annoyed her.

As soon as her jeans were dry, she put them on and said she wanted to leave. Frank drove her to the station. In all, she was home about three hours.

"Boy, was she mean and nasty," said Frank when he got back.

"Boy, is she the same," said Suzy.

"Boy, am I glad she doesn't live here anymore," said David.

"I got a job, Mom!" Nancy told me excitedly over the phone one afternoon.

"Wonderful!" I exclaimed.

"Yeah, I don't have to worry about money anymore. And you don't have to take care of me. I'll be good for two or three hundred a *night!* Do you *believe* it?"

I didn't. "That's a lot of money, sweetheart. What kind of job is this?"

"Dancin'," she replied. "Kinda sleazy places, but that's cool. An agency sets me up with gigs."

She was a go-go dancer. She danced topless in Times Square hustle joints.

"I have to drink with some of the customers afterwards. You know the old routine, right?"

"Uh, no."

"They think they're buyin' me champagne. Champagne! It's ginger ale." She laughed. "Fuckin' ginger ale."

I guess her new profession fit all of the criteria Nancy had for a job. It was lucrative and, while not illegal, it was socially unacceptable. It took her into a hard, unsavory, and dangerous world. And it allowed her to sleep all day and be up all night.

It was, to us, repellent. Knowing about it made us feel dirty, ashamed. When people asked us what Nancy was doing for work in New York, we didn't tell them. Only my friends Janet and Susan knew. Suzy and David kept it from their friends. They, too, were ashamed.

Of course, we were perfectly aware that these clubs were also operating bases for prostitutes. The one thing, dancing, led to the other thing, hooking. We shut our eyes to this possibility. It was too horrible to conceive. We wanted to believe that Nancy was *only* dancing, and so we believed it. That was bad enough.

Recently Karen told me that she called Nancy one morning that March to tell her that her father had died. Nancy coldly told her, "I have to hang up—I have a customer here." And hang up she did.

So I suppose I must face the fact that my daughter probably did work as a prostitute. She was certainly capable of it. Sex meant nothing to her. It hurts me to think about it. But I can deal with it now. Nancy is at peace now. I couldn't deal with it then.

Karen told me she was very hurt after talking to Nancy on the phone. Nancy had rejected her. She wasn't there for Karen when Karen needed her. My daughter had stopped caring about people. Frankly, I think this upsets me more than the thought of Nancy selling her body.

Nancy was able to pay her rent and bills herself now that she was working. She was very proud of this. She was also able to afford the fast track to self-obliteration. With the two to three hundred dollars she was making a night, she became a hard-core heroin addict.

I found out in the early spring when Frank and I took the kids to New York to see Nancy's apartment and take her to dinner. They hadn't been up there since the move.

She looked tired and down. She wore old jeans and a baggy, oversize turtleneck sweater that came to the very tips of her fingers.

She hadn't cleaned her apartment. It wasn't a pigsty, but the ashtrays and litter box were overflowing. She showed Suzy and David around rather mechanically. They played with her cat for a minute. It went for David's throat as if it wanted to kill him. We didn't stay long.

We went to a restaurant in the neighborhood. I sat next to Nancy, who immediately began to doze off right there at the table. Her eyes closed, her head lowered, and off she went into slumberland. I nudged her. She sat up, confused, then fell asleep again. So we talked around her. We talked about the food. We talked about the weather.

At one point she slumped onto the table. Her elbow went into the untouched spaghetti I'd ordered for her. The sauce got all over her sweater. I roused her, suggested she take the sweater off so I could dab at the sauce before it stained. She did. She had a T-shirt on underneath.

That's when I saw the track marks. They ate away like a cancer at the insides of her elbows and the backs of her hands. The sight made me so sick to my stomach that I almost vomited. Those were her baby arms and hands to me, pudgy, soft, innocent. Now they were covered with the needle scars of an addict. She was so out of it, she didn't notice or care that I saw them.

Frank saw them, too.

"There's nothing we can do to help her," he said to me later that night, choosing his words slowly and painfully.

"Nothing?" I begged.

"Not until she wants to be helped."

He took me in his arms. I held back my tears.

I had a nightmare that night, the nightmare I was to have so many times over the next three years. I dreamed we were back on Welsh Road. Nancy was five. She was running up to me in the living room, excitedly waving her hands in front of her face.

"Look what I have, Mommy!" she exclaimed. "Look what I have!"

What she had were track marks all over her little girl' hands and arms, the track marks I'd seen in the restaurant.

Then she began to cry.

"Help me, Mommy!" she sobbed. "Help me!"

I tried to reach out to her, but my arms wouldn't move no matter how hard I strained.

I awoke from the nightmare with a start.

Seeing Nancy's track marks haunted me in daylight, too. A few days later Frank and I went to his friend's house, where a *briss* was being held for the baby that he and his wife had just had.

The proud mother held the lovely pink baby in her arms. When I saw it, I nearly screamed. I saw needle marks on that baby's pudgy little hands. I saw my Nancy's baby hands covered with track marks. I saw my sweet-smelling, innocent infant with a pink ribbon in her hair, the infant who had grown up to be a receptacle of unendurable pain. Maybe this baby would too. Some would. Too many. I couldn't blot out that realization, that fear.

I had to leave the room. I thought I'd get hysterical if I stayed in there with that baby for another second. I tried to compose myself in the dining room. Frank found me in there a few minutes later.

"What's wrong?" he asked.

"I'm having a . . . a problem in there."

"What kind of a problem?" he asked, turning me around to face him.

"If I look at that . . . at that baby for one more second I'm going to break down."

Our foreheads touched. He understood what I meant. Somehow he always did.

"We'll go, Deb. We'll just go."

Frank told them I wasn't feeling well and we left. When his friend asked us over for dinner the following week, Frank told them we were busy. I could not see that baby again. Or any baby. From that day on, if I saw one in the grocery store or being wheeled down the street in a carriage, I was immediately seized by the same hysteria. I began to avoid places where I thought I'd see babies. It was no use. There are a lot of babies in the world.

I gritted my teeth and kept going.

* * *

Nancy reached out for help toward the end of April. She phoned me several times, highly agitated, to say the city was getting to her and she had to get out, just had to.

"I'm going to Jamaica, Mom," she said. "I have money. Saved up. I'm going to Jamaica. Have a round-trip ticket."

"Why Jamaica?" I asked.

"It's warm there."

"It's warm in New York. It's spring."

"I'm going to Jamaica, Mom."

"Okay."

I had to be in Chicago then on business. When I got in touch with Frank my first night there, he told me he was about to drive to New York to get Nancy. He said she'd phoned several times, very upset, sobbing, barely coherent. She didn't want to go to Jamaica anymore, she said. She wanted to come home. She'd begged him to come and get her. He refused, surprised that she was even speaking to him.

"Please, Daddy. Please come. *Please.*"

She hadn't called him "Daddy" in over a year. He figured this meant she was pretty serious. He agreed to come get her.

She clung to him when he arrived.

She looked horrible, her clothes ratty, her hair stringy. She was wiped out and ravenously hungry. He took her to an all-night diner, where she wolfed down two hamburger platters, then they got in the car and drove home. She slept the whole way, slept most of the next day. She was barely stirring when I got home from Chicago. She was having a bowl of cereal in the kitchen.

"What happened with Jamaica?" I asked.

"I tried to get the money back. The fucker wouldn't give it back."

"Who?"

"The travel agent."

"But why didn't you want to go anymore?"

She shrugged.

"Nancy?"

"What?"

"Why didn't you want to go anymore?"

"I . . . I got scared."

"Of what?"

She shrugged, went back to her room, and closed the door. For the rest of the evening she didn't come out.

"Why is Nancy here?" asked Suzy at dinner.

"I haven't the slightest idea," I replied.

I awoke with a start in the middle of the night. Nancy stood over me. She was tugging at my nightgown.

"Mom," she whispered.

"Nancy? What is it?" I yawned.

"Do you have any Valium?"

"Any what?"

"Valium. I can't sleep."

Now Frank was awake.

"What's wrong?" he asked.

"Valium," she repeated. "I can't sleep."

"I don't have any."

"You must!" she demanded, clutching my nightgown. "You *have* to!"

"Nancy, I told you, I don't have any. Now go back to bed. Let us sleep, please."

"But *I* can't sleep. I gotta have Valium!"

"You slept all day," Frank said. "Maybe you should read a book for a while."

"Call your doctor!" she cried, wide-eyed now. "Tell him it's for you! Lie!"

"No," I said. "I won't."

"Then give me the keys to the car. Lemme go downtown. I'll buy some. On the street."

"No. Nancy, you're not making sense. Go to bed."

*"Fuck you! Fuck both of you!"* She stormed out.

I heard Frank sigh in the darkness. We turned over and tried to get back to sleep. The next thing I heard was a terrible thumping in the hallway, followed by a strangled moan and then a scream. We dashed into the hall, turned on the light.

Nancy was writhing on the hallway floor.

*"Nancy!"* I cried out.

Suzy and David rushed out of their rooms, blinking at the light. When they saw Nancy, their eyes widened in horror.

"What's wrong?" Suzy gasped.

"I'm trying to . . . I'm tryin' to . . ." Nancy rolled around on the floor, clutching herself. "I'm tryin' to . . . *kick.* I'm on smack. I'm tryin' . . . tryin' to get off. That's why. That's why I was goin' to Jamaica. Valium. I need Valium. So I can sleep . . . I gotta get off. Can't work no more. Nobody wants me. Keep firin' me. Guys don't dig the tracks. Gotta kick!"

I knelt down next to her, felt her forehead. Supposedly, the most obvious drug withdrawal symptom was shivering and sweating. Nancy's forehead was cool and dry. I was very confused.

"Valium . . . need Valium," she repeated desperately.

I had a strong gut-level hunch that Nancy was not actually withdrawing, that we were witnessing some sort of acting job. Possibly she just wanted me to call my doctor and get her some Valium so she could sleep. But if she *was* really serious, if she *was* trying to get off, I didn't want to slap her hand away.

"You have to get me Valium . . . you have to help me. It's your fault. Your fault."

"What's our fault?" Frank demanded.

"You made me an addict!"

"No way!" I snapped.

*"Did!"* she yelled.

"You're down there on the damned floor because you want to be there!" I yelled back. "It's *your* fault!"

"Don't you love me?" she asked.

"Of course we love you," I replied.

"Then why don't you stop me? Stop me! *Stop me! Look at me!"* She pulled up her nightgown. There were track marks behind her knees and ankles. It was horrifying.

"*You* have to stop yourself!" I yelled.

"I want to!" she cried. "I want to!"

"We'll take you to a drug hospital."

"No! No! I'll do it myself! No hospital!"

"You can't!" I said. "You need medical supervision!"

"No!" she cried.

"Nancy," I said. "If you're serious about getting off drugs, we're here for you. We'll do everything we can to help you. But *you* have to be serious. *You* have to want help."

"I am!" she protested. "I am!"

"No, you're not," said Frank, his voice harsh. "If you were, you'd get professional help. Go to a hospital. Not come up with some cockeyed scheme about going to Jamaica."

"You don't know what it's like!"

"I know you're not doing yourself any good this way," Frank said. "I'm going back to bed."

With that, he turned and went back to bed. We all did, except for Nancy. She just lay there alone on the hallway floor for a while. Then she went in her room, threw some things around in anger. Then she was quiet. At dawn she came in again, tugged at my sleeve, and begged me to call my doctor for Valium. Again, I refused.

She stayed with us for the next day and night, edgy and unhappy, though—seemingly—not suffering withdrawal symptoms. Evidently she had some heroin with her.

"I can't work, Mom," she said. "The tracks."

"Then *do* something about it, Nancy," I begged. I felt so powerless.

"I'm thinkin' about it. Maybe I will."

"We're with you, sweetheart. But you're an adult now. You have to initiate it. It has to be a decision *you* make. We're behind you a hundred percent."

She took a train back to New York after staying with us for two nights. She made some calls to city methadone clinics. She tried to get into an in-patient program, but came up against a shortage of beds. However, she was able to latch onto an out-patient program in Greenwich Village. It called for her to be at the clinic for her methadone every morning at eight. She did it. She went on the program early in May.

A sales award breakfast banquet I put together for Western Union brought me to New York City during the second week of Nancy's methadone maintenance program. Frank came with me. I had worked hard to make the banquet a success, and it was.

"You did a wonderful job," said the woman who sat next to me at the banquet.

She was my boss's wife, a tan, cool, perfect blond in her mid-forties with nice tan, cool, perfect blond children. All tennis players.

"Thank you," I replied.

"How are your children doing?" she asked me.

Ordinarily I kept my problems with Nancy set apart from work. My work was my refuge from her. On this day it spilled out. I was tired, and I was upset over the death of my favorite aunt the day before.

"My husband and I are about to go see our daughter, Nancy. She's a heroin addict. Now she's on methadone. We want to give her as much support as we can."

She shook her head sadly. "It must be so difficult. You must feel so . . . so . . ."

"Alone. We feel very alone. And helpless."

"I feel so fortunate," she said. "It's my greatest fear that it will happen to one of my children. It hasn't, at least not yet. You must be a very strong person—to cope with it."

"Not really. You can cope with a lot you never thought you'd be able to, if you're forced to."

She smiled sympathetically.

I wished I were her. I wanted so desperately to trade places with her at that moment. She was so calm and cool and in command of her life. She'd gotten what she wanted. I'd gotten something I'd never asked for.

When the breakfast was over, Frank and I checked out of our hotel and went to see Nancy. It was a gorgeous May afternoon, a Sunday. The city's sidewalks were filled with people out walking, enjoying themselves, enjoying life.

She was much improved. Her apartment and her appearance were neat. She was cheerful. She wore a short-sleeved blouse and I could see that the track marks were starting to heal.

"Hey, I'm okay," she confirmed. "A guy at the agency said I can come back to work next week. It's all right. This methadone thing is all right. I'm not hooked anymore. See? Look at my arms!" She eagerly showed me the wounds that were healing on her arms. "See? Look at my hands. Aren't you proud of me, Mom?"

"Yes, sweetheart."

"Are you really? Are you *really* proud?"

I hugged her. "Very proud."

She hugged me back, her eyes filling with tears.

I know that the debate over methadone rages on. Its opponents say it is merely a heroin substitute rather than a cure. They say it is not the answer. I can only speak for one heroin addict I've known—Nancy. When she was on methadone, she was able to work, pay her bills, get out and do something besides agonize over where her next fix was coming from. The phone calls, the paranoia, abated. She had a more positive self-image and her overall physical health improved. Methadone helped Nancy.

Admittedly, it didn't attack the problem of substance addiction. But it couldn't. Nancy had been escaping life's pain with drugs from the age of three months. She had been overmedicated. Society, as Cott told us, had offered her no other way to cope with her pain. She had grown up drug-dependent; now she was easing her pain through self-prescription.

Nobody had ever gotten to the root of Nancy's pain, her basic emotional disturbance. We tried. Lord knows, we tried. We spent her whole life—and, seemingly, ours—trying. But we'd been unable to find answers. There was no label for Nancy. She fell between the cracks, somewhere between neurotic and psychotic. She displayed flashes of schizophrenia, then she was fine, then the flashes would come back. There were fireworks going on inside her brain, yet nobody ever found an organic cause for them. I still believe she suffered neurological damage at birth. But no doctor ever said, "I want to know what makes this girl tick. I won't let her mind be wasted." And we were never able to help her on our own.

No one cared about my daughter until she was found under a hotel sink with a hunting knife in her stomach, and only then because they perceived her as some kind of freak. Am I angry? You bet I am.

I'm angry at the medical profession. Confronted with a child who fit no mold, doctor after doctor stuck his head in the sand. Each refused to look outside his own parameters. Each rejected her after a few months, told us to "take her somewhere else."

Even worse was the fact that we were lied to. They didn't understand what was wrong with her. Instead of telling us that, they told us nothing was wrong with her. "She's very bright, Mrs. Spungen," they said. "She'll outgrow it, Mrs. Spungen," they said. "Take her home and love her, Mrs. Spungen."

I'm angry at myself for accepting what they told me. I knew something was wrong with Nancy. She cried constantly from birth. She was acutely nervous and angry. She wouldn't sleep. But I didn't follow my instincts. I accepted what they told me. And Frank and I went ahead with our lives as if she were the normal child they told us she was. We had two more children. We tried and failed to have the life we wanted to have, unaware that what was tearing us apart was a decidedly abnormal child. They didn't warn us that Nancy was disturbed and would require special attention. They kept us in the dark. That was wrong. If we had known what we were getting into with Nancy, we might not have brought two more children into the world. We placed an unfair burden on them. And on each other.

When Nancy reached adolescence, they told us that what was wrong with her was us. It was *our* fault. We were bad parents. This caused us great anguish. A year later the clinic we'd taken her to revised its diagnosis to one of possible schizophrenia. Did they tell us this? No. We went on through the remainder of Nancy's life saddled with the burden of guilt for our child's problems. That was wrong.

We are not alone. Doctors continually lay this horrible guilt trip on other parents. Recently I saw a mother and her three children in a grocery store. Clearly, she was a caring mother. Two of the children were neat, bright-eyed, and well behaved. The third was wrecking the store—knocking merchandise off the shelves, screaming, refusing to listen to his mother's firm commands. No matter what she said or did, the boy would not be controlled. Finally, in tears, she had to call out for her husband to take the boy out to the car. She noticed me looking at her.

"I don't know what I'm doing wrong," she sobbed. "He's so . . . *difficult*. My others are fine. I wish I knew what I was doing wrong."

"I don't think you're doing anything wrong," I said.

She blinked, surprised. "My doctor says it's me. That I'm handling him wrong."

"It might not be the case," I said. "Some children are like that and there's nothing you can do about it. My daughter was like that. I know."

"Thank you," she said. "Thank you so much. You know, I've always believed that, but I needed to hear it from someone else. I needed someone to tell me I was doing the right thing."

She needed her doctor to tell her that.

To the medical community I say: Be more open with parents. Communicate with them, share your insights. If you don't have answers, don't pretend you do. Say so. Nothing is gained by handing out platitudes like lollipops. Or guilt. On the contrary—much can be lost.

To parents I say: Don't give up on your instincts. You know your child best. If you don't agree with your doctor's diagnosis, press on. Get more answers. See another doctor. Don't accept what you're told at face value. My biggest regret is that I did. Demand the truth—even if that truth turns out to be the painful realization that nothing can be done. You'll still be better off than Frank and I were. Believe me. You won't torment yourself like we did, wondering what you're doing wrong. You won't blame yourself. You'll know that yours is an abnormal child. You'll know that yours is a child for whom you can do nothing. Except love.

I'm not saying Nancy's life would necessarily have turned out differently if I knew then what I know now. Chances are, she still would have ended up in an institution, or in prison, or dead. But we would have been aware of what we were getting into. Maybe we'd have found a place for her, someplace where she could have had her books and her records. Maybe the wounds inflicted on the four of us would not have cut so deep or taken so long to heal.

Something happened to Nancy in the first twenty-four hours of her life. I know it. There was neurological damage. I've met parents with children who had problem births like hers—prolapsed umbilical cord, a high bilirubin level. Many of them are just like Nancy: angry, aggressive, in pain. This is no coincidence, and doctors now acknowledge it. At Children's Hospital in Philadelphia, for example, therapists now follow problem-birth babies closely for the first two years of their lives. They observe them at home, test their progress every few months. That's good. Maybe they'll get a body of information together. Maybe they'll improve their ability to detect neurological damage. Maybe they'll be able to help someone else's baby. It's too late for Nancy, a generation too late.

It's good to see people opening their eyes to this syndrome that has no name. You tend to close them until it happens to your child. There is no such thing as a child who is not worth saving.

At this point in Nancy's life she couldn't be saved. Methadone kept her alive a little longer. It was the next best thing to a cure and we applauded it.


We took her out to dinner. Her choice for a restaurant was Grotta Azzurra in Little Italy. We'd taken all three kids there for dinner years before and had a nice meal. This night Nancy enjoyed herself, enjoyed the food. But after about an hour a little timer seemed to go off in her head. She got restless. It required great effort for her to play the part of good daughter, and she'd run out of energy.

"I wanna go," she said, putting her fork down.

"Don't you want to finish your dessert?" I asked.

"I wanna go."

Actually we were anxious to get back home. This was the first time we'd left Suzy and David for a weekend without a baby sitter.

So we left. We dropped her off at a friend's apartment in the Village and headed on out. When we stopped for gas on the New Jersey Turnpike, I called home. Suzy answered. She sounded upset, frightened.

"What's wrong, Suzy?"

"Nothing, Mom."

"Why do you sound that way?"

"We had a party and—"

"You were told not to have a party!"

"—and we smashed your car."

It was the last straw. I couldn't stand to hear anymore. I hung up on her. I got in the car and told Frank, then totally withdrew. We drove all the way home without speaking. I didn't have the strength to deal with this. Or the desire. I decided to resign. As a mother. As a human being.

When we got home, the car was sitting in front of the house. It was so badly smashed that I could not look at it. Suzy and David were waiting for us in the foyer, cowering. I didn't greet them.

"Frank," I said. "You handle it. I quit."

They all looked at me, shocked. I had always been strong enough to deal with whatever came along. Not this time. I'd had it. My limit had finally been reached. I went upstairs and closed myself in the bedroom. I thought about grabbing a suitcase and filling it and running away. Then my mind went blank. I just lay on the bed, staring at the ceiling, limp, drained. Eventually I slept. Frank crawled into bed next to me sometime during the night. We didn't speak.

I felt okay in the morning. I asked Frank for the details. He gave them to me. The kids had thrown a beer bash by the pool. Sometime during the evening they'd loaned the car to a friend who asked for it (which they were forbidden to do) and he had proceeded to wreck it along with two other cars.

We did, of course, lose our car insurance again. This time we were forced to take out a high-risk policy at triple the rate.

Left on their own for the first time, Suzy and David had done just the sort of thing Nancy would have done. They were getting to be the age she had been that awful last year she'd spent at home. They were testing us, testing to see if they could get away with the kind of behavior Nancy had. They couldn't. We would not tolerate this sort of recklessness and irresponsibility from them. History was not going to repeat itself. We came down on them very hard. They were grounded until they left for camp in July. Unlike Nancy—thank god—they took their punishment, cowed by our anger, apologetic.

We'd gotten Nancy away from them, but her specter remained.

# ☐ Chapter 17

Nancy stayed on the methadone program for about four weeks.

I didn't hear from her very often. One time, the strip club she was dancing at was raided for a liquor license violation, and she was busted. She was stuck in a cell for a couple of hours until the club owner bailed her out. She ended up having to pay a $150 fine. She didn't have the money so I paid the fine for her. I couldn't stand the idea of her going to jail.

Then she met a guitarist named Jerry at Max's. She liked him a lot. She wanted me to meet him. I don't know if he returned her ardor. I somehow doubt it, since he broke it off to move to London and play in a band there. Nancy was pretty down about his leaving, but seemed to be coping until she discovered that her friend Phyllis was flying to London for two weeks—mainly to see Jerry.

She called me, sobbing hysterically.

"Do you *believe* her? That rotten. . . . She was my friend! She's fucking *my guy! My . . . guy!* He's *mine!*"

"I'm sorry, Nancy."

"Do you *believe* somebody would do that!"

"It happens. People do that."

"To you?" she demanded.

"Well, no. But you have to accept it."

"I don't have to accept a fucking thing."

She slammed down the phone.

And went back on the smack. I could tell from her slurred voice on the phone a few days later.

"You're shooting again, aren't you?" I said.

"Uh . . ."

"Aren't you?"

"Well . . . yeah. Like, uh . . . well, yeah. I am."

"Oh, Nancy, why? Why did you start again? You were doing so well."

"Jus' figured I'd do it one time, Mom. One little ol' time, ya know?"

"Nancy, that's so stupid! Totally stupid! You're an addict! You *can't* just go back to it once!"

"I . . . yeah. Well, you know what they say: Never trust a junkie. Not even your own daughter."

She hung up, chuckling sadly to herself.

Nancy stayed on heroin through June and July. By then Suzy and David had left for camp. Every evening Frank and I sat at opposite ends of the pool, both of us in our own oasis. Silence.

One afternoon she called the house while I was on my way home from work. She told Frank to have me call her at once. She wouldn't speak to him, wouldn't answer his questions. She sounded terrified, he said.

I called. There was no answer.

"How long ago did she call?" I asked Frank.

"Five minutes, tops."

I called again to make sure I had the right number. I let it ring a couple of dozen times. I was about to hang up when she picked it up. I heard heavy breathing, then a muffled moan.

"Nancy!" I cried out.

There was a long pause.

"Huh?"

"*Are . . . you . . . okay?*"

"Tired . . . just tired, Mom."

"Are you sure?"

"Uh-huh."

She hung up. A few days later she called to thank me for saving her life. She'd OD'ed. My call had roused her enough to call Lance Loud for help. He'd taken her to the hospital.

"You saved me, Mom. You saved your Nancy's life."

I didn't know if I had done her a favor or not. She seemed to think so. But I believe that she knew, deep down inside, what I myself was becoming certain of: Only in death would she find peace.

After that incident she swore off smack, though. Not that she let on that there was any connection.

"It's just no good, Mom," she told me on the phone. "Gotta get off. Nobody likes the way I look. Gotta get off so I can keep workin'."

She spoke about kicking her heroin addiction as if it were like taking off ten extra pounds.

"And it's really expensive. I'm gettin' off."

"I want you to know we're with you. Anything we can do . . ."

"I'm glad."

"Same program?"

"Uh-uh. State of New York ran out of money. Big surprise, right? But I found another one. Flower Fifth Avenue Hospital. Goin' up there tomorrow mornin'."

"Good luck, sweetheart."

"Thanks, Mom."

My job no longer took me to New York regularly. I made arrangements to take a personal day off so I could go up and see her. I thought it was important to give her positive reinforcement.

She was very enthusiastic about my coming. Truly, the change in her when she was on methadone was remarkable.

"Come in really early, Mom. We'll spend the whole day together, you and me."

"Will you be awake?"

"Call me from Penn Station. I'll be up!"

Unfortunately the day I chose to come to New York fell in

the middle of a horrendous August heat wave. It was already ninety degrees and muggy when I got on the train at eight in the morning. It was close to a hundred by the time I got to New York. I wore a loose-fitting T-shirt and jeans. As I sat there on the train, I fantasized that Nancy had just graduated from Penn and gotten a job in New York. She and I were going to shop for the new business suits she'd need. We'd try Bloomingdale's. And Saks, of course. And Bendel's . . .

The train plunged into the blackness of the tunnel and then we were in Penn Station. I called Nancy from a pay phone. She was up and raring to go. I bought some fresh hot bagels and a bunch of daisies at the station, then took a cab to her apartment. She was showered and dressed. She wore a tight T-shirt, black jeans, and platform sandals. She hugged me and squealed with delight over the flowers. She carefully arranged them in a pitcher, then made a pot of coffee. We had breakfast.

"You've *got* to see Fiorucci's," she jabbered excitedly. "That's where these jeans came from. And then we'll go to Bloomingdale's, okay?"

It was just like my fantasy. A real mother-daughter day.

"Great," I exclaimed.

"But first I get my booking for tonight."

"Okay."

"And get some kind of blood test at a city health center in Harlem. To do with my methadone thing. Ya know, to make sure I'm clean."

"Okay."

"And then get my methadone."

"Okay."

"But we'll have plenty of time to shop. *If* we get moving, lady!"

"Okay, okay!" I laughed. "Let's go."

The go-go club booking agency was in a sleazy office building in the West Forties. The hallway outside smelled; inside it was very hot and dingy. There was a large room with a number of men at desks working the phones. Hardened young women were coming in and going out. There was a big blackboard on one wall with about fifty women's names listed.

It was all so foreign to me, so bizarre, so sick, so inconceivable. Never had I imagined I'd ever find myself in a place like this—especially with my eldest daughter. The daughter had *brought* me here.

"See, Mom, there's my name!" Nancy exclaimed, pointing to her name on the board. She wrote down her assignment, then said, "Hey, you gotta meet my boss!"

"That's really not—"

"C'mon."

She dragged me into a small office where a fat middle-aged man was on the phone. He was sweating profusely. His shirt stuck to him. One shirttail was out. Nancy waved to him. His response was annoyance. He gestured for her to go away and not bother him.

"Let's go," I whispered.

"No way," she replied.

He got off the phone. "What is it?" he demanded impatiently.

"I want you to meet my mother," Nancy said proudly.

His head snapped back when he heard the word *mother*. He smoothed back his hair, tucked in his shirt. Then he politely introduced himself and shook my hand. He was greasy.

"A real pleasure. A real pleasure indeed." He beamed. "What brings you to New York?"

"She came to see me," Nancy answered.

"Right. Well, enjoy your stay, Mrs. Spungen. Come again."

I wondered what kind of person he thought I was. I didn't ask. We left. When we got back down onto the burning pavement, I asked myself, *How many mothers in America are doing this today?*

It was now about eleven o'clock. Time to go to Harlem for Nancy's blood tests. We took the subway. It was a long, crowded, chokingly hot ride. When we got off, we had to walk several blocks crosstown, past burned-out tenements and abandoned cars. The sidewalk was littered with broken glass. Some men slept in doorways. Others loitered on street corners and in doorways. They appraised us as we walked past. Nancy's jeans were *very* tight. She wore no bra and well, what breasts there are in the family, Nancy got. They whistled and hissed after us, made kissing noises and very detailed, very obscene comments about what they'd like to do with us.

"Fuck you!" Nancy yelled back at a bunch who sat on a stoop, drinking beer and smoking marijuana.

"Nancy!" I whispered fiercely, walking faster. "Let them be!"

"You're not afraid, are you, Mom?"

"Yes, I am."

"Hey, don't worry. I won't let anything happen to you." She took my hand and held it until we got to the health center.

It was an absolutely horrible place—hot, filthy, and mobbed. There were alcoholics, addicts, bums, people with hacking coughs.

The man in line ahead of us at the reception desk told the nurse, "I has this here, like, discharge from my penis, ya dig?"

My skin began to crawl.

We were told to wait. There were no empty seats in the waiting area, which was just as well. I was afraid if I sat down I'd catch something. It was so hot in there it was hard to breathe. A man came over to us. I was frightened. He only wanted a light. I gave him some matches. When he tried to give them back to me, I told him to keep them.

Nancy and I stood there for two hours. I felt like everyone in the place was staring at us. We did kind of stand out, being the only two white people there.

"Sorry about this, Mom."

"It's okay."

"No, I really am."

"Don't worry about it."

We stood there until Nancy couldn't stand waiting anymore. She spat out "Fuck this shit" and plowed her way down the corridor and around the corner toward the examining room.

"Miss!" the receptionist called after her.

Nancy evidently grabbed the first man in a white coat she found and let loose. I could hear her quite plainly.

"You sonofabitch! You stupid motherfucker! We've been waiting for *three* fucking hours. My *mother* is with me. We're not gonna wait another fucking minute! Three fucking hours for a lousy fucking ten-minute blood test! *Now!* Take me now!"

He took her right into the examining room. She came back out ten minutes later, grabbed my hand, and yanked me toward the front door.

"Let's get out of this fucking hellhole!"

I breathed a sigh of relief as we emerged onto the street. Even the street was better than being in the health center. We walked back crosstown, past the same men—they remembered us—and caught a bus down to Flower Fifth Avenue Hospital, which was on Fifth at 106th Street. Once again I asked myself, *How many mothers in America are doing this today?*

We were only in the hospital a few minutes. We took the elevator up to the methadone clinic. Nancy handed over an ID card that had been stamped at the Harlem health center. The nurse gave her back the card, then gave Nancy her paper cup of methadone.

She downed the orange liquid, handed back the cup, and said to me, "Let's get some lunch."

By now it was already past three o'clock. Nancy had to be at work at six, and change her clothes first. So our day was pretty well shot. We had lunch at Joe Allen's in the theater district. We took a cab. I had had enough mass transit for one day.

The restaurant was so heavily air conditioned, it felt like a meat locker. I loved it. We both gulped down two gigantic iced teas. It was the best iced tea I'd ever tasted. We ordered hamburgers and dove into them when they came.

"I'm really sorry things turned out this way, Mom. I wanted us to go to Bloomingdale's and Fiorucci's. They have these pants that'd look good on you."

"It's okay. We had a day together, that's the main thing."

"Yeah, but we wasted it, waiting in that hellhole."

"We'll shop some other time."

She grinned. "Okay."

The cab dropped me at Penn Station. I gave Nancy enough money so she could take the cab home and pay the driver.

"Good-bye, Mom. I'm sorry everything got loused up."

"Don't worry. It was fun. I had a nice time. Not quite what I expected. But nice."

"Really?"

"Uh-huh."

We embraced. Then I got out and the cab took off down Seventh Avenue. Nancy waved to me through the rear window. I waved back.

There were no seats left on the train, and the air conditioning was broken. I stood the whole way home, crammed between two commuters, sweat streaming down my back and my legs.

"How'd it go?" Frank called when I came in the front door.

I didn't answer. I was too busy peeling off my wet clothes in the foyer.

He appeared from the kitchen. "What are you doing?"

I went past him, found my bathing suit in the laundry room, jumped into it, and dove to the bottom of the pool. I stayed down there as long as I could. When I came up, Frank was waiting by the side of the pool with an iced tea. I drank it. Then I went upstairs and washed the day off of me in the shower. Or tried. Only then was I able to tell Frank about it. In the telling, I found humor in my adventures. By the time I was done describing my day, we were both roaring with laughter there by the side of the pool.

You had to laugh, if you wanted to survive.


Nancy stayed on the methadone through the fall. The lease on her apartment came up for renewal at the end of November. She had now been in New York a year. When we talked about renewing it, she balked. She had a different idea.

"I don't know, Mom. I don't know if I wanna lock myself into New York."

"Why not?"

"Just don't."

"Is there somewhere else you want to go?"

"A lot of bands are going over to London. A lot of my friends are just sort of clearin' out, going there. Debbie's goin' there. The whole music thing from here is there now. I've never been there. Everybody's been there."

"I haven't been there."

"Randi has. Phyllis. I wanna go, too."

"I don't understand what this has to do with your lease, Nancy. You still have to have a place to live."

"Well, I don't know. I was thinking I'd like to work in the music business there. You know, live there."

"But you've never been there. How do you know you'll like it?"

"All the bands are there. It's cool there."

She didn't renew the lease. Instead she rented the apartment on a month-to-month basis and talked continually about moving to London. She began to save up for it.

I asked her if she wanted to come home for Hanukkah/Christmas, but she said she had to stay in New York and work. So the four of us decided to spend the day after Christmas in New York with her, a prospect that delighted her. She was especially excited about buying gifts for all of us. She loved giving and getting gifts. As Christmas neared she called me anxiously for gift suggestions for Frank (she was now actually speaking to Frank occasionally) and for the kids. She was so happy about what she'd bought me that she wanted to tell me what it was right there on the phone. I had to talk her out of it. Then she wanted me to tell her what I'd gotten her. She begged and teased and giggled like a little girl.

I bought her a lot of little gifts. She didn't care how much you spent on her. It was the *idea* of getting the gifts—opening the boxes, discovering their contents—that she loved. I knew it would give her pleasure to tear open so many boxes. She was so rarely happy. This would make her happy for a few minutes. What more could I give her?

It was a raw, gray day as we drove to New York, and we had to keep both the car heater and our coats on. We mapped out our day. Suzy and David wanted to go to a museum after we opened the presents. Frank and I agreed that I'd take

Nancy to a movie if she didn't want to go to a museum. Then the five of us would have an early dinner before she had to leave for work.

"Think she's really going to do this London thing?" Frank wondered aloud.

"It sounds pretty farfetched to me," I said. "I can see her going over for a vacation. You know, two weeks. But not staying there for good. She may not even like it there."

"If she wanted to stay," Suzy asked, "would you let her?"

"Nancy does what Nancy wants," I answered with a shrug.

"How come *we* can't?" Suzy asked.

Frank and I exchanged a quick look, weighed a reply. The kids waited for it. It got very quiet in the car.

"Nancy doesn't live by the same set of rules the rest of us do," Frank said. "Not me, not Mom, not any of your friends' parents. She won't lead a life like other people. She just won't. She's determined to be different, and there isn't much that Mom and I can do about it anymore."

"How come?" David asked.

"Because she's disturbed," I replied. "Nancy has serious troubles. You know that. You both know that. Her way isn't the right way. Believe me, it isn't. Maybe our way isn't, either. But we think it is. That requires a certain amount of faith on your part. You have to trust us. But you're not kids anymore. You can look at Nancy. You can see she's not happy."

"Are *you* happy?" Suzy asked.

"Good question," Frank admitted.

"Are you?" she repeated.

"Sometimes," I said. "Sometimes, we are. Yes."

We got to Nancy's apartment at about noon and she greeted each of us with bear hugs. She was in great spirits and the place was spotless.

She absolutely would not open her gifts until we had each received our gifts from her.

I went first. I couldn't believe what I saw when I opened the little box. It was an Elsa Peretti necklace—a small silver vase that hung from a sterling silver chain. I had long admired Elsa Peretti's jewelry, but I'd never imagined I'd get to own a piece. It must have cost Nancy $150.

"It's real, Mom." Nancy beamed. "The vase, I mean. It holds water. You can wear a fresh flower around your neck every day."

I was flabbergasted, it was so beautiful.

Underneath it, folded into the cotton, was a note. I opened it.

> *Dear Mom,*
> *I love you very much and you know why. There is noth-ing else I can say. Merry Christmas.*
>
> > *Love, Nancy*

I looked up at her beaming face. She was so proud. For a moment the source of the necklace—the kind of work she'd done to make the money—crossed my mind. But I let the thought go. I hugged and kissed her and thanked her.

"Do you *really* like it?" she begged.

"Oh, Nancy, I *love* it."

"Really?"

"Really."

She asked twenty times. I answered twenty times. The answers never seemed to compute.

Frank went next. His box was from Bloomingdale's. Inside was a gorgeous dress shirt to wear with his new suit.

"That's great, Nancy," he said enthusiastically. "Just great."

"Does it fit? Does it fit?" she begged.

Unfortunately it was not the right size. Frank hesitated. Obviously, it crossed his mind not to tell her.

"I'll take it back," she said, guessing it was the wrong size. "I'll take it back. Maybe they're open now."

"No, no, it's beautiful, Nancy. I love it. I'll . . . I'll take care of it."

"You sure?"

"Positive."

"You like it?"

"Love it."

"What if they don't have it in your size? What will you do?"

"I . . . I'm sure they will."

"It's a big chain, Nancy," I said. "They'll have Daddy's size somewhere, at one of their branches."

"Right," Frank agreed. "Somewhere."

"Oh," she said. "Okay."

Then it was the kids' turn. From Nancy, Suzy got a monogrammed canvas bag for her art supplies and books. David received several pairs of bikini briefs in assorted colors.

"You're already gorgeous," Nancy advised her baby brother. "But now you'll be *sexy,* too."

Now it was time for Nancy to open all of her boxes. She sat down on the floor, legs crossed, and fanned them out around her. Then she tore into them with childlike glee, ripping the paper and ribbons, giggling and gasping.

We gave her a makeup mirror, an ashtray, a cake of perfumed soap, a bottle of toilet water, an address book, stationery, a scarf, and a book about cats.

"So many presents!" she exclaimed. "So many presents! It's just like Christmas! It *is* Christmas!"

It was a treat to see her so happy—the best Christmas present I could ask for.

We went out for a nice lunch. As it turned out, Nancy did not want to go to "any lousy museum," so she and I went to see *Voyage of the Damned* at a theater on Thirty-fourth Street while Frank took the kids to the museum. She got restless afterward at dinner. She could spend only so many hours with us. She was tired of being pleasant, so she became hostile and argumentative. We drove home to Philadelphia right after dinner.

Gradually, Nancy was weaned off the methadone in January and February. By the time she turned nineteen on February 27, 1977, she was off drugs completely. And on her way to England. The dream had formulated into a plan. She was set to leave the first week of March.

As it happened, she hadn't been able to save enough money for her plane fare. She'd spent too much on our Christmas presents. However, she, Suzy, and David had each been given a $1,500 savings certificate by their great-grandfather to be cashed when they turned twenty-one. I was the guardian of the certificates. Nancy asked if I would let her have $500 for her plane fare and deduct it from her certificate. I told her I'd have to think about it.

Actually it wasn't a difficult decision. There was no point in saving money for her. True, she was off drugs at the moment. But for how long? How much time did she really have left? Not much, I believed. Her emotional problems hadn't gone away. She wanted to travel, to enjoy herself. She wanted to go to England. It was a trip I'd wanted to take when I was nineteen. Still wanted to take. I hadn't had the chance but I wanted her to have it. So I let her have the money for her plane fare.

After her death I read in a well-known magazine that Nancy had worked as a prostitute in order to earn her plane fare to London. Not true. The money came from me. I paid it directly to the travel agent—an open-ended round-trip ticket to Amsterdam, which was the cheapest fare.

She gave up her Chelsea apartment, stored her furniture, gave away her cat. Her treasured record collection was entrusted to her friends Felipe and Babette. (As far as I know, they still have it. They disappeared shortly before Nancy came back from England and she was unable to reclaim it.)

Frank and I made plans to see her in New York a few days before she left for a combination bon voyage and birthday dinner. We bought her some luggage as a present. She looked radiant. Her blond hair was piled neatly on top of her head; her color was good, her complexion clear. Her track marks were completely healed. I told her how fabulous she looked.

"I'm clean, Mom," she said. "That's why."

We had a lovely dinner at the One Fifth Avenue restaurant. Nancy chattered nonstop through the meal, she was so excited.

". . . and Debbie's gonna come over. And Jerry's there. The whole *thing* is there. It's like everybody from here is there now. That's where it's all happening. *Everybody's* there! You wouldn't *believe* it! I'm gonna get a job. Maybe in an office or something."

"Sounds great," Frank said.

"It will be." She beamed. "It really will be."

Another of Nancy's fresh starts. Only this time her last.

After dinner we hugged and kissed and said good-bye. She promised to write us from London. She had a reservation in a small hotel for one week. She hoped to get settled quickly.

Actually Frank and I thought she'd be back in two weeks.

She didn't come back for eighteen months, and when she came she wasn't alone.

# ☐ Chapter 18

Nancy had trouble from the minute she got off the plane in Amsterdam. She missed her connecting flight to London and called me from the airport—angry, bewildered, panicking.

"The fucking plane's *gone!* I couldn't find it! Nobody in this fucking place speaks English and I went the wrong fucking way and now it's gone and I'm stuck here! What am I gonna do?"

"Take the train to London," I suggested.

"I haven't got enough *money.* The plane was *paid* for. Fucking travel agent. It's his fucking fault. I want you to sue his—"

"I'll send you the money, Nancy. To American Express in London. Okay?"

She didn't answer.

"Nancy?"

"All right," she said, disgusted.

She phoned the next day to report that she'd made it to London.

"It's okay here," she said. "At least they speak English."

She reported in again two days later. She seemed to need to report in.

"I walked around," she said. "Found some really great shops. You'd like them, Mom. And I saw Jerry, remember him? The guitarist? He introduced me to some people, and I saw some other people I know."

When her week at the hotel was up, she phoned again.

"I'm gonna move in with some friends tomorrow. For a while."

"How is your money holding out?" I asked.

"Okay, for now. I think I actually have a gig lined up."

"A gig?"

"Yeah. Playing bass fiddle in an all-girl band. They're goin' on tour. France, Germany, and Belgium."

"Nancy, you don't know how to play bass fiddle."

"They're gonna teach me. They said it's easy. There's really a lot goin' on here, Mom. Music. People. I'm meeting a lot of people. You know who I met at a party last night? You won't *believe* it."

"Who?"

"Sid Vicious."

*"Who?"*

*"Sid Vicious."*

"Who's he?"

"A punk rocker. He's with the Sex Pistols, Mom."

"Who are the Sex Pistols?"

"They're the biggest band in England. They're great. The best."

"Oh."

"He's nice. Really nice. I really like him. I think he likes me, too."

"What kind of a name is that, Sid Vicious?"

"I met Johnny, too."

"Johnny?"

"Johnny Rotten. The singer."

"He's with the Sex Pistols, too?"

"Uh-huh."

"That's very nice." Needless to say, I felt a little out of it.

"I'll let you know when I get settled at my friend's place. Like I said, I may be goin' on the road right away with this group."

At dinner that night I asked Suzy and David if they'd ever heard of the Sex Pistols. Suzy rolled her eyes.

"They're terrible," she said. "Really sick and bad."

"What do they play?" asked Frank.

"It's punk," David added. "Only, well, to tell you the truth, it's not even music. It's one step beyond. It's nothing you'd like too much. Why do you ask, Mom?"

"Nancy likes one of the fellows in the group."

"Figures," said Suzy.

"Never heard of them," Frank said.

"Are they popular here?" I asked.

"No," said David.

"But they will be," said Suzy, "if Nancy's into them."

I paid no further attention at that time to the subject of punk music or to the musician Sid Vicious. I assumed he was just another of her fleeting, one-sided attachments. There was no reason then to think otherwise.

Within two weeks Nancy's projected tour with the all-girl band had fallen through. And she was, it appeared, back on heroin. She denied it, but on the phone her voice was slurred. She was paranoid and didn't make a lot of sense. And she was out of money.

"I can't stay with my friends no more, Mom. They don't like me. Don't want me there. They hate me."

"So where are you staying?"

"On the street. In a car. Your Nancy's sleepin' in a car. And I got no food. Nothing to eat. No money, Mom."

"You're back on."

"No, it isn't that."

"Nancy, don't lie to me."

"I'm not."

"You told me never to trust a junkie."

"I'm your *daughter*."

"*Even* my daughter."

"I'm not on junk. I *swear*. It's just that . . . that nobody *likes* me. And I'm sleepin' in a *car*. No place. No food. I need

money, *please*. The money from my certificate. Send me
some of it. There's a thousand left, isn't there? Please, Mom.
*Please.*''

"Maybe you should think about coming home."

"No! I won't! I'm not ready!"

"But you're not hacking it over there."

"I'm okay. I just need money. I just need . . . I need
*spring*. It's so *cold* here. So *moldy*.''

I told her I'd have to think about it.

I agonized over it. I felt more helpless than ever before.
She was so vulnerable, so incapable of taking care of herself.
And so far away. If she'd been in New York I could have
driven up to see her. I could have brought her food. I could
have helped her survive. Now she was several thousand miles
away—broke and homeless. A street urchin.

I'd sworn I'd never send her money if she was on drugs.
But where was the right and wrong here? Where was the
truth? *Was* she clean? Even if she wasn't, how could I let her
starve?

I sent her a hundred dollars. I knew she might use it on
drugs but I felt she was also without the necessities of life. I
had to try to provide those for her. I had to try to keep her
alive. She was my baby.

Meanwhile, Suzy also needed me.

She was in her senior year of high school and wanted to attend art school after she graduated. Now was the time to apply. The schools asked to see slides of the student's work as
part of the application. Suzy had the slides made, but balked
when it came to sending them in. She couldn't seem to get her
finished applications into the mail. She'd start crying. She
was insecure. She had a confidence problem—springing,
doubtless, from all of those formative years spent being belittled and beaten down by Nancy. She'd been through a lot.

Frank and I sat her down. We suggested she work for a year
before applying to art school. We wanted to take the pressure
off her, give her some time to grow on her own. She liked our
idea. She seemed relieved.

Toward the end of April my friend Susan went to London
for a vacation. She had known and cared about Nancy since

Nancy had been a baby. I gave Susan a hundred dollars and asked her to deliver it to Nancy.

"She's going to ask you for more money," I told Susan. "Don't give it to her, no matter what she says."

Susan promised she wouldn't.

She gave me a report when she returned from her vacation.

"Nancy came to my hotel the first day I got there," Susan said. "I gave her the money and she immediately asked for more, just like you said she would. I told her I didn't have any. She got really angry. She refused to believe I didn't have any more money. When I offered to buy her lunch, she stomped off."

"How did she look?" I asked.

Susan hesitated. "Not well. Her hair was uncombed. She was pale and had dark circles under her eyes. She looked really out of it, Deb."

No doubt about it now—she was on heroin again. Finding herself in a foreign environment, encountering situations she couldn't handle, she'd prescribed a painkiller to ease the discomfort.

We didn't know what to do. The situation seemed hopeless. Frank and I discussed my going over there to bring her back. I wasn't sure I'd be able to handle her alone. If Frank went alone, she'd fight him. If we both went, well, we both couldn't afford to go. We decided to wait and see, try to handle it by phone and by sending her small amounts of money.

She called constantly. As before, she would only speak to me. It seemed as if she always called when I was in transit. When I got home from work, I could always tell if Nancy had called by the tension on Suzy's and David's faces. If they'd taken a call and then gone out, the procedure was to leave the note with Nancy's latest phone number stuck on the refrigerator. Checking the door of the refrigerator when I got home became automatic. So did my physical response while I waited for the overseas operator to place my call. The adrenaline would surge through me. It would take forever, it seemed, for the operator to connect me to Nancy's latest crisis.

Toward the beginning of May I came home to find the kids and Frank waiting in the foyer for me, upset.

Frank said, "She's in the hospital."

"Why?" I cried.

"She has to have some kind of operation," he said. "On her spine. You just missed her call. She wants you to call her right away."

"Her spine! Where's the phone number?"

"In your bedroom," David said. "On your pillow."

I dashed up the stairs two at a time, my heart pounding. I turned on the light in the bedroom and went to the pillow. There was no note on it. I searched the bed, the nightstand, the floor. I flung the bedspread aside. I could find no piece of paper with Nancy's number on it.

"David!" I shouted. "I can't find it! Where is it?!"

"On your pillow!" he called from downstairs.

*"Where!"* I screamed, my cool starting to vanish.

All three of them came up to the room.

"It's on your pillow, Mom," David said. "Honest, I wrote the number down and put it right there on your pillow."

"Then find it!" I shrieked. Nancy needed me. Without that number, I couldn't help her!

David got down on the floor and began to search under the bed, behind the bed. We all searched, crawling around frantically for that elusive scrap of paper.

"It's gotta be here somewhere," David said.

"What hospital!" I screamed, seized by panic. "What was the name of the hospital!"

"I don't remember, Mom. Saint . . . Saint . . . something."

"Do you realize how many saints there are!"

"Calm down, Deb," Frank commanded. "She'll call back."

"How do you know that!"

"She always calls back."

I scampered across the rug for the phone. "I'll call every hospital in London until I get her!"

"No!" barked Frank, wrenching the phone from me. "You'll just tie up the line."

His words bounced off me. I could only think of Nancy in trouble somewhere, and my inability to do a thing about it.

*"David, where is that paper?"* I yelled. *"Where is it? Find it!"*

"I don't know what happened to it, Mom," he protested, his voice quavering.

*"Find it!"*

"I can't!"

"I can't find my baby and it's your fault! My baby needs me! Find it, goddamnit! *Find it!*"

I picked up a bottle of lotion that was on the nightstand and hurled it blindly in David's direction. I missed him. It smashed against the wall, lotion spraying everywhere.

David looked to Frank helplessly. Frank stood there looking at me, wide-eyed. So did Suzy. They'd never seen me like this. I'd never freaked before.

My head was spinning. I was out of control. I collapsed on the floor in a heap, screaming, *"My baby! My baby! My baby!"*

The phone rang. I dove for it, answered it. It was the overseas operator.

"A collect call from Nancy."

"Yes! Yes!"

"Hi, Mom."

*"Where are you? What's wrong?"*

"There's something wrong with my spine," she said. "I can't sit. I can't stand. It hurts so much. They have to operate on it tomorrow morning. Please come and be with me, Mommy."

I realized at once what the problem was—Nancy had been born with a pilonidal opening at the base of her spine. It is not a serious condition, simply an incomplete closure. However, her first pediatrician had warned me that a pilonidal cyst will often develop there after puberty. Very, very painful, but a minor surgical procedure to remove.

I heaved a huge sigh of relief.

"Don't worry, Nancy. It's a cyst. It's not anything serious. You'll feel much better after he takes it out. It won't hurt any more."

"Promise?"

"Uh-huh. I'll call you right afterward."

She gave me the doctor's name so I could call him.

"I love you, Mommy."

"I love you, sweetheart."

I hung up, totally drained. I looked up. My family was watching me apprehensively. David swallowed and looked down. He was very upset. He was so reliable, and I loved him so much. He didn't deserve the fury I'd unleashed on him.

I went over to him, put my arms around him.

"Please forgive me, David. I'm sorry. I'm really so sorry."

We hugged, holding on to each other for several minutes, both of us feeling such incredible sadness.

Then he and Suzy went downstairs.

"You okay?" Frank asked, still concerned.

I nodded.

He went downstairs with the kids. I cleaned up the mess I'd made with the lotion, then slid into bed and fell asleep. I awoke at five a.m. and called Nancy's physician in London. It had indeed been a pilonidal cyst, and he'd removed it without complications. I spoke to her later in the day. She was groggy from the painkillers, but fine. I sent her flowers. Three days later they sent her home.

Trouble was, she had no home. She was crashing in someone or another's dirty flat from week to week, stoned and without a source of income apart from what I was sending her. We had wired her the $1,000 balance from her certificate, and it ran out in June. Then the money started coming out of the household budget.

As far as I know, she had no regular place to live until midsummer, when she phoned to inform me that she and Sid were moving in with his mother.

"Sid?" I asked, not placing the name.

"From the Sex Pistols, Mom. Sid Vicious. He's the biggest rock star in the world. And he's all mine. Isn't that great?"

"So you two are . . . ?"

"We've been crashing at people's flats for a couple of weeks but it's no good."

I heard a man's voice in the background.

Then Nancy said, "Here, Mom. Sid wants to say something."

There was a rustling and then a young man with a heavy English accent said, "Hello, Mum."

"Hello, Sid," I said.

"How are ya?" He had a flat, placid-sounding voice.

"Fine. How are you?"

"Fine. Your daughter looks so pretty. I bought her shoes."

"That's nice."

"And fancy underwear."

"That's very nice, Sid," I said. "Sid?"

"Yes, Mum?"

"Could I speak to Nancy again?"

"Yeah, sure. Okay. But could you send us money? For Nancy?"

"I'll talk to her about that."

"Oh, okay. Here's Nancy. Nice talking to you, Mum."

"Nice talking to you, Sid."

" 'Bye, Mum."

"Good-bye, Sid."

Nancy got back on. "Isn't he great?"

"He sounds very pleasant."

"Oh, he is. He's a very nice lad, Mum."

Nancy was starting to pick up an English accent.

"With that name," I said, "you'd expect he'd be, I don't know, kind of rough."

"Oh, no. That's just for the act. He's nothing like what the papers say. That's all made up. Would your daughter go out with someone like that?"

I decided then and there to find out what it was that the papers said about the Sex Pistols.

"Is he on heroin?"

"No."

"Are you?"

"Yeah, but I'm going on meth again. Sid wants me to. See how good he is? Can you send me some money? So we can get settled? Sid's broke, too."

"If he's such a big success why doesn't he have any money?"

"I think they're holding out on him."

I told her I'd think about it. I ended up sending her fifty dollars.

I started reading whatever I could find about the Sex Pistols, punk music, and its devotees. It was quite a lesson in commercial exploitation.

The group and its image had been created by Malcolm McLaren, a shrewd young London University art school graduate who portrayed himself as an avant-garde artist and the group as his art form—a new, living art form for the postindustrial age.

In the early 1970s McLaren opened a shop on Chelsea's King's Road that specialized in 1950s clothing and records. The store was a hit with working-class teenagers, who liked the tough, greasy Elvis look and sound. It became a popular hangout.

Over the next couple of years economic hard times hit England. Job opportunities dried up, especially for the workingclass teens who formed McLaren's clientele. They became increasingly sullen and angry. They were hostile toward the queen. They saw no future for themselves. Immediate thrills—anything shocking and exciting—became all that they were interested in.

McLaren, meanwhile, had his eye on something potentially more profitable than '50s clothing. And definitely more avant-garde. He turned his store into a sex shop, stocking it with kinky leather and rubber clothing and bizarre, sadomasochistic sexual apparatus—everything from handcuffs to chains to metal-studded leather collars. He now called his store simply Sex.

His old clientele of disaffected teens liked his new merchandise even better than the old. They began to wear his black leather clothing and metal-studded cuffs on the streets of Chelsea. It was shocking and mean-looking stuff. It turned heads. Malcolm McLaren had given birth to a fashion craze, a big enough one to attract the attention of members of the New York Dolls—friends of Nancy's who had gone over to London to perform during the year she lived in New York. They visited his shop. He heard them play and they hit it off.

McLaren followed the Dolls back to New York to manage them.

There he heard the raw underground rock that Nancy was so excited about. (He also, I later read, came in contact with Nancy for the first time.) When the New York Dolls broke up a few months later, McLaren returned to his London sex shop with the idea of forming a band incorporating the nasty leather look he'd popularized along with the tough, hard rock he'd heard in New York. After all, the bored, restless teens who hung around his shop were hungry for a new sound, something angry, nihilistic, shocking. In other words, a sound to go with the clothes.

And so a craze was born.

McLaren came up with a name for the group, the Sex Pistols, and hired four of the teenagers hanging around his shop to be its members. Johnny Lyman was given the job of lead singer.

"He looked good in my clothes," McLaren reportedly explained.

"But I can't sing on key," Lyman reportedly protested.

"That's what I want," McLaren reportedly replied. He gave Lyman a new name to go with his outfit: Johnny Rotten.

The Sex Pistols began performing in London clubs in the spring of 1976. They were an immediate sensation. Not, apparently, for their music, which critics described as "nonmusic." ("The Sex Pistols weren't into music," McLaren was later quoted as saying.) No, what attracted attention was their manners, which were described as outrageous. Instead of singing lyrics, the Sex Pistols shouted vulgarities at the audience, snarled at them, spat at them, called them and the queen dirty names. Supposedly, they took bad taste beyond any level seen before in public. They vomited on stage. They stuck themselves in the face with safety pins. They practiced "pogo dancing," which consisted of hopping up and down in place, arms spastically flailing. They advocated "squelching," which was making love without any show of emotion.

My stomach churned as I read and heard about all this.

Maybe it was only an act, as Nancy had warned me, but it was a disgusting one nonetheless.

With McLaren encouraging them to "let it all hang out," the Sex Pistols whipped themselves and their audience into such a state of frenzy that their early performances ended amid fistfights and property damage. "Their public persona wasn't a gimmick," McLaren later said. "It expressed their real attitude toward life. They were into chaos."

For McLaren, it was a kind of living theater of the absurd, a statement about the decline of English civilization. And a gold mine. A more than able promoter, McLaren got the outrageousness of the Sex Pistols enough exposure for the record companies to take notice of them. Britain's EMI Records signed them up.

(To measure McLaren's promoting skills, consider that by the time they broke up less than two years after he created them, the Sex Pistols had signed two million dollars in recording contracts even though they could not, in reality, play. In all, they would record two albums and perform less than fifty times in public.)

Sid, whose real name was John Simon Ritchie, was not part of the original foursome. He was a childhood friend of John Lyman and an ardent early fan of the Sex Pistols. He was exactly the sort of person McLaren had designed the group to appeal to. He was, McLaren said, "a living example of the bored, frustrated kids in London looking for a scene."

When the group's original bass player dropped out, McLaren gave John Simon Ritchie the name Sid Vicious and handed him the job. The fact that Sid did not know how to play the bass was apparently not an issue. His appearance was the important thing. At 6 feet 2 inches and 135 pounds, he was tall and gaunt. He wore his black hair standing straight up on his head in a spiky fashion. One eye drooped. He already wore McLaren's clothes.

One of the magazine stories I read had a black and white photograph of him. He didn't look particularly threatening or evil in his photograph. He looked like a typical skinny English rock musician.

Black and white photographs can be very deceptive, I was soon to realize.

The Sex Pistols' first album, *Anarchy in the U.K.*, was released in England in November 1976. The group first came to the attention of the mainstream British public a few days after its release because of an appearance on a national television talk show. Its host, Bill Grundy, asked them to say something outrageous to the viewing public. They obliged by letting loose with a string of snarled obscenities, resulting in front page news the next day, as well as the suspension of Grundy.

By the time Nancy arrived in London four months later, the Sex Pistols were the biggest sensation in England. Their album was atop the charts, their exploits the toast of the thrill-hungry British tabloids. The press reported that several members of the band had vomited at the KLM ticket desk at Heathrow airport while en route to Holland. More headlines came as a result of a press conference held in front of Buckingham Palace to announce that the Sex Pistols were signing with A & M Records for their second album. Johnny Rotten, the press reported, spat vodka all over the director of A & M Records, as well as members of the press corps. Within a week A & M cancelled the contract. More headlines.

As big as the Sex Pistols were at that time in England, their popularity was confined there. The group was not well known here, and then only for their outrageous reputation. No U.S. record distributor had picked up *Anarchy in the U.K.* The U.S. record industry and press seemed to regard the Sex Pistols as a sick sort of Bristol social phenomenon, a fad that figured to be short-lived.

But it was only natural that Nancy would like the Sex Pistols, want to be involved with them. They were angry and violent. They were the newest thing on the musical horizon, the next step past the underground New York punk scene. They were celebrities. Later, when she herself would become a punk celebrity, journalists would characterize her as a girl who took to punk because it was a repudiation of middle-class life. Not so. They didn't understand Nancy. She loved being middle-class. She was making no social statement, issuing no challenge. It was simply the music that attracted Nancy to punk. Always, it was the music. It was her flame. All she wanted was to get close to it. As close as possible.

I didn't know yet how ugly and frightening that flame was. I hadn't heard the music. I hadn't seen the Sex Pistols or their followers in action. I didn't until later that summer, when a network television magazine show did a feature on them. The four of us gathered around the TV set in the den to watch it.

The report opened with some Chelsea street scenes, focusing on the punk teens there. They were some of the most bizarre-looking human beings I'd ever seen. They wore narrow wraparound sunglasses and weird spiky haircuts—one young man wore his hair in a mohawk, dyed green. The young woman with him had cascading purple hair, purple makeup, and a tattoo on her upper arm. They were skinny and pale and wore Hell's Angels-type black leather clothing and black motorcycle boots. One young man wore a set of handcuffs in his belt. Another carried a truncheon. They looked like futuristic Nazi stormtroopers. They were repellent.

Ten years earlier some people had called hippies with beards and long hair "freaks." Those were not freaks. Those were sincere, peaceful people who were trying to make a statement. *These* were freaks.

Over the street scenes was played the music of the Sex Pistols. Only it wasn't music. It was an unpleasant, atonal cacophony of sound. It was antimusic. It was *noise*.

"Great stuff, huh, Mom?" David said.

I was too stunned to reply.

"Why would anybody want to look like that?" Frank asked as a young man with a black leather collar and no shirt clenched his fist at the sidewalk camera.

"I guess it's some kind of statement," said David.

"Of what?" Frank pressed.

"They're saying that everything stinks, is all I can figure," David said.

"They look dumb," Frank said. "Really dumb."

Then the report took us to a Sex Pistols concert. First the camera focused on Johnny Rotten as he snarled and spat at his packed house of followers. All of them were, seemingly,

menacing punks. All of them were, seemingly, eating his ac
up and dishing it right back at him with their own snarling an
ger. Here was the opposite of Woodstock. If that had been a
love-in, this was a hate-in. Rotten, to me, came off sort o
like Mick Jagger in a bad mood. An untalented Mick Jagger

Then the camera moved in on Sid.

I couldn't believe it. The newspaper photos hadn't pre
pared me. He was extremely tall, pale, and cadaverous. With
his drooping eye and malevolent expression, he had to be the
creepiest-looking young man on the face of the earth. He
looked like Frankenstein's monster. My daughter was living
with Frankenstein's monster.

"Too bad," Frank said, "she couldn't find somebody
more outrageous."

"It's all an act," Suzy said as Johnny stomped around on
stage. "It's fake. It's show biz."

Indeed it was an act. A Sex Pistols concert was a perfor
mance, and the band members performers. But they seemed
to be caught up in this angry, hateful act just as much as the
crowd was. There was something dangerous about all of the
hostility being let loose in that concert hall, something that
was almost out of control. It scared me.

Then the camera panned across the foot of the stage, at the
punks who were crowding close to the Sex Pistols, clapping
cheering, yelling obscenities back at them. There, clapping
her hands high over her head, was Nancy Spungen.

"That's my sister!" cried Suzy.

At least it almost looked like her. If you could picture
Nancy with a wild mane of hair bleached white, and gian
smudges of black makeup around her eyes. And black leathe
clothes.

She was one of those freaks. I couldn't believe it. I couldn'
believe it was my baby, that I was the mother of that girl.

I wasn't. That wasn't my Nancy. My Nancy had slipped
away. My Nancy was gone.

That face on the TV was a doomed face. The face of the
terminally ill. Her days were numbered. Her wish was com
ing true. I knew it for sure as soon as I saw her that night.

She'd gotten too close to the flame.

My immediate response was to cross the bridge before I came to it. From that evening on I began to daydream about the details of Nancy's death. I didn't wish her dead. I just knew she soon would be. I was preparing myself. I knew that no matter what she had done, how much I had hated her and wanted to smack her sometimes, it would hurt. A lot.

She would be back from London. It would be a golden, sunny autumn day, her favorite day, her favorite kind of day. The New York Police Department would call me to say that Nancy had overdosed and was in critical condition. I would phone Frank, Suzy, and David with the news. The four of us would rush to the New York hospital. There, we would find her in her bed, conscious. She would say good-bye to each of us, then die peacefully in my arms.

Then it would be time to make arrangements. First I would have to have her body moved to Philadelphia. I would arrange that. I would call the funeral director and give him all of the instructions. Next I would phone my dear friends Janet and Susan, and my mother. Janet would go to our house immediately and be waiting there for us when we got back. So would my mother. Susan would be out. Or could be. I had to be prepared for that. I would leave a message with her son, that's what I would do. I would ask him to tell Susan that "something's happened" and to come over. When we got home, I would make arrangements for the visitors who would come by. I would order assorted deli platters from Murray's Delicatessen. I would sit down with Frank so we could decide what should be said at the funeral. A rabbi. We'd have to talk to a rabbi.

My daydreaming occupied my mind whenever I was alone—driving to work, shopping for groceries, or trying to fall asleep at night. Sometimes I felt guilty about having these daydreams. I wondered if it was wrong. I didn't know.

I was very, very strong in my daydreams. I acted in a calm, detached, businesslike manner. I just did what I had to do. I fantasized Nancy's death so many times that when a business contact asked me at one point how many children I had, I automatically answered, "Two." It just fell out of my mouth. It was as if she were already dead. I was ready for it, I thought. I was prepared, so prepared that when the inevitable happened, it wouldn't hurt.

How foolish I was.

Nancy phoned toward the end of the summer. I told her we'd seen her on TV.

"Didn't I look great, Mom? My hair?"

"It was exciting to see you," I replied.

"Did you hear the band?"

"Yes."

"Aren't they great?"

"Uh . . . to tell you the truth, it's not really my kind of thing."

"That's cool. Aren't you proud of me, Mom? I've made it! I've really made it!"

She genuinely believed she had achieved something. I understood her pride, but I didn't share it. Having an affair with Sid Vicious was not my concept of doing something worthwhile with your life. But she was proud. Her rock fantasy was coming true.

She called the following week to tell me that she and Sid had gotten married.

## Chapter 19

"Aren't you happy for us?" she cried, excited.

Shocked was a better word.

"When?" I asked. "Where?"

"Now you can send us a gift," she said.

"When were you married?" I repeated.

"We'd prefer money to things. Tell everyone in the family, okay? No gifts. Cash."

The amount of emphasis she placed on money made me doubt her story.

"Nancy, can you prove you and Sid are married? I mean, if he's such a big celebrity, how come it wasn't publicized?"

"We didn't want the press to know. It'd be bad for his image."

"Can you *prove* you're married?"

"Don't you believe me?" she snapped angrily. "Don't you believe your own daughter? I'm *happy*. *You* should be happy, too. Instead you're calling me a bloody liar."

"I'm not—"

"I'll send you the bloody wedding pictures, *okay?* Now send us our wedding gift."

She hung up.

I told Frank the news. We discussed it. We were confused. We didn't know whether to believe her or not.

She called again two days later.

"Did you send the money, Mom?"

"No."

"What's wrong, don't you believe me? You don't think I'd lie about something like this, do you?"

"I don't know, Nancy. You told me never, ever to trust a junkie when they ask for money."

"But Mom, this is different. We're *married.* Your Nancy is *married.*"

We sent her a hundred dollars. My mother sent her fifty.

We had been conned. The wedding pictures never came and Nancy never referred to her "marriage" again. (After her death our lawyer was in London and checked the records. As far as he could determine, there had been no marriage.)

We were angry at ourselves for having been taken in. The incident also heightened our mixed feelings about Nancy. It was getting to be so hard to love her. It seemed sometimes like all we got in return for our love was untruth and crap. I'd never do something like that to her. How could she do it to me? And why?

But I kept remembering something my housekeeper had once told me: "Your child is your child, no matter what she does or is. She is still your child." It was true. No matter what Nancy did, I still loved her.

Soon after this I had a nightmare. I was walking in a cemetery. Suddenly I came upon several men who were working on a new tombstone beside a freshly dug grave. They were chiseling a person's name on the stone. A first name and middle name were already there: NANCY LAURA. So was a date of birth: FEBRUARY 27, 1958. Nancy's date of birth. One of the men put his chisel to the stone to begin the first letter of her last name.

"*Stop!*" I cried in my dream. "I don't know what her last name is! I don't know if it's Spungen or Vicious! And Vicious isn't his real name!"

I awoke from the nightmare in confusion. Frank was sleeping peacefully by my side.

I had not, I realized, looked at the date of death on the tombstone.


Nancy and Sid stayed with his mother for less than two months. She and Nancy apparently didn't get along. So Nancy and Sid moved into a hotel. Nancy phoned me from her new place of residence. From her calls, I learned that she was becoming exposed to the violence that surrounded the Sex Pistols.

"I got beat up, Mom," she moaned. "My nose is broke somethin' 'orrible. It's all over my face. It hurts."

"Who did it?" I asked.

"The Teddys. They don't like us."

"Who are the Teddys?"

"Assholes who hate punks. They attacked us on the street. They gave me two black eyes, too. Sid got knifed. But we're okay. And I'll be ready for 'em next time. Sid bought me a truncheon."

Two weeks later she phoned to say she and Sid had moved to a different hotel. When I asked why, she replied that the manager of the hotel had asked them to leave.

"Sid got mad," she explained, "and dangled me out the window. I was screaming at him to let me back in and I guess it pissed off the other people in the hotel."

"Are you okay?" I asked. What else could I say?

"Oh, yeah. It was nothing. He was just upset."

I did not yet know Sid or understand Nancy's relationship with him. But this incident clearly indicated to me that it had an ugly, violent streak. It made me wonder if perhaps Sid was the actual source of the beating Nancy had blamed on the Teddy boys. I didn't ask her. I couldn't. I didn't want to know. Besides, she kept assuring me his name and on-stage manner were an act, that he was in reality a "sweet lad." Indeed, the few times I'd spoken to him on the phone he'd seemed pleasant.

They got in another reportedly violent quarrel in a different

London hotel room at the end of November. Again, Nancy's screams brought the manager. This time the British press was also alerted. The papers reported that the manager went up to Nancy and Sid's room to find a bloodstained bed, a near naked Sid bleeding from cuts on his arms, and broken glass all over the carpet. There was a bottle of pills on the nightstand. A police inquiry was launched.

Nancy had a different version.

"It was nothing," she told me over the phone. "The manager didn't like us and he wanted us out is all. The pills were a prescription."

"Do you need a lawyer?"

"There's nothing to worry about, Mom," she insisted "Forget about it. Malcolm's lawyer will take care of everything."

"Are you sure you're okay, Nancy?"

"Of course. It was *nothing*. Sid was just upset. Something to do with the group."

However, because of this second run-in with a hotel manager, Nancy and Sid decided to find a place of their own. She told me a few days later that they'd rented a small carriage house in the Maida Vale section of London.

"It's our own little house," she gushed, "with our own little furniture. We bought a sofa. You'll love it. It's great You'll *have* to come and stay."

It was domestic bliss, punk style.

There was a second consequence to this hotel incident. A British reporter phoned us for some background information on Nancy. We gave it to him. We never heard from him again or saw the article. It was our first contact with the press, our first inkling that Nancy was becoming a celebrity in her own right. Why, we couldn't imagine. The hotel room story was not picked up by the American press. The Sex Pistols were still not very big here, nor was punk.

The group was bigger than ever in England. A second album, *Never Mind the Bollocks*, was recorded on the Virgin Records label. A film project, *Who Killed Bambi*, was in the works with financing from Twentieth Century-Fox. Responding to the incredible popularity of the Sex Pistols in En gland, America's Warner Records finally got in on the act that winter. They invested in a U.S. release of *Never Mind the Bollocks* to be tied in to a winter Sex Pistols concert tour of the United States. McLaren had arrived in the big money.

Nancy phoned to tell me the news about the U.S. tour. She was very excited about being able to come back and see us. She was anxious for us to meet her Sid.

Our feelings were mixed. Yes, we wanted to see our daughter. But she was very far away from us now. We had a life of our own, a life that no longer had a real connection to her. Frank and I had a social life now. We had people over to the house for dinner, something we'd never felt comfortable doing before. We had spent some money on the house, installing wallpaper and a sliding door from the kitchen to the patio. I had a new job and enjoyed it. David was now in his junior year at prep school and doing well and Suzy had found a job cooking in a health food restaurant, which she enjoyed, and was hard at work on her painting. Meanwhile, the four of us were planning a winter vacation to Saint Thomas.

All of a sudden I had visions of Nancy dragging us to a Sex Pistols concert. I had visions of her inviting the band and its entire following to our house, and of not being able to get rid of them.

As it happened, it was a false alarm. Malcolm McLaren refused to allow Nancy to come with the group on the U.S. tour. Apparently he did not like her. He found her disruptive and a challenge to his authority over Sid. Reportedly, he blamed her for introducing Sid to hard drugs.

"Sid wants me to come," she told me over the phone, "but they won't let me. They said nobody else is bringing women so he can't."

"Maybe it wouldn't be fun anyway," I said. "After all, he'll be working."

"Yeah, but it means I'll be alone on my birthday. All the fuck alone."

"I'm sorry, sweetheart."

I *was* sorry she couldn't come. And relieved at the same time. As it happened, she was not alone for her birthday. The much ballyhooed U.S. tour of the Sex Pistols was an unqualified disaster. It was aborted midway through, and Johnny Rotten left the group.

The tour got off to a roaring start. The band members got surly and walked out on an interview on the *Today* show. Then they headed for a concert swing through the Deep South, where it was believed they would get the maximum mileage out of their shock value and hopefully arouse the kind of rage they were able to with England's punk teens. At first they did. In Atlanta the audience threw plastic cups and popcorn at them. In Dallas, Johnny Rotten called the audience "redneck cowboy faggots" and Sid had his lip bloodied.

In Memphis the house was packed and rowdy. But within thirty minutes the audience was streaming out. Why? Because people had come to see the much publicized freak show, and, apparently, a lot of it was hype—always had been. There was no on-stage vomiting, for example. The Sex Pistols were simply not as outrageous as the reputation that preceded them. Additionally, they were terrible: Johnny Rotten could not sing; Sid Vicious did not know how to play the instrument he was holding on stage.

Without a punk following, without any musical talent, the Sex Pistols were not a success in America. Far from it. They were a joke. A bad joke. By the time they got to Los Angeles, the tour was off and the band shattered by business and personal squabbling.

Still, they drew headlines. When they got to New York, Sid had to be carried from the plane unconscious. Reportedly, he had overdosed on drugs and alcohol.

He was back in London in plenty of time for Nancy's twentieth birthday. And for his and Nancy's arraignment on drug charges stemming from the hotel room incident at the end of November. As far as I've been able to learn, the charges against them were dismissed. As they left the courtroom the British photographers snapped a picture of Nancy and Sid. She was, according to one account, "wearing stiletto-heel boots, a mop of wild, white hair, and a defiant pout."

We had always called it That Look.

Coming as it did on the heels of the Sex Pistols' much heralded failed tour, the arraignment photo made the U.S. pa pers. Some featured it on the front page. Here was a nice, fresh angle—Sid apparently had a violent, drug-related romance going with an American girl. The Philadelphia papers jumped on it with particular zeal. Hometown girl makes bad.

Nancy was now a celebrity. Our life would never be the same.

The reporters started calling. Eight or ten of them called the day after the photo appeared, from Philadelphia, from New York, from California. All of them wanted to know about us, about Nancy's history, about her drug background. I said I didn't care to comment. As far as I was concerned, our lives were none of their business.

This was my first brush with the American press, and I was appalled. Several reporters were abusive and nasty to me, suggested they would simply go ahead and print what they knew to be hearsay and fabrication if I didn't cooperate with them. I repeated that I did not care to comment. I had the right not to.

"Why should anyone be interested in Nancy anyway?" Frank muttered at dinner that night. "It's nonsense. She's no celebrity."

The next day my statement that I did not care to comment came out in more than one paper as "When informed of her daughter's arrest in London on drug charges, Mrs. Spungen replied, 'I don't care.'" Several of our neighbors had also been contacted and quoted. They told me that they, too, had been misquoted.

I can't generalize about the practices of the American press, but in our case many reporters were unethical. Before my involvement with them, I'd always believed reporters were there to report the news. Now I realize that they are also given the license to manufacture it.

The press made Nancy into a celebrity. No fascination in her existed until the reporters stepped in, created an aura about her and Sid, and then milked it for all it was worth to sell papers. The press portrayed Sid and Nancy as Romeo and Juliet in black leather, roaring into hell. Sid was seen as a pop star associated with manufactured violence who was living it out for real. Nancy was seen as a coarse tramp who took whatever Sid dished out and gave it right back to him. Together they were portrayed as the living embodiment of the punk movement.

In reality there was no sensational story there. All that was there was illusion, a somewhat sick illusion but mostly just very sad. In reality there was a bright, mentally disturbed twenty-year-old girl whose misguided ambition it was to be associated with a famous rock musician. She had realized her ambition, she thought. Only her rock musician wasn't *really* a rock musician. He, like Nancy, believed he was. But he wasn't. In reality he was a talentless twenty-one-year-old kid off the streets whose pop celebrity had been achieved by means of hype and fakery. Sid was *not* a musician. He was simply a celebrity, a nonphenomenon—someone who had spat and snarled at an audience and become famous as a result.

In reality each was living out a dream via the press. Each was living up to a press-created image. I couldn't understand why anyone cared to read about them. The Sid and Nancy story was not one I myself would have read in the newspapers. But others, apparently, did.

The most painful story came out in the Philadelphia *Inquirer* a few days later. The newspaper had followed up the arraignment photo and story by assigning a reporter, Julia Cass, to probe into Nancy's past. She succeeded in opening up our private odyssey with Nancy to the public—by going around us. She spoke to Nancy's friend Karen, to Mr. Sylvester at Darlington. She retraced Nancy's route to Avon, then to Colorado and back again.

And she spoke to Nancy in London. She asked Nancy if she was a groupie.

"I am not or never have been a groupie," Nancy replied in the article. "If a groupie came up to Sid, he'd kick her in the face."

She asked Nancy about her domestic life.

"I sleep all day and go out to the shops, you know, for bread and milk. I don't cook. This place isn't a pigsty or anything, but I'm not into cleaning."

She asked Nancy about her future plans, now that the band had broken up.

"I never think about the future," Nancy replied.

Nancy then asked the reporter to send me a copy of the article when it came out. She wanted me to see how well she was doing.

We were extremely hurt and angry over this article. It is one thing to give up your privacy. It is another to have it taken from you. We felt victimized, like our family's dirty laundry had been snatched and hung in public. Moreover, we couldn't understand why anyone would want to read about us. But read they did.

At the office the following day I could tell that everyone had seen the article. They didn't say so, but I could tell. They looked embarrassed. They should have been. It was none of their damned business.

We began to get obscene phone calls as a result of the article. David, who was home sick with the flu, took one from a man who said, "Tell your parents it's all their fault. They should have taken the Pill." Other callers simply cursed at him and hung up.

We also got obscene mail. One was simply a copy of the Julia Cass story with various words circled and obscenities written next to them. We called the police.

This public response baffled and upset us even more. Sixteen-year-old David took it upon himself a few days after the publication of the article to phone Julia Cass at the newspaper. He told her that she had hurt our family, that we'd been receiving obscene calls and letters, and that it wasn't justified based on the relative unimportance of the story. We were glad that David called. We appreciated it. We also thought it was a mature thing for him to do. He had something he'd wanted to get off his chest and he had. Julia Cass vigorously defended the story to him, though she later admitted to me that his call had affected her profoundly. By then we had become good friends. Still are. I can now ask her why anyone cared about Sid and Nancy, since I still cannot fathom it. And she, a veteran journalist, can simply reply, "They were the ultimate tabloid news story—amusing, amazing, freaky."

David spoke to Nancy a few days later. She called to find out if the story had come out. David told her it had, and that we'd been suffering as a result. She apologized, then asked

him for a copy of the article for her portfolio. Then she sai
Sid had something important to say, and put him on. What Si
had to tell David was that while he'd been touring Americ
with the Sex Pistols, he'd had sex with a transvestite. All c
the gòry details followed.


Soon after our unpleasant brush with the press and notoriety,
received one of the two letters I got from Nancy while she wa
abroad. Actually, what she sent me was a Mother's Day card
It was only March, but the British celebrate Mother's Da
earlier in the year than we do. It was a standard Mother's Da
card with a couple of standard rhyming verses about ho
sweet and thoughtful a mom I really, truly was. Underneat
and across the back, she scrawled:

> *Dear Mommy,*
> *Happy Mother's Day from both of us. I guess this card
> pretty much sums up the way I am and I feel. If you
> don't know it, Sid thinks the world of you, too. Believe
> me, that's rare. He rarely takes a liking to anyone. And
> he wants to meet you very much.*
>
> *I miss you very badly and I hope we'll see each other
> soon. You know, just between us, that you're the only
> one in the family that I really care about. Now, I have
> two best friends that I love—you and Sid. I hope you're
> happy your daughter finally found a guy and settled
> down! It's our anniversary on March 11th. One year al-
> ready since we met. I can't believe it. But we both love
> each other very much and take care of each other and
> we have a very beautiful relationship that you would be
> proud of.*
>
> *The reason my writing is so shaky is because my
> Sidney is playing bass right next to me and the bed is
> bouncing like hell. Well, enough about us. Have the
> happiest Mother's Day of anybody. We'll be thinking of
> you. We both love you, Mommy!*
>
> > *Love, XOXOXOXO*
> > *Nancy*

Underneath, in his own childlike scrawl, Sid wrote:

*Luv from Sid XXXXXXX*

And underneath that, Nancy added:

> *P.S. We both love you again and hope we'll be together soon!*

I read the letter over several times in amazement. This was clearly not the letter of a girl who was repudiating her upbringing. Far from it; this was a girl who hoped her mother was happy that her daughter "had finally found a guy and settled down." Had I not known the circumstances, I'd have been justified in jumping to the conclusion that her "Sidney" was a nice Jewish dentist.

Something else about the letter amazed me—its tone. It was unfamiliar. After I'd read the letter over again, I realized what it was.

Nancy was genuinely happy—possibly the only time she had been in her entire life.

She stayed that way for a short time. A very short time. The life that she and Sid had together was constructed around drugs and his fleeting fame and wealth. They could stay happy only for as long as they were able to hold on to their health and his money.

She phoned me from Paris that spring, her voice filled with childlike enthusiasm.

"I'm traveling, Mum," she exclaimed. "Just like I always wanted to. It was so bloody moldy in London and it's so *beautiful* here."

"It sounds wonderful, sweetheart," I said.

It did sound wonderful. I'd always dreamed of being able to go to Paris in the spring.

"Oh, it is! My Sid bought me real French underwear. *Black.*" She giggled. "And shoes. *Charles Jourdan.* And we eat every night in this great little restaurant and have wine and they're so bloody *nice* to us. They don't make any kind of big deal over us or anything. They're just *nice.*"

I got a postcard from her a few days later. It was a pictur
postcard of the Eiffel Tower. On the back she wrote:

> *Dear Mom,*
> *Love Paris. It's a really beautiful city with pretty parks*
> *and squares. Have been here for 3 weeks, so we had a*
> *chance to really look around. I bought so many*
> *things—clothes, French make-up, jewelry, etc. Send*
> *my love,*
>
> *Love, Nancy and Sid*

Now it sounded like she and her dentist were on their hon
eymoon.

She and Sid spent an idyllic month together in Paris. Inevi
tably things began to turn sour for them when they got back t
London.

First Nancy's health gave out. It was sometime in June, a fe
weeks after they got back. A hysterical phone call woke me i
the middle of the night. A child was screaming and crying.

"My baby! She's my baby! She's in pain! My baby's i
pain!"

I finally realized that child was Sid.

"Sid? Is that you?"

"Yes, Debbie," he sobbed. "Nancy. She's in pain. I don
know what to do. Tell me. Oh, please. Tell me."

"What is it, Sid? *What's* bothering her?"

"Her insides!"

"Have you called a doctor?"

"A doctor?"

"Can you call a doctor, Sid?" I asked, very slowly.

It was morning there. The doctors would be in their offices

"Yes," he replied. "Yes. A doctor."

"Okay, Sid. Take Nancy to a doctor. And have the docto
call me. Can you do that, Sid? Can you take Nancy to the doe
tor?"

"Yes, a doctor. I'll do that, Debbie. I'll do that."

The doctor phoned me a few hours later to say that Nanc
was suffering from a severe infection of the fallopian tubes

"I'm afraid I'll have to hospitalize her, Mrs. Spungen," h

.id. "But she'll be fine, I think, in a few days. And there's a
ery nice young man here who's very worried about her."

Nancy stayed in the hospital until she was well enough to
ant out. Sid took her home to their little house in Maida
ale and vowed to be her nursemaid. He also promised to call
e every day at the same time to report on her progress. He
ept both promises.

"She's already doing better, Debbie," he said on her first
ay back. "I fed her yogurt with a spoon and gave her her
edicine. I'm taking care of her. I gave her lemonade. Here,
e wants to talk to you. Here's Nancy. Here's our little girl."

Nancy got on the phone.

"Hi, Mum," she said weakly. "He's so sweet, isn't he?
n't my Sid sweet?"

"Is everything all right, Nancy?"

"I'll be okay. My Sidney's here. I miss you, though. Can't
ou come over? Can't you be here to take care of me, too?"

"I . . . I don't know. I'll have to let you know."

I wanted to see her. I hadn't seen her for fifteen months,
nd she was ill. But I was afraid. She'd told me about the
eatings she and Sid had suffered.

"Would I be safe?" I asked.

"Nobody will touch you, Mum," she assured me. "I'll
atch out for you."

I wasn't so sure. Hers was an alien life. There was danger
it. I was against going—until I got a letter from her a few
ays later. This was her second and last letter from abroad.
ctually it was a list. She catalogued the twenty-one places
e wanted to take me in London, everywhere from Trafal-
ar Square to Harrods ("the English Bloomingdale's") to
nightsbridge ("fancy shopping area") to Oxford Street
"more shopping"). At the bottom of the list she concluded,
Don't forget to bring this list with you. Can't wait to see
ou. Everything is fine here."

Now I was thinking I would go. She seemed so up and anx-
us to see me. We could have a good time together. A
other-daughter time.

I was just about to check out the fares to London when
ancy called me with a complete change of plans.

The second problem had arisen to doom Nancy and Sid's little life together: Sid's career. The Sex Pistols had broken up and he was having trouble catching on as a solo act in London—understandable, considering his lack of talent. He'd cut a single called "My Way," but it failed to take off. His money was running out. Meanwhile, Malcolm McLaren had apparently lost interest in his creation. Clearly, Sid's novelty value had passed. (And genuinely talented performers—from Elvis Costello to Graham Parker to the Clash—had emerged to grab hold of the punk audience.) But Nancy and Sid failed to see it that way. They both thought he was a bona fide rock star, one who was simply in need of fresh, inspired management.

"I'm managing Sid's career now, Mum," Nancy told me over the phone. "He's gonna be even bigger as a solo."

In retrospect, here was a pathetic show business fantasy, one akin to Norma Desmond's hopeless dream of a return to screen glory in *Sunset Boulevard.* It wasn't going to happen. In retrospect, here was also rather touching loyalty. If Nancy had simply been a groupie, as some still suggest, this would have been the time to dump Sid—his career, such as it was, had ended—and move on to greener pastures. But she didn't. She stuck by him.

"He'll do better in the States, I figure," she declared firmly. "So we're comin' back for good. End of August or so. As soon as we get to New York, I'll bring Sid down to meet the whole family. We'll stay for a while. Won't that be great?"

Nancy was coming home.

The prospect stirred bad memories. Not memories of the public Nancy, the punk Nancy, but memories of our private Nancy, the one we'd grown up with. That experience was far more frightening than anything I'd ever read about the punks.

Nancy was coming home.

I was afraid. I was afraid of my own feelings. I was afraid I'd get hysterical when I saw her, that I'd cry for that sweet smelling baby, that lost Nancy.

Nancy was coming home.

We could not deny her that right. All we could do was try to control the situation. We decided to put them up at a nearby Holiday Inn rather than have them stay in the house with us. I

ade practical sense anyway, what with Nancy's room now
eing Frank's office.

I informed Nancy of this when she called just before she
nd Sid cleared out of London. She got very upset—she
ought I was telling her she couldn't come. I explained that
e and Sid were welcome to stay as long as they wanted, but
at we'd thought they'd be more comfortable at a hotel.

"Oh, okay, Mum," she said. "That's all right. Listen, I'll
e sending some of our stuff to your house to keep until we
et a flat in New York, okay? We'll be staying at the Chelsea
hen we get in. Our flight is on August the twenty-fourth.
hat's a Thursday. We'll check in at the hotel, then come
own Friday. Doesn't that sound great?"

A knot formed in my stomach as a response.

Everyone in the family grew more and more anxious as the
y approached. It so happened that at this time Suzy was in
e process of moving into her own small studio apartment in
iladelphia. She was now nineteen. Her year off from
hool had been good for her confidence. She had applied to
d been accepted by several art schools. She'd chosen the
iladelphia College of Art and was all set to start that fall.
nce her classes were early in the morning, she'd decided to
ke an apartment in the city. I kept myself occupied during
e days before Nancy's return by helping Suzy furnish it. I
lped her pick out a platform bed and table. We bought a
ower curtain. We packed up her clothes and things and
ank moved them by the carload.

It was a little sad helping her move. It meant that there was
ly one child home now. David, who'd spent the summer
ay as a camp counselor, was about to enter his senior year
high school.

Suzy was about halfway moved into her own apartment the
y that Nancy and Sid came to visit in suburbia:

# ❏ Chapter 20

Frank and I were at the Trenton train station on time, bu
the train from New York was twenty minutes late. I was s
agitated I couldn't sit still. Same with Frank. We paced u
and down the platform in opposite directions, each of us los
in our thoughts.

"I hope the weather's nice this weekend," Frank muse
aloud at one point when our paths intersected.

"What?" I snapped.

"The weather. Nice."

"What for?"

"So they can use the pool."

"Oh, right."

We resumed pacing.

The train pulled in. Commuters spilled out of the doors an
shoved their way across the platform to the escalators. 
craned my neck in search of my Nancy. I couldn't spot he

Then the air was pierced by a loud *"Mum!"*

It was Nancy's voice. My eyes sought her out and foun
her.

I was not prepared for how much she'd deteriorated—even from when I'd seen her on TV. She looked like a Holocaust victim. She was much thinner. Her skin was a translucent bluish white. Her eyes had sunk deep into their sockets and had black circles under them. Her hair was bleached white, and along the hairline there were yellowish bruises and sores and scabs. She wore a black leather jacket with a torn, filthy T-shirt under it, tight black jeans, and spike heels. Around her neck was a charm necklace—silver charms of gargoyles and snakes.

She looked like the walking dead.

Behind her lurked Sid. I say "lurked" because he was at least a foot taller than her, and his spiky hair stood straight up on his head. He too was bluish white and painfully thin. He wore a black leather jacket with no shirt under it, black jeans, black motorcycle boots, and a matching black leather collar and cuffs with pointed metal studs.

Frank and I just stood there gaping at them. We weren't alone. Everyone, but *everyone*, on the platform was staring at them. They stood out as much as if they'd just arrived from another planet. There was a total absence of life to them. It was as if the rest of the world were in color and they were in black and white.

They were totally oblivious to the scene they were causing.

Nancy came toward me and I toward her. We met halfway and embraced.

"My mum!" she cried as she held me tight. "My mum."

But it wasn't my Nancy I held in my arms. I felt as if I were holding a stranger. I wanted my Nancy back. But my Nancy was gone. A sob welled up in my throat.

We released each other.

"Mum," she said, "this is Sid. Sid, this is my mum. Isn't she beautiful? Just like I told you."

He stuck out his hand. I shook it. It was wet and limp, a boy's hand. He *was* a boy, shy and more than a little confused by the strange surroundings.

" 'Allo, Mum," he said quietly.

"Hello, Sid," I said.

He wasn't so evil-looking once you got used to the sight of

him. It was partly his drooping eye that made him appear so malevolent. His presence, however, was not malevolent. It was subdued. My initial impression was that he simply wasn't very bright.

"And this is my dad, Sid," Nancy said. "Dad, this is Sid."

"Pleased to meet you, Sid," Frank said, shaking Sid's hand vigorously. Sid's arm seemed as if it were made of rubber.

"Pleased to meet you," Sid said, shifting uncomfortably from one foot to the other.

Frank grabbed their bags and we found our car, blazing a path straight through the stunned crowd on the platform.

"I thought we'd go straight home," I said as we got in the car. "I made a reservation for you at the Holiday Inn. We can go over there after dinner."

They sat in the back seat, holding hands, not replying.

"I thought we'd go home and have dinner now," I repeated. "Suzy's on her way home from town. David's already there."

I was the only one talking. I plowed on about nothing, afraid to stop, afraid of what the silence would feel like. I chattered the whole way home.

As we slowed in front of the house to turn into the driveway, Nancy began to clap her hands like a little girl.

"See, Sid?" she exclaimed. "That's it! That's my house!"

"It's a fuckin' palace," he gasped, genuinely awestruck by our housing tract colonial with its brick-faced first floor and aluminum-sided second floor—literally hundreds exactly like it spanning for block after block.

"It *is*," he said. "It's a fuckin' palace."

We pulled into the garage. Nancy jumped out of the car excitedly and dragged Sid inside by the wrist.

David waited in the foyer. His jaw dropped in shock at the sight of them. Nancy, totally unaware, hugged him.

"Sid, this is my little baby brother." She giggled because David was about six feet tall. "This is David."

David and Sid shook hands.

"Okay," she exclaimed. "Now you *have* to see the house!

This is the foyer, okay?'' She dragged him from room to room by the wrist. "Here's the living room, Sid. And here's the den.'' He went along, as if he were a docile child. "This is the kitchen. Now we get to go upstairs.''

They went upstairs. I could hear her guiding him from room to room. Then they came back downstairs and she took him out back to show him the garden and the pool.

"Isn't it beautiful, Sid?'' she asked.

"It's a fuckin' palace,'' he replied.

"I better get going,'' David observed. "Gotta pick up Suzy at Bethayres Station.''

"Oh, can we come, too?'' Nancy begged.

David shot Frank an inquiring look. Frank nodded.

"Sure,'' David said.

"Oh boy!'' Nancy cried gleefully. "C'mon, Sid. We're gonna pick up my baby sister at the station!''

The three of them got in the car and drove away. I began to get dinner ready.

"I think,'' Frank said, "they're going to be the biggest thing that's ever hit Bethayres Station.''

"Frank, what are we going to do with them?''

"Maybe Sid plays golf,'' he said, attempting to lighten my mood. I was not amused. "I sure don't know,'' he admitted.

They came back in about twenty minutes. Suzy rolled her eyes when she walked in the door—it was her way of saying she couldn't believe how Nancy looked.

"Guess who we saw?'' cried Nancy as she came in with Sid. "Aunt Susan and Holly. They were on the *same exact* train as Suzy. Do you *believe* it? Boy, did Holly grow up!''

The "Aunt Susan" Nancy referred to was my friend Susan, the one who had delivered the money to Nancy a year before in London. Holly was Susan's daughter. Later Susan told me she and Holly had gotten off the train and noticed a tremendous commotion—a commotion caused by the sight of Sid Vicious and Nancy Spungen leaning against the car, waiting for Suzy. Susan said Nancy had changed so much in the past year that she hadn't recognized her. Holly had—from the pictures in the Philadelphia papers.

Nancy and Sid each requested a vodka and tonic. Frank

made them. They sat on the den sofa and held hands, sipping their drinks. Suzy went into the den and presented her sister with a batch of chocolate chip cookies. They were a love offering from Suzy.

"Oh, my favorites!" cried Nancy. "Oh boy, oh boy!"

She opened the foil package and removed two cookies. One she popped joyfully in her mouth. The other she handed to Sid.

"You can have *one*, Sid," she said. "I'm gonna wrap up the rest and take 'em back to New York. Oh, thank you, Suzy!"

"You're welcome," Suzy said.

Sid sat there on the sofa holding his cookie.

"Eat it, Sid," Nancy told him.

He bit into it obediently. We watched as he chewed and swallowed it. He said nothing.

"How is it?" Nancy prompted him.

"It's fuckin' delicious," he replied. He took another nibble. Suzy rolled her eyes.

Dinner was served.

I barbecued a steak and served it with corn on the cob, salad, and garlic toast. We ate outside on the patio, under our green-and-white-striped awning, seated around our glass-topped wrought-iron table with its six matching wrought-iron chairs.

Nancy cut Sid's meat for him. Apparently she always did. Then he dug in. He ate ravenously for a few minutes, his face in his plate.

"Fuckin' good food," he said. "Fuckin' good, Debbie. Never have I had a meal like this. Never. Used to be I lived in a place with rats. Had to tie the food up in bags. High up, so they couldn't get at it. Never have I had a meal like this."

"I don't cook much." Nancy giggled.

"But that's okay," he said. "She's so fuckin' good to me."

"That's very nice," I said.

We ate in awkward silence for a moment.

"So what are your plans?" Frank said.

"Well, we just got in," Nancy said.

"First class," Sid pointed out. "We flew first class. I paid or the tickets. Nancy should always fly first class."

"We're loaded." Nancy smiled. "Money to burn."

Sid stopped eating. He'd lost interest in the food after only consuming about a third of it. So had Nancy. They lit cigarettes and sipped at their vodkas while the rest of us ate.

"We're at the Chelsea Hotel for now," she said. "We're gonna get a flat. I thought I'd see if my old one is empty. Our stuff is on the way. Our sofa and clippings and Sid's gold record and his knives and . . ."

"Knives?" I asked uneasily.

"Wish I had me knives," Sid lamented. "Never know when you might get cut. That's how I got this eye, you know. n a fight."

"Everything's on the way," Nancy said. "I had it sent ere. Didn't know where we'd end up, you know. I have to et my stereo and my records back."

"Then what?" Frank asked.

"Once we get settled, I'm gonna promote my Sid," she aid. "I'm his manager now. I'm a professional. Oh, I'll have o show you my portfolio after dinner! I'm a star! Can you beieve it? I made it! I really did!"

We all smiled and nodded and continued to eat.

"Oh, and we have to find a methadone clinic in New York. We brought some back, but it'll run out pretty soon. You now how we got it past the customs guys?"

"No," I said.

"Guess," she said. "I poured it in a bottle of dish soap. airy Lotion, it's called. They didn't think to look in it. Wasn't that stupid of them? I knew they wouldn't. They're so nbelievably dumb." She lit another cigarette. "So Suzy, ow are you doing, love? You moved into the city?"

"Uh-huh."

"Like it?"

"Uh-huh."

"That's grand. Just grand. And David? You're in private chool?"

"Yeah, that's right."

"My brother's very smart," Nancy proudly informed Sid.

"I didn't much like school," Sid said. "Teacher used to hit me. I didn't like school." He turned to Nancy. "Have you a guitar?"

"Sid wants to *play*," Nancy said excitedly. "David, do you still have your guitar?"

"Yeah," he said. "I'll get it." He went inside to get the guitar from his bedroom.

"Do you know our music then?" Sid asked us.

We nodded.

"Do you like it?"

We nodded yes.

David returned with the guitar, handed it to Sid.

"Let's go in the den, Sid," Nancy said.

They grabbed their cigarettes and got up.

"Best fuckin' food I ever ate," Sid said.

"Thank you, Sid," I said.

"Debbie?"

"Yes, Sid?"

"Is *Sha Na Na* on? On the telly?"

"Do you mean right now?" I asked uncertainly.

"Yes."

"They're on tomorrow, Sid," David told him. "Saturdays at seven."

"Oh," Sid said. "Don't want to miss *Sha Na Na*. They're my favorites."

He and Nancy went inside.

The four of us ate our food in silence, glancing occasionally at the remains on Nancy's and Sid's plates.

"She really looks awful," Suzy finally said, breaking the silence.

"She treats him like a little boy," David said. "She cuts his meat for him."

"He *is* a little boy," Frank said.

"And what's with her stupid accent?" Suzy asked.

"She always picks them up," I said. "Remember the time she got the southern accent from the boy at Avon?"

"When are they going back to New York?" Suzy asked.

"I don't know," I said.

"We can't throw them out," Frank said.

"I really don't know her anymore," David said. "That person is not my sister."

We finished our meal in silence.

"Best fuckin' steak I ever ate, Mum," David concluded.

"Come inside!" called Nancy. "Come in and hear Sid play!"

We went inside to hear Sid play. He and Nancy sat close to each other on the sofa, fresh vodka and tonics in front of them. They'd left the last ones half finished.

"Sid has something he wants to show you," Nancy said. "Okay, Sid. Go ahead."

Sid proceeded to bang out two chords, clumsily and with great difficulty. Then he stopped and looked up, grinning crookedly. That was it. That was what he wanted to show us. Our cat could have played it.

The four of us just stood there, staring at the two of them.

"Ain't that great?" asked Nancy.

We agreed it was great.

"Daddy used to play the guitar for us when we were little," Nancy said. "Remember how you used to play for us, Daddy?"

"I remember," Frank said.

Sid held the guitar out to Frank. "Here," he said anxiously, "play."

"No, I'm a little rusty," said Frank. "Haven't touched the guitar in years. David plays. He took lessons."

Sid offered the guitar to David, who took it reluctantly, sat down, and began to strum the Beatles song "Eleanor Rigby." He'd taken lessons for six months. At that, he was ten times the guitarist that Sid was.

"That's grand," said Nancy. "Sing, too."

David shook his head.

"C'mon," she urged.

He shook his head again. "I have a terrible voice."

She looked to Sid for support, but he had begun to melt into the sofa, half asleep.

"Perhaps," I suggested, "I should take you to the hotel."

"Okay," Nancy said. "No, wait. You haven't seen my portfolio yet. You have to see my portfolio."

She jumped up and went to the foyer to get it. Then she
came back and cleared a spot on the coffee table. We gathered
around the table to be shown her portfolio. Sid perked up, sort
of.

Her portfolio was actually a scrapbook in which she had
neatly pasted newspaper photos and stories about herself and
Sid, as well as publicity shots of the two of them.

"Don't I look beautiful in this one?" she asked.

In it, she was by Sid's side, one fist clenched at the camera,
teeth digging into her lower lip. Sid was shirtless and snarling.

"So beautiful," Sid agreed, putting his arm around her
proudly.

"It was taken at a press conference," she said. "The photographer told me I could be a professional model if I
wanted."

She looked half dead in the picture. The statement was so
pathetic I winced.

"I bought her those shoes," Sid pointed out. "I bought her
everything she ever had."

She showed us the other pictures in her portfolio. Some of
them predated Sid. There was the photograph of her with
Debbie Harry, a picture of our cats, a picture of her friend Sable.

"Oh, Sid!" she exclaimed suddenly. "You haven't seen
my baby pictures!"

She went to the desk and got out her baby pictures. There
was one snapshot of her curled up nude on our bed at seventeen months that was particularly cute. Sid gazed at it fondly.
So did I.

"Wasn't I adorable?" she asked him.

"So pretty," Sid said. "So, so pretty. Debbie, may I keep
this? I want it."

Frank and I exchanged a look. Frank nodded.

"Sure, Sid," I said. "It's yours."

He happily slid it into the pocket of his black leather jacket.
Then he yawned. It was about eleven o'clock. I again suggested taking them to the hotel. Sid said he'd like that. I drove
them while Frank, Suzy, and David cleaned up.

Nancy positioned Sid in the back seat, where he immediately began to doze. Then she joined me up in front.

"Great to be back, Mum," she said as I pulled out of the driveway.

"Nice to have you."

"Hated the bloody weather in England. Damp. House looks nice."

"Thank you."

"How come you have sliding glass doors in the kitchen now?"

"It's easier."

We drove in silence for a while.

"So when are you going back to New York?" I asked.

"Sunday night. That okay?"

"Fine."

"We have to find a methadone clinic on Monday."

We said nothing the rest of the way to the Holiday Inn. We really had nothing to say to each other.

The parking lot was deserted. Businessmen usually stayed there, but not on weekends. I pulled up right next to the front door.

"Come on, Sid," Nancy commanded. "We're here." She got out, clutching Suzy's cookies, and opened the door for Sid, who followed us inside groggily.

The desk clerk stared at them, incredulous.

"I registered you under your real name," I told Sid. "I thought it would be better."

"That's fine, Debbie," Sid said.

I filled out the registration form for them. For their address, I put down "Chelsea Hotel, New York, N.Y." Then Sid signed it. I paid for the room. The clerk handed me the key, still staring at them. They seemed not to notice. They never did.

"Do you . . . do you want a bellboy?" the clerk stammered.

I said no. Then I turned to Nancy and Sid.

"Well, I guess I'll be seeing you tomorrow," I said. "What time should we pick you up?"

"Wait, Mum," she begged. "Walk us to our room. Please."

They were like two lost, frightened children standing there in the Holiday Inn lobby. I wondered how they had survived for so long on their own. I helped them find their room. Then I unlocked the door for them and put the key on the bureau. I half expected Nancy to ask me to tuck them in.

Sid immediately started to get undressed for bed. Off went the leather jacket. As I mentioned, he had nothing on underneath it. He had a hairless, concave chest. His ribs stuck out. There were a couple of long, thin scars on his back and side. Knife wounds, possibly.

"So what time should we pick you up tomorrow?" I asked.

"Call us at noon, please, Mum," Nancy said.

We kissed each other good night.

Sid started to take off his pants. I headed for the door.

"Wait, Mum," Nancy said.

"What is it, Nancy?" I asked.

"You forgot to kiss Sid good night."

I went over to him, averting my eyes from his unbuckled trousers. I turned my face. He kissed me lightly on the cheek. I shuddered.

"Good night, Mum," he said.

"Good night, Sid."

Then I drove home.

The dinner dishes were all cleaned up.

"So when are they leaving?" Suzy wanted to know first thing.

"Sunday," I replied.

"Early?" she asked.

"Late," I answered.

"He's not nearly as threatening as I thought he'd be," David observed. "He's too zonked."

"I'll tell you one thing," Frank said. "If he can make a million dollars with that guitar-playing of his, I should be able to make a hundred million."

"At least she's calm around him," I said. "Motherly, almost."

We went to bed. As he turned out the light Frank said,

"Every time I look at the two of them, I keep thinking the same thing."

"What's that?"

"That neither one of them looks like they're long for this world," he said sadly.

I couldn't sleep. I just lay there in the darkness, thinking, groping toward some kind of grasp on Nancy's relationship with Sid, her only lasting relationship.

They were two lost souls who had found each other. Their relationship came out of their inability to find what they wanted in the outside world. They were on the same wavelength. They fit each other's needs.

Both had trouble getting along with most people. Both were troubled and angry. Sid had the capacity to lash out in anger at others. Nancy tended to direct her anger at herself. She needed to have everything her way. Sid needed to have somebody tell him what to do. She was bright and aggressive. He was, seemingly, withdrawn and not particularly verbal. If you'd have asked Sid what sort of social statement he was making by the way he performed and looked, he'd have been hard-pressed to articulate a response.

They were dependent on each other. They cared for each other. To them, what they had together was genuine love. It was the only time for Nancy. Sid was the one great love of her life. She was twenty years old, he a year older. They were basically the same age Frank and I had been when she'd been born. That was hard for me to imagine. They seemed like children to me, immature and incapable of taking care of themselves—much less another human being. Maybe Frank and I had been, too, when we were that age, and just hadn't known it.

No, I refused to believe that. We had not been Nancy and Sid. We had devoted ourselves to building, not tearing down.

I tossed and turned the entire night.

Happily, it was bright and sunny the next morning. I phoned them at noon and woke them up. Nancy asked me to call back in an hour. I did and woke them again.

"We'll get up," Nancy said. "Come for us in an hour."

David picked them up. They weren't in the lobby when he

got there, he later informed me. So up he went up to their room and knocked on the door. Nancy called for him to come in. They were still in bed, naked, watching Saturday morning cartoons. When David walked in they got out of bed, put on their rumpled clothes from the previous night, and took a swig each of methadone from the Fairy Lotion bottle. Then Nancy said, "Let's go." Neither of them got washed or brushed their teeth.

David said he walked fifty feet ahead of them down the corridor and out to the car. He noticed the people noticing them. He was, he said, embarrassed to be seen with them.

About halfway home Sid tugged at Nancy's sleeve and whispered something to her.

"Sid wants a hamburger," Nancy informed David.

"McDonald's be okay, Sid?" David asked.

Sid whispered his reply to Nancy.

"That'd be fine," Nancy told David.

David pulled into McDonald's and waited outside in the car while Nancy and Sid went in to get Sid's hamburger. As he waited the people who came out were all pointing inside in amazement, laughing, pulling their hair straight up. After a few minutes Nancy and Sid came out with Sid's hamburger, blinking at the sunlight.

Sid picked at his hamburger as they drove home. He was still working on it when they arrived.

Nancy wanted to swim. Neither she nor Sid had suits. I gave her one of mine. David found a pair of jogging shorts for Sid, who could barely keep them on, he was so thin. His legs were incredibly pale. I doubted that they'd ever been exposed to the sun before.

They jumped in the pool. We sat by the side and watched them. They splashed and frolicked like two little kids. They dunked each other and giggled and tossed a beach ball and attempted zany dives off the board. They were without a care in the world. It was a typical suburban scene, just like a million others you'd have seen around America that summer afternoon. The only difference was that we were the only suburbanites in America who had Sid Vicious of the Sex Pistols in our swimming pool.

He was exhausted within ten minutes.

The two of them stretched out in the sun on lounge chairs. zy had made plans to visit her friend Laura, so she left. ank, David, and I had lunch on the patio. Nancy and Sid id they weren't hungry.

He was green after five minutes in the sun.

"I don't feel very well," he said weakly.

"He's probably not used to the sun, Nancy," I said. Maybe he should sit in the shade."

She helped Sid move to a chair in the shade. When he still lt ill, I suggested she take him inside where it was air- nditioned.

"Stretch out on the sofa in the den, Sid," Frank said.

"May I watch the telly?" Sid asked.

"Sure," Frank said.

"Any cartoons on, Frank?"

"Don't know. Probably."

"How about *Sha Na Na.* Is it on?"

"Tonight, Sid," David told him. "At seven."

Nancy took him inside, laid a towel down on the sofa to otect against his wet suit. He stretched out. When I came in- de she was sitting on the end of the sofa, stroking his head, hich was in her lap.

"How does he feel?" I asked her.

"A little better," she replied.

"Does he want something cold? Sid, would you like a ink? A cold drink?"

"Please, Mum."

I brought him some juice. He thanked me and drank it. en he sat up and lit a cigarette. Nancy turned on the TV and und some cartoons for them to watch. They sat there on the fa for the remainder of the afternoon, chain smoking, star- g at the TV, glassy-eyed. They seemed stuporous. Occa- nally they would nod off, lit cigarettes in hand.

After the first time a live ash had tumbled onto the oatmeal eed sofa and begun to smolder, I stayed in the den with m, watching them carefully, vaulting across the coffee le every once in a while to catch the falling ash in an ntray before it did any damage.

Toward the middle of the afternoon Suzy returned with her friend Laura. They were very close, and Suzy wanted her to meet her big sister. Laura had been prepared for how they looked, and acted as if she didn't notice.

"Hi, Nancy!" exclaimed Laura, so cute and perky, so alive.

"Hello," said Nancy quietly, barely noticing her.

"And this is Nancy's boyfriend, Sid," Suzy said. "Sid, this is Laura."

"Pleased to meet you, Sid," she said.

Sid didn't notice her at all. He just looked right through her.

There was an awkward silence. Then Suzy and Laura went outside.

A little later the phone rang. It was a friend of David's, a fellow counselor from camp who happened to be visiting some relatives in Huntingdon Valley. David suggested he drop by for a few minutes.

I wish I had a picture of Bob's face when he walked into the den, unsuspecting, to find Sid Vicious on the sofa with our daughter. Bob's eyes widened and for a moment he looked as if he were going to choke. Then he swallowed and, with terrific effort, held on to his cool. After exchanging pleasantries with us, he was introduced to them.

"Hi, Nancy," Bob said.

She nodded.

"Nice to meet you, Sid," Bob said, sticking his hand out.

Sid stared at the hand, uncomprehending for a moment, then up at Bob. Finally he stuck out his own hand and they shook.

David took Bob outside to shoot some baskets. As they went out the back door I could hear Bob saying, "I can't believe it! Sid Vicious is in your den watching cartoons!"

It *was* pretty hard to imagine.

Another ash fell onto the couch.

"Nancy, your cigarette!" I cried.

"Huh?" she said.

"Nothing," I said, swatting at the dead ash on the upholstery. "Forget it."

went into the kitchen—stomach knotted, teeth clenched
o find something to do. I couldn't sit there anymore look-
at the two of them.

What I really wanted to do was shake her and scream,
ook what you've become! You're not my Nancy! Where's
Nancy? I want my Nancy back!''

There was no point in saying anything to her. I couldn't
ch her. She was lost to me. My arms ached to hold the
by Nancy, ached for a fresh start.

I didn't know how much longer I could stand having them
re. I wanted them gone.

Suddenly Nancy appeared behind me.

"Mum, would you take me to the hospital?" she asked.

"What for?" I demanded, alarmed.

"I, uh, got beat up by the Teddys a few weeks ago and they
led my ear off. A doctor sewed it back on, you know, but I
got to get the stitches out. Just remembered."

"Here, let me see," I said.

She pulled back her hair and turned so I could get a good
k. First I noticed the yellowish bruises and open sores
ng her hairline. Then I saw the ear. Revulsion swept over
as I saw the row of stitches that ran along the back of her
, all the way from the top, where the ear met the skull, to
bottom, where it joined the neck.

It did, however, look clean and healed.

"We'll have an awfully long wait at the hospital," I said.
Not to mention another scene.

"How about your doctor, Mum?"

"It's Saturday. He's off. Tell you what, I can take them
. There's really nothing to it."

"Okay."

I went upstairs to fetch a pair of small toenail scissors. I
shed them in alcohol, took them downstairs with the bottle
alcohol, some cotton, and antibiotic ointment. Nancy was
iting for me in the kitchen.

"Stand next to the window," I said. "The light is better."
She obeyed.

"Okay, now don't move," I said.

"I won't."

She stood perfectly still for me as I cut the little catgut kno
one by one and pulled the stitches out. I worked smoothly a
calmly, as if I took out stitches every day. In actuality, I h
never done it before. When I was done, I cleaned the ear a
put ointment on it.

"It looks fine," I said.

"Thanks, Mum. Could you make me an appointment wi
a plastic surgeon? These scars all over my arms. I'd like to g
'em off."

"We'll see," I said.

I sensed another presence in the room. I turned to find S
looming in the doorway.

"Mum," he said, "I need a doctor for me eye. It wou
stay open, you know. Could you make me an appointmer
too?"

I looked at her, then at him. I felt myself getting suck
into their universe. Now there were two of these helple
souls for me to take care of. My burden was doubled. I took
deep breath, let it out.

"I'll try, Sid," I said.

"Thank you. That'd be very nice of you. I don't like r
eye, you know. I got it in a fight. People always want to fig
with me. Teachers. Policemen, Teddys. Everybody. I do
want to, but they do."

"He's really a very sweet lad, Mum," Nancy said.

They returned to the sofa and began to nod off again.

When it got to be about six, I asked Nancy what she and S
felt like for dinner.

"Can we go to the Village Inn, Mum? I want to take S
there."

The Village Inn was an old family favorite, a neighborho
Italian restaurant we'd taken the children to many tim
through the years. Evidently Nancy had fond memories of t
place. However, to go into the Village Inn dining room mea
walking through the bar, a popular blue-collar conservati
hangout. It would be impossible to take Nancy and S
through there and emerge unscathed.

Frank and I exchanged a worried look.

"I don't know, Nancy," I improvised. "It's gotten to be o crowded."

"I don't mind," she said.

"We'll have to wait a long time," I said.

"I don't mind," she said.

"Sid will miss *Sha Na Na* at seven," Frank pointed out.

"*Sha Na Na?*" said Sid, perking up. "I don't want to miss *ha Na Na*. They're my favorite."

"We could order takeout and eat it here," Frank suggested. I blew him a kiss when Nancy agreed.

David took the orders—both Nancy and Sid wanted spahetti and meatballs—phoned them in, and went to pick them up with Frank.

Nancy and Sid helped themselves to vodka and tonic and egan to kiss and grope at each other on the den sofa. I didn't ke watching Sid touch her. It wasn't that I hated him, beause I didn't. Actually, I felt kind of sorry for him. He eemed like a victim of Malcolm McLaren's promotion mahinery. For a brief time he'd been a star. Now he didn't now who or what he was. He seemed like a genuinely conused kid. No, the reason I didn't like watching him touch her as because the two of them were totally oblivious to my resence in the room. I felt I was witnessing an intimacy I asn't supposed to see, really didn't *want* to see. It made me ant to avert my eyes. It gave me the creeps.

They lived in their own little world, Nancy and Sid did.

I went into the kitchen to set the table in there for the four of s. Nancy and Sid would eat in the den before the TV. Suzy ollowed me in there. She was angry.

"How can you stand this!" she demanded. "How can you atch them? How can you watch her dying like that? Why on't you *do* something?"

I wanted to say "Suzy, if I let myself react at all, my head ill simply blow off." But I didn't want her to know I was so pset. And I was too upset to explain myself. I shut her out. I ouldn't have, but I did.

"They'll be gone tomorrow," I said. "Let's just get rough the weekend, okay?"

She glared at me. "I don't see how you can put up with it. Your own daughter." Then she stormed out.

Frank and David came back with the food. Suzy came downstairs grudgingly and we four ate silently in the kitchen while Nancy and Sid ate in the den, watching *Sha Na Na,* of course.

"Debbie?" Sid called.

"Yes, Sid?"

"Best fuckin' food I ever ate. Best fuckin' ever!"

"We think it's good, too, Sid!" I called back.

He ate, at most, a third of it. He had little appetite for food it seemed. After dinner the four of us watched the two of them nodding off on the sofa, ever alert to the falling cigarette ashes.

Suzy was still angry. She glared at her sister with a combination of curiosity and disgust. Nancy caught her.

"If you look at me like that one more time I'll cut your fucking face up," she snapped viciously, her eyes cold.

Suzy froze. There was total silence. I couldn't stand the tension in the room, so I went into the kitchen. Suzy followed me in there, wide-eyed.

"Do you think she will?" Suzy whispered, terrified.

"I don't know," I replied. "I really don't know."

Suzy went up to her room. She was so scared she went back to her apartment early in the morning, before Nancy and Sid came back from the hotel. Suzy never had the chance to see or speak to her sister again. That little scene they'd played out in the den was their final communication.

Frank took them to the hotel that night. I picked them up on Sunday at about one o'clock. Just like David had the day before, I found them naked in bed. They got up, pulled on their now filthy clothes, gulped their methadone, and were set to go.

"Don't you want to pack?" I asked, wary that they'd changed their plans and were going to stay longer.

"Oh, right," remembered Nancy, heaving their few possessions carelessly into an overnight bag. "All set, Mum."

I checked them out of their room and brought them to the

ouse. Frank had picked up lox and bagels for Sunday
runch, per Nancy's request.

Nancy piled cream cheese and lox onto her bagel and began
evouring it with gusto. Sid just nibbled on a dry bagel.

"Have some lox, Sid," Frank offered.

"Oh, no," he said. "No . . . I can't eat *that*. "

In midafternoon, Nancy decided it was time for them to
atch a train back to New York. We drove them to the station.
rank and I got in the front seat, David in the back seat with
Nancy and Sid. Nancy said nothing in regard to Suzy's ab-
ence, though she did clutch her sister's offering of chocolate
hip cookies.

"Thank you so much for having me," Sid said as we
ulled out of the driveway.

"Our pleasure, Sid," Frank said.

"I didn't know people lived like this," said Sid. "In a
uckin' palace."

We drove in silence for a while. Then out of nowhere,
Nancy quietly said, "I'm going to die very soon. Before my
wenty-first birthday. I won't live to be twenty-one. I'm never
onna be old. I don't wanna ever be ugly and old. I'm an old
ady now anyhow. I'm eighty. There's nothing left. I've al-
eady lived a whole lifetime. I'm going out. In a blaze of
lory."

Then she was quiet.

Her words just lay there like a bombshell. No one wanted
touch them. She hadn't issued a threat, simply made a flat
atement. We all believed her. Even Sid.

We got stared at by everyone again at the platform. When
e train pulled in Nancy hugged me.

"My beautiful mum," she said softly. "My beautiful
um."

She released me. "Didn't I tell you she was beautiful, Sid?
'asn't I right?"

Sid nodded.

We hugged again and kissed. Then she kissed Frank and
avid. Sid kissed me again on the cheek, and again I shud-
ered. Then he shook hands with Frank and David.

"Very nice to meet all of you," he said.

"Don't forget to call when our stuff comes," she said.

They got on the train. We watched from the platform as i pulled away. She waved from the window. We waved back

She'd issued a warning to us in the car, but I had no inkling that this was the last time I'd see her alive. I felt only relie that she and Sid were gone.

"I honestly can't understand her," David said as we drov home. "She's dying. She knows it. Why won't she stop her self?"

"She doesn't want to," Frank said sadly. "She wants t die. She has for a long, long time. It's been her goal."

"But why?" asked David.

"She hates being alive," I said. "She hates her pain. Sh hates herself. She wants to destroy herself."

"Isn't there anything you guys can do?" asked David.

"Yes," I said.

"What?"

"Watch her die."

# ❑ Chapter 21

Nancy lived out her rock fantasy in New York, sharing the bed and the career of a star. But she and Sid were running out of time.

He collapsed in the lobby of the Chelsea Hotel their first week there. Nancy phoned me from the hospital in hysterics.

"Save him, Mum!" she cried. "Save him! The doctor says his brain might be damaged! What do I do? Help me! Oh, please!"

As always I calmed her down. And as always it left me a wreck.

"The doctor will take care of him, Nancy. He'll be fine. You'll see. Call me tomorrow, okay?"

She did. Sid was okay.

Nancy did manage to find them a methadone center, but the lines were long and every day Sid was taunted and provoked by the other addicts. He got mad. He got in fights.

"They keep hasslin' my Sid," Nancy reported. "He's got his hot button, Mum, and they just won't leave it alone."

She went to work on Sid's career.

She tried to line up recording contracts for him, but found little interest from the record companies. Sid had no actual career. All he had was a claim to fame. But neither she nor Sid realized that.

"It's not workin' out the way we thought," she told me over the phone. "Nothing's happening. Sid's real depressed."

They went back on heroin.

Two weeks after we'd put them on the train, she was calling for money—stoned, incoherent, paranoid.

"Won't let us work," she mumbled. "Don't like us. M'Sid. Me. Don't like us. Won't let us work. No money."

"Where's Sid's money?" I asked.

"Supposed to get some. England, Mum. It's in England. Don't have it, though. Don't have any. No money. Problems. Just problems."

I refused to send them money. She hung up, more dazed than angry.

The following week she did somehow manage to get Sid some club work. She lined up three nights for him at Max's Kansas City in mid-September, and also booked him into the Hive, her old Philadelphia hangout, for the last weekend of October.

"If you see Karen," she told me, "tell her I hope she comes. Wanna see her. Wanna see Karen."

Sid's first couple of performances at Max's were sellouts, thanks to his notoriety. But he did not cut it in his U.S. solo debut. There were catcalls and boos. People walked out.

He and Nancy sank deeper into drugs and despair. I spoke to her about once a week and each time she sounded lower. She and Sid went out of their room at the Chelsea less and less. One night one of them nodded off in bed with a lit cigarette and set the mattress on fire. Reportedly, a hotel employee rushed up to their room with a fire extinguisher to find them wandering around, oblivious to the smoldering mattress. The manager moved them to another room, room 100.

Their packages began to arrive at our house from London toward the end of September—each package addressed to a different family member. For some reason Nancy thought this would speed up delivery. I got a roll of newspapers—Sid's clippings. David got a box filled with metal-studded leather collars and cuffs. Inside the box there was also a note from U.S. Customs: "Three knives were removed from this package by U.S. Customs agents. Please contact if you wish to appeal." We didn't wish to. Frank got Sid's gold record, the glass covering shattered. The sofa didn't come. It never did.

I phoned Nancy to tell her their stuff had come.

"What stuff?" she asked, stoned and confused.

"Sid's clippings and his leather, uh, *things.* And his gold record."

"Oh, right."

"The glass on the record is broken."

Sid got very upset when she passed this bit of information on to him. I could hear him cursing in the background.

"We'll get it fixed, Mum. We'll fix it here. Is Daddy gonna be here? Can Daddy bring it?"

I checked. Frank had to be in New York on business the following Wednesday and said he could drop the stuff off. I told her.

"Can you come, too, Mum?"

"No, Nancy. I have to work."

"Oh, okay. We'll see you Wednesday."

"Nancy, I'm not coming."

"Why not?"

"I just told you. Work."

"Oh. See ya, then. See ya . . . whenever."

On Wednesday, Frank loaded Sid's things into his car along with his briefcase and headed into New York. He stopped at the Chelsea Hotel first thing. He didn't want to take the chance of having Sid's gold record stolen from the car. He got there at about noon.

He checked in with me by phone when his mission had been accomplished.

The hotel lobby, he told me, was seedy and shabby. The desk clerk directed him to room 100. He took the stairs up to the second floor, found their room, and knocked on the door. There was no answer. He knocked again, louder. Nancy hollered for him to come in. He went in.

They were still in bed, watching cartoons on TV. It was very dark in the room, the lights out, the shades drawn. And it smelled. Half-filled takeout food containers and soda cups were piled everywhere. So was dirty laundry.

They were both so out of it they didn't seem completely aware of his presence in the room. They just continued to stare at the TV.

Frank said he cleared a spot on the dresser, put down the things he'd brought, and said he'd be going.

"Thank you, Daddy," Nancy said, looking right through him.

Sid said nothing.

Frank left.

"I couldn't wait to get the hell out of there," he told me. "It was so depressing. They're even worse than they were before. Totally out of it. They're barely alive."

I was sorry Frank had seen her like that. But I was glad I hadn't.

It rained that Sunday, October first. It was a dreary day, the kind that makes you want to be somewhere else, doing something else. I decided to clean out some closets. I started with Nancy's. It had remained untouched for over three years. I had put off cleaning her things out. I guess, deep down inside, I had wanted to believe she'd come back someday and live with us, live happily. Now I knew this was never going to happen. There was no point in keeping her old papers and hippie clothes around. Knowing that, I wanted to get the job over with.

There were three shelves built into the right side of the closet. These were crammed with school papers from Darlington and Colorado, crammed with keepsakes, crammed with junk. Most of it went into the trash. I saved whatever I thought might be important to her. I saved her newspaper from the day after JFK's assassination. I saved her *Life* magazine issue about Woodstock. I saved her old doll. It had been my doll before it was hers. I saved her little stuffed tiger, which Frank had bought for me when he was away in the army, and which I had given to her when she was little because she adored it so. I saved her scholastic awards from elementary school and her books. It occurred to me, as I made a stack of the dog-eared paperbacks, that she hadn't looked at a book or magazine the weekend she'd been home. She had stopped reading, given up on her intellect.

Suzy came by that afternoon and helped me go through Nancy's clothing. We packed most of it into cartons to give away. We felt certain there was nothing there that Nancy would want to wear anymore. Suzy kept a couple of the blouses for herself. Then we took the cartons downstairs to the garage.

I went back upstairs to survey my work. The closet was empty and clean now—all except for a garment bag hanging way in the back. I hadn't noticed it until now. I unzipped the bag. Inside was that slinky, lime-green dress Nancy had bought for her Darlington prom. I zipped the bag up again and left it hanging there in the closet. I didn't feel like making another trip downstairs. Then I closed the closet door and surveyed the room. It was an office now, with Frank's desk and filing cabinets. The evidence that Nancy had lived here was all but erased. But the memories—the screaming, the demons, the pain—were not. Those I couldn't give away to Goodwill.

She phoned the following Sunday, October eighth.

"I'm sick," she said weakly. "My kidneys. I'm sick from my kidneys. Can you send money? Can you send me money?"

"You know the deal, Nancy. Go to the doctor and tell him to send the bill to me. I'll pay him directly. What's wrong with your kidneys?"

"Wait, Mum. Sid wants to talk."

Sid got on. "Debbie?"

"Yes, Sid."

"Why won't you help your daughter?" he demanded. He sounded different—harsh and unpleasant.

"I will, Sid. I'll pay her bills directly to the doctor. That's always been our—"

"Her health comes first!"

"I *know* that, Sid. I *will* pay her medical bills. *Directly* to the doctor."

"But it's your daughter's health!" he snapped angrily.

"Sid, I—"

"We need three thousand dollars right now! For the doctor! Send it at once!" he ordered.

"No."

"We *must* have it!" he insisted.

"I said no, Sid! Please put Nancy back on."

"What kind of mother are you? How can you do this to your own fuckin' daughter?"

"Sid, in the first place, I haven't got three thousand dollars. In the second place, a doctor's appointment doesn't cost that much! Now would you *please* put Nancy back on?"

"It's your daughter's health!" he repeated angrily. "Your daughter's fuckin' health!"

"Sid, would you please put—"

*"No! I won't put Nancy on! Not until you—"*

"Put Nancy on or I'm hanging up!"

*"How can you do this to your own fuckin'—"*

I hung up on him, shaken. This was a side of Sid—hostile and belligerent—I hadn't seen before. He frightened me.

The phone rang immediately. I wouldn't answer it. Frank and I had made dinner plans with my mother. I told David not to answer the phone if it rang while we were out. It was ringing when we left. When we returned, David said it hadn't stopped ringing the whole time we were gone.

It immediately started to ring again.

"See?" David said.

I decided to answer it. It was Nancy.

"Mum, what happened before between you and Sid?"

"He was very nasty. I warned him I was going to hang up."

"Wait, hang on." She turned away from the phone to talk to Sid. "Here's your match. Now light your cigarette and leave me the fuck alone," she said to him. Then she was back. "He's very upset, Mum. A very upset lad. He has a lot of problems."

"Where is he now?"

"Right here. But he's out of it. You don't have to worry about him."

Her voice was calm, her speech clear. It was the most lucid he'd sounded in a long time.

"Are your kidneys really bothering you, sweetheart?"

"Yes. I think I have an infection. I'll be all right, though. I'll go see a doctor tomorrow. What kind do you go to for kidneys?"

"A urologist. Go to the emergency ward of the hospital tomorrow and ask for one. If there isn't one there who can treat you, call me. I'll get you the name of someone in New York to see."

"Okay, Mum, I will. Thank you." She paused. "Mum?"

"Yes?"

"Did Daddy ever beat you?"

I was so taken aback by the question, I didn't know how to answer it. I made a joke out of it. "No, but *I've* thrown a few things at *him.*"

There was silence from her end.

"Nancy, why do you ask?"

"You know all the times I told you I got beat up by the Teddys in London? Got my ear torn off? My nose broken?"

"Yes."

"It was Sid who was really doing it. And . . . and now he's started doing it again."

"Why?" I gasped, horrified.

"He's upset."

"Nancy, why do you put up with that? Why don't you leave him?"

"Because . . . well, he's having a terrible time. He's getting hassled. He can't get work. He's depressed. He's not himself."

There was a long pause.

"Maybe one of these days you *will* find me on your doorstep," she said softly.

"We're always here for you, Nancy. If you ever hit the bottom and need us, we're here to help you. You can count on 
"

"I *am* at the bottom, Mum. This is it."

She'd come out of her fog. She was rational. We were communicating.

"Mum, do you remember that detox hospital, White Deer Run? It's somewhere in Pennsylvania. Our next-door neighbor had to go there, remember?"

"Yes."

"Do you think Sid and I could get in there? We have to get off. Just have to. Could you call? Could you find out for me if it's locked? I don't want to go if it's locked. I can't stand being locked up."

"I know. I'll call tomorrow and find out."

"Thanks."

"Let me know how you are. Let me know what the urologist says, okay?"

"I'll let you know."

"Good."

"Mum?"

"Yes?"

"Does Daddy love me?"

"Of course he loves you. He's always loved you very much."

"He doesn't act that way."

"How does he act?"

"Like he's afraid of me."

"That's because he has to walk on eggs with you, sweetheart. Everyone has to. You're very sensitive. But that doesn't mean he doesn't love you. Do you understand?"

"Yes, Mum. I do. Tell Daddy I understand. And . . . and . . ."

"And what?"

"Tell him that I love him."

"Okay, sweetheart. I will."

"How's *your* mom? How's Essie?"

She hadn't asked about her grandmother in three years.

"She's fine."

"Send her my love, will you?"

"I'll do that."

"Good-bye, Mum."

"Good-bye, sweetheart."

As I hung up the phone I heard her yell, "I love you, Mommy! I love you!"

I wanted to tell her that I loved her, too, but it was too late. The connection was broken.

I gave Frank her message.

"Nancy said that?" He was surprised and touched.

"Uh-huh. It was a very strange call, Frank. Spooky, kind of. It was almost as if she were saying good-bye."

I called White Deer Run on Monday afternoon from the office. The woman I needed to speak with in admissions was out sick. I was told to phone later in the week.

Nancy didn't call on Monday night. I supposed she had nothing to report about her kidneys.

On Tuesday I met Suzy after work at her haircutter's. It was located right near the clothing store where Nancy's friend Karen worked. Suzy and I stopped in to tell her Nancy would soon be coming to town for Sid's appearance at Artemis.

It was hard to imagine that she and Karen had once been friends. Karen was responsible, hardworking, and sober. Her appearance was very neat. But she got excited at the prospect of seeing Nancy again.

"Tell her I'll be there!" she exclaimed. "That'll be great! I haven't seen her in years. I keep wondering if she really looks like that. You know, like she does in the papers."

"More so," I said.

"You mean you've seen her?" Karen asked.

"*And* Sid," replied Suzy, rolling her eyes.

We filled Karen in on our weekend with the two of them. Karen looked down, suddenly very serious. "You know, 's such a waste. She was so smart and read so many books. She could have been anything she wanted."

Nancy didn't call on Tuesday night, either. I had a vague uneasiness, but I didn't give in to the temptation to call her. If she was coping with her problems, I didn't want to interfere with the process. She knew where to reach me.

She didn't call on Wednesday, either. Wednesday was Yom Kippur. I became more uneasy.

On Thursday morning it was glorious and crisp, a beautiful autumn day. I drove to the office early, my mind on all of the work piled up on my desk. I made a mental note to phone

White Deer Run for Nancy, but crises kept coming up at the office and I still hadn't had a chance to call at two o'clock.

I was coming out of the computer room and crossing the main office to my own office when one of the secretaries said, "Debbie, you have a call. The receptionist wants you to buzz her before you take it."

I buzzed the receptionist.

"It's a Lieutenant Hunter from the Lower Moreland police," she told me. "I just thought you'd like to know."

I wondered what the local police wanted of me.

I thanked her, went into my office to take the call. As I sat down at my desk I glanced at the calendar page for that day, October 12, 1978. On it I'd scrawled "Call White Deer Run re: admission Nancy, Sid." Had to remember to take care of that, I told myself. And call Nancy that night if I hadn't heard from her.

I picked up the phone.

"This is Deborah Spungen," I said. "Can I help you, Lieutenant Hunter?"

e sounded very uncomfortable.

"Your . . . next-door neighbor told us where to find
ou," Lieutenant Hunter said. "We were out at your
ouse . . ."

"What's this about?" I asked.

"The, uh, New York Police Department would like to
eak to you. Something has happened to your daughter
ancy."

"What happened to her?" I pressed, confused by his
gueness.

He didn't answer me. Instead he gave me the name of a de-
ctive and a number to call in New York. Then he was silent.
Suddenly my face felt very hot.

"Lieutenant, please tell me what happened. It's okay. I'm
dy for anything. Believe me. But I will not hang up this
one until you tell me what has happened to my daughter."

"Mrs. Spungen, I'm sorry to tell you that your daughter is
ad."

My first reaction was disbelief. We'd been through so

343

much together over the past twenty years. I had thought I'd somehow *sense* her death. I did not.

But it *was* over, really over. My head seemed to swell up in response as if someone were using a bicycle pump on it. My fantasy was coming true. It must have been a drug overdose. What else could it have been?

Since I shared my office with someone else, I went to look for my boss to ask him if I could call the NYPD from his office. He wasn't in his office. I went out into the main office. There were a hundred or so people working and talking out there. They made no noise. Their world was soundless. I felt like I was floating, my head up somewhere near the ceiling.

I did find a vice-president, talking to someone at a desk. stood beside him for a minute, but he didn't seem to notice me. I thought about just waiting there until my head exploded all over the place. Then he'd notice me.

I didn't wait. "Nancy's dead!" I shouted. "Can I use Joe's office?"

He turned and stared at me, stunned. Everywhere people looked at me. He nodded.

I went into Joe's office, shut the door, and dialed Detective Brown in New York. My dialing finger shook. I was reacting with a bit more emotion than I'd expected, but I was in control.

"I'm sorry to tell you your daughter has been murdered, Mrs. Spungen," Detective Brown said in a kind voice.

*Murdered.*

My baby. Murdered. It couldn't be. It wasn't supposed to be this way. Besides, Frank and I were supposed to be together. I needed him, but he was on the road, somewhere on his way between Philadelphia and a convention in New York.

"Her boyfriend, Sid Vicious, has been arrested," Detective Brown said.

He must have beaten her again. He must have gone too far.

"My husband," I said. "My husband's on his way to New York."

"Can you get word to him, Mrs. Spungen? Quickly? I'm afraid it's on the news already. I'm sure he'd rather hear from you than the car radio."

"Yes, yes, I'll tell him. And then he . . . he should meet ou?"

"No, not today. There's nothing either of you can do here oday. We would like to see the two of you tomorrow morn-ng, though. Say, ten o'clock."

"What for?"

"We have to ask you some questions. Strictly routine. And f course you have to identify the body."

*The body.* Not *her* body. *The* body. Nancy was no longer a erson. She was, officially speaking, an "it."

"There'll be a preliminary hearing and . . . and, again my ondolences. Mrs. Spungen, there is one detail you need to ke care of as soon as possible."

"Yes?"

"Do you have a pencil?"

"Yes, I do."

"Okay, I'm going to give you a name and number. It's the edical examiner's office."

I wrote down the information.

"When you make arrangements with the funeral home, ey'll need to phone this number to arrange the pickup."

"The pickup?"

"Yes, the body, Mrs. Spungen."

"Why can't she . . . ?" I trailed off. I was about to ask hy she couldn't just hop on the train. I swallowed. "Yes, of ourse."

"It'll be sometime over the weekend. After the autopsy, of ourse."

"Of course. The autopsy," I repeated woodenly.

He gave me directions to the precinct house.

"So I'll see you tomorrow morning at ten. I'll make sure ou're taken everywhere. We'll get it over with just as uickly as possible."

I hung up the phone. Joe, my boss, appeared in the office oorway. He'd heard the news. He held his arms out. I went him and buried my face in his chest. It felt good to be held r a moment. He said nothing.

I said, "Thank God it's over."

Then I called Frank's office. His secretary answered.

"Nancy's dead!" I blurted out. "Please try to find Frank right away!"

She said he was due at the St. Moritz in forty-five minutes.

"You've got to get word to him," I said.

She said his partner was already there. She'd phone him and tell him to ask Frank to call home right away. He would not give Frank the news. I needed to be the one to do that.

I hung up, noticed I was clutching a piece of paper in my hand. The phone number of the medical examiner's office. Right, I had to contact a funeral home. I had chosen one already in my fantasy. All taken care of. The name. I couldn't remember the name. Why couldn't I remember it?

I looked it up in the Yellow Pages. I had trouble focusing on the print—it kept transforming from written language to meaningless wriggles on a page. But I found it. I called. The director was out; he would call me later at home. I gave the man on the phone the message about the medical examiner's office. He took down the number and said they'd take care of the transportation arrangements.

Okay, I was in control again. I had been thrown, briefly, but now I was all set to follow through on my fantasy. I phoned Janet.

"Please get to my house right away. Nancy is dead," I said quickly.

Then I called my friend Susan. Her son said she was out. Good thing I was prepared for that.

"Tell her something has happened," I said, "and to come over right away."

I wrote instructions for what needed to be done at work over the next three days. I gave it to my secretary. Now I was ready to go home. David would be there soon from school. Suzy? That would take some doing—she had some late afternoon classes. Frank would call soon. Home. Time to go home.

I gathered up my briefcase and my purse and went out into the main office. There was some kind of catered party going on out there now. Tables were heaped with food. People were standing around eating little meatballs with toothpicks. They stopped chewing and talking when I glided through on a cloud, feeling nothing, hearing nothing.

I found my car in the lot. I started it up and headed home. It ok me two days to get there—or so it felt. Time seemed to ave stopped. There were no cars or people anywhere. The reets were devoid of life. It was as if everyone had died ex- pt me.

*"I'm sorry to tell you your daughter has been murdered, rs. Spungen."*

It was sunny and bright. I rolled down the window, felt no ind on my face.

*"Her boyfriend, Sid Vicious, has been arrested."*

I screamed. No sound came out.

*"And, of course, you have to identify the body."*

The car seemed to be driving itself. I thought about taking y hands off the wheel and just letting it. Then I panicked. I alized *I* was driving and I was in no condition to drive. Why dn't anyone offered to give me a ride home? Or had they, d had I just not heard it?

I was about halfway home. No turning back. I kept going, ghting to hold on to the rational me, the one who knew that ancy was finally at peace, the one who was taking care of siness. There was another me I hadn't anticipated. This as the me who wouldn't accept her death. The me who was eaking down.

Somehow I found our block and then our driveway. Janet as there. I got out of the car. We hugged. She cried. I didn't. wanted to, but I couldn't. There was too much to do.

Janet made some coffee. Susan arrived a few minutes after at. She cried when she got the news. Again, I did not.

Janet and Susan told me they were available to do anything asked of them. They were there for me. True friends are.

I called Suzy's college and told the administrative secretary it as urgent I talk to my daughter. The woman checked Suzy's rd, found out what room she was in, and sent someone for her. eld the line. The woman got back on a minute later to say she uldn't help. Suzy had not shown up for class that day.

I called her friend Laura. She wasn't home, either.

I was getting unglued. I couldn't find anyone in my family. The phone rang. Frank! I dove for it.

It wasn't Frank. It was a reporter from the New York *Daily*

*News.* "I'm sorry your daughter was murdered," he said
"Do you want to make a comment about it?"

I was stunned by the insensitive intrusion. My daughter ha
been murdered. Her father didn't even know yet.

I snapped, "No comment." Then I slammed the phon
down.

Here was my first inkling that the press would be eve
more interested in Nancy in death than in life.

Frank called a few minutes later.

"Hi," he said cheerfully. "What's up?"

He hadn't heard it on the radio, thank God.

"Nancy's dead. She's been murdered. I love you. Pleas
come home right away."

"Wha-who?" he stammered.

"Sid's been arrested."

He was silent for a moment. "Are you okay?" he asked

"I need you."

"Should I call the police or go over there or what?"

"Tomorrow. Come home."

At that moment David came home. He looked at Janet an
Susan's grief-stricken faces, then at me. He knew immedi
ately that someone had died. He put his books down, put hi
arm around me protectively.

"Is it Daddy?" he asked softly.

"Daddy's on the phone," I said. "It's Nancy. She wa
murdered."

He turned white. We stood there with our arms around eac
other, his eyes filling with tears, Frank connected to us by th
phone.

"David knows now," I told Frank.

"I'm on my way home," he said.

"Try and get someone to drive you," I urged, reme
bering my own trip.

He said he would. "I love you," he said. Then he hung u

I asked David to try to locate his sister. He began to ma
some calls. Janet, Susan, and I sat down to make lists of wh
needed to be done. There are so many details to be taken ca
of when someone dies. Friends and relatives needed to be n
tified. A rabbi had to be found for the funeral. We didn't b

ong to a synagogue at that time, but we remained loyal to the
aith and I thought Nancy should have a Jewish funeral. This
vas a Thursday. We figured on a Sunday funeral. The food
ad to be ordered for the people who would come by. Deli
latters, coffee cake.

I was back in my fantasy again, with one crucial difference.
he phone rang repeatedly. Every time it rang, it was a differ-
nt reporter. Every time I said "No comment," then hung up,
eized by fear. I wasn't sure what I was afraid of. All I knew
vas that Nancy's death was supposed to be pretty and peace-
ul. But it wasn't pretty. She'd been murdered—beaten to
eath, I assumed. Murder was something that happened to
ther people in other places. Not to us. And it wasn't peaceful
r private. Not with the press calling.

After the first few calls Janet and Susan decided to take
harge of incoming calls. Our official response: "No com-
nent."

Then the doorbell began to ring. Again and again. TV re-
orters were on our front porch trying to get some film for the
vening news. Again, Janet and Susan responded with "No
omment."

I peered out the living room window and gasped. At least
wo dozen reporters and photographers and cameramen were
warming around at the edge of our property—they were cog-
izant of our legal rights, if not our human ones. Some rang
eighbors' doorbells. Others just joked and talked with each
ther, smoked cigarettes, waited for something to break.

Me, perhaps.

I phoned our neighbors and asked them to please refuse to
omment. They had all been misquoted by the press in Febru-
ry. They were happy to oblige. They respected our privacy.

Why couldn't the reporters? How could a human being
tick a microphone in another human being's face at a time
ke this, asking—no, *demanding*—that I help them sell pa-
ers, boost their ratings? How could they invade, harass, use?
Vhy was anyone even interested? Why did anyone care?
Vhy couldn't we just be left alone? We had never sought the
melight. We were an ordinary middle-class suburban fam-
y. Our daughter wasn't an actress or a singer. She'd never

done anything exceptional except take heroin. Why couldn't they leave us alone to mourn her? Why rob us of our privacy?

I was bewildered and frightened. I had always seen Nancy's death as the end of our odyssey. It wasn't going to be. Sid would doubtless be put on trial. This would go on for weeks, months, *years*. It wasn't supposed to happen this way.

An ache formed in the center of my chest. I quickly breathed in and out several times, the pain more than I could bear. It didn't go away. I took aspirin. They didn't help.

I began to call friends and relatives. Some called me. They'd heard the news on the radio. Others just came by. I greeted each one in the foyer. Few words were spoken. Mostly, we embraced. People often say they don't know what to say to someone like me at a time like this. Nothing need be said. The presence of those you care about is comfort enough; a warm embrace communicates far more than words do.

David finally located Laura. She knew where Suzy was— with friends. Laura left her own job, went to Suzy, and told her Nancy was dead. Suzy called at about five o'clock, crying. I asked her to come home. She said she would. Laura offered to make the trip on the train with her.

My mother, Nancy's only living grandparent, had to be told. Trouble was, she was visiting *her* father, who was ninety-six, at his senior citizens' home. I didn't want to phone her there for fear of upsetting him too much. Then I remembered that one of my cousins was with her. I arranged to have my cousin pulled aside and informed of the news. As soon as my mother had concluded her visit, she was given the news by my cousin, who then brought her by. She was shocked and confused by all the press outside the house. She'd been living in the Virgin Islands for the past ten years and was largely unaware of Nancy's collision with heroin, punk rock, and celebrity. We had protected her from Nancy's problems.

Frank was still on his way. It seemed to be taking him forever.

Details. So many details. I knew there would be a generous outpouring of gifts and flowers from our friends. In lieu of flowers, I felt there should be a place for money to be donated someplace appropriate to Nancy's life. Frank's nephew Dean

suggested the Eagleville Hospital, a nearby drug and alcohol re-
habilitation center. A friend of Dean's worked there. Dean
phoned him. His friend said no such fund existed at Eagleville at
that time, but that he'd be happy to set one up to receive dona-
tions in Nancy's memory. I gave him the go-ahead. I wanted to
do something for the other Nancys. Now that she was dead, it
was a priority to find a way to save someone else.

Fortunately this much was clear then. Within a few weeks I
would not be capable of such rational thinking.

The man from the funeral parlor called. He said he had spoken to the medical examiner's office in New York. The
body—that phrase again—would be released Saturday. He
concurred with a Sunday morning funeral. He'd be able to
meet us at the funeral home that night about nine thirty so we
could make all of the arrangements.

Janet found a rabbi who was available for a Sunday funeral.
He agreed to come by on Saturday to talk about Nancy. I
thought it important that he know about her. For him to say
something standard like "We mourn the loss of this beautiful
child who gave all of us much" just wouldn't be appropriate.
Nancy would have said, "Cut that bullshit out!" I wanted
him to talk about Nancy as she was—in pain, incapable of living productively, incapable of returning our love. I wanted
him to convey our own pain and sadness. I wanted her to
know she was still loved.

I also thought something appropriate should be read. David
and I began to search through the lyric sheets of all of the rock
albums in the house, hoping to find one song that would
somehow capture Nancy's life. We examined all of the
Beatles albums in particular. I was especially fervent in my
search. I guess I was hoping I'd find some words to explain
the meaning of her short, unhappy life.

When our search yielded no such song, Dean asked if it
would be okay if he wrote a poem for Nancy. I said "Of
course." He went into the den. Ten minutes later he returned
with it. I read it. It was beautiful. Indeed, it captured Nancy's
life in a few verses. I embraced Dean. I thanked him and said I
would share it with the rabbi and ask him to read it at the funeral.

Then Frank came home. He stood in the open front door-

way framed by the lights of the news minicams. He appeared
calm in front of the reporters clamoring for attention on our
front lawn. He waved them off, said "No comment" in a
clear, controlled voice. Then he shut the door on them and
reached out for David and me. We embraced in the foyer.

David put his arms around the two of us, adopting the role
of the strong one, the protector who would shield us from further pain.

"I felt like it was my job to be there for you," David later
told me. "Whatever I was going through, I knew it was ten
times worse for you."

In fact, this role also allowed him to bury his own powerful
and conflicting emotions over Nancy's death. Later they
would surface on their own.

Frank's emotional response was immediate. He began to
cry standing there in the foyer. I'd never seen him cry before.
He didn't stop. He sobbed and sobbed and sobbed, deep, gut-
wrenching moans coming out of him along with the tears. It
all came out at once for Frank—the twenty years of frustration
and pain, the realization that what he'd wanted for our first
child was never going to happen. He sobbed for twenty minutes. Never have I heard another man cry like that. It was the
saddest crying I've ever heard.

I stood there holding him as his grief came out in a torrent.
envied his ability to let it loose. My eyes were moist, but
could not cry outwardly, not with all of those reporters on the
other side of the door. I cried on the inside, filling within with
tears. It hurt to cry like that. It made that ache in my chest
even more intense.

Frank cried until there were no more tears in him. He dried
his eyes and the three of us went into the living room to join our
family and friends, many of whom were now sharing Frank's
extraordinary outpouring of grief by shedding tears of their own.

Suzy came home about half an hour after Frank. She was
up set and in tears, but also on guard.

"What are all these people doing here?" she demanded
indicating not the press but our family and friends in the living
room. "Half of them don't even *know* Nancy. What do they
want?"

"To be with us," I said.

"What for?" she said.

"To share our loss. They care about us and—"

"How long are they going to be here?"

"The funeral is on Sunday," I said. "We found a rabbi fortunately. Then we'll sit *shivah* for a few days."

"Nancy wouldn't like this," Suzy said angrily.

"What do you mean by 'this'?" asked Frank.

"*This.* This Jewish fuss."

"She's not here anymore," Frank pointed out.

"She'd want to be cremated," Suzy insisted.

"She left no instructions," I said.

"And she's not here anymore," Frank repeated gently. "It's what *we* want."

Today Suzy understands. "I realize now that it was for you guys that those people were there," she told me recently. "But at the time I resented it. Nancy wasn't a normal person and I didn't think she should be mourned like one."

So Suzy went off to the living room, spoke to a couple of close relatives, then sat by herself, grumbling. Nancy's death had triggered a powerful emotional conflict in her, too. This was the first sign of problems that, like David's, would take a while to surface.

Someone made dinner. We sat around the dining table and had something to eat. The phone and doorbell rang constantly. Most of the time it was reporters. They simply would not quit. With each ring I was seized by that fear I'd felt earlier. Now it bordered on panic.

Suddenly I realized what was frightening me. Each ring was taking me further and further from the fantasy I'd written to desensitize myself to Nancy's inevitable death. As a result, I was moving further and further out onto an emotional high wire with no net under me. I could feel myself losing my balance. That's why I was afraid.

Mercifully, the reporters and cameramen had temporarily gone on to another story when Frank and I left for the funeral parlor. Frank drove slowly. We held hands, not talking for a while. It was the first chance we'd had to be alone. It felt good.

"You know," Frank said, "when I was driving into New

York this afternoon, I was actually thinking about going to that hotel and getting her away from there and that guy. Dragging her out of there over my shoulder if I had to. Bringing her home.''

"It wouldn't have made any difference," I said. "She would have gone right back."

"Yeah, that's what I figured. Still . . .''

"Don't do that to yourself."

He shrugged. "Anyway," he said, letting out a deep sigh, "I guess she made it."

I knew what he meant. "She didn't see twenty-one," I agreed. "She knew better than all of us. I still can't believe it happened this way, though. *Murder.* What happens now? What will they do to us tomorrow?"

"Whatever we have to do, we'll do. Don't be afraid. I'll be with you."

"But then there'll be a *trial.*"

"So there'll be a trial. It doesn't matter. She's dead."

"What if she's not?" I asked, suddenly clinging to her existence.

"Huh?"

"What if it's not her? What if it's someone else? It could all be a horrible mistake. It's happened."

"It's her," he said softly. "We'll see tomorrow."

When we pulled into the funeral home parking lot, there was only one other car there. Inside it was dark and deserted. Rather eerie. Just the funeral director, us, and the dead. He took us into his office, offered his condolences, and got down to business.

The plot came first. We had no family plot. We arranged for one near where Frank's parents were buried. It cost about two thousand dollars. It all cost. It seemed there was a rule or regulation for everything, each one designed with the purpose of lining someone's pocket. We had to pay a fee to a New York mortician for securing the body from the medical examiner's office and releasing it to our mortician—the New York City ME's office would not release a body to an out-of-state mortician. We had to pay to transport Nancy to Pennsylvania.

We had to pay a fee to open the gravesite. State law. So was paying for a concrete outer burial casing.

"For what?" I asked, in reference to the latter.

"To keep the wood from rotting," he replied.

"Wood?" I asked, confused.

"The casket, Mrs. Spungen."

I shuddered, decided to ask no more questions.

"Will you want it open or closed?" he asked.

"Closed," Frank said.

"What will she wear?"

"Well, we don't have anything of hers," Frank said. "I suppose we could buy her a dress."

"No, wait," I broke in. "We have her prom dress. The green one."

"Shoes?" the man said. "Have any of her shoes?"

I shook my head.

"We can take care of that. She needn't wear any. We'll cover her feet."

"The dress," I pointed out. "It's rather, well, it has a bare midriff."

"We'll arrange it," he assured me. "The next item is flowers. White flowers? Fall flowers?"

"Fall flowers," I said. "Those were her favorite."

"Fine. We'll cover the casket with amber and copper mums. They look lovely. Then there's the matter of the announcement in the newspapers, the paid advertisement."

"We're having some problems with the press," Frank said. "This is an unusual case. A murder. We don't want them there."

"I can't keep them out," he said. "But if you're concerned about your privacy—"

"We are," Frank and I said.

"Then we can wait and put the announcement in on Monday, the day afterward. Of course, that means you'll have to personally contact anyone you wish to attend."

"That's all right," Frank said. "We'd prefer that. We just don't want this thing to end up a circus."

"I understand. I hope you'll understand though that if people want to come, they'll come. A funeral home is open to the public.''

"Isn't there anything you can do?'' I begged.

"Well, I can put you in a side room off the chapel before the service to protect your privacy. And then close off the six rows of the chapel immediately behind you so no one can bother you. How would that be?''

It seemed so unfair to have to be distanced from our friends and relatives like that. I wondered if anyone else had to take such a precaution.

We said that would be fine.

Then the funeral director went on down his checklist. He was trying to be as sympathetic and understanding as possible, but I found the whole business morbid and awful. Going over all of these details seemed so unnecessary. Frank was used to it. He'd done it before for his parents' funerals. I hadn't.

Then there was the matter of choosing a casket. He took us down a flight of stairs, flicked on a fluorescent light switch to illuminate an immense subterranean showroom filled with caskets—a macabre supermarket. Some were featured on individual pedestals. Some were raised to display the blue satin within. It was positively ghoulish.

I had never known a room like this existed outside of *The Twilight Zone.*

The director took us from one model to the next, explaining the relative merits, fingering the brass handles, running his hand lovingly over the fine satin wood just like the model on *Let's Make a Deal* would caress the smooth, shiny hardwood dining set behind door number two.

He opened and closed each one for us, then gave us the price. They ran in cost from $1,200 to $10,000. When he had shown us all of them, he waited courteously for our decision.

"Which one do you want?'' Frank said.

"I don't know,'' I said. "I don't care.''

"Do you think she'd want something plain? Fancy?''

"Maybe we should wait,'' I said. "What if she's not dead? I mean, it's not like we have any real proof. Just somebody telling me on the phone. It's not like we've *seen* her.''

"I believe she's dead,'' Frank said. Then he took my hand

d took charge. He chose an $1,800 model of cherry wood.
hen we went back up to the office and the director added up
e list.

The total cost of Nancy's funeral was a little over $8,000.
rank told the man that would be fine. We didn't have nearly
at much money in our savings account, though if we had a
ollar for every newspaper article that referred to us as "afflu-
t" we'd have just about covered it.

We would get the money somehow. Have to.

We got home just before eleven. The street was once again
mmed with cars and vans. Our house looked as if it had
en seized by enemy troops. Reporters, photographers, and
meramen were everywhere.

Frank pulled into the driveway. We got out and made a
sh for the house.

"There they are!" shouted someone.

"Wait, folks!" cried someone else. "We need a live feed
r the late news!"

"Just your reaction!"

Frank waved them off. We slammed the door on them. The
ll rang immediately. He opened the door, firmly stated
No comment," and closed it. Someone on the porch cursed.
I wanted to scream at them, "Go away and leave us alone!
ve you no compassion? Can't you see what's happened to
r family?" But I kept quiet. Anything I said or did would be
ptured by their minicams and sent out live over the air.

Besides, they wouldn't understand. To them, this was a big
ry, a sensational death. As Julia Cass of the *Inquirer* later
t it to me, "It was sex, drugs, rock 'n' roll, and murder—
perfect culmination of the punk movement."

Our friends and family greeted us inside our refuge. We de-
ed to watch the late TV news and see what was being said
ut us and our daughter. We turned the set on in the den and
down.

We didn't have long to wait. Nancy's death was the lead
al news story. The news was far worse than I could have
agined. "Punk girlfriend" Nancy Spungen hadn't been
ten to death, as I'd assumed. She'd been stabbed in the ab-
nen with a seven-inch hunting knife.

*Stabbed*. A big, ugly knife had been plunged into m▮ baby's stomach. There was blood. There was pain. I winced chest aching. It was more real now, more awful.

Sid had been arrested and charged with the murder. A film▮ report from outside the Chelsea Hotel showed Sid being led ▮ by the police, wearing handcuffs, real handcuffs this time. ▮ was pale and dazed. There were scratch marks on his face.

"I'll smash your cameras," he snarled at the press.

According to Manhattan Chief of Detectives Martin Duffy Sid had awakened at 10:50 a.m., still feeling the effects ▮ Tuinal, a depressant he had taken the night before.

Nancy was not in bed next to him. Rather, the bed was co▼ ered with blood. Her blood. A trail of it led from the bed ▮ the bathroom. Nancy was on the bathroom floor, under th▮ sink, clad only in her fancy black underwear, a stab wound ▮ her stomach. She'd bled to death.

The Chelsea Hotel switchboard, the police spokesman ad vised, received an outside call at about this time asking tha someone check room 100 because "someone is seriously i▮ jured." It was not clear if the call had come from Sid.

Hotel employees went up to the room to find signs of struggle, and Nancy's body. Sid was not in the room. He r▮ turned a few minutes later, before the police got there.

Hotel neighbors reportedly heard Sid tell police, "Yo can't arrest me. I'm a rock 'n' roll star."

One of the arresting officers reportedly replied, "O▮ yeah? Well, I play lead handcuffs."

An unidentified friend of the couple, the TV newsman r▮ ported, said he had been out with them that night until fo▮ a.m., at which point Nancy had begged him to come back ▮ the Chelsea with them because Sid was "acting strange." Si▮ had, the friend said, pressed a hunting knife against Nancy throat. "He beats her with a guitar every so often," the r▮ porter quoted the friend as saying, "but I didn't think he wa going to kill her."

Then the news broadcast cut to our house for a live repor▮ There were the cameras and reporters we'd just seen. Ther▮ was our house, the one we were hiding in as we tried to mou▮ our dead child.

A reporter stood out front, saying we were inside, in seclu-
, and had no comment to make.

id would be arraigned the following day.

We turned the television off, stunned into silence by the
ly details of Nancy's murder. I hated violence. Movies
h blood and gore in them were abhorrent to me. I avoided
m. This I could not avoid. This was real life. It didn't feel
it. It was inconceivable that this was really happening.
it was.

he phone rang almost immediately. Frank picked it up.
meone shouted into the phone, "She was a no-good twat!"
then hung up. Frank put the phone down, shaken. It rang
in. A different caller hollered, "Cocksucking cunt bitch!"
hung up. Frank took one more of these awful, hateful
s before he decided to leave the phone off the hook.

We were bewildered by this turn of events. My God,
cy had not murdered anyone. *She* was the victim. Yet,
ehow, the murder suspect and his victim were inter-
ngeable in this case. The media had made Nancy and Sid
personifications of the punk movement. Some people
ntified with them. Others hated them. Her murder seemed
tir up both sides.

n death, Nancy was bringing out people's anger, just as
had in life.

t was unnerving. We decided to call the phone company
next day and ask for an unlisted number.

rank peered out the window. The reporters were gone. All
r. Our friends filtered out and the four of us went to bed,
nb and drained.

rank and I just lay there holding hands. The only words of
nfort we could give each other were "I love you." After a
ile Frank began to cry again. I cradled him in my arms and
sobbed and moaned uncontrollably like he had before in
foyer. I cried some more on the inside. I still couldn't cry
the outside.

Nor could I sleep. I was thinking about what we'd have to
tomorrow. I was inching further and further out onto the
h wire, trying to hold on to my balance, trying not to look
wn. Fear kept me awake until just before dawn.

# ❑ Chapter 23

The police precinct house in New York was on East Fifty-
first Street between Lexington Avenue and Third Avenue. We left the car in a lot a few blocks away and walked
over.

The world felt different. It looked and sounded uglier and
crueler than it had before. But *it* hadn't changed. *I* had. I was
different. My world was different. I felt very cut off from the
activity on the streets around me. I felt numb.

When we got to the station, Frank took my hand and we
went inside. It was a dreary place. It smelled.

We approached the desk sergeant, who was chattering with
a plainclothesman.

"Press cleared out, huh?" the plainclothesman said.

"Yeah," said the desk sergeant, who seemed not to notice
us standing there.

"Some nutsy story, huh?" said the plainclothesman.
"Nutsy rock star. Nutsy broad. Jesus, what kind of broad
would wanna fuck a guy like that."

"Dunno," said the sergeant, shaking his head.

"A slut, I guess you gotta figure," the plainclothesman
id, "your basic druggie slut."

I wanted to scream "That's my daughter!" but the words
ick in my throat.

"Excuse me," Frank said, voice quavering slightly.

"You see the hair on that sonofabitch?" continued the
ainclothesman, ignoring Frank. "What a fuckin' weirdo."

"Looks like he stuck his finger in an electric socket,"
reed the desk sergeant.

They both had a hearty chuckle. Then the sergeant noticed
. Frank cleared his throat, asked where we'd find Detective
own. We were directed upstairs.

Lieutenant Brown was a thin man in a rumpled green suit.
 was in his late forties. Shock registered on his face when
 saw us standing there in his office doorway. I don't know
iat he expected Nancy Spungen's parents to look like, but
 were not it. Frank wore a dark suit and tie. I wore a som-
r business outfit. We looked very respectable.

Then he adopted a look of genuine sympathy.

"Thank you for coming," he said. "I realize this is hard
r you."

We sat down. Two other detectives squeezed into the tiny
fice. They questioned us for about an hour, asking about
incy's drug background, relationship with us, with Sid.
ey asked us if we knew who their friends were. We told
m whatever we knew and they were kind enough not to
sh us. When they asked if we could pinpoint the last time
 'd spoken to Nancy, I told them about our phone conversa-
n the previous Sunday, when she confessed to me that Sid
d been beating her, and that she might leave him.

"Was she afraid of him?" one detective asked.

"Nancy wasn't afraid of anyone," I replied.

Then I told them what happened when Sid got on the line,
it instead of his usual passive, polite manner he was rude
d belligerent—a different person.

"What was he angry about?" Detective Brown asked.

"Money," I replied. "They needed money and he wanted
 to send some."

"Hmm," Brown said. "We'd been led to believe they al-

ways carried large amounts of cash on them. In the tho
sands.''

''Maybe they did when they had it,'' Frank said. ''But th
didn't have it. They were broke.''

''Are you sure about that?'' Brown asked.

''They asked us for money,'' I said.

The three detectives exchanged a look. Apparently this w
a valuable piece of information. (Later there would be son
speculation that Nancy had been murdered by a third party,
robber who was after Sid's bankroll. There was no su
bankroll. I don't know who thought it existed or upon wh
basis, but evidently it was someone who'd spoken to the p
lice.)

Detective Brown lit a cigarette, sat back in his chair. ''Y
folks must have a million questions of your own. Now i
your turn. Fire away.''·

''Did she have any pain?'' I wanted to know.

''She died right away,'' he told me.

''How many wounds?'' I asked.

''Just the one.''

''Do you think Sid did it?'' Frank asked.

''He *said* he did right when we got there. Of course, he w
also totally out of it. A good lawyer will say he was out of I
head with grief and get it thrown out. Can't take a confessi
like that to court. We're working on it, though. We'll buil
case.''

''Did he say why he did it?'' I asked.

''He said, 'Because I'm a dog. A dirty dog.' I'll tell yo
he was pretty incoherent. Still is. We got him out at the dr
detox ward on Riker's Island. Our theory right now is it wa
lover's quarrel that went too far. Seems to go with what v
know about their relationship. It appears she bought the kni
On Tuesday. Place in Times Square.''

''What will happen to him?'' I asked.

''His hearing's this afternoon. His manager is flying ov
for it.''

''Nancy was his manager,'' I pointed out.

''His ex-manager then.''

''What will happen at the hearing?'' Frank asked.

"He'll probably be let out on bail."

"What if he comes after us?" I asked, stricken with sudden
d to me very real terror.

"I wouldn't worry about that, Mrs. Spungen. I doubt
u're on his mind. Even if you were, there's no reason to be-
ve he'd want to kill you."

But I did worry.

We had no more questions.

"Okay, here's what's gonna happen," Detective Brown
d. "We're gonna drive you over to the medical examiner's
fice to identify your daughter's body. Then we'll take you
er to the DA's office. More questions, I'm afraid. But we'll
ke good care of you. It won't take long. Then you can go
me to your family."

We squeezed into an unmarked police car with four differ-
t plainclothesmen, all of them well fed. They joked about
w small and poorly equipped the car was—it had no siren or
lio. They did their best to keep us amused and to keep our
nds off the terrible business that lay ahead. They were kind
n who had seen the worst of life and knew what we were
ing through.

The New York City medical examiner's office is housed in
orbidding glass and tile building on First Avenue in the
st Thirties, next to the sprawling Bellevue Hospital com-
x.

It was very cold inside. We were left on a bench in a large
iting room with about twenty others who were there to
ntify their dead. Some were crying. Others seemed to be in
ock. At one end of the room there was a door. Every few
nutes it would open and some poor grief-stricken soul
uld emerge, an officer at his side for physical support.
ose of us who sat waiting would look up apprehensively,
it for the officer to call out the next name on the clipboard.
en one of us would get up and go through that door while
rest of us settled back to wait again. New people arrived in
waiting room for everyone who left it. A lot of people die
New York in one day.

Frank and I sat in tense silence. My chest still ached. Now
stomach did, too. I don't think I blinked once.

After about an hour the woman next to me struck up a co
versation.

"I just got here from Texas," she said, clutching a tissue
her white-knuckled hand. "My son. He's been missing. Th
asked me to fly up and see if it . . . if it's him."

I nodded.

"Why are you here?" she asked.

"My daughter. She was murdered."

She nodded in sympathy. I noticed several other such co
versations going on in the waiting room. Total strangers we
exchanging information, sharing the vigil. All of us faced t
same experience. All of us had to go through that door.

Our name was finally called. It was our turn.

The door led into a large office with about a dozen desks
it. At the other end of it was *another* door.

We were led to the desk of an assistant medical examin
who wore a white coat. She didn't acknowledge our presen
She was too annoyed.

"Are you trying to tell me," she demanded of a man acr
the room, "that I have to type this thing myself?"

The man nodded.

"So where the hell are the stenos?" she hollered.

"At lunch!" he hollered back.

"You believe it?" she asked, of nobody in particul
"First some shithead steals my car keys. Now I can't ge
typist in this place."

She snatched a form from a pile, rammed it angrily int
typewriter. Then she finally looked at us. She gestured for
to sit down.

"I'm going to be performing the autopsy on the body,"
said brusquely. "I need some information about it."

Frank nodded.

I shuddered. That was not a body. That was not an "i
That was my daughter.

"Date of birth?"

Frank gave it to her. She started to type it in. She mad
mistake, struck over it, then cursed, ripped the paper o
wadded it up, and hurled it at the wastebasket.

"God, why are you punishing me like this?" she asked the ceiling. "What did I do to deserve this?"

Frank and I exchanged a look of utter dismay. Who had the problem here?

She put a fresh form in the typewriter, typed in Nancy's name. A man came in from outside, took off his coat, and sat down at the next desk. He began to pick his lunch out of his teeth with a toothpick.

"Have you seen my car keys, Jack?" she asked him.

He shook his head.

"Some fucker stole 'em," she said.

He nodded his head, spat into his wastebasket.

She turned back to us. "What did you say the date of birth was?"

Frank repeated it. She typed it in. Then she asked for "the body's" height, weight, and eye color.

"Fucking car keys," she muttered as she typed in our responses. "Why me? Why me?"

Then she asked about distinguishing marks or scars.

"She has a number of them on her arms," I said.

"What kind?"

"Long ones."

"Lateral?"

"Yes."

She typed in my response. "Any other ones?"

"Behind her right ear," I said, "there's a scar from where he had the ear stitched on. That's fairly recent."

The woman looked at me, incredulous. "How do you now all that about that piece of shit?"

I sucked in my breath. I looked at Frank, who gripped my hand tightly. I think he wanted to dive across the desk and kill the woman with his bare hands. I know I did.

"She's . . . she's my *daughter*," I finally managed to say.

My reply went right by her. She removed the paper from the typewriter. "Do you want a copy of the autopsy or just the death certificate?"

"We don't need to see a copy of the autopsy," Frank said.

The woman nodded, motioned impatiently for two detectives who were waiting nearby.

"Okay," one of them said to us, indicating the door at the far side of the room. "It's time to identify the body."

Frank and I got up to go with him.

"Wait," the other detective said to me. "Not you. You can't go in."

"W-why?" I asked.

"You're the mother," he said.

My mind raced. *You have to let me see her!* I screamed at him. *I gave birth to her! I have to know it's her! I have to see her! Let me go! Please let me go!*

But nobody paid any attention to me. The words weren't coming out of my mouth. They were stuck in my throat.

Frank and I reluctantly let go of each other. He was taken through a door. I was led to a different waiting room, a smaller one. I was the only person in it. I sat down on the hard bench.

Frank joined me in there five minutes later. He was very pale. Horror registered on his face.

"Was it her?" I asked.

"You know, it's been almost five years since I quit, but I sure do feel like a cigarette right now."

"Was it her?" I repeated.

"Yes, it was her."

"How did she look?"

He sat down next to me. "She was in a body bag. Just her head was showing. She was blue white. She didn't look like our Nancy." He swallowed. "You're better off. It was awful. You wouldn't have wanted to see her."

But I *had* wanted to see her. I *needed* to see her with my own eyes, not just be told about it. It was important to me. I had to see her dead. Otherwise I couldn't accept the reality and so commence my mourning. I had a *right* to see her. I was furious at being denied that right.

I still am. Why was I less prepared than a man to view her body? Why was I weaker? And why separate us at a time like that—when Frank needed my support as much as I needed his. We'd been through the pain of her life together. Why couldn't we be together for the pain of her death?

I know other mothers whose children were murdered

They, too, were denied the right to see the body by the medical examiner's office. I suppose the officials are well-meaning, but we should have been given our options. To me it was important.

So was being treated with simple human consideration. I fully realize that the coroner's office in a major city is inundated with death and that the people who work there must become hardened to it in order to function. But this does not excuse the way that particular medical examiner spoke to us. She did not deserve to have her job.

I haven't spoken to a parent of a murdered child who had quite so awful an experience as we did with that woman, but they did have to suffer through the same dehumanizing labeling. They, too, had to hear their child referred to as "the body." This is a horrible thing to hear. We do not think of our child as an "it." The coroner's staff people are undoubtedly too overworked to remember every deceased person's name, but couldn't they at least take the trouble to say "your son" or "your daughter" or even "your child"? Anything but "the body."

Obviously, no one can make an experience such as this pleasant or easy. No one can bring your dead child back. But some measure of awareness and sensitivity by those who work at the medical examiner's office would go a long way in easing a parent's burden. If Frank and I had been treated with simple human consideration that day, I would not have been left with such nightmarish memories, memories I still carry around.

"Can we go home now?" I begged Frank.

"I wish we could. The rest of it—the DA, the trial—doesn't mean a thing. None of it makes any difference. She's dead."

I rested my head on his shoulder. He put his arm around me. We sat there like that for an hour before the policemen finally came to fetch us and drive us downtown.

The New York City district attorney's office was on Centre Street, a large, worn, public building surrounded by other large, worn, public buildings. There was a soda vendor out front. I was thirsty. I asked one of the detectives if there was

time to get a drink. He insisted on buying sodas for both
Frank and me and told us to go ahead and relax for a few minutes on the retaining wall out front. After I drank my soda I
called home.

Janet answered warily. She was relieved that it was me.
There had, she said, been several more obscene calls. In addition, the press had been calling frequently—from as far away
as London—to find out when the funeral would be. She had
not told them.

Janet said she had spoken to the phone company. We
would be given a new, unlisted number, but not until Monday, unfortunately. She ran down the list of friends and relatives she'd informed about the funeral. Susan, she said, had
delivered Nancy's green dress to the funeral parlor. I thanked
her for all that she and Susan had done. Then I spoke briefly
with Suzy and David. So did Frank. Then the detectives came
to take us inside.

There was a tremendous amount of commotion in the long,
dark corridors. People were rushing in and out of offices, up
and down stairways. I was afraid we'd get swept away. It was
a battle to stay with our police escort. Finally we got to the
office of the assistant district attorney who was handling our
case. Two uniformed officers waited outside. They introduced themselves and shook our hands. They were the ones
who had answered the call at the Chelsea and found Nancy.

"Oh, are you Nancy's parents?" asked a businesslike
woman next to them.

"Yes," I said.

"What do you do for a living?" she asked me.

"I'm in direct mail advertising," I said, puzzled by her interest.

"For who?" she asked.

"Well, I just did a campaign for *Newsweek*—"

"*Newsweek*?" she said. "What a coincidence. I'm *from
Newsweek*—"

A reporter.

"Hey, don't bother these people!" ordered one of the uniformed officers.

"I'm not bothering her," the woman insisted.

He grabbed Frank and me and herded us into the assistant
A's office.

"C'mon in here, folks," he said. "You don't have to be
ssled."

I thanked him.

"You gotta watch out for those people," he warned.
Moxie's what they get paid for."

We sat down at a battered conference table. Soon Detective
own and three others came in, then the assistant DA, who
as young, aggressive, and rushed. He shook our hands.

"Mr. and Mrs. Spungen, thank you for coming. I want to
fer you my condolences while I have the chance. I feel very
d for both of you. Please understand that I have a job to do.
nay seem hard-hearted. I'm not. It's the job. I hope you'll
derstand."

We both nodded. I thought it was considerate of him to say
is.

The assistant DA quizzed us for about forty-five minutes.
 asked us basically the same questions Detective Brown
d. Our replies were the same.

"Okay," he said, breaking off the session with a glance at
 watch. "I have to be down at Sid's bail hearing in ten min-
es. You folks want to come?"

"No, please," I begged, paralyzed by fear at the thought
 having to see Sid. I didn't care if the police thought fear
sn't warranted. I had it. "Can we not?"

"No problem," he assured me.

Then he rushed out. The detectives took us down a back el-
ator and stashed us in someone's private office.

"Nobody will find you in here," one of them said.

We sat there for an hour. When the detectives returned for
 they filled us in on what had transpired at the hearing. I was
d we hadn't gone.

The courtroom had been mobbed with reporters, many of
m from England. Malcolm McLaren was there, dressed in
red plaid jacket. Also in attendance were the Idols, ex-
embers of the New York Dolls who'd been Sid's backup
nd for his dismal solo debut at Max's Kansas City.

Sid, clad in black suit jacket, black shirt, black pants, and

black shoes without socks, had to be led into the courtroom by
two people.

"Boy, I don't know whether he was stoned or sick or
what," said one of the detectives, "but he was in really bad
shape. His eyes were glazed over; he was shaking. The guy
could barely stand up."

The assistant DA argued that Sid, who wasn't an American
citizen, should be denied bail on the ground that he might flee
the country. Sid's lawyers ("a real fancy Park Avenue
bunch," the detective said) argued that New York was now
where Sid worked, and that he would not leave it. The judge
set a cash bail of $50,000. It was a low figure, but all of it had
to be raised in cash—not the ordinary one-dollar-for-every-ten
bail ratio. This made it the equivalent of $500,000 regular
bail.

"Did Sid say anything?" I asked the detective.

"One thing," he replied. "He said he wanted to get out on
bail right away so he could come to Nancy's funeral. He
really wants to be there."

"W-will he try to come?" I gasped, horrified.

"When is it?" the detective asked.

"Sunday," said Frank. "We're not making it public."

"Well, I'd say it's not too likely. Would you,-Murphy?"

The other detective nodded. "Nobody can raise that kinda
cash on a weekend."

"Not even a guy like McLaren?" asked Frank.

"Monday. That's when he'll get out, most likely."

"Anyway," added the other detective, "say he does get
out Saturday. He can't leave the state."

"Who's going to stop him?" I asked.

"He'd be in violation of his bail," the detective said.

"Who's going to stop him?" I pressed.

"We do the best we can, Mrs. Spungen," he said.

I couldn't believe this. The bail process made no sense to
me, still doesn't. They were saying they thought he'd murdered my daughter, but they were setting him free in exchange for some cash—free to come to Nancy's funeral, to
our home.

He knew where we lived.

The detectives led us back to the car and drove us back
town through rush-hour traffic. At one point an ambulance
s stuck in the traffic with us, even though its siren was on
d its lights were flashing. Nobody would get out of its way.
When the ambulance passed us, I saw that there was a per-
a being attended to in it. For an instant I saw Nancy in that
bulance, her life bleeding out of her. I shuddered, gripped
nk's hand.

Then we were back in our own car, heading home on the
w Jersey Turnpike. The awful day was over.

The whole way home, I dwelled on a strange realization—
t for me this day, the day after Nancy's death, was so much
e the anxious day after her cyanotic birth. Both days had
nd me spending endless hours in grim, institutional
rridors—hurting, confused, uncertain of the future. My
ld was lost to me. She was in someone else's hands, some
powerful official. Both days had been Fridays.

It seemed like a bizarre kind of life cycle. Nancy was even
same age at her death that I'd been at her birth. Our fami-
s life was just starting then. Now hers was over.

There was one big difference. Twenty years before, I'd
n waiting for the beginning. On this day I was waiting for
end: her funeral. I was anxious for it to be over. Only then
uld she be at peace.

All I could see ahead was her funeral. Beyond that, I saw
hing.

The press was clustered in front of our house again. We
de our dash inside.

"Wait, folks! When's the funeral?"

"We need to know!"

"No comment," said Frank.

"Why?"

tried to close the door. A reporter's foot was in it.

"Please," he said in a British accent. "When is it?"

"No comment," I repeated.

"I'll be back," he warned.

"Why?" I demanded.

He was thrown by that. He removed his foot, puzzled, and
t back to his comrades.

I noticed that the four of us avoided making eye contac
with each other as we ate dinner. To see the pain in the othe
person's eyes was to compound your own.

All of us, friends and relatives included, were disgusted b
the vulgar way Nancy was being demeaned in the press. T
them, she was Nauseating Nancy, some rich, thrill-hungr
druggie slut. They knew nothing of her troubles. Nor did the
seem to care.

Frank wondered aloud about the possibility of giving ou
our side of the story, as an effort to counteract all of the fals
crap that was being written. (No legal recourse existed, sinc
libel law does not protect the dead.) It was, he felt, importar
to restore Nancy's dignity. Or at least to try.

We were all in agreement. One of my friends had a frien
who was a feature writer for the Philadelphia *Bulletin*—a sei
sitive, intelligent woman. She was contacted and she agree
to our terms. We would not discuss Sid or punk rock or th
murder.

She came on Saturday morning. The four of us sat with h
and gave her our side of the story. We were not looking fe
sympathy, just understanding. After about an hour Suzy su
denly jumped to her feet, cried "Enough! That's it!" ai
stormed out in tears. The reporter closed her notebook ai
left. (We were pleased with the article when it appeared in tl
*Bulletin* the next morning, the morning of Nancy's funera
Though the story didn't come even close to stemming the ti
of public opinion against Nancy, we were glad we'd done i

I found Suzy on her bed, dabbing at her eyes with a tissu

"I don't have a sister anymore," she said quietly.

I sat down next to her. "You haven't had one for a lo
time, Suzy."

She looked startled.

"I'm not saying you shouldn't cry for her," I said. "Al
mean is you could have cried for her a long time ago."

She mulled that over. "I know. But I also know . . . I
never see her again."

She began to cry again. I tried to hug her but she pull
away from me, seemingly repulsed by my touch.

"I *did* feel a physical revulsion," she recently admitted

. "I didn't want to be touched or told I was loved. I wanted be separated from you."

Neither of us understood why at the time. I was baffled and rt by her rejection of my love. I got up and started to leave r room.

"Mom?" she said. "What will they do to her?"

"What will *who* do to her?"

"The funeral parlor," she said, looking down.

"I don't know. She'll be wearing her green prom dress d, well, I suppose she'll look as nice as possible. Why?"

"Do you think they can do something with her hair. It was beautiful before. Could they dye it back from that horrible ite?"

She didn't want to remember her sister as she'd been at the d. It seemed important to her.

"Okay," I said. "I'll call them. Maybe they can."

I could hear the funeral parlor director gulp when I passed Suzy's request over the phone. Apparently it was an unial one.

"We . . . *can* do that, Mrs. Spungen. Yes. What color s your daughter's hair?"

"It was chestnut."

"Chestnut."

"Yes, with these sort of, uh, gold highlights."

"Uh-huh. Okay, I understand. It may not be exact, but 'll do our best."

The rabbi came that afternoon. The four of us sat with him he den and explained to him that Nancy's life had been as ch of a tragedy as her death. She had lived a life of pain l had brought pain to those who loved her. She had left rs.

showed him Dean's poem. He read it and was deeply ved.

He said he would write the service around it. Then he left. were satisfied that our wishes would be fulfilled.

slept poorly that night. I awoke ten or twelve times; every e I thought I heard a noise outside. The press was out re, I feared. Each time I checked the clock to see how ny more hours it would be until the limousine came to take

us to Nancy's funeral. I had a nightmare at one point, t
same old one I'd had off and on since the first time I saw t
track marks on Nancy's arms.

"Look what I have, Mommy!" exclaimed my eager fiv
year-old Nancy. "Look what I have!" Then I saw the tra
marks, and she cried, "Help me, Mommy! Help me!"
reached for her but my arms were paralyzed.

The limousine was due at nine thirty. We were all up ho
before that.

"Will he come?" I asked Frank anxiously as we dresse
"Will Sid be there?"

He shrugged unhappily. It was the eighth time I'd ask
him. I couldn't help myself.

There were no reporters outside when the limo came.
climbed inside and glided silently through the deserted Su
day morning streets. The kids and my mother looked out t
window, lost in their private grief. Frank and I held han
tightly.

I saw a lot of our friends waiting outside the chapel. Mer
fully, I saw no reporters or cameras.

The funeral director escorted us to a small private room
the side of the chapel. The front door of the chapel was s
closed. No one was in there yet, aside from Nancy. He ga
Frank and David yarmulkas to wear. Then he cleared
throat.

"I know you requested a closed casket, but it's a state l
that you identify Nancy before we close it." He turned
Frank. "It's only necessary for one of you to do it."

"I want to, too," I said.

"Me, too," said David.

So did Suzy and my mother. We all went into the cha
and approached the open casket. When we got near it, a fo
seemed to pull us collectively away. It took a mighty effor
fight it off. We inched toward the casket, clinging to one
other for support. I saw her feet. They were covered w
flowers. I saw her legs and her stomach, draped in her gr
dress. Then I saw her face.

It wasn't her. She was at peace. The pain was missing fr

r face. She had no more pain. Without it, she looked almost
e a different person. She wasn't angry anymore.

"Now I know how much she really suffered," I cried out.
Ier pain was greater than ours, greater than all of our
in."

The scars and bruises were gone. So was the white hair.
ey'd dyed it almost to its natural color.

Frank's eyes filled with tears. Suzy and David wept
enly. Once again I cried only within, a knot in my throat,
ache in my chest. None of us moved any closer. None of us
iched her.

We returned to the side room, still clutching one another.
ank nodded to the funeral director.

He disappeared into the chapel. A moment later I heard the
sket slam shut with a bang. Forever.

Then the chapel was opened and our friends filtered in. The
bi joined us in the private room. He pinned a black button
each of us, then tore off a piece of black cloth affixed to
-part of the Jewish grieving ritual. Then he said a prayer
d we all went out to the chapel.

My eyes searched the rows of mourners for unfamiliar
es, for Sid's spiky hair. Happily, I saw only the familiar
es of our loved ones. Some had driven three hours to be
re. They cared. I felt good knowing that.

We sat in the front row holding hands, the six rows behind
cordoned off just in case anyone tried to bother us. I re-
ited the precaution, resented that a distance had to be kept
ween us and those who loved Nancy and us enough to
ne.

Her casket was now covered with lovely fall flowers. The
bi approached the pulpit, looked at all of us with genuine
lness in his eyes, and began. As is the Jewish custom, his
narks were brief.

"We were all deeply shocked by the tragic death of Nancy
ungen," he said. "We extend our deepest sympathies to
bereaved family. The burden of grief is always difficult to
ir. Yours is uniquely painful—not only the loss but the
owledge of circumstances which led to this end.

'I would not be so presumptuous as to tell you how to cope

with your sorrow. This is a time when words do not easily tr
off the tongue nor ease the burden. Words of comfort ri
hollow in the deepest abyss of life's sorrow. It is not by wor
but by the presence here of friends—loved ones—who
hearts and hands reach out to you that solace will come.''

I could hear our friends crying behind us. Sobs and sniffl
seemed to fill the chapel. Possibly, everyone there was cryi
with the exception of myself.

''And yet,'' the rabbi continued, ''not to speak some wor
of tribute would be to deny the life that was, the goodness a
sweetness she brought. The years she lived must not be lost
us in the shadow of her death.

''What I am about to say is her family's tribute to Nanc

''From the time of her birth, Nancy was a special, gifte
and troubled girl. Despite the love, caring, and concern of h
family she experienced an inner torment and disquietude. S
turned to drugs not for sensationalism, but for relief from t
pain that afflicted her. She knew herself, but was not respo
sible for the consequences of her actions. She lived for ea
hour, each day, and consequently much living was crowd
into the years of her life.

''She was capable of compassion, and of perception ra
and unusual for her age. These are signs of her special gif

''The following was written by her cousin, Dean Becker
captures the feelings Nancy would have wanted to expre
about herself to her family:

> ''Don't misunderstand me!
> What I do has purpose
> A meaning you may not see.
> I know what I'm doing.
> Please don't judge me
> From where you stand.
>
> ''My life is my own
> My decisions are in my hands
> Don't try to make your dreams
> A part of mine
> For I have my own.

"Don't misunderstand me!
Be happy in your thoughts.
Your recollections of our happiest hours
Will be enough to help you forget
The bad times—the hard times
The sadness you feel today.

"Nancy is now at peace," the rabbi continued. "She saw, heard, felt what others did not and could not. She was different.

"May her family go forth from their pain of separation, to strengthen each other, to face the ongoing tasks of life with courage. And with love for each other, and remembrance of the goodness and happy hours you shared."

I felt very comforted by what he said. We all did. It was beautiful and right.

The pallbearers removed her casket. The limousine took us to her gravesite, where chairs had been set up under a canopy. The rabbi said a few more words, then she was lowered slowly into the ground.

I reached over and broke off a yellow chrysanthemum from the blanket atop her casket. I needed it. It stayed on my nightstand for three nights. Then I pressed it into her Darlington yearbook, where it remains.

I felt incredible relief as we rode home. Nancy was safe and protected now. For her, the fight was over.

For the four of us, the battle was just beginning.

# ❑ Chapter 24

Sid's mother phoned that night.

Janet took the call. She approached me in the living room
where I sat on a folding chair, talking quietly with friend
who had come by to help us sit *shivah*, the Jewish period o
mourning.

"Debbie," whispered Janet, her face ashen, "it's Ann
Beverley. She wants to talk to you."

I froze. "W-what does she want?"

"She says it's very important."

I took a deep breath, let it out. I motioned for Frank. H
came over. I told him.

"Talk to her," he suggested. "Get it over with. If yo
don't she'll keep calling."

"Are you sure it's her?" I asked Janet. "It could be
prank."

"She has an English accent," Janet said.

I turned to Frank. "Come with me?"

He nodded. We went to the phone in the kitchen. I picked
up and said hello.

"Mrs. Spungen? It's Anne Beverley," she said. "Thank you for giving me a moment. I'm in New York. I'm here to be with my son. He'll be out tomorrow on bail, you see."

I said nothing.

"Mrs. Spungen, I wanted you to know that my boy wouldn't do such a thing. He couldn't."

"I don't want to talk about it," I said. "There's no point in talking about it."

"Our Sid and Nancy were very special people. I didn't understand her. I was sorry I didn't. And I'm very sorry for you."

"Thank you," I said woodenly.

"I hope we can meet someday. Under better circumstances, of course."

"Thank you for calling, Mrs. Beverley."

I put the phone down and began to tremble. Frank held me. When I didn't stop trembling, he held me tighter. I was okay in a few minutes. Then we returned to our mourning.

Our friends stayed late. A couple of them who live far away stayed over. It was one of them who answered the doorbell when it rang the following morning at about ten. Frank and I were still upstairs getting dressed. I was bleary-eyed. It had been another sleepless night for me.

"Who is it?" I called from the top of the stairs.

"A friend who came to see you," our guest called back.

Frank and I came downstairs to greet the friend.

A total stranger stood there.

"Good morning, Mr. and Mrs. Spungen," he said quickly, handing us his card.

It identified him as a correspondent of *People* magazine.

"I'm working on a story about your daughter. We're running—"

"Look, pal," snapped Frank angrily. "Why don't you just get the hell out?"

"I'm so sorry!" cried our friend. "He said he *knew* you. He said he was an old friend!"

The man did not deny it. Rather, he said, "I thought you'd want to know: We're running a whole feature on your daughter. If you don't talk to me, it's going to be an unflattering portrait. I'm sure you'll find it very upsetting. If you'd only give me

a few minutes, well, I'll say whatever you want me to say. It's i
your interest to talk to me. I mean, if I were you I'd want to mak
sure my daughter's side of the story was told."

What easy marks we were that day. What a smoothie h
was. He was, in effect, saying, "Give me an interview o
your daughter gets screwed in print." But we were so vulner
able, and he was so sympathetic on the surface, that we fe
for it. We gave him the interview. It wasn't until he'd bee
gone an hour that we realized we'd been coerced into it, falle
for a sleazy journalistic tactic.

We were angry at ourselves. And even angrier than befor
at the press. A number of them seemingly played by no rule
of civilized human conduct. Felt they were above them,
guess. No sooner had we finished breakfast than a taxi-load o
British reporters showed up on our front porch. They wante
to know what we thought about Sid's being released on ba
that morning. They refused to leave when we told them w
had nothing to say. One of them actually began to nos
around in the backyard.

"Yeah, there's a pool all right!" he called to one of h
buddies.

Frank phoned the Huntingdon Valley police. A patrol ca
came at once. Two officers escorted the reporters off ou
property. They got in their cab and drove off, shaking the
fists at us.

I began to wonder how this, the first day after Nancy's fu
neral, could possibly get any worse. It wasn't long before
found out.

The phone rang. At least *it* had been quiet that day—th
phone company had finally given us our new unlisted num
ber. I answered it.

It was a special operator. She said she realized our numb
was now unlisted but she had an urgent message to pass on
us.

"What's the message?" I asked warily.

"Sid Vicious wants to talk to you," she said. "He says it
very, very important. I have a number you can reach him at.

I calmly took down the number and hung up. Then
screamed *"Frank!"*

He came running.

"It's Sid!" I cried. "He called the operator. He wants to to me. What do I do?"

"Do you want to talk to him?"

"Of course not. But what if I don't call him? What if he is angry or something?"

We stood there looking at each other. Neither of us could lieve it. I was about to phone the man who was accused of y daughter's murder. I had no choice. I was afraid to do it, t even more afraid not to.

I dialed the number. It was a hotel switchboard. I was put ough to Sid's room. It rang.

"Hullo?" said Sid.

"Sid?" I said, my voice cracking. "It's D-Debbie Spun-n."

"Oh, Debbie, thank you. Thank you so much for calling. I nted you to know, Debbie, how very, very sorry I am I uldn't come to the funeral."

"That's okay," I said. I couldn't believe how calm he inded.

"I wanted to so very much," he said, "but they wouldn't let out. They wouldn't let me say good-bye to my Nancy."

"Uh-huh."

"I'm sorry she's dead, Debbie. So sorry."

Suddenly there were so many questions I wanted to ask n. Had he done it? Why? How? But I was afraid to ask m. I remained silent.

"Debbie, I don't seem to . . . I don't know why I'm alive more, now that Nancy is gone."

"I understand," I said.

"I knew you would, Debbie. You're the only one who ild."

"Sid, I . . . I can't talk anymore."

"May I call again?"

"I . . . I'll have to think about it."

"You know, Debbie, you're the only real friend I have . Thank you for talking to me. Good-bye."

"Good-bye, Sid."

I hung up. Then I caved in. Frank held me again until
stopped trembling.

For the first time, it occurred to me that I might not surv
this ordeal, that I might lose my mind before it was over,
I might lose it *soon*.


I felt the same way on Wednesday, the day we tried to
back to the rest of our lives.

The four of us had breakfast together. The house was qu
our friends and relatives gone. A number of lovely con
lence notes had arrived in the morning mail. We read tl
aloud while we ate. When we were through we sat there f
moment, staring at each other.

Then Frank said, "Maybe I'll go to the office for a cou
of hours."

"I'll pack up the folding chairs for the funeral parlor,"
David, "so we can get them out of here."

"I guess I'll be heading back to the city," said Suzy.

I didn't seem to have anything to offer. I mumbled son
thing about how much I was looking forward to putting
kitchen things back where they belonged.

I couldn't believe it. Here I was, falling apart right before t
eyes, and *nobody noticed*! I was unable to sleep, barely abl
eat. I was frightened. I was in pain. I was inert. I felt cut off f
everyone—the outside world, my family, my old self. I wa
*me* anymore. I was somebody I didn't know, somebody lost
scared, somebody whose life seemed to have no focus. And
body noticed! How could they not notice?

The doorbell rang. I answered it.

It was the same group of English reporters. Their
waited for them on the street. One of them waved a Xe
copy of a London tabloid. On it was the banner headl
NANCY WAS A WITCH!

"Care to deny it, Mrs. Spungen?" one of them said.

Why was this happening to me?

"N-no comment," I stammered, starting to close the de

"People will assume it's fact if you don't deny it,"
warned.

'They'll believe she *was* a witch,'' agreed another.

But I was on to this trick now.

'No comment,'' I repeated.

closed the door. Before it shut, the reporter managed to
w the sheet of paper inside the hallway. It lay there on the
r next to my feet, headline shouting at me. I left it there.

Frank left for the office. Suzy went back to the city.
he British reporters returned.

'You took our property!'' charged one of them. ''We want
ack!''

'W-what property?'' I asked.

'Our paper! Our piece of paper! You took it! Give it
k!''

'Or we'll call the police,'' said another.

David appeared behind me. ''What is it, Mom?''

'I . . . I . . .'' I couldn't answer him. I was quivering all
r. I couldn't take this, I just couldn't take it.

'What do you guys want?'' David demanded.

'Our clipping,'' one of them replied. ''She has it.''

'I . . . I . . . *don't* have it,'' I whimpered.

'Then we're getting the police,'' one of them said.
Ve're calling the police and telling 'em you stole our prop-
y.''

'Leave us alone,'' David said angrily.

'Of course,'' one suggested, ''you *could* just give us a
tement about—''

'Get off our property!'' David ordered.

'Look, sonny—''

David hurled the door open, charged out onto the porch,
-faced. He was taller and huskier than any of them. Their
s widened.

*''You get the hell off our property,''* he screamed, *''or so
p me I'll beat the living crap out of you!''*

They took off. Then David came back inside, slammed the
r shut, and phoned the police. They said that if we could
d the clipping they'd come over to pick it up, then deliver it
he reporters, who'd just phoned from their motel.

'Do you know where it is, Mom?'' David asked.

was still standing in the foyer, frozen.

"Mom?"

"Huh?"

"The clipping. Where is it?"

"I . . . left it. Here, on the floor."

"I don't see it, Mom."

I just stared at him.

"Mom?" he said. "I don't see it."

"Then I don't know where it is," I said.

David checked the wastebasket to no avail, then ca
Frank. Frank hadn't seen it. Then David tried Suzy. She h
On her way out she'd taken it outside and thrown it in a gar
trash can. David found it, called the police, and handed i
them when they arrived. They took it away.

"Those guys won't come back," one of the officers pr
ised. "We'll make sure of it."

But I was sure the reporters were still out there. They w
hiding somewhere. Behind the bushes, maybe. I heard a
door slam a few minutes later. My heart began to pound,
chest to ache beyond belief.

As I stood there in the foyer, watching David calmly
efficiently fold up the chairs in the living room, I fell off
high wire. I managed to grab it with my hands and hold on
dear life, but I had to do something fast. I had to talk to so
body, somebody who would listen, somebody who would
derstand. I could not go on like this for one more second.
didn't talk to somebody right now I would lose my grip
fall all the way down. I would break into a million
pieces. Nobody would be able to put me back together ag

I made a dash for the kitchen phone and dialed a therap
knew.

"I have to talk to you!" I cried. "I have to talk to yo

"Come," she said. "Come at once."

I blurted something out to David, got in my car, and s
away. It was a forty-five-minute drive to her office. I ope
the window and let the cold air blow on my face. I inhal
deeply. I turned the radio on full blast.

I looked at the people in the other cars. I couldn't beli
they were just going on about their lives—their soft, tri

ves—as if nothing had happened. The world had changed.
ancy was dead! How could no one care?

The therapist, Paula, embraced me warmly when I got
ere.

"I feel so badly for you," she said soothingly. "The pa-
ers are doing such an awful number on you."

"Yes," I said. "Yes, they are."

I felt calmer already, just being with someone who under-
ood, someone who was on my side.

"Sit down," she said. "Tell me what's bothering you."

I told her. I poured it all out in a nonstop forty-five-minute
rade—my anxiety, pain, isolation, nightmares, paranoia. I
ally don't remember much of what I said. All I remember
as that I kept telling her how *afraid* I was.

"I thought it would be over," I said. "It's not over. It
eeps coming at me. And there's going to be a trial. It'll last
or months. We might have to actually go. I can't take it. I'm
private person. I need my privacy."

She nodded sympathetically.

"You also need your family's support at a time like this,"
he said, "and you feel like you're not getting enough of it."

"Everyone's been fine," I said. "It's just that nobody
eems to notice how much trouble I'm having, or to care."

"Usually, in times of stress, members of a family are there
or each other," she said. "You each count on the other. But
a case like this, when you *most* need to rely on one another,
ou aren't there for the other. Do you know why?"

I shook my head.

"Because *each* of you is in the same kind of pain. *Each* of
ou feels grief and pain. Your whole family is going through
crisis. One of you isn't there anymore. One of you has been
urdered."

"Yes, yes," I said, eager for her insights.

"Because of all the notoriety surrounding Nancy's death, you
ren't being allowed to weather the crisis. You aren't being al-
owed to grieve as you should. The normal grief cycle is being
isturbed. This is confusing you and causing you problems. It's
robably setting all of you off, in your individual ways."

"And each of us is used to leaning on the other," I muse aloud. "But *can't,* because the other's in the same boat."

"Right. You're all hurting. You're feeling your own pai real bad right now. But I'm sure you're not alone in that. Yo just feel alone."

"What do I do?"

"We have a program called crisis intervention counseling We try to help you to restore the normal cycle, let it happen s you can get on with the rest of your life. I want to see yo twice a week. I'd suggest individual therapy for the othe members of your family, too, but that's up to them. Then, a ter you've each handled your grief, I'd recommend famil network therapy, so you can rebuild as a unit.

"I'm going to get you a prescription for a very light dosag of Valium. It's to help you sleep. It's just enough to break th cycle of wakefulness you're in."

"What about my chest? It hurts so much."

"I don't want you to take anything strong—no tranquilize or painkillers. It'll be best for you in the long run if you fe the pain *now.* It's a rough time, but you have to get through without the aid of drugs. You can do it. Okay?"

"Okay."

"Do you mind if I tell you what I'd do if I were you?"

"No, go right ahead."

"Get away for the weekend. The four of you. Go to th mountains. Someplace where nobody will bother you. Clea your heads. Get some perspective and some rest. Then try get back into it on Monday."

That sounded like an excellent idea. I suggested it to Fran that night. He agreed. Then I told him who the suggestion ha come from.

"I just really needed to talk to somebody," I said. "I' upset, and we, well, we talked."

Frank was very supportive. "Do you think she can he you?" he asked.

"Yes. I'm going to see her for a few weeks. She sort suggested we all might need some help getting through this."

He nodded noncommittally. He still harbored a distaste fo therapy, one that had in no way been tempered by our trac

ecord with Nancy. He was not interested in seeing a thera-
ist. He felt pain, but he also felt he could handle it. And
uuch of his grief had already poured out of him in an
ncomplicated torrent of tears. With me, it had stayed inside
nd was seeping into all the cracks and crevices. The same
iing was quietly happening to Suzy and David.

Frank made reservations for all of us at one of the big resort
otels in the Catskills, where the meals and recreation are all
id out for you. No effort is required on your part. David en-
orsed the trip heartily. Suzy did not. She refused to come
ith us. She had withdrawn to her apartment and her paints.
I needed to be away from you,'' she recently told me. ''I
eeded to not talk to you.''

I was perplexed by her apparent desire to keep her distance
om us, but I respected it. However, I didn't like the idea of
er being alone the entire weekend. She agreed to spend the
eekend with a cousin.

The three of us were blessedly anonymous in the Catskills.
Ve hiked in the crisp, clean fall air, ice-skated, swam, and
ut away one giant meal after another. I even slept pretty
ell. The Valium helped.

The tension did not vanish, though. On Saturday afternoon
got a massage at the health club.

''You ought to relax more, dearie,'' the masseuse clucked.
Your neck and shoulder muscles are like granite.''

I tried to relax. We all did. But something always seemed
prevent it. At dinner on Saturday night a photographer ap-
roached our table and said, ''How'd you like to have your
icture taken?''

''No pictures!'' I screamed.

''Beat it!'' commanded Frank.

We all hid behind our menus like fugitives.

''Wait, folks!'' protested the startled photographer. ''You're
ot *obligated* to buy 'em!''

He was an innocent hotel photographer. We'd mistaken
im for a member of the press. We declined his offer more
almly, then burst into relieved laughter as he went off to the
ext table, totally confused.

After dinner Frank and I went to see a movie. David spent

the evening with some teenagers he'd met at the hotel. He di
not tell them his last name. They all ended up in one of thei
rooms watching *Saturday Night Live*. While watching it
David had the misfortune of encountering a cruel sketch abou
Sid Vicious and Nauseating Nancy. As his friends howled
with laughter, David broke down and began to sob. The
didn't know why. He told them, then fled from their room an
appeared at our door, tears still streaming down his face.

"They were in total shock," he said. "I had to get out o
there. *Had* to."

I put my arms around him.

"I'm okay now," he assured me, quickly putting his fam
ily protector mask back on. "It's just that it's not *fair*. That'
what it is. It's like no matter how hard you try to get awa
from it, you can't. Are you guys okay?"

"This thing really is going from bad to worse," muttered
Frank. "I just don't see how far people will go."

"I'm going to write them a nasty letter," I vowed.

(And I did. An NBC vice-president sent me a letter of apol
ogy. I also fired off a letter to Johnny Carson a few days late
after he continually made crude jokes about Nancy in hi
monologues. He did not respond to the letter.)

I dreaded our return home. I felt the same intense uneas
ness as soon as we turned onto our street. My eyes darte
from one parked car to the next, checked the shadows behin
bushes, the fluttering curtains in neighbors' windows.

I waited until Frank had gone in the house before I woul
go in. I was subtle about it—he never noticed how terrified
was that there might be cameramen in there.

There was quite a lot of mail, much of it condolence notes
One letter was addressed to me personally in large, shak
handwriting with little circles over the *i*'s instead of dots
There was no return address. I feared it was an obscene letter
I took a deep breath and opened it.

It was from Sid.

*Dear Debbie,*
*Thank you for phoning me the other night. It was so*
*comforting to hear your voice. You are the only person*

who really understands how much Nancy and I love
each other. Every day without Nancy gets worse and
worse. I just hope that when I die I go the same place as
her. Otherwise I will never find peace.

Frank said in the paper that Nancy was born in pain
and lived in pain all her life. When I first met her, and
for about six months after that, I spent practically the
whole time in tears. Her pain was just too much to bear.
Because, you see, I felt Nancy's pain as though it were
my own, worse even. But she said that I must be strong
for her or otherwise she would have to leave me. So I
became strong for her, and she began to stop having
asthma attacks and seemed to be going through a lot
less pain. [Nancy had had asthma since she was a
child.]

I realized that she had never known love and was
desperately searching for someone to love her. It was
the only thing she really needed. I gave her the love that
she needed so badly and it comforts me to know that I
made her very happy during the time we were together,
where she had only known unhappiness before.

Oh Debbie, I love her with such passion. Every day
is agony without her. I know now that it is possible to
die from a broken heart. Because when you love someone as much as we love each other, they become funda-
mental to your existence. So I will die soon, even if I
don't kill myself. I guess you could say that I'm pining
for her. I could live without food or water longer than
I'm going to survive without Nancy.

Thank you so much for understanding us, Debbie. It
means so much to me, and I know it meant a lot to
Nancy. She really loves you, and so do I. How did she
know when she was going to die? I always prayed that
she was wrong, but deep inside I knew she was right.

Nancy was a very special person, too beautiful for
this world. I feel so privileged to have loved her, and
been loved by her. Oh Debbie, it was such a beautiful
love. I can't go on without it. When we first met, we
knew we were made for each other, and fell in love with

*each other immediately. We were totally inseparable and were never apart. We had certain telepathic abilities, too. I remember about nine months after we met, I left Nancy for a while. After a couple of weeks of being apart, I had a strange feeling that Nancy was dying. I went straight to the place she was staying and when I saw her, I knew it was true. I took her home with me and nursed her back to health, but I knew that if I hadn't bothered she would have died.*

*Nancy was just a poor baby, desperate for love. It made me so happy to give her love, and believe me, no man ever loved a woman with such burning passion as I love Nancy. I never even looked at others. No one was as beautiful as my Nancy. Enclosed is a poem I wrote for her. It kind of sums up how much I love her.*

*If possible, I would love to see you before I die. You are the only one who understood.*

*Love, Sid XXX*

*P.S. Thank you, Debbie, for understanding that I have to die. Everyone else just thinks that I'm being weak. All I can say is that they never loved anyone as passionately as I love Nancy. I always felt unworthy to be loved by someone so beautiful as her. Everything we did was beautiful. At the climax of our lovemaking, I just used to break down and cry. It was so beautiful it was almost unbearable. It makes me mad when people say "you must have really loved her." So they think that I don't still love her? At least when I die, we will be together again. I feel like a lost child, so alone.*

*The nights are the worst. I used to hold Nancy close to me all night so that she wouldn't have nightmares and I just can't sleep without my beautiful baby in my arms. So warm and gentle and vulnerable. No one should expect me to live without her. She was a part of me. My heart.*

*Debbie, please come and see me. You are the only person who knows what I'm going through. If you don't want to, could you please phone me again, and write.*

*I love you.*

I was staggered by Sid's letter. The depth of his emotions,
 sensitivity and intelligence were far greater than I could
ve imagined. Here he was, her accused murderer, and he
s reaching out to me, professing his love for me. His an-
ish was my anguish. He was feeling my loss, my pain—so
ich so that he was evidently contemplating suicide. He felt
vould understand that. Why had he said that?

I fought my sympathetic reaction to his letter. I could not
pond to it, could not be drawn into his life. He had told the
lice he had murdered my daughter. Maybe he had loved
r. Maybe she had loved him. I couldn't become involved
th him. I was in too much pain. I couldn't share his pain. I
dn't enough strength.

I began to stuff the letter back in its envelope when I came
on a separate sheet of paper. I unfolded it. It was the poem
d written about Nancy.

Nancy

You were my little baby girl
And I shared all your fears.
Such joy to hold you in my arms
And kiss away your tears.
But now you're gone there's only pain.
And nothing I can do.
And I don't want to live this life
If I can't live for you.
To my beautiful baby girl.
Our love will never die.

felt my throat tighten. My eyes burned, and I began to
ep on the inside. I was so confused. Here, in a few verses,
re the last twenty years of my life. *I* could have written that
em. The feelings, the pain, were mine. But I hadn't written
*Sid Vicious* had written it, the punk monster, the man who
l told the police he was "a dog, a dirty dog." The man I
red. The man I should have hated, but somehow couldn't.
How was I supposed to react? What was I supposed to do?
The Valium did not help me sleep that night.

* * *

Frank put in a full day at the office on Monday. Suzy a
David returned to classes. I made my first appearance at wo
On Sunday night Suzy and David had mentioned that they we
nervous about how people would react to them. I was, too.

They weren't quite looking at me, I realized, as I stro
through the main office. But they were extremely aware of n

I sat down at my desk. The calendar page was still open
October twelfth, on which I'd written "Call White Deer R
re: admission Nancy, Sid." I turned the page and began
clear off my desk. There were a number of condolence no
and phone messages. As I began to answer them, co-work
gradually came in one at time to offer a few words of symp
thy. Several of them inadvertently called me Nancy instead
Debbie. Then they got flustered and *I* ended up comforti
*them.*

I had trouble getting back into my work. I couldn't seem
concentrate on it. Sid's presence was too strong. I kept thir
ing about his letter and poem. I kept worrying about his tria
kept trying to figure out what had gone on that night in ro
100 of the Chelsea Hotel.

I constantly caught myself staring out the wind
wrapped up in these thoughts. I tried to shake myself free
them. "Please go away," I begged. "Just for five minut
Let me think of something else." But I was unable to.

I ran out of steam at about three o'clock. This puzzled m
usually have tremendous stamina. I decided to go home ea
My work had waited for me for a week. It could wait
more day.

When I turned onto our street, I slowed the car down t
crawl so I could look inside each parked car. I checked
neighbors' bushes and windows. I stopped in front of
house, hesitated, kept going. I circled around the blo
Maybe the reporters were hiding there.

I found a car with a New York license plate parked on
next block. My eyes searched the windshield and bumpers
some sort of press sticker. None. Seemed innocent enou
but how to know for sure? I returned to our street, got to
house again, idled outside. Someone honked behind me
jumped, looked in the rearview mirror. It was a neighbor

ng to get by—I was blocking the road. I pulled over so the car could pass. I looked our house over for any signs of forced entry. It appeared secure.

But I couldn't get myself to go inside. Not until somebody else was home. I drove to Murray's Delicatessen and had a cup of coffee at the counter. Then I called home. No one was here yet. I had another cup of coffee. I called again. David was back from school. Relieved, I drove home.

I told my therapist, Paula, about this fear the next day. She advised me that in order to overcome it I'd first have to get in touch with its cause.

I already knew it, I told her—the press genuinely made me feel as if I were walking around the house stark naked with the window shades up. I said I didn't see how I'd be able to get back on track until I was sure the reporters were gone—for good.

And they were far from gone. The second week after Nancy's death the story merely entered its second phase: PROMOTERS OF VICIOUS TURN SLAYING INTO HYPE read the Philadelphia *Inquirer* headline that week. The story quoted McLaren as saying Sid was set to finish a film about the Sex Pistols, record a brand-new album, and begin to make some TV talk show appearances. A Sid Vicious concert tour was in the works, reported the Philadelphia *Daily News,* commencing with that October 27–28 appearance at Artemis in Philadelphia that Nancy had booked for him. David Carroll, owner of Artemis, joined McLaren in denying that he was exploiting Nancy's murder. Rather, Carroll described himself as a personal friend of Nancy's. "Now that she's gone," Carroll reportedly portedly said, "I have to ask, what would she have wanted him [Sid] to do? She would have wanted him to play rock 'n' roll."

The press showed up on our doorstep, hoping we'd vent our outrage over Sid's being allowed to perform in Nancy's hometown just two weeks after her death. We *were* outraged, but we kept quiet. Fortunately others spoke for us this time.

An editorial in the Philadelphia *Bulletin* angrily denounced the tasteless profiteering. "The very idea of new promotions of Sid Vicious based on his current notoriety leaves us aghast," wrote the *Bulletin*'s editors. "Still, we suppose it

isn't all that surprising that the folks who brought us punk
rock would now look for an even more disgusting way to line
their pockets.''

Our friends rallied in our support, offering to go down and
picket Artemis for us. We appreciated this and might have
taken them up on it had it been necessary. As it turned out, i
wasn't.

On October 23, eleven days after Nancy's death, Sid tried
to kill himself in his room at New York's Seville by slashing
his wrists with a broken light bulb. He also tried to jump out
the window. Anne Beverley, said the newspapers, quoted her
son as screaming "I want to die! I want to join Nancy! I didn't
keep my part of the bargain!" Sid was admitted to the psychi
atric ward at Bellevue Hospital, and the reporters were back
on our front porch. Had there been a Nancy-Sid suicide pac
they wanted to know. Or were these false dramatics on Sid
part to lay the foundation for an insanity plea. Again, we kep
quiet.

Based on the contents of his letter to me, I felt Sid's suicid
attempt was a genuine one. This belief was confirmed tw
days later when Sid phoned me from Bellevue, again goin
through an operator with an urgent message. I returned hi
call for the same reason I had the first time—fear of what h
might do to us if I didn't.

"I can't live, Debbie," he said weakly. "I tried to kill my
self."

"I know."

"I tried, but they wouldn't let me. Now I sit around her
and do nothing. They're afraid I'll try again. And I will. Ca
you come visit me, Debbie?"

"I can't, Sid."

"I so want to see you."

"I can't," I repeated.

"Please call me then. *Please*."

"I have to hang up now."

"I love you, Debbie."

"Good-bye, Sid."

A few days after that I got a second letter from Sid, this on
even more anguished than the first. Sid's second letter al

ave me some insight into what might have happened that
ight at the Chelsea.

*Dear Debbie,*
*I'm dying. Slowly, and in great pain. My baby is gone,*
*without her I have no will to live. I love her so desper-*
*ately. I know I can never make it without her. Nancy*
*became my whole life. She was the only thing that mat-*
*tered to me.*
   *I'm glad I could make her happy. I gave her every-*
*thing she ever wanted, just for the asking. When we*
*only had enough money for one of us to get straight, I*
*always gave it to Nancy. It was less painful to be sick*
*myself than it was to see her sick.*
   *When you love someone that much you cannot lose*
*them and still be able to go on. I know that if I lived to*
*be a thousand years old I would never find anyone like*
*Nancy. No one can ever take her place. I love Nancy*
*and Nancy only. I will always love her. Even after I am*
*dead.*
   *I have only eaten a few mouthfuls of food since she*
*died. I may die of starvation in this place. I just hope it*
*comes soon, so that I can be with Nancy again.*
   *We always knew that we would go to the same place*
*when we died. We so much wanted to die together in*
*each other's arms. I cry every time I think about that. I*
*promised my baby that I would kill myself if anything*
*ever happened to her, and she promised me the same.*
*This is my final commitment to the one I love.*
   *I worshipped Nancy. It was far more than just love.*
*To me she was a goddess. She used to make me kiss her*
*feet before we made love. No one ever loved the way we*
*did, and to spend even a day from her, let alone a whole*
*lifetime, is too painful to even think about. Oh Debbie, I*
*never knew what pain was until this happened. Nancy*
*was my whole life. I lived for her. Now I must die for*
*her.*
   *It gave me such pleasure to give her anything she*
*wanted. She was just like a child. She used to call me*

*"daddy" when she was upset, and I used to rock her to sleep. When I was upset, I used to call her "momma" and she used to nurse me at her breast and call me her "baby boy."*

*I tried to kill myself but they got me to hospital before I died. Nancy knows that I will soon be with her. Please pray that we will be together. I can never find peace until we are together again.*

*Oh Debbie, she was the most beautiful person I ever knew. I would have done anything for her.*

*Nancy once asked if I would pour petrol over myself and set it on fire if she told me to. I said I would, and I meant it. If you would happily die for someone, then how can you live without them. I can't go on without her. She always said she would die before she was twenty-one, and I never doubted it.*

*Goodbye, Debbie. I love you.*

*Sid XXX*

There was a friend's address on the back of the envelope, case I felt like writing Sid a reply. Again, I was so terrib confused. On the one hand, I truly felt sorry for Sid. He was victim of his celebrity. He had loved Nancy and was now pain. On the other hand, I had no doubt he had killed her. wanted him punished. I wanted not to feel anything for hi but anger and hate.

I kept rereading two sentences from the last paragraph his letter:

*Nancy once asked if I would pour petrol over myself and s it on fire if she told me to. I said I would, and I meant it.*

From that, it wasn't hard for me to imagine what went that night at the Chelsea. It wasn't hard to visualize Nan handing Sid the knife she'd bought and ordering him to pro his love for her by using it on her. By shutting my eyes could almost hear her say the words: "I don't believe y love me. If you really loved me, you'd help me die." The could hear his protestations. And then her screams.

No one will ever know for sure what happened that nigh Based on Sid's letters, my knowledge of Nancy, and the p

e's disclosure that she was the one who bought the knife, it
my belief that she engineered her death. She wanted to die,
d for years. She was ready to die. So she made Sid the in-
ument. She egged him into stabbing her by convincing him
was the only possible way he could prove his love for her.
rtainly, she was capable of manipulating him. Certainly,
was capable of being manipulated. Sid was the patsy, per-
ps unwittingly, perhaps not.

In a figurative sense, I feel Nancy committed suicide, the
ath she'd long wanted but had been unable to bring about
her own. In a literal sense—in a legal sense—I don't be-
ve you can regard this as suicide. Nancy did not plunge a
ven-inch hunting knife into her own stomach. Another hand
1, and the law said that hand had to be held accountable for
actions, no matter the degree of outside persuasion or ine-
ation.

But that was and is *my* belief. I realized at the time that
ters might not agree, that here was cause for genuine debate
d food for vivid courtroom drama. I realized again how
ich I was dreading Sid's trial.

I didn't write back to Sid or phone him again. I never heard
m him again. I kept his letters to me a secret from everyone
cept Frank. I felt that if I disclosed them to the police,
mehow they'd end up in the newspapers, end up being sen-
ionalized. I didn't want that. They were private, personal
ters. He made no threats in them. He bared his soul. The
ters weren't meant to be shared.

I disclose them now because I feel they shed light on what
ppened that night and might help others to understand what
ncy and Sid really meant to each other outside the lime-
t. I disclose them now because both Nancy and Sid are
e. They can no longer speak for themselves.

# ☐ Chapter 25

David's protective armor began to peel away the week a
Sid's suicide attempt.

He went out with friends on a Friday night. He came ho
after only an hour, troubled.

"I just didn't want to stay out," he said. "I don't see h
anyone can have a good time."

The very same thing happened the next night, only he ca
home even more upset.

"I tried to talk about what was bothering me," he said.
tried to talk to Bobby. He's my best friend, right? I spilled
guts out to him. Know what? He got really uptight.
changed the subject. He's, I mean, he's my *best friend*.

David went up to his room and sat in there by himself
was unusual for him to be unable to communicate with
friends. It was unusual for him to want to be alone. He
becoming depressed and isolated. Frank and I were c
cerned.

Then at dinner a few nights later he suddenly froze with
fork halfway to his mouth. The fork began to shake. His h

s shaking. He stared at it as if it belonged to someone else.
en he began to tremble all over.

"What's wrong?" asked Frank.

David burst into tears, hurled his fork down, and ran up to
 room. We followed him up there.

"What is it, David?" I begged. "Tell us. Talk to us."

"I just . . . I just don't know what to do," he sobbed. "I
 't go to school. I start to go, and then I just *can't*. I can't sit
re in class with everybody else. They all *know*."

"So what are you doing?" asked Frank. "Where are you
 day?"

"In the library. I hide out in the library. At first I figured
 start working on this big term paper I have to do, you
 ow? But I couldn't do that, either."

"How come?" I asked.

"Because it doesn't mean anything. It doesn't matter. It's
 t so stupid. All of it is. I'm supposed to take the SAT's in a
 ple of weeks, and I don't want to do that, either. All I do is
d. That's all I do. Read about death. There's this tribe in
 rica, you know? When somebody you love dies, they build
 rieving hut for you way off in the woods and put you in it
 a year. Then they come get you and bring you back.
 u're healed."

"Sounds pretty good," I said. "I wouldn't mind that at
 "

He began to cry again. "I can't figure out what to do."

He went into therapy. However, he came home from his
 t few sessions even more upset than before. He refused to
 his therapist anymore. He requested mine, Paula. She
 k him on. With Paula's help, David made some progress.
 was at least able to get in touch with what was upsetting
 .

"I was really angry at Nancy for so much of what she did to
 " he said recently. "I wouldn't let myself grieve for her. I
 ght it. I didn't think it was right to grieve for her. That
 ly messed me up, because I also loved her. She was my
 er."

This was a start. He began to work out his conflicting emo-
 s. However, he continued to cut his classes and feel alien-

ated from his friends. We made an appointment at his sch
and the three of us sat down with the admissions officer a
David's counselor. As it happened, the admissions offi
was very understanding of the trouble David was having v
his schoolwork—his own sister had died when he was sixte

"All I ask," he said to David, "is that you try. Come
you can't stay, then tell us and go on home. If you're havii
bad day, if you can't take a test, just come on in and tell
As for the SAT, you tried taking it as a junior and did v
well. I'd just use that score and forget about taking it ag;
Life is tough enough for you right now."

The admissions officer's support was crucial at this ti;
And it went on for the next few months. With it, David be
to mend. Without it, there's no telling how long it would h
taken David to get back on track.

I shared one of David's problems. I was beginning to
the same way about my job as he did about his schoolworl
didn't seem to matter. It wasn't important—to me or to a
one else. I was having trouble getting out of bed and on
way in the morning. I seldom got into the office before
thirty. Or stayed past three. I tired easily. My energy—
drive to succeed—seemed to have vanished.

About a week after I got Sid's second letter, my job t
me to New York for the day. This was my first trip there si
the day after Nancy's death, and it was an awful experienc
was ill at ease from the second I got off the train in Penn
tion. It was even worse out on the street. Each time I hea
siren, I saw Nancy in the back of an ambulance. She
being rushed to the hospital, her life bleeding out of her.
ward the middle of the afternoon I was seized by chest-acl
panic at the thought of being caught in New York City a
dark. I felt I was going to hyperventilate at a sales mee
and had to flee to the ladies' room. When the meeting
over, I high-tailed it to Penn Station and got the hell ou
New York. It was no longer an exciting city, with jazz
ballet and theater. It was Sid and Nancy's New York.

I had to go to Washington the following week for a two-
conference. It was my first solo overnight trip, also the
time I had to meet new people and be charming. I trie

alked around the banquet room with a frozen smile on my
ace and a little nametag stuck on my chest. I felt like I was
eally wearing a banner headline on my forehead: MURDERED
IRL'S MOM.

Sure enough, I hadn't been there an hour before a middle-
ged businessman recognized my last name.

"Spungen," he said, staring at my nametag. "Spungen.
pungen. I know that name."

I said nothing.

"Hey, I got it," he exclaimed. "Did you know that girl?
he one that was murdered?"

No more frozen smile.

"Yes," I replied.

"How?"

"She was my daughter."

He laughed. "Don't be ridiculous. That wasn't your
aughter."

"You're right," I snapped. "That was my dog."

His eyes widened. He walked away. So much for my at-
mpt to be charming. I went up to my room. I needed to call
ome. I needed to hear Frank's voice.

Nancy's death had made us closer than ever before. I later
scovered that few marriages are the same after a child is
urdered. The divorce rate among the parents of a murdered
iild is very high: nearly four out of five couples split up.
hey look at each other and see only their pain. In a sense,
rank and I had already gone through that years before, when
ancy was growing up. Now we were in the minority, the
ie out of five couples who grab on to each other as a result of
eir child's murder and don't let go.

I told him what had happened downstairs.

"It just won't seem to go away," I said.

"Try to roll with it," he suggested. "Don't take things to
art. A lot has happened, but one thing hasn't changed—
ere's always going to be plenty of assholes in the world."

I still wasn't ready to go back down after Frank and I were
rough speaking, so I phoned Suzy to see how she was
ing. She was by herself in her apartment, continuing to
ep her distance. As soon as I said hello she began to cry.

"Oh, Mommy, it's so awful," she wailed. "I'm havin such a bad time. I need to be with you."

"But I'm in Washington, sweetheart."

"Come home, please."

"I can't. I have meetings tomorrow. What happened? Te me what's wrong."

"I can't be around other people. I just can't. I went to clas today. Political science. The professor called the roll, okay And when he got to my name he said 'Spungen. No relatior of course, to Nancy Spungen, killed by Sid Vicious at th Chelsea Hotel.' He thought he was being funny. He didn know. Some of the people laughed. I started to cry. Tha made everyone around me freak. I ran out. I just can't b around other people."

"Tomorrow you're going to go right back into the clas room and tell that professor—"

"I can't stand it, Mom! I can't! What am I gonna do?"

"Maybe you should think about seeing someone."

"You mean a shrink?"

"Yes."

"No way. No!"

"Why?"

"Nancy went to shrinks. No way. I'm not Nancy."

"I'm not saying you are, Suzy. Just because you need hel doesn't mean you're Nancy. David's seeing one. So am I.

She said she'd think it over. When I got back to Philade phia, Frank and I went to see her. We discussed the subje again and she grudgingly agreed to see a therapist.

Her problems began to come to the surface. Much of wh bothered her was what plagued David—the conflict betwee her grief and her resentment. But in Suzy it ran much deepe Nancy had heaped more abuse on her. There had been inten jealousy and rivalry between them. Suzy had often truly d tested her older sister. At the same time, she had looked up her and sought her approval. She still loved Nancy. And sl wondered how much of Nancy's influence guided her. He was a powerful struggle. It still is.

If Suzy and David had been able to communicate, the might have helped each other at this time. They were goir

rough the same problems. But Nancy had driven a wedge
tween them. They did not have a close relationship.

Besides, Suzy was keeping all of us at arm's length. With
r therapist's aid she began to understand why. Someone she
ved had gone. It hurt. She was reacting to her hurt by push-
g us away. A defense mechanism triggered revulsion when
: tried to embrace her. After all, she loved us, too. She
dn't want to open herself up to being hurt again.

d was released from Bellevue after a couple of weeks.
ward the end of November he appeared at a preliminary
aring, at which he pleaded not guilty to charges of second-
gree murder. (First-degree murder in New York applies
ly to the killing of a police officer.)

The famous attorney F. Lee Bailey was retained to defend
m. Bailey's defense, the press speculated, would center
ound Nancy's past history of drug abuse and attempted sui-
le in an attempt to prove she'd brought her murder on her-
lf. This pained me. It meant that she, not Sid, would be on
al. She would be painted as someone who deserved what
e'd gotten, just like a rape victim. Except a rape victim can
there to defend herself. Nancy wouldn't be.

I didn't think I'd be able to handle Nancy's public crucifix-
n, especially since I might be asked to get up on the stand
d help. I decided I would not go to the trial. I told Frank.
: understood. He said he was unsure about himself.

"Can they make me go?" I asked our lawyer.

"If you get a subpoena," he replied, "you have to go."

"What if they make me testify?" I asked. "What if they
k me all sorts of awful questions about Nancy?"

"Worse comes to worse," he said, "You put your hands
er your face and start screaming, 'Leave me alone! Leave
: alone! My child is dead!' And they'll leave you alone."

I didn't think I could behave that way in public.

I began to worry more and more about the trial. It loomed
ead. It made it impossible for me to get on with my life.

In the beginning of December, Frank and I were asked to
ne to New York to be questioned by the new assistant dis-

trict attorney assigned to the case, Allen Sullivan. Unlike his
predecessor, he had prosecuted a number of major homicides
and had the reputation of being a heavy hitter. Bailey's presence for the defense necessitated such a man for the prosecution.

I asked our lawyer if he thought he should accompany us to
the questioning. He said it wouldn't be necessary.

"You haven't done anything wrong," he said. "You
haven't got anything to hide. I can't see why you need an attorney with you."

He was trying to save us money. That was nice of him. Unfortunately it was a mistake.

Sullivan was in his late thirties, tall and brusque. He immediately put us on the defensive. He made no effort to acknowledge our loss. Rather, he declared, "I'm going to question
you witnesses separately. Which one of you wants to go
first?"

Frank and I held hands tightly. We looked at each other,
confused.

"Well? Speak up!" he commanded.

"We'd rather not be separated," Frank said.

"You *will* be separated," he insisted, glaring at us.

"We came here voluntarily," Frank said. "We have nothing more to tell you than we've already said twice before.
We'd prefer to stay together."

"We're *going* to stay together," I said.

Sullivan looked at me, then at Frank. Then he threw down
his pencil in disgust. "Okay. *This* time. But next time I sep-
rate you. Understand? Now, when was the last time you saw
your daughter?"

Frank protested, "We've already—"

Sullivan cut him off. "I want the answers again," he
snapped, as if we were naughty children. He pointed a finger
at us. "I want you witnesses to answer my questions," he
thundered.

Why did he keep calling us witnesses? Witnesses to what?
We hadn't witnessed anything. We were the parents of the
victim. Why was he putting us in an adversary position? Why
was he yelling at us?

We were sorry our lawyer wasn't with us. We were intimi-
d and rather lost. We had no idea what our rights were.
realized Sullivan had a job to do, but we didn't under-
nd where we fit into it.

e threw questions at us for about two hours. He didn't ask
ny that we hadn't heard twice before. Unlike the police
his predecessor, however, he was not satisfied with the
nt of our knowledge. If we didn't know the answers, he
ssed us, bullied us, belittled us.

"Has either one of you ever been arrested?" he demanded
en he was through.

"No," Frank said.

"Never," I agreed.

"Positive?"

"Yes," we said.

He eyed us skeptically. "I'm going to question you sepa-
ly about that."

He didn't believe us!

"I'll be in touch," Sullivan said. "And then I'll see you at
trial. April, probably."

So many more months before this would be over!

"I'm not planning to come," I said.

"You *have* to," he said.

"Why?" I asked.

"You *have* to," he repeated.

"I don't want to."

"Then I'll subpoena you," he said.

We limped out of there. When we got home, I checked
h our lawyer to see if there was any way to avoid being
poenaed.

"Yes," he replied. "Stay out of New York. They can't get
if you're out of state."

That was a relief, but it was small consolation. I was flab-
gasted by our meeting with Sullivan. Prior to that, I'd al-
ys thought the district attorney's office represented the
tim. It doesn't. It represents the state. Who represents the
tim? Nobody. The suspect is taken very good care of. He
s free counsel if he can't afford it. His rights are vigilantly
eld and monitored. As for the victim, well, the victim has

no legal rights. Nobody watches out for the victim's famil
Society places a very heavy burden on it. Too heavy. A
even though, in retrospect, we needed a lawyer with us at c
meeting with Sullivan, we would have been forced to pay 1
it ourselves. That hardly seems fair.

Still, it would have been worth it. Sullivan would ha
been less likely to treat us as he had. I have since spoken
many other parents all over America whose children we
murdered. They have similar horror stories to tell about t
way they were treated by prosecutors. Our experience w
Sullivan is not the exception.

Why did he treat us that way? Maybe he was trying to p
pare us for what it would be like to be grilled on the stand
F. Lee Bailey. If so, he should have explained himself.
would not take that much more effort to show some sensiti
ity. Maybe Sullivan was a fine prosecutor. Maybe he wa
warm, caring human being who found it necessary to shie
his emotions. Maybe he was under too much pressure to bu
a case. Whatever the situation, it was not necessary to treat
with such disdain and hostility. We were still reeling from t
shock of our daughter's violent death. The prospect of
lengthy trial was extremely painful. It would not be flatteri
to Nancy. It would keep us in the public eye. It would prolo
the grieving period. The prospect of *attending* the trial w
even more painful. A great emotional price would have to
paid. Some explanation for why this sacrifice was requir
would have been appreciated. We were given none.

I beg prosecutors to remember the other victims
murder—the victim's family. There are a lot of us out the
More of us every day. We hurt and bleed, too. Our rights a
feelings must be dealt with in a better way than they are no

Sid stayed in the papers.

In the second week of December he was jailed again, t
time for allegedly slashing the face of musician Todd Smi
brother of singer Patti Smith, with a broken beer bottle. T
incident occurred at a rock club where the musician's ba
was performing. Reportedly, Sid liked the looks of Smit

lfriend, a guitar player in the band. He gave her a lewd
ch and she complained to Smith. Smith told Sid to leave
alone. In response, Sid broke his beer bottle on a table and
shed Smith.

'He is hell-bent on living up to his image,'' McLaren was
oted as saying.

Sid was arrested for the attack the following morning when
made his daily check-in with the police—a requirement of
bail. He wore a torn black T-shirt, black jeans, and boots.
'I doubt that he'll be let out on bail again,'' the papers
oted a police spokesman. ''But he could be.''

is bail was revoked. He was sent back to Riker's Island.
gain, we got a visit from the press corps. Again, we said
ing.

few days later I was sitting in my office, staring out the
dow, when the phone rang. It was a secretary in personnel
Western Union where I had worked. She thought I'd want
know that a man who said he was with the FBI had phoned
uesting background information on me. Her boss had read
personnel folder to the man over the phone—what I
ned, weighed, did. Everything.

I was aghast. I phoned the FBI in Philadelphia. They said
re was no reason for them to be involved in the Sid Vicious
e. In addition, I was told they would never approach a
npany for a personnel file over the phone. They'd do it in
son.

I called Sullivan in New York. He said he'd look into it and
back to me. He never got back to me.

I went home. David was there, but still I circled the house
eral times before having the nerve to pull into the drive-
y. When I finally did dart inside the house, I kept my coat
and my keys in my hand—just in case I had to make a run
it. David was upstairs in his room. I sat down at the dining
m table, chest aching beyond belief. I heard a car door
m outside and I panicked. I took off out the back door,
ped in my car, and sped away. I had no destination in
d. Just away.

ended up at my therapist's office. I burst in. Fortunately
was there.

"You've got to give me something," I begged. "I have
take something. I can't stand it anymore! I'm losing my mi
Give me a pill!"

"No," she said simply.

"Please! I've got to get rid of it! I've got to calm dowr
can't do it on my own. A pill *please!*"

"Sit down, Deb."

"I'm begging you!"

*"Sit down!"*

"I don't *want* to sit down!"

"Fine, then stand! You want to know why your ch
hurts? Because your daughter is dead. That hurts. You
feeling the pain. You *have* to feel it! And you *have* to stand
That's the way it is."

I took several deep breaths, tried to calm myself. I
down.

"No pills."

"No pills," she said. "You have to feel it sooner or lat
It may as well be now."

"Couldn't we put it off? Until after the trial?"

"No."

"Two months?"

"No."

"One month?"

"I'm not going to bargain with you."

"Will you do me one small favor then?" I asked.

"What?"

"Find me another mother whose child was murdered. F
me a woman who has gone through what I'm going throu;
I'd really like to talk to her. I'd like to find out how she s
vived."

"Okay," she said. "I'll try. But offhand I can't think
anyone."

"That's not very comforting."

"All I mean is that I've never handled a murder before.
find you somebody. I'm sure there's somebody out there v
knows what you're going through. You're not alone."

I didn't contradict her, but I felt certain she was wrong. I

dy else had gone through this. Nobody else had felt my
in.

I went home and made dinner and felt the pain. There was
lly only one way it would go away, I realized. It would
nish only if I were dead. Then I would be free of pain, at
ace.

As I stood in the kitchen, chopping vegetables, I seriously
ndered if I'd be better off dead. Then I remembered some-
ng Sid had written in his first letter. I found the letter, and
 passage:

*Thank you, Debbie, for understanding that I have to die.
eryone else just thinks that I'm being weak.*

I *did* understand. I *did* see what he was talking about. The
n *was* too much. Only in death could one be free of it. Just
Nancy was.

Suicide? Me? Never. How could I do it? Stick a pistol in
 mouth? Swallow a bottle of Drano? Where would I find
 nerve?

No, I couldn't do it. I had to survive the pain, that's all. Su-
de was not a practical alternative. Tantalizing, yes; realis-
, no. No way.


esigned from my job right around the holidays. I didn't
nt to work anymore. I no longer had any desire to succeed
business. It simply wasn't important.

I held on to a slim connection. I was a consultant one day a
ek. But the rest of the week was my own to do with as I
ased. Most of the time I sat around the house in my coat,
ys in hand. I stared at the walls a lot. I was very lethargic,
thdrawn into my own suffering. I also felt very isolated
m Frank. We didn't talk much now. I didn't talk to my
ends at all.

January was a very dreary month. It seemed the sun never
ne out. Life held no hope for me, no meaning. Only night-
res. Only pain. With each passing day my desire to be
ve waned.

I thought about suicide again, though I didn't mention it to
ula. She'd just get mad at me. No, I kept it to myself. And I

began to write scenarios in my head. I began to fantasize
own death, just as I had Nancy's. I checked into guns, call
some shops I looked up in the Yellow Pages. You had to ge
license in order to get a gun. It seemed too time-consumi
and complicated. And it would be messy for whoever fou
me. Pills? There weren't enough in the house. Poison? I ca
fully read the contents of all of the cleansers and polishes
the house. There were several that could do damage.
would I be able to swallow enough of it?

Then one day one of our neighbors, a man I didn't kno
hanged himself. Successfully. He used the metal support
the garage door. If it held his weight it would hold mine
took this as a message. Somebody was trying to tell me son
thing. Hanging was the way to go.

There was no rope in the house, but I did find a length
heavy, rubber-encased wire. It would serve my purp
nicely. The only question now was when.

Tomorrow. Always, it was tomorrow. A part of me k
saying; *Tomorrow you'll be your old self again; tomorr
you'll find a reason to be alive; tomorrow you'll be ready
start living again.* I lived from day to grim day, cut off fr
everyone. All I could think about was that I wanted my p
to stop.

On February third, the day of Sid's death, I was at the b
tom.


He'd been released on bail again from Riker's Island. Rep
edly, he celebrated that night with a party at a frien
Greenwich Village apartment. He had a few beers and
feeling pretty good. At about midnight he decided to shoot
some heroin. It was too much. He died in his sleep later
night. Sid was found in bed, face up. It was ruled an accid
tal overdose. He was twenty-one years old.

And then the reporters were back on our front porch w
their microphones and bright lights and minicams. They w
ringing the doorbell over and over and over again, demand
a comment.

And then Sid's mother was on the phone. I wondered h

'd gotten our unlisted number. I didn't ask. She had a
estion. Could she bury Sid next to Nancy? No, I said. She
led up having him cremated.

And then I was certain it was time for me to hang myself. I
s ready now, really ready. I'd had it. This nightmare was
ver going to end. I couldn't take it anymore. No more. No
morrows. I went out to the garage, got that piece of wire. I
ught it back into the house, tied a noose around my neck,
od in front of the dining room mirror.

And then, as I stared at myself in the mirror, reality sank
I realized I was not going to kill myself. I didn't need to. It
s over now. The odyssey was truly over. Sid was dead.
ere would be no trial. Nothing else could possibly happen.
e press would leave us alone, forget about us.

I could start to live again. It wouldn't be easy. But I wanted
now. I had to. I suddenly realized I had to give purpose to
those years of anguish. I owed it to myself. I also owed it
Nancy. I had to keep my promise. I could do it. I was
gh. I'd made it this far. Somehow I was going to make it
rest of the way. Somehow I was going to survive.

I removed the noose from around my neck, called Paula.

"I just heard the news," she said. "How do you feel? Re-
ved?"

"Empty," I said hoarsely. "I feel empty."

"You're off the hook now. You have your privacy back.
ur life."

"I know," I said. "But I have no life."

"What do you mean?"

"I was thinking about suicide a little while ago," I said,
gering the noose in my lap.

"Are you still?"

"No."

"Good. That's not an answer. That's quitting."

"I know. It's just that, well, like I said. I have no life."

"You've made real progress. I'm glad to hear you say
t."

"You are?"

"Yes. It means you're coming to grips with the reality of
ncy not being here anymore. You built your old life around

Nancy. Everything you did was a response to her. That w
your old life. Now you need a new life.''

"You mean, I have to build my life around someth
else.''

"Exactly.''

"Like what?''

"You'll find it.''

"I may need help.''

"You've got it.''

"Have you found me another mother?''

"Not yet. Still looking.''

I hung up, heard a creak on the stairs. I turned, saw Nar
coming down from her room to model the new ski outfit sh
brought back from Colorado.

The house was haunted. Everywhere I went in it, I still s
Nancy. Everywhere I went outside of it, I saw phantom
porters jumping out from behind bushes. I saw neighb
whispering.

We had to move out. That would be step one of my n
life. A fresh start. Rooms that Nancy had never been
Chairs she'd never sat in.

I wanted to move back to the city. I was born and rai
there; it was my home. I wanted out of suburbia—out of N
cy's house, out of Nancy's street, out of the markets a
stores where people murmured about Nancy when t
thought my back was turned.

My mind made up, I went back to the garage and loo
the noose around the support I'd planned on using. I lef
there for three weeks. I left it because I wanted someone
see it and realize how much pain I was in. And to help
But nobody noticed it. Not Frank, not Suzy, not David. T
were in too much pain themselves.

That night I told Frank I wanted to move. I didn't tell
that moving was crucial to my survival. But that much
could see.

"If it's something you feel strongly about,'' he said, "t
go ahead and take a look.''

Frank's niece was a realtor in an area I liked called Soc
Hill. It had quiet, tree-lined blocks of renovated townhou

joining an old market square, near the water. I called her mediately and made an appointment to drive around the xt day and look at houses. I was determined to find a place t first day, and I did. I asked Frank and David to come and k at it that evening. They were overwhelmed by my urncy, but they agreed. Suzy refused. She saw moving out of r house as a betrayal of Nancy.

"You wanna sell my sister's house right out from under r," she snapped.

It particularly bothered her that the house I liked had only ee bedrooms, not four. But I didn't concern myself with zy's feelings, or anyone else's. I couldn't see past my own rvival.

We bought the house. Our house in Huntingdon Valley— r dream house—was sold in a week. So was the furniture. I nted everything to be new.

The builder was still putting the finishing touches on our w house. As soon as the paperwork was settled, I drove into wn to check out his progress and see how soon we could ve in.

It was a sunny winter day. There wasn't too much traffic on expressway. The heater was on in the car; my hat and ves were off. I was feeling a little better, now that I could k forward to being in a new house. My chest still ached, t I felt I could endure it. I was no longer contemplating sui- le.

Suddenly I felt something hot on my hands.

I looked down. My hands were drenched with tears. I ked at myself in the rearview mirror. Tears were rolling wn my cheeks. Twenty years' worth. They were finally uring out on their own. I couldn't stop them. My vision be- n to blur. I was afraid I'd lose control of the car. I pulled er to the emergency lane, barely able to see the other cars the road. When I'd come to a safe stop and turned off the tor, I broke down and sobbed. I sobbed and sobbed uncon- llably. I cried a torrent of tears. Tears of frustration, anger, n, grief.

cried for my baby.

Finally, I had time to cry for my baby.

# ❏ Chapter 26

I encountered a great deal of heel-dragging when [t]he new house was ready for us to move into. Nobody would h[elp] me pack up our things. Frank, it turned out, had changed [his] mind. He said he loved our home and was sorry we were le[av]-ing it. David echoed that sentiment.

"So why didn't you speak up? Why didn't you stop [me] from buying the other place?" I demanded of them. "W[hy] didn't one of you say 'Don't do it'?"

Frank shrugged. "I didn't think I cared one way or [the] other."

"Me neither," said David.

"But now that the time has come," added Frank, "I gu[ess] I do."

"It's too late now," I protested.

"I know," he replied sullenly.

I packed up our things and arranged for the move itse[lf. It] was not considered "our" move. It was "my" move. S[o be] it. My friend Susan came over the day the movers arriv[ed to] help me transport the cats and the valuables. Then we g[ot]

414

car and drove off to the new house. I never looked back at
ncy's house.

There were no carpets or drapes in the new place yet and,
en after the movers had unloaded everything from our old
use, very little furniture. I spent part of my first afternoon
the new house hanging sheets over the bare windows so
'd have some privacy after nightfall. Then I walked around
neighborhood a bit. I went in and out of the nearby shops.
ought some groceries. And a bottle of champagne. Nobody
ognized me. Nobody knew me. I was starting from scratch
d I liked the feeling. It felt right.

I popped open the champagne when Frank got to the new
use after work. I thought a small celebration was in order.
didn't. He drank down one glass of champagne, then dered, "I don't like it here."

"Please, Frank," I pleaded. "Give it time. It'll be nice.
ce we have carpets and drapes."

He looked around for a place to sit down. There wasn't
.

"And furniture," he pointed out.

"And furniture," I acknowledged.

"Tell you what," he said, gathering up his coat. "I'm
ng to the Holiday Inn. Call me when the place is ready to
in."

waited for him to crack a grin. I thought he was kidding.
wasn't.

managed to talk him into staying. David arrived. He was
y positive. He assured me that the place was nice and he'd
ery happy in it. I could tell he hated it. The three of us had
lent dinner at a nearby restaurant, then Frank and I went
to look at furniture.

'd been looking forward to this. I thought we'd have fun
pping together for pieces for the new house. We had some
ney—we'd gotten more for the old place than we'd spent
the new one. But Frank was very noncommittal when I
ted out living room furniture that appealed to me. He just
gged. Then he began to yawn. He took a walk while I
ed at furniture.

When he came back he said, "Next time you want to g look at furniture, go without me."

"Why?"

"I don't have the time."

"But what should I buy? How will I know if you'll li it?"

"Just buy whatever you want."

This was not working out at all. I tried to get Frank to op up, but he wouldn't. We had nothing to say to each other bed that night, or the following morning. The doorbell ra about an hour after he and David had gone.

I opened the door to find two police officers.

"Mrs. Spungen?" one of them asked.

I nodded. I was devastated. They'd caught up with us one day. Surely, the press would be quick to follow. The was no pulling away, no fresh start. They wouldn't let us liv

"We wondered if we could ask you a few questions."

"About what?" I asked, hoarsely.

"The murder."

"I've already been over it a hundred times with the NYP the DA's office—"

"This is a local matter, Mrs. Spungen," said one of the ficers, confused.

"What is?" I demanded, equally confused.

"There was a woman murdered in this courtyard l night."

"There was?"

"Yes. We were wondering if you'd seen or heard a thing."

"N-no. Nothing."

They asked a few more questions, but I had no informat for them. I closed the door. I was relieved that our notori hadn't followed us, but frightened that violence had.

Later I met one of my neighbors, a particularly nice yo woman who lived next door with her husband. She invited over for coffee. When we were inside her house, she dis peared into a bedroom for a second. When she returned was carrying a three-month-old baby girl.

She cooed at her groggy little baby, tickling and caress

. I couldn't handle it. I couldn't stand to look at the baby. I
saw my own baby, my little Nancy, with needle marks on
soft baby hands.

"My goodness, what's wrong?" asked my new neighbor,
rmed.

Tears were pouring down my face, just as they had in the
. A puddle was forming on this poor woman's dining room
le.

"N-nothing," I blubbered.

"Did I do something to upset you?"

"No. Nothing. I have to go. I'm . . . I'm expecting a de-
ery."

I took a raincheck on the coffee, left hastily for my own
use. She was confused and a bit insulted, I think. Once I
s inside my own home, I sobbed and sobbed. I wished I
ald look at a baby again. Would I *ever* be able to? Would
wounds heal?

This crying business was starting to become a regular
ng. It seemed that now that the floodgates had opened I
aldn't close them. All those tears I'd shed inwardly were
ming out. That afternoon, for instance, there was a story on
local TV news about a seven-year-old girl who would die
on without a kidney transplant. I felt her pain. Tears started
stream down my face again.

I cried on February 27, 1979, the twenty-first birthday
ncy vowed she would never live to see. The four of us vis-
d her at the cemetery. We laid flowers on her grave. All of
cried, then we put our arms around each other for support.
ddenly Suzy broke away from our little circle and moved
eral steps away. She did not want to be part of us. There
s anger in her face.

A wave of incredible sadness washed over me. It saddened
that Suzy could not make peace with Nancy, with herself,
with us. It saddened me that our family seemed to have
ne apart even more than before. I wondered if we would
r be whole again.

Paula was pleased that I was starting to cry a lot. She said it
s a positive sign that I was releasing my grief.

Then I told her the family wasn't doing very well.

"We're not talking," I said. "Frank just sort of grumbles and complains. David isn't communicating his feelings to me, which isn't like him. Suzy is turning her back on us."

"Do you know why?" she asked.

"At first I thought everybody was mad about the move. I don't think so now. I think it's more than that."

She nodded. "You've been through a lot of trauma and change. You still have to adjust to it as a family."

"How?"

"Remember when you first came to me, I suggested you might need family network therapy after each of you had handled your individual grief?"

"Yes, I remember. Do you think it's time for that?"

"I do. We have to make you a family again. A family of four."

I was all for it. So was David. Frank groused but went along. Suzy was the hardest to persuade. She agreed to come only with the understanding that she need not speak if she didn't feel like it.

Her therapist and Paula joined the four of us. We sat around in a circle.

"Let's get started, shall we?" said Paula.

We all nodded in assent. This was followed by silence. Then more silence. The four of us suddenly seemed very uncomfortable with one another. Throats were cleared. Eyes wandered. We were like strangers.

"Go ahead," Paula urged.

"What exactly are we supposed to do?" I asked.

"Talk to each other," she said.

"About what?" asked Frank.

She thought this over. "Perhaps a little direction might help. A starting point. How about if we go around the family, and each one of you gets something off your chest. Why don't each of you mention something you really regret. Whatever comes to mind."

Suzy started to speak.

"Other than the fact that you're here," Paula said, anticipating Suzy's comment with a chuckle.

We all laughed. That broke the ice a little.

"Frank, why don't you start," said Paula. "What do you egret most?"

"About Nancy?"

"About anything to do with the family."

Frank thought it over. "Okay," he said. "I regret . . . the ing I regret most is that Nancy and I were never able to get gether. We were always at each other's throats. We were ever able to just hug each other and say 'I love you, even if e don't always see eye-to-eye on things.' I'm sorry that ever happened . . . and, well, that it never will."

"Okay," said Paula. "Comments?"

The rest of us just looked down. We had nothing to say.

"Suzy?" asked Paula.

"Yes?"

"Would you like to share your regret with us?"

"Yeah. I'm pissed that my folks moved out of our house so st. It's like, well, it's like they want to pretend Nancy never isted. I don't think she'd like that. It was just really hasty. nd they didn't talk it over with us. No explanation, noth- g."

"I did, too," I protested.

"Did not," Suzy insisted.

"I did," I said. "I told David why I needed to move."

"Excuse me," said Paula. "Why didn't you tell Suzy?"

"Because she was upset about it," I replied.

"Obviously," said Paula. "So why didn't you talk to her out it?"

I looked from Frank to David to Suzy. Then I turned to ula. "I guess I was afraid of her reaction. We all walk on s with each other. We always have, because of Nancy. u see, with Nancy, to confront her about something she s angry about, or you were angry about, well, that would tty much guarantee an explosion. So if I got mad at her I'd l Frank, and then he'd tell her. Or vice versa."

Frank nodded.

"By using a go-between," I went on, "we could limit the e of the explosion. We've always used go-betweens for ch other in our family. It's just our way. It's automatic. I n't even realize it anymore. It's not conscious or anything

like that. I guess that's why I told David about why I needed
to move, instead of Suzy—figuring she was mad about it, and
it would work out better if she heard it from him. She wasn't
mad at him. He could explain it without the explosion.''

"But I still didn't understand your reasons," objected
David. "And Suzy and I really haven't had a chance to talk
much lately, anyway."

Suzy turned to me, scowling. "You could have talked to
me about it directly," she said. "I'm not Nancy, you know."

Paula suddenly got up, grabbed an empty chair and made
room for it in our circle.

"As long as Nancy's here," she said, "we may as well
pull a chair up for her and ask her to sit down."

We all stared at the empty chair.

"What I'm saying," Paula went on, "is that Nancy is *not*
here anymore. She's loved and she's missed. But she's *not
here*. The purpose of these sessions is to get rid of that chair,
for you to stop behaving and making decisions around her.
You're a family of four now, not five. What we've just been
talking about here is a perfect example, this walking-on-eggs
business. You seem to have gotten into the habit of talking in
triangles with each other instead of talking one to one. Maybe
it was necessary before. Whether it was or not isn't the issue.
The main thing is, it isn't anymore. Nancy's not here. You
*can* talk to each other. I'm not going to tell you *how* to talk to
each other. All I'm saying is, you're *not*.''

The four of us nodded at one another in acknowledgment.
She was right. Nancy's presence was built into the way we in-
teracted as a family. The roles we adopted, the manner in
which we thought and communicated, all dated back to the
way our house had been during Nancy's formative years.
Without realizing it, we'd stayed in our Nancy-oriented
patterns—even after she'd gone off to Darlington, then Col-
rado, then New York, then London. The patterns were still
with us now, even though she was not.

We met several times in family network therapy over the
next few weeks and became increasingly aware of how Nancy's presence was built into how we were with each other. We
didn't just talk in triangles. We also tended to hold on to o

ersonal preferences and opinions about things rather than
oice them—this in deference to Nancy, who had always
nded up getting her way. After so many years spent giving in
 what Nancy wanted to do, we'd all gotten accustomed to
ist saying "I don't care" instead of voicing our true feelings.
 had been easier that way. But now it served only to keep us
part. We were strangers with one another.

We were wary of showing affection for one another, for
ar that Nancy would get jealous. She needed all the love we
id. She needed *everything* we had. This, too, was a prob-
m.

So was the fact that Suzy and David now expected us to do
e same things for them that Nancy had forced us to do for
r—send money, for example. They resented it if we
ouldn't or couldn't give them what we'd given Nancy. It
as necessary for us to explain to them that Nancy had been
e exception to the rule. Then we had to tell them what the
le was.

Our problems as a family were by no means solved over-
ght. But this was a start.

Unfortunately, in my own case, I found it hard to concen-
ate totally on the family's problems. I still needed to solve
y own. The major one: finding something new to build my
e around. Furnishing our new townhouse wasn't enough.
or was my one day a week of work. I still felt purposeless. I
ll had trouble getting out of bed in the morning. I had no
ive.

One morning I just decided to stay in bed. I was feeling a
 under the weather anyway. I turned on the TV set and
iwled back under the covers with a cup of coffee. I flicked
ound, settled on the Phil Donahue show, then into the pil-
ws. Four couples were on. They all belonged to a group
led Parents of Murdered Children. As they talked, I sat up
ruptly in bed, moved closer and closer to the set until I was
 more than a foot away, hanging on their every word.

I was not alone.

Bob and Charlotte Hullinger, POMC's founders, were on
  show. Bob is a Lutheran minister in Cincinnati. Their
ighter had been bludgeoned to death by her boyfriend

while the two of them were exchange students in Germany
The family had been devastated. Bob, a clergyman, said h
had been unable to find any words of comfort for them. The
son, who was David's age, began to cut classes and stoppe
doing his term papers. Charlotte said she had felt totally ise
lated from everyone.

"My biggest wish," said Charlotte on the show, "was t
find another mother to talk to who'd gone through what I wa
suffering."

So she contacted one whose loss she'd read about in th
newspaper. They spoke several times on the phone. The fam
lies met to comfort and support each other. And they kept
it. That's how POMC began. Chapters were now sproutin
up all over the country. Wherever children were murdered

One couple on the Donahue show had launched a chapt
on Long Island. Their teenage son had come home fro
school one afternoon to find robbers in the house. The robbe
stabbed him. The boy stumbled onto the front lawn, cried f
help. The robbers pursued him, stabbed him again, this tin
fatally. The men were apprehended, tried, convicted, an
sentenced, but the boy's mother said she could not rid herse
of the fear that they might come back and "finish the job."
took her a long time to convince herself that she wasn't goir
crazy.

Donahue asked them why they decided to start a POM
chapter.

"We felt a responsibility," replied the boy's father. "W
managed to survive, so we were obligated to show other pa
ents how."

An Arizona couple spoke about what had happened to th
nineteen-year-old daughter. A stranger had followed h
home from a shopping center, shot her on her front porch
right in front of her father—then fled. The girl's mother sa
she had had so many bizarre thoughts over subseque
months—paranoid thoughts, thoughts about suicide. Sh
seen a therapist, she said, but therapists didn't really and tru
understand what the parents of a murdered child were feelir
Only other parents of murdered children did.

I could not believe what I was watching. There were otl

milies out there who had gone through what we'd gone
rough, felt the same feelings. Ordinary people, good peo-
le, who had joined together so they wouldn't feel so alone in
e world, so marked.

At the end of the program the Hullingers gave their phone
umber in Cincinnati in case anyone wanted to call about
ining the group. I dove for a pencil and wrote the number
)wn, excited.

I called. I spoke to Bob Hullinger for about ninety minutes.
:old him how remarkable it had been to hear the couples talk
)out things on the program that I thought nobody else had
xperienced except us. I asked him if there was a POMC
apter in Philadelphia.

"Not yet," he replied. "Would you like to start one?"

I said I didn't know, I'd have to think that over. A few days
:er I phoned the Hullingers again and spoke to Charlotte.
iere was a remarkable bond between us, a kinship between
o strangers. Both of us had suffered so many of the same
notional problems, and felt totally alone in doing so. I'd fi-
lly found that other mother who'd survived. I felt like I'd
und a sister. She, too, asked me if I wanted to start a Phila-
lphia chapter of POMC.

It was a hard decision for me. I had never been the sort of
rson to get involved in causes. I was not a joiner. Further-
)re, we had at last found the measure of privacy and ano-
mity we craved. Starting a POMC chapter would mean
;ing that. It might mean losing a piece of myself, too.

Then I remembered what that Long Island father had said
the Donahue show: "We felt a responsibility. We man-
:d to survive."

I was a survivor. I still had troubles, but I was going to
ike it. It was incumbent upon me to be there for the others
they wouldn't have to go through that private hell. After
, nobody else understood.

I sat down with Frank and we discussed it. He was with
:. We were committed.

Shortly after that, Charlotte Hullinger called me to say she
s about to appear on a local Philadelphia talk show to speak
)ut POMC.

"I don't want to pressure you," she said, "but would yo
like to go on with me as the representative of the new Phila
delphia chapter?"

"Yes," I said without hesitation.

I met Charlotte at the TV studio. We embraced each othe
like long-lost relatives. Then we went on the air. It was no
easy for me. I had hidden from the cameras and bright light
now I was seeking them out. The talk show host didn't mak
it any easier by introducing me as the one mother in Americ
"who knows the most about sex, drugs, and rock 'n' roll.
But I steered clear of the circus elements surrounding Nancy
murder. I talked about what pain and isolation our family ha
gone through, and how valuable it was to reach out to som
one who understood.

I perspired freely and my voice quavered, but I did it.
was important. It needed to be done. I gave out Frank's offic
number at the end of the show. He got seven phone calls fro
local parents of murdered children in the first hour, anoth
ten throughout the day. I couldn't believe there were so ma
in our own town. Frank took down their names and numbe
and said I'd phone them back.

And the Philadelphia chapter of POMC was in business

It was difficult for me to call these parents. Each was sha
ing their pain with a kindred soul for the first time. I felt th
pain over the phone. I invited each of them to a meeting at c
house. Most of them were eager to come. Only one wom
said she wasn't ready for that kind of thing yet. Her daugh
had been murdered in 1964, but her husband still would
discuss it or release his grief. He got very angry at her wh
she cried about it. He would not attend such a meeting.

"If you have any literature or anything," she said, "plea
send it to me. You'll have to send it unmarked, or my hi
band will throw it away. If you don't have anything,
okay. Just knowing you're there and I can call you is enou
to get me through the day."

She wept. I wept with her.

Then Frank came in and wondered if I was ever going
knock off.

"Why?" I asked, finding the next number on the list to phone.

"You've only been on the phone for something like seven hours," he said, grinning.

I wasn't tired. I'd found my old intensity again. My energy was back.

Seven couples came to the Philadelphia chapter's first meeting. Like us, they were ordinary middle-class couples. Some were blue collar, some were white collar. One of the couples was black.

It happened to be raining particularly hard that night.

"God is crying for us," someone said.

We all put on nametags and milled around the living room, having coffee and cake. Nervous with one another, we weren't quite sure how to get started.

We ended up sitting in a circle and sharing our experience, one couple at a time. As each story unfolded I realized the Bungens did not have the market cornered on suffering.

One couple had been on vacation with their two children. Their nine-year-old son was grabbed by a man in the motel corridor when he went to buy a newspaper. The man, who turned out to be an illegally discharged mental patient, dragged the boy into a room and slit his throat over the toilet. The couple had cried over it every night for five years. They still could not get over it, could not get on with the rest of their lives. Nor could they overcome their fear of letting their remaining child out of their sight.

One couple's sixteen-year-old son had turned up missing. His disemboweled body was found in the woods twelve days later. They read about it in the newspaper. It turned out to be their son. No one was ever arrested for the crime, though there had been a suspect—the mother's uncle. As a result, the family had been torn apart while it grieved. The damage was irreparable.

An older couple had had their son, daughter-in-law, and both of two grandchildren murdered. Now they were raising the surviving grandchild—a girl who had witnessed the murder of her parents and sister.

Another couple's son had been murdered. Their other son

then went out and murdered the murderer. Now he was se
ing a jail sentence. In effect they had lost both sons.

The room was very quiet as we listened to one anothe
stories. There was just the rain pattering against the window
And the sound of many of us crying for one another's pai

When it was our turn Frank and I told our story. I me
tioned this awful pain that had developed in my chest, a pa
that wouldn't go away. Three other mothers spoke up as or
They had felt the exact same pain.

Though Frank had been able to purge himself more eas
than I, he still harbored great anger toward Sid. He worri
that he would never be free of it. He talked about it oper
and discovered that his lingering anger was felt by others
well.

This was the key. This was why it was so therapeutic to
with others who had suffered. We didn't feel like freaks ar
more. We didn't shock each other, didn't find people gett
embarrassed, looking away, trying to change the subject. \
could mention our dead children's names without feeling
apart, without having to hear platitudes like "You should
still be dwelling on that" or "So often the good die young

We had found refuge in one another. We felt safe enough
share, to cry, to laugh.

We have stayed together. Our refuge has grown. There
now fifty couples in the Philadelphia chapter, thirty su
chapters around America. We are there for one another.

We don't just sit around airing our grief. We reaffirm l
We say that we are ready to live again and what we want i
find out how.

We help one another cope. Each of us must find our c
way. I cannot tell others how to cope. I can only say I've
vived.

Taking a cue from Women Against Rape, we've launc
a court accompaniment program in Philadelphia. A ph
network connects all POMC members. When the suspe
murderer of the child of one of our members comes up
trial, we go to the trial with the parents. We go with ther
help give them the strength to endure it. I hadn't wanted t
to Sid's trial. The thought terrified me. But I would have b

ong to hide from it. I now realize it is crucial for us to go to
child's murder trial, and to bring as many relatives and
nds as possible. Our presence reminds the judge and the
y that there was a victim, a victim who can no longer speak
who nonetheless has the right to see justice done. It re-
nds them that a crime was committed, and that the appro-
ate price should be paid by the one who committed it.
ing to the trial is the one thing—the last thing—we can
e our child. For our presence does make a difference.
lges and juries do think twice before they administer a mere
p on the wrist when we are there.

In addition, our chapter has mounted a concentrated effort
spare future parents from the wounds inflicted on many of
by the outside world immediately after our losses. So much
the nightmare Frank and I went through was caused by our
n ignorance of the legal system and by the ignorance and
ensitivity of the people we had to come in contact with.
r the parents, we at POMC are presently assembling a
idbook of victim's legal rights. This way, they will know
at's going on around them each step of the way. They will
ow their role and their options—whom they need or need
talk to, where they do or do not have to go. And they will
ow why. For the others, we are putting together a sorely
ded sensitivity packet, which we will distribute to district
orneys, police officers, medical examiners, radio and TV
vs directors, newspaper editors, and therapists. The packet
l, we hope, give them a better understanding of exactly
at parents of murdered children are feeling. It might con-
ce them to show more humanity in the future. No one
uld have to hear his or her child called "the body."

Meanwhile, a major victory for the rights of families of
rder victims was recently scored in a New York City fed-
l court. A jury awarded $40,000 to the parents of Bonnie
rland, a Yale University music student who had been
ten to death several years before by her boyfried, Richard
rrin. The award came as a result of a civil suit the parents
l filed against the convicted killer for payment of their
ighter's medical and funeral expenses, as well as their own
fering.

A legal precedent has been set. Parents need not absorb
of the cost of suffering themselves. Now the killer must, lit
ally, pay the price.

At the time of Nancy's death our lawyer advised us that
could try to file suit against Sid in civil court for such da
ages. We were opposed to the idea because we feare
correctly so—it would only bring us more publicity. I appl
the Garlands for their courage in filing suit. I pray their v
tory will prove to be a victory for all parents of murdered c
dren.

I have found a mission. I'm trying to spare others from
nightmare. I'm trying to get the word out. This book is par
that mission.

In addition to our involvement with POMC, Frank an
have kept Nancy's fund at Eagleville Hospital alive. To d
we've raised $20,000. That's enough for a three-bedrc
suite in the women's wing. Maybe one of the young wor
in one of those beds will overcome her drug or alcohol dep
dency and go on to lead a useful life.

It has taken time. But by helping others, I feel myself
ing. I know my work is having a positive effect on peo
lives and on the system. The fear and anger and feelin
powerlessness are leaving me. A sense of purpose is repla
them. My life is forming again. I am rebuilding.

I am not the same person I was before. My priorities I
changed. Success has a new definition for me. Pers
achievement—doing well in school and in business—use
be a major factor in my life. I was always driven to acc
plish something. A big title and salary seemed import
They don't anymore. Making a positive difference in the l
of other people—my adopted POMC family, my own fam
my friends—is now how I define accomplishment. Th
what makes me go.

I am much more serene than I used to be. I value peace
quiet. I used to get so upset by a leaky faucet, and then by
inefficient repairman who came late to fix it, and didn't.
longer. I have perspective now. I ask myself if anybo
going to die because of it. If not, it isn't worth get
steamed about. That's my bottom line now—if anybody

e. From where I sit, there really isn't that much to get upset
out. When I'm stuck in a traffic jam, I look around at the
eople honking and screaming in the other cars, and I wish
ey could see that being five minutes late to a meeting isn't
gnificant.

I think I value life itself more now. I am more aware of its
fts than I used to be. A beautiful sunny day makes me soar
th happiness. Biting into a ripe peach is cause for ecstasy.
the other hand, a gray day can fill me with more sadness
an it once did. I guess I just *feel* more than I used to. I feel
joy of others and the pain of others. My tears continue to
w freely. I don't try to stifle them. I'm not ashamed to feel
mpassion.

My healing is not complete. I still jump whenever the
one rings—somehow I still instinctively feel it's my child
ling for help, help I cannot give her. I still have hurts. It
ts that my Nancy suffered so and brought suffering to my
er children. It hurts that her gifts went for nothing: it's not
if we have too many brilliant, compassionate people in this
orld. It hurts that we couldn't save her. Some wounds will
ver heal. I know that as long as I live, Nancy's birthday will
a bad day for me. So will the day of her death.

Frank has changed, too. He doesn't push himself at work
e he used to. It isn't important to him anymore to be a big
ot. He is content to do less and to enjoy it more. We have
th learned to savor life. Recently, I noticed him sitting on
e deck in the sun reading the paper. He sat there like that for
urs. He didn't used to be able to do that. He is also more
mmunicative. He used to get moody in the old days, with-
awn, closed off. Now he is much more open. He airs his
elings.

We crave each other's company. We're like newlyweds to-
ther. We share and talk and love with incredible zeal. We
joy doing things together. We take long walks together,
ork out at a health club together, cook nice meals together.
e finally took our first trip to Europe.

We truly enjoy Suzy and David and appreciate their indi-
dual gifts. We love their company. At the same time, we
joy the fact that they're basically on their own now. Inde-

pendence is as wonderful for us as it is for them. I think t
Suzy and David, both of whom are now older than Nan
ever lived to be, understand that.

I think the four of us communicate pretty well now. We
a warm open family—at least, much more so than we used
be. We respect one another's feelings and are sensitive
them. You won't see us bickering or picking at each other li
other families. Our tendency to behave or make decisio
based on Nancy's presence is gradually being erased.

"The hardest thing for the family wasn't Nancy's death
David observed recently. "It was all of those years with her
the middle and the four of us on the outside. It has take
long time not to be that way, not to hold back our affectio
Now I believe the four of us are genuinely happy together.
our story has a happy ending, and I think it does, that's wha
is."

Relations between Suzy and David have begun to tha
David has only one sister now. He cherishes her that mu
more. It has not been easy for Suzy to openly love him ba
Recently she was able to say to him, "You know wh
You're my brother, and I love you." She could not, howev
put her arms around him.

She is now twenty-three. Still finding herself, she has ye
cut completely loose from Nancy's influence. Suzy still fe
big sister Nancy looking over her shoulder. She didn't fin
up at Philadelphia College of Art. Instead, like Nancy, s
moved to Colorado. She lived in Aspen for a while, su
porting herself as a waitress. Recently she moved to N
York. She has an apartment in Greenwich Village, is wo
ing, and is considering resuming her college education.

She has some challenges ahead of her. She still resists lo
ing back, examining the hurts, searching for explanatio
She is, for instance, bitterly opposed to my writing this bo
I have told her it is necessary, and hopefully she will one
understand why.

David got into the University of Pennsylvania, our al
mater. His grades for his senior year of high school were na
rally a bit spotty. However, his admissions officer wrot
very sensitive letter of recommendation on David's beh

e letter detailed David's family crisis and the mature way
which David handled it. I believe the school admitted him
the strength of that letter. David is twenty-one now. He
s a mustache and a girlfriend. He lives off campus in an
artment with a gang of other fellows. They have mustaches
d girlfriends, too. He is boisterous, athletic, and does well
his classes. Truly, David seems remarkably well adjusted
nsidering all he's been through. "I used to be dominated by
ncy's presence," he told me recently. "I couldn't break
ay from it. Now I can talk about her but walk away from it.
n not detached. I still cry. But I'm not controlled by it."

Sometimes David thinks he'd like to be a psychologist
en he graduates. I'm told this is not an uncommon ambi-
n for the youngest member of a family that has had trou-
s. Other times, he thinks he'd like to be a chef. Whichever
ection he chooses, we're confident it will be the right one
him.

With help and love and fresh commitment, we have all be-
n to heal. We cannot erase the scars. We cannot rewrite the
st. We cannot forget. But we can get on with the rest of our
es.

Ultimately, time does heal, too. There is no other explana-
n for the small miracle that happened to me one recent
ght.

Frank and I were at a neighborhood zoning council meet-
. There were about five hundred concerned citizens there.
I listened to a speaker I became acutely aware of the sound
an infant gurgling in the row behind me. Wary, I turned in
seat to find a beautiful little baby girl nestled contentedly
her mother's arms.

I didn't get upset. I didn't see my baby Nancy with needle-
rks on her hands. I was not overcome by incredible pain
d sadness. Instead I just saw a lovely little baby girl, her
ole life ahead of her.

I turned farther around in my seat and touched the baby's
n. I stroked the soft, pink skin inside her forearm, and the
s of her tiny hands. I willed them to be forever free of
rs. She grabbed at my index finger with her fist and smiled
me.

Frank noticed what was happening and turned to watch

"What's her name?" I whispered to the baby's mother

"Amy," the mother whispered back.

Amy held on to my finger until the meeting was over a people were getting up and starting to leave.

"She's a lovely baby," I told the mother.

She thanked me.

"My daughter was murdered," I said. "She was a her addict. Looking at babies, touching them, has been very pa ful for me. But I'm touching Amy. It doesn't hurt."

"Would you like to hold her?" she asked me.

"Could I, please?"

She handed the baby over to me, tears forming in her ey

I pressed Amy over my heart. She nestled her head into side of my neck, clutched at the collar of my blouse with hands. She looked into my eyes, trusting me.

I stroked her soft skin, smelled her sweet baby sm kissed her silky hair and face. It was just the two of us the exactly like it had been the first time I'd held my baby Na in my arms. Only that time I'd been saying hello to Nan Now I was saying good-bye. I was letting go.

Yes, there was a Nancy. Yes, there will be more Nanc But not all babies will feel her pain. Their world need no one of sadness. For them there is a future. There is ho There is a world out there filled with beauty and happin and love.

"Do you know how beautiful you are, Amy?" I murmu to her, my throat constricting. "You are. You're a beaut baby. You beautiful, beautiful baby."

I reluctantly handed her back to her mother and thanked woman for giving me this moment. She tried to say somet to me, but couldn't. She was crying.

Then I turned to Frank. Tears were streaming down face, too. Tears of joy.

# About the Author

**Deborah Spungen,** born in Philadelphia, has been the owner of a natural foods store, a direct mail consultant, and a member of the Philadelphia Crime and Elderly Coalition. She now lives in Philadelphia with her husband, Frank, and has two children, Susan and David.